.75

Good Housekeeping

Light&
Healthy
Cookbook

Good Housekeeping
Light & Healthy Cookbook

375 Delectable Recipes for Everyday Meals

From the Editors of Good Housekeeping

Hearst Books
A Division of Sterling Publishing Co., Inc.

Library of Congress Cataloging-in-Publication Data

Good Housekeeping light & healthy cookbook : 375 delectable recipes for everyday meals from the editors of Good House-keeping.

   p. cm.

   ISBN 1-58816-271-0

   1. Cookery. 2. Low-fat diet--Recipes. I. Title: Good House-keeping light and healthy cookbook. II. Good Housekeeping Institute (New York, N.Y.)

   TX714.G6496 2003

   641.5'638--dc21

                                                           2003006899

10 9 8 7 6 5 4 3 2 1

Published by Hearst Books, a division of
Sterling Publishing Co., Inc.
387 Park Avenue South, New York, N.Y. 10016
© 2003 by Hearst Communications, Inc.
Distributed in Canada by Sterling Publishing
c/o Canadian Manda Group, One Atlantic Avenue, Suite 105
Toronto, Ontario, Canada M6K 3E7
Distributed in Australia by Capricorn Link (Australia) Pty. Ltd.
P.O. Box 704, Windsor, NSW 2756 Australia

Good Housekeeping
Editor-in-Chief: Ellen Levine
Food Director: Susan Westmoreland
Associate Food Director: Susan Deborah Goldsmith

Edited by Pamela Horn
Designed by Liz Trovato

Printed in China

ISBN 1-58816-271-0

Photograph on page 6: Peruvian Seafood Soup;

Photograph on page 8: Bow Ties with Cannellini and Spinach

Photo Credits

6, Mark Thomas; 8, Steve Mark Needham; 15, Brian Hagiwara; 19, Rita Maas; 23, Brian Hagiwara; 24, Brian Hagiwara; 26, Ann Stratton; 29, Ann Stratton; 33, Mark Thomas; 35, Ann Stratton; 39, Ann Stratton; 40, Mark Thomas; 43, Ann Stratton; 47, Mark Thomas; 51, Mark Thomas; 52, Mark Thomas; 54, Steve Mark Needham; 55, Ann Stratton, 57, Mark Thomas; 58-9, Brian Hagiwara; 63, Mark Thomas; 65, Mark Thomas; 70, Alan Richardson; 71, Brian Hagiwara; 73, Brian Hagiwara; 75, Alan Richardson; 76, Brian Hagiwara; 82, Mark Thomas; 85, Mark Thomas; 87, Alan Richardson; 89, Alan Richardson; 91, Brian Hagiwara; 93, Mark Thomas; 95, Mark Thomas; 99, Charles Gold; 100, Mark Thomas; 102, Ann Stratton; 105, Zeva Oelbaum; 107, Martin Jacobs; 109, Brian Hagiwara; 113, Mark Thomas; 118, Charles Gold; 119, Mark Thomas; 121, Brian Hagiwara; 123, Brian Hagiwara; 124, Brian Hagiwara; 127, Alan Richardson, 130, Lisa Koenig; 131, Brian Hagiwara; 133, Lisa Koenig; 134, Brian Hagiwara; 137, Lisa Koenig; 138, Brian Hagiwara; 140-41, Brian Hagiwara; 143, Brian Hagiwara; 146, Brian Hagiwara; 148, Brian Hagiwara; 149, Rita Maas; 151, Brian Hagiwara; 152, Brian Hagiwara; 154-55, Brian Hagiwara; 157, Rita Maas; 158, Ann Stratton; 163, Mark Thomas; 165, Steve Mark Needham; 166, Rita Maas; 173, Brian Hagiwara; 174, Mark Thomas; 175, Brian Hagiwara; 177, Alan Richardson; 180, Mark Thomas; 182, Jonelle Weaver; 187, Brian Hagiwara; 188, Brian Hagiwara; 190, Tex-Mex Cobb Salad, GH 365 Days , pg 73, Jan 1997; 192, Ann Stratton; 193, Brian Hagiwara; 195, Jonelle Weaver; 198, Rita Maas; 199, Rita Maas; 200, Rita Maas; 202, Jonelle Weaver; 203, Jonelle Weaver; 205, Rita Maas; 206, Ann Stratton; 208, Mark Thomas; 211, Ann Stratton; 215, Rita Maas 217, Beatrix Da Costa; 222-23, Alan Richardson; 227, Brian Hagiwara; 230, Brian Hagiwara; 237, Steve Mark Needham; 240, Ann Stratton; 241, Steve Mark Needham; 243, Ann Stratton; 248, Steve Mark Needham; 251, Steve Mark Needham; 252, Steve Mark Needham; 258-59, Ann, Stratton; 261, Ann Stratton; 263, Ann Stratton; 266, Brian Hagiwara; 267, Steve Mark Needham; 268, Ann Stratton; 269, Mark Thomas; 271, Peter Ardito; 275, Brian Hagiwara; 278, Brian Hagiwara; 281, Alison Miksch; 283, Mark Thomas; 284, Steve Mark Needham; 286, Brian Hagiwara; 289, Mark Thomas; 292-93, Ann Stratton; 294, Mark Thomas; 295, Mark Thomas; 297, Mary Ellen Bartley; 299, Steve Mark Needham; 303, Rita Maas; 305, Rita Maas; 309, Rita Maas

Contents

Welcome to Good Housekeeping's collection of Light & Healthy recipes.

We all want to eat nutritious meals. But sometimes it's hard finding easy, healthy recipes that everyone in your family will love. (As the mother of two sons, I know!) That's why I'm so pleased to present this cookbook.

The 375 entrees, appetizers, side dishes and desserts in the book are sure to be crowd pleasers at home. Each has been triple-tested by the pros in the Good Housekeeping kitchens, so you can be sure they'll come out great. In every recipe, fewer than 30 percent of the calories come from fat. That's right in line with the USDA's dietary guidelines for healthy eating. We also offer dozens of terrific tips and shortcuts from our expert cooks to make your light and healthy food preparation easier.

You'll quickly discover that cooking with an eye towards good health doesn't mean sacrificing taste. Roasted chicken, mushroom risotto, flatbread pizza and sinful desserts such as baked Alaska with raspberry sauce—all of these can be light and nutritious.

Happy, healthy cooking for you and your family!

—Ellen Levine
Editor-in-Chief
Good Housekeeping

The message is simple: Eat well to stay well. The good news is you don't need a nutritionist's skills to eat well. With the help of the USDA Food Pyramid (on the following page), common sense, and the recipes in this book, you can easily balance your daily diet. You'll see that it's not hard to get the nutrients you need without too much saturated fat, cholesterol, sugar, sodium, or calories.

Dietary Guidelines for Americans

The U.S. Department of Agriculture recommends that everyone eat a wide variety of foods to get the calories, protein, vitamins, minerals, and fiber needed. In addition, the agency recommends that you:

- Balance the food you eat with enough physical activity to maintain or improve your weight.

- Choose a diet that is low in saturated fat and cholesterol and moderate in total fat.

- Eat plenty of vegetables, fruits, and grain products, especially whole grain.

- Limit your consumption of sugar and salt, and drink alcohol in moderation.

Nutrients: The Big Three

Our bodies need three essential nutrients: carbohydrates, proteins, and fats. Carbohydrates are the body's major source of energy. Complex carbohydrates (composed of starch and fiber) are very important and should comprise the bulk of a healthful diet. Simple carbohydrates (sugars) have limited use, so their consumption should be restricted. Proteins are needed to help produce new body tissue. Fats store the energy the body needs, but too much of the wrong kind can lead to health problems, including cardiovascular disease.

Most health professionals suggest balancing your daily food intake with 50-60 percent carbohydrates, 25 to 30 percent fat, and 15 to 20 percent protein. The fat quota is controversial, however: In truth, the *type* of fat in the diet is more important than the actual amount, but keeping a cap on total fat can make it easier to maintain a healthy weight. Keep in mind that fat is an essential nutrient, so don't cut back too much.

To calculate the amount of fat you can consume each day and still meet a 30 percent limit, divide your ideal body weight (your doctor can provide you with this number) by 2. For example, if your ideal body weight is 120 pounds, limit your total fat intake to 60 grams (120 lbs ÷ 2 = 60).

The USDA Food Pyramid

The Food Pyramid outlines what to eat each day. This research-based plan, developed by the U.S. Department of Agriculture, shows the relative importance of various foods and is meant to serve as a general guide—not a rigid prescription—to help you create a healthful diet tailored to your food preferences.

The pyramid calls for eating a variety of foods to get the carbohydrates, proteins, and fats you need, along with the right number of calories to maintain a healthful weight. It focuses on controlling fat intake, because most American diets are too high in fat, especially saturated fat. The most servings should come from the foods shown in the two lower sections of the pyramid, with moderate amounts of meat and dairy foods and small amounts of fats, oils, and sweets, which are located in the top section.

Each group provides some—but not all—of the nutrients needed for a balanced diet. The foods in one category can't replace those in another (and no one group is more important). For good health, you need them all.

When planning meals, choose fresh or minimally processed foods whenever possible. Highly processed foods tend to have fewer nutrients and higher amounts of fat and sodium; check the labels to make sure the fat content fits your fat budget.

Within each section of the pyramid, the suggested range of servings is given. The number that's right for you depends on your calorie needs, which in turn depend on your age, sex, size, and activity level.

Bread, Cereal, Rice, and Pasta

Grains form the base of the pyramid. They provide complex carbohydrates, vitamins, minerals, and fiber. You need the most servings (6 to 11) of these foods each day. One serving

About the Recipes in This Book

The recipes in *Good Housekeeping's Light & Healthy Cookbook* make it easy to set yourself in the right direction for eating right. That's because every recipe fits into a healthy eating plan—most contain less than 30 percent calories from fat (part of the USDA's guidelines). So take your pick from the appetizers, pastas, main dishes, salads, sides, breads, and desserts in this book—they're all good for you.

You can also use our Light & Healthy recipes to balance out your long-time favorite higher-fat dishes, so you can indulge in personal favorites and still stay on your healthy eating plan. For example, if you'd like to make your grandmother's lasagna one night, serve it with a salad tossed with our Buttermilk-Chive Dressing (0 grams fat, page 231) and then bring out Lemon-Anise Poached Pears (1 gram fat, page 267) for dessert.

At the end of every recipe, you'll find complete nutritional information about the recipe, including calories, carbohydrates, protein, total fat, and saturated fat. This information will help you plan your meals and balance your intake of carbohydrates, protein and fat. (See "Nutrients: The Big Three" [page 9] and "Understanding Food Labels" [page 14] for the recommended daily nutrient levels.) Keep these points in mind when using our nutrition information:

- Our nutritional calculations do not include any optional ingredients or garnishes.

- When alternative ingredients are given (such as margarine), our calculations are based on the first item listed.

- Unless otherwise noted, whole milk has been used.

equals: 1 slice of bread, 1 ounce ready-to-eat cereal, or ½ cup cooked rice, pasta, or cereal. The recommendation of 6 to 11 servings may seem high but it adds up quickly. A generous bowl of cereal or pasta could easily equal 2, 3 or even 4 servings!

Starchy foods are often blamed for adding extra pounds, but high-fat toppings (butter on bread, cream sauce on pasta) are more likely the culprits. Stick with lean carbohydrates, like peasant bread or pita bread, instead of rich croissants and buttery crackers. Whole-grain breads and cereals offer the most fiber.

Fruits and Vegetables

Eat fruits (2 to 4 servings) and vegetables (3 to 5 servings) for your daily intake of vitamins, minerals, and fiber. For the widest range of nutrients, don't eat the same fruits and vegetables day after day. Include choices high in vitamin C (citrus fruits, kiwifruit, strawberries) and those rich in vitamin A (carrots, winter squash, spinach, kale, cantaloupe). Research links cruciferous vegetables, such as broccoli, cabbage, cauliflower, and Brussels sprouts, with reduced risk for certain cancers, so be sure to eat them several times a week.

Meats and Dairy Foods

Most of the foods in this section of the pyramid are animal based. The "meat" group includes meat, poultry, fish, dry beans, eggs, and nuts. Meat, poultry, and fish are rich in protein, B vitamins, iron, and zinc. Dry beans, eggs, and nuts provide protein along with vitamins and minerals. Dairy foods (milk, yogurt, cheese) provide protein, bone-building calcium, and other nutrients.

Most individuals should aim for 2 to 3 servings daily from each of these groups. Many of these foods, especially meat and cheese, are high in calories, so it's easy to accidentally overdo the portion size. Weigh out the suggested portions at least once to get a visual idea of the amount. For example, a 2- to 3-ounce piece of lean cooked meat is approximately the size of a deck of cards. Other suggested portions are: 1 cup (fat-free or reduced-fat) milk or yogurt, 1 1/2 ounces natural cheese or 2 ounces process cheese, 1/2 cup cooked dry beans, 1 egg, 1/3 cup nuts, or 2 table-spoons peanut butter. The fat in nuts and seeds is very healthy. People should not limit them because of the fat. They are much better than many other snacks.

In general, animal products are higher in fat than plant foods, but it's not neces-sary to cut out all meat and dairy products to keep your saturated fat intake low. Low-fat dairy foods, lean and well-trimmed meat, and skinless poultry provide the same amounts of vitamins and minerals as their fattier counterparts. Skinless poul-try, fish, dry beans, and split peas are the "slimmest" foods in this category. By removing the skin from poultry, you reduce the fat by almost one-half. Most fish and seafood is low in fat and rich in beneficial omega-3 oils, which have been linked to a lower risk of heart disease. Dry beans also provide the body with fiber, which is important for digestion and may help you feel fuller with fewer calories.

You can enjoy red meat if you choose lean cuts and trim away all the visible fat (marbled fat cannot be trimmed away). Here are some good choices.

Beef: eye round, top round, tenderloin, top sirloin, flank steak, top loin, ground beef (choose ground sirloin: it's 90 to 93 percent lean)

Veal: cutlets (from the legs) and loin chops

Pork: tenderloin, boneless top loin roast, loin chops, and boneless sirloin chops

Lamb: boneless leg (shank portions), loin roast, loin chops, leg cubes for kabobs

Vegetarians can substitute servings of dry beans and nuts for their protein needs but will also need fortified foods, extra servings of plant foods (especially grains), and/or supplements to get adequate amounts of calcium, iron, and vitamin B12.

Fats, Oils, and Sweets

At the top of the pyramid are foods such as oil, cream, butter, margarine, sugar, soft drinks, candy, and desserts. To maintain a healthful weight, eat these sparingly and aim for a total fat intake of no more than 30 percent calories. Beyond that, it is essential to understand the kind of fat you are eating. There are three types of fatty acids: satura-ted, monounsaturated, and polyunsaturated. Saturated fat (found in meat, dairy

The Mediterranean Diet

For centuries, the traditional diet of the sunny Mediterranean countries has succeeded in prolonging life and preventing disease. Health experts have taken notice and suggested that the culinary habits of these countries can help Americans in their quest to cut fat and eat more nutritiously. The result is the "Mediterranean Diet," a plan not too different from the Food Pyramid. Both have a foundation in grains, vegetables, and fruits. But the Mediterranean model highlights beans and other legumes, limits red meat to a few times a month, and promotes the use of olive oil. This diet also encourages daily exercise and even a glass of wine with dinner.

What makes olive oil so great? It is predominantly a heart-healthy monounsaturated fat. When substituted for more saturated fats, it tends to lower artery-clogging LDL cholesterol while maintaining good levels of protective HDL cholesterol.

Wine with meals is traditional in Mediterranean cultures. Studies have shown that moderate drinking (defined as one drink per day for women, two for men), raises "good" cholesterol levels and may make blood less likely to form clots in arteries. But moderation is the key: One drink is a 4-ounce glass of wine, a 12-ounce serving of beer, or 1 ounce of hard liquor.

Quality of life, however, can't be overlooked as a contributing factor to health and happiness. In the Mediterranean, meals are savored along with the company of family and friends, and physical activity is a part of daily life.

products, and coconut, palm, and palm kernel oils) should be limited to less than 10 percent (about one-third of your total fat intake) or less; too much raises cholesterol and the risk of heart disease. Monounsaturated fats (found in olive, peanut, and canola oils) and polyunsaturated fats (found mainly in safflower, sunflower, corn, soybean, and cottonseed oils and some fish) are healthier.

Trimming the Fat

Here are some tips for trimming excess saturated fat and extra calories from your diet:

- Choose lean cuts of meat and trim all the visible fat before cooking. Remove skin from poultry before or after cooking.

- Broil meat on a rack so the fat can drip away.

- Substitute ground chicken or turkey for ground beef. Be sure the package is labeled "meat only," or it may contain skin and therefore have as much fat as ground beef.

- Substitute protein-packed dried legumes, like beans and lentils, for meat in casseroles.

- Chill soups and stews overnight so you can remove all the hardened fat from the surface.

- Be skimpy with fat. Use nonstick pans and nonstick cooking spray, or "sauté" in a small amount of broth or water. Don't just pour oil into a skillet; it's easy to add too much. Measure or use a pastry brush to coat pans with a thin layer of oil. When baking, coat pans with a spritz of nonstick cooking spray instead of oils or fats. (Kitchenware shops now carry oil sprayers you can fill with your favorite oil.)

- Experiment with low fat or skim milk, low fat sour cream and cheese, and nonfat yogurt: They provide the same amounts of calcium and protein as the whole-milk varieties but with less fat or none at all.

- When making dips, use nonfat yogurt instead of sour cream.

- Use fresh herbs and zesty seasonings liberally.

- Choose angel food cake instead of pound cake, especially when making cake-based desserts like trifle.

- To reduce fat and cholesterol, you can substitute 2 egg whites for 1 whole egg in recipes, but don't substitute egg whites for all the whole eggs when baking: The dessert will have better texture and flavor if you retain a yolk or two.

- Replace sour cream with buttermilk or yogurt in baking.

Understanding Food Labels

Food labels help you make informed choices about the foods to include in your diet. The Percent Daily Values reflect the percentage of the recommended daily amount of a nutrient in a serving (based on 2,000 calories daily). You can "budget" your intake of nutrients by adding up these percentages. For example, a typical label for corn chips may show 13 percent of the daily value for fat.

If the next food you eat has a 10 percent daily value for fat, you've already had 23 percent of your total fat allowance for the day. When it comes to fat, saturated fat, sodium, and cholesterol, it's a good idea to keep the daily values below 100 percent. Fiber, vitamins A and C, calcium, and iron are listed because diets often fall short; aim for 100 percent or more of these nutrients. (Other vitamins and minerals may also appear on labels.)

The Daily Values footnote includes a chart that shows some Daily Values for diets containing 2,000 and 2,500 calories. Use these numbers as a guide. Your own daily values may be higher or lower, depending on your calorie needs.

Food labels are required to have an ingredients list. The ingredients are listed in descending order according to their weight. This enables you to easily discern which food products contain larger amounts of ingredients that are healthful.

Nutrition Facts	
Serving Size 2 pieces (29g)	
Servings Per Container 15	

Amount Per Serving	
Calories 150	Calories from Fat 80

	% **Daily Value***
Total Fat 8g	13%
Saturated Fat 5g	27%
Cholesterol 25mg	8%
Sodium 115mg	5%
Total Carbohydrate 18g	6%
Dietary Fiber 0g	0%
Sugars 6g	
Protein 2g	

Vitamin A 0%	•	Vitamin C 0%
Calcium 2%	•	Iron 2%

* Percent Daily Values are based on a 2,000 calorie diet.

Backyard Bruschetta, page 16

Backyard Bruschetta

Prep: 15 minutes   Grill: 10 minutes

Easy appetizers of grilled bread and your choice of two Italian-style toppings.

  **Tuscan White Bean Topping or Tomato-Goat
  Cheese Topping (below)**
1 **loaf (8 ounces) Italian bread**
2 **garlic cloves, peeled and cut in half**
1 **tablespoon olive oil**

1. Prepare one of the toppings; set aside.

2. Cut off ends from bread; reserve for another use. Slice loaf diagonally into 1/2-inch-thick slices.

3. Place bread slices on grill over medium heat. Grill, turning occasionally, until lightly toasted, 8 to 10 minutes. Rub one side of each slice with cut side of garlic. Brush with oil.

4. Just before serving, assemble bruschetta by topping toast slices with either white bean mixture or goat cheese then tomato mixture. Makes 16 bruschetta.

Tuscan White Bean Topping

1 **can (151/2 to 19 ounces) white kidney beans,
  rinsed and drained**
1 **tablespoon minced fresh parsley leaves**
1 **tablespoon lemon juice**
1 **tablespoon olive oil**
1 **teaspoon minced fresh sage leaves**
21/4 **teaspoons salt**
1/8 **teaspoon coarsely ground black pepper**

In medium bowl, with fork, lightly mash beans, parsley, lemon juice, oil, sage, salt, and pepper until combined.

Tomato-Goat Cheese Topping:

1 **package (6 ounces) soft low-fat goat cheese**
1 **teaspoon minced fresh oregano leaves**
1/4 **teaspoon coarsely ground black pepper**
2 **ripe medium tomatoes, seeded and diced**
2 **teaspoons minced fresh parsley leaves**
1 **teaspoon olive oil**
1/8 **teaspoon salt**

In small bowl, with fork, mix goat cheese, oregano, and pepper until blended. In medium bowl, mix tomatoes, parsley, oil, and salt.

Each bruschetta with white bean topping: About 80 calories (23 percent calories from fat), 3g protein, 11g carbohydrate, 2g total fat (0g saturated), 0mg cholesterol, 175mg sodium.

Each bruschetta with goat cheese topping: About 70 calories (13 percent calories from fat), 3g protein, 7g carbohydrate, 1g total fat (0g saturated), 2mg cholesterol, 100mg sodium.

Prosciutto with Melon

Prep: 10 minutes

The marriage of sweet ripe melon and slightly salty prosciutto is a classic combination. Imported prosciutto di Parma, available at Italian grocers and specialty food markets, is much milder than the domestic varieties of this ham. It's worth seeking out.

1 small honeydew melon or 1 medium cantaloupe, chilled
4 ounces prosciutto, thinly sliced
freshly ground black pepper

1. Cut melon in half through stem end and remove seeds. Cut each half into 4 wedges; cut off rind.

2. Arrange 2 melon wedges on each of four plates; arrange prosciutto to side of melon. Sprinkle pepper on each serving. Makes 4 first-course servings.

Each serving: About 150 calories (24 percent calories from fat), 9g protein, 22g carbohydrate, 4g total fat (1g saturated), 23mg cholesterol, 548mg sodium.

10 Guilt-Free Before-Dinner Snacks

- Celery stuffed with nonfat bean dip
- Dried fruit (apple rings, strawberries, cherries, cranberries, apricots, or raisins)
- Fat-free cinnamon-raisin bagel chips
- Fresh tangerine or Clementine sections
- Low-fat caramel or Cheddar rice cakes or popcorn cakes
- 1% or skim milk with chocolate syrup
- Pretzel sticks or whole-grain pretzels
- Red- or green-pepper strips, cucumber spears, or peeled baby carrots with salsa
- Reduced-fat mozzarella string cheese
- Toasted pita wedges with shredded reduced-fat cheese melted on top

Firecracker Mix

Prep: 10 minutes plus cooling   Bake: 30 minutes per batch

A spicy party snack so addictive, you can't eat just one hand-ful! Omit the ground red pepper for kids or guests with a mild-taste preference. Make up to a week in advance—store in ziptight plastic bags.

1/4 cup Worcestershire sauce
4 tablespoons margarine or butter
2 tablespoons brown sugar
1 1/2 teaspoons salt
1/2 to 1 teaspoon ground red pepper (cayenne)
12 cups popped corn (1/3 to 1/2 cup unpopped)
1 package (12 ounces) oven-toasted corn cereal squares
1 package (8 to 10 ounces) thin pretzel sticks

1. Preheat oven to 300°F. In 1-quart saucepan, stir Worcestershire, margarine, brown sugar, salt, and ground red pepper over low heat until margarine melts.

2. Place half each of popped corn, cereal, and pretzels in large roasting pan (17" by 11 1/2"); toss with half of Worcestershire mixture.

3. Bake popcorn mixture, stirring once halfway through baking, 30 minutes. Cool mixture in very large bowl or on counter covered with waxed paper. Repeat with remaining ingredients. Makes about 25 cups.

Each 1/2 cup: About 65 calories (14 percent calories from fat), 1g protein, 13g carbohydrate, 1g total fat (0g saturated), 0mg cholesterol, 245mg sodium.

Chinese Dumplings

Prep: 45 minutes   Cook: 10 minutes

Steamed dumplings are fun to make at home. Serve as a first coarse of an Asian feast, or have them for brunch (that's the way the Chinese enjoy them).

   2 cups packed sliced Napa cabbage (Chinese cabbage)

   8 ounces ground pork

   1 green onion, finely chopped

1¹/2 teaspoons minced, peeled fresh ginger

   2 tablespoons soy sauce

   1 tablespoon dry sherry

   2 teaspoons cornstarch

  36 wonton wrappers (9 ounces)

   1 large egg white, beaten

   Soy Dipping Sauce (below)

1. Prepare filling: In 2-quart saucepan, heat 1 inch water to boiling over high heat. Add cabbage and heat to boiling. Cook 1 minute; drain. Immediately rinse with cold running water to stop cooking. With hands, squeeze out as much water from cabbage as possible. Finely chop cabbage. Squeeze out any remaining water from cabbage; place in medium bowl. Stir in pork, green onion, ginger, soy sauce, sherry, and cornstarch until well blended.

2. Arrange half of wonton wrappers on waxed paper. With pastry brush, brush each wrapper lightly with egg white. Spoon 1 rounded teaspoon filling in center of each wrapper. Bring two opposite corners of each wonton wrapper together over filling; pinch and pleat edges together to seal in filling. Repeat with remaining wrappers, egg white, and filling.

3. In deep nonstick 12-inch skillet, heat ¹/2 inch water to boiling over high heat. Place all dumplings, pleated edges up, in one layer in skillet. With spatula, move dumplings gently to prevent them from sticking to bottom of skillet. Heat to boiling. Reduce heat; cover and simmer until dumplings are cooked through, about 5 minutes.

4. Meanwhile, prepare Soy Dipping Sauce.

5. With slotted spoon, transfer dumplings to platter. Serve with dipping sauce. Makes 36 dumplings.

Each dumpling without sauce: About 40 calories (23 percent calories from fat), 2g protein, 5g carbohydrate, 1g total fat (1g saturated), 5g cholesterol, 103g sodium.

Soy Dipping Sauce

In small serving bowl, stir ¹/4 cup soy sauce, ¹/4 cup seasoned rice vinegar or white wine vinegar, and 2 tablespoons peeled fresh ginger, cut into very thin slivers, until blended. Makes about ¹/2 cup.

Each teaspoon: About 4 calories (0 percent calories from fat), 0g protein, 1g carbohydrate, 0g total fat, 0mg cholesterol, 221mg sodium.

Chili Corn Chips

Prep: 5 minutes   Bake: 8 to 10 minutes

1/4 **teaspoon ground cumin**

1/4 **teaspoon chili powder**

1/8 **teaspoon salt**

4 **(6-inch) low-fat corn tortillas**

nonstick cooking spray

1. Preheat oven to 400°F.

2. In cup, mix cumin, chili powder, and salt. Spray 1 side of each tortilla with nonstick cooking spray; sprinkle with chili-powder mixture.

3. Cut each tortilla into 8 wedges and place on ungreased large cookie sheet. Bake tortillas until crisp, 8 to 10 minutes; cool on wire rack. If not serving right away, store in tightly covered container. Makes 32 chips or 4 appetizer servings.

Each serving: About 60 calories (15 percent calories from fat), 2g protein, 11g carbohydrate, 1g total fat (0g saturated), 0mg cholesterol, 110mg sodium.

Quick Quesadillas

Prep: 10 minutes   Bake: 5 minutes

Serve as an accompaniment to Spicy Black Bean Soup (page 37) or as the first course of a Southwest-style meal.

8 **(7- to 8-inch) flour tortillas**

1 **jar (7 ounces) roasted red peppers, drained and thinly sliced**

2 **small green onions, thinly sliced**

1 **ounce Pepper Jack cheese, shredded (1/4 cup)**

3/4 **cup loosely packed fresh cilantro leaves**

1. Preheat oven to 400°F. Place 4 tortillas on large cookie sheet. Sprinkle one-fourth of roasted peppers, green onions, cheese, and cilantro on each tortilla; top with remaining tortillas to make 4 quesadillas.

2. Bake quesadillas until heated through, about 5 minutes. Cut each quesadilla into 8 wedges. Serve warm. Makes 32 appetizers.

Each appetizer: About 34 calories (26 percent calories from fat), 1g protein, 5g carbohydrate, 1g total fat (0g saturated), 1mg cholesterol, 56mg sodium.

Black Bean Dip

Prep: 5 minutes   Cook: 3 minutes

Simple to whip up—even when you're pressed for time. Serve with toasted pita points or crudités.

4 garlic cloves, peeled

1 can (15 to 19 ounces) black beans, rinsed and drained

2 tablespoons tomato paste

2 tablespoons olive oil

4 1/2 teaspoons fresh lime juice

1 tablespoon water

1/2 teaspoon ground cumin

1/2 teaspoon ground coriander

1/4 teaspoon salt

1/8 teaspoon ground red pepper (cayenne)

1. In 1-quart saucepan, place garlic and enough water to cover; heat to boiling over high heat. Reduce heat to low; cover and simmer 3 minutes to blanch garlic; drain.

2. In food processor with knife blade attached, puree garlic, beans, tomato paste, oil, lime juice, water, cumin, coriander, salt, and ground red pepper until smooth. Spoon dip into serving bowl; cover and refrigerate up to 2 days. Makes about 2 cups.

Each tablespoon: About 20 calories (45 percent calories from fat), 1g protein, 3g carbohydrate, 1g total fat (0g saturated), 0mg cholesterol, 55mg sodium.

Green Goddess Dip

Prep: 10 minutes   Cook: 3 minutes

A less complicated version of the famous dressing for salads and fish makes a delicious dip for crudités.

2 garlic cloves, peeled

1 container (8 ounces) fat-free sour cream

1 cup fresh parsley leaves, chopped

2 green onions, minced

2 tablespoons light mayonnaise

2 teaspoons fresh lemon juice

1 1/2 teaspoons anchovy paste

1 teaspoon dried tarragon

1. In 1-quart saucepan, place garlic and enough water to cover; heat to boiling over high heat. Reduce heat to low; cover and simmer 3 minutes to blanch garlic; drain. Mince garlic; place in medium bowl.

2. Stir in sour cream, parsley, green onions, mayonnaise, lemon juice, anchovy paste and tarragon. Cover and refrigerate up to 2 days. Makes about 1 cup.

Each tablespoon: About 20 calories (45 percent calories from fat), 1g protein, 2g carbohydrate, 1g total fat (0g saturated), 1mg cholesterol, 40mg sodium.

Crudités

Crudités served with a lower-fat dip can be a calorie-watcher's best guiltless indulgence. And while these two dips rise a bit above our "less than 30 percent calories from fat" rule, they do have just 1 gram of fat per tablespoon—and when you serve them with naturally low-in-fat veggie crudités, they fit right into your eating plan.

Why not go beyond the same-old carrots and celery, and try some more unusual vegetables? Consider blanched asparagus spears, blanched snap peas, whole cherry tomatoes, bite-size purple, yellow and red pepper strips, tiny romaine lettuce leaves, jicama strips, generous-size red radishes, and English (seedless) cucumber strips.

Sweet Pea Guacamole

Prep: 10 minutes

The perfect impostor: all the flavor and none of the fat found in traditional guacamole. Serve with baked tortilla chips for the full effect.

- **2 packages (10 ounces each) frozen peas, thawed**
- **3 tablespoons fat-free chicken or vegetable broth**
- **2 tablespoons light mayonnaise**
- **2 tablespoons fresh lime juice**
- **2 tablespoons chopped fresh cilantro leaves**
- **2 teaspoons chopped, seeded jalapeño chile**
- **1/4 teaspoon ground cumin**
- **1/4 teaspoon chili powder**
- **salt to taste**
- **2 tablespoons chopped tomatoes and green onions for garnish**

1. In food processor with knife blade attached, puree peas, broth, mayonnaise, lime juice, cilantro, jalapeño, cumin, chili powder, and salt until just smooth.

2. Spoon guacamole into serving bowl; garnish with tomatoes and green onions. Makes about 3 cups.

Each tablespoon: About 10 calories (0 percent calories from fat), 1g protein, 2g carbohydrate, 0g total fat, 0mg cholesterol, 30mg sodium.

Canyon Ranch Guacamole

Prep: 15 minutes

This asparagus guacamole has been served at Canyon Ranch since the day it opened. Serve it with fat-free baked tortilla chips for your next fiesta.

- **2 cups chopped, lightly steamed asparagus (about 12 ounces)**
- **2 1/4 teaspoons fresh lemon juice**
- **3 tablespoons chopped onion**
- **1 large tomato, chopped**
- **3/4 teaspoon salt (optional)**
- **1/2 teaspoon chili powder**
- **1/4 teaspoon ground cumin**
- **1/4 teaspoon coarsely ground black pepper**
- **1 garlic clove, pressed or minced**
- **dash hot pepper sauce**
- **1/3 cup light sour cream**

1. In blender, combine all ingredients and blend until smooth.

2. Transfer guacamole to a bowl. Cover tightly and refrigerate several hours, or overnight, before serving. Makes 3 cups.

Each serving: About 11 calories (0 percent calories from fat), 0g protein, 2g carbohydrate, 0g total fat, 0mg cholesterol, 145mg sodium.

Skewered Chicken with Papaya Salsa

Prep: 30 minutes plus marinating   Grill: 6 to 8 minutes

These make the perfect light treat at a cocktail party. The refreshing papaya salsa can be prepared several days in advance and refrigerated until ready to use.

- 2 **tablespoons seasoned rice vinegar or balsamic vinegar**
- 2 **tablespoons Asian sesame oil**
- 1 **tablespoon fresh lemon juice**
- 1 **tablespoon reduced-sodium soy sauce**
- 1 **tablespoon hoisin sauce**
- 1 **teaspoon minced garlic**
- 1 **teaspoon minced, peeled fresh ginger**
- 1 **pound skinless, boneless chicken breast halves, cut into 1-inch cubes**
- 6 **(12-inch) bamboo skewers**

PAPAYA SALSA:

- 2 **teaspoons olive oil**
- 2 **shallots, finely chopped**
- 2 **teaspoons minced, peeled fresh ginger**
- 1/2 **teaspoon curry powder**
- 1 **large ripe papaya, peeled, seeded, and finely chopped**
- 2 **tablespoons fresh lime juice**
- 1 **tablespoon finely chopped fresh cilantro leaves**
  - **salt to taste**
  - **lime wedges for garnish**

1. In large ziptight plastic bag, combine vinegar, sesame oil, lemon juice, soy sauce, hoisin sauce, garlic, and ginger; add chicken, turning to coat. Seal bag, pressing out as much air as possible. Place bag on plate and refrigerate 1 hour to marinate, turning occasionally. Soak skewers in water 20 minutes.

2. Meanwhile, prepare salsa: In nonstick 1-quart saucepan, heat olive oil over medium heat. Add shallots and ginger, and cook, stirring often, until softened, 6 to 7 minutes. Stir in curry powder; cook 1 minute.

Transfer mixture to food processor with knife blade attached. Add papaya, lime juice, cilantro, and salt; pulse until just blended. Do not overprocess. Spoon salsa into bowl; serve at room temperature. If not serving right away, cover and refrigerate salsa up to 2 days. Bring to room temperature before serving. Makes about 2 cups.

3. Prepare grill. Thread chicken onto skewers without crowding. Place skewers on grill over medium heat and grill, turning occasionally, until chicken cubes lose their pink color throughout, 3 to 4 minutes a side. Arrange chicken skewers on platter; serve with salsa and lime wedges. Makes 10 appetizer servings.

Each serving, chicken only: About 70 calories, 11g protein, 1g carbohydrate, 2g total fat (1g saturated), 29mg cholesterol, 65mg sodium.

Each 1/4 cup salsa: About 35 calories (26 percent calories from fat), 1g protein, 6g carbohydrate, 1g total fat (0g saturated), 0mg cholesterol, 75mg sodium.

Mussels with Tomatoes and White Wine

Prep: 20 minutes   Cook: 25 minutes

This saucy dish should be served with plenty of good crusty bread for dipping.

  1   **tablespoon olive or vegetable oil**
  1   **small onion, chopped**
  2   **garlic cloves, finely chopped**
  1/4 **teaspoon crushed red pepper**
  1   **can (14 to 16 ounces) tomatoes**
  3/4 **cup dry white wine**
  4   **pounds large mussels, scrubbed and debearded**
  2   **tablespoons chopped fresh parsley**

1. In nonreactive 5-quart Dutch oven, heat oil over medium heat. Add onion and cook until tender and golden, 6 to 8 minutes. Add garlic and crushed red pepper and cook 30 seconds longer. Stir in tomatoes with their juice and wine, breaking up tomatoes with side of spoon. Heat to boiling; boil 3 minutes.

2. Add mussels; heat to boiling. Reduce heat; cover and simmer until mussels open, about 5 minutes, transferring mussels to large bowl as they open. Discard any mussels that do not open. Pour broth over mussels and sprinkle with parsley. Makes 8 first-course or 4 main-dish servings.

Each first-course serving: About 104 calories (26 percent calories from fat), 9g protein, 6g carbohydrate, 3g total fat (1g saturated), 18mg cholesterol, 277mg sodium.

Chinese Steamed Clams

Prep: 10 minutes   Cook: 10 minutes

Serve this flavorful dish with white rice.

  1   **tablespoon vegetable oil**
  2   **green onions, finely chopped**
  1   **tablespoon minced, peeled fresh ginger**
  1   **garlic clove, finely chopped**
  2   **dozen cherrystone or littleneck clams, scrubbed**
  1/2 **cup water**
  3   **tablespoons dry sherry**
  2   **tablespoons soy sauce**
  2   **tablespoons chopped fresh cilantro**

In 8-quart saucepot, heat oil over high heat. Add green onions, ginger, and garlic; cook until green onions are tender, about 1 minute. Add clams, water, sherry, and soy sauce; heat to boiling. Reduce heat; cover and simmer until clams open, 5 to 10 minutes, transferring clams to large platter as they open. Discard any clams that do not open. Pour broth over clams on platter and sprinkle with cilantro. Makes 4 first-course servings.

Each serving: About 131 calories (27 percent calories from fat), 14g protein, 5g carbohydrate, 4g total fat (1g saturated), 36mg cholesterol, 576mg sodium.

Homemade Sushi

Prep: 1 hour 30 minutes plus chilling   Cook: 25 minutes

All our suggestions for homemade sushi use cooked fish, such as shrimp or smoked salmon, and/or vegetables. You can make the sushi rolls up to 6 hours before serving.

FILLINGS:

- 4 ounces cooked shelled deveined shrimp, thinly sliced lengthwise
- 4 ounces imitation crab sticks (surimi), cut lengthwise into pencil-thin sticks
- 4 ounces thinly sliced smoked salmon
- 1 ripe medium avocado, cut lengthwise in half, then thinly sliced lengthwise
- 1 medium carrot, peeled and cut crosswise in half, then lengthwise into pencil-thin sticks
- 1 small cucumber, cut lengthwise into 2" by 1/4" matchstick strips

GARNISHES:

- black sesame seeds
- white sesame seeds, toasted
- minced chives

ACCOMPANIMENTS:

- pickled ginger
- soy sauce
- wasabi (Japanese horseradish)

SUSHI RICE:

- 2 1/2 cups water
- 2 cups Japanese short-grain rice
- 2 tablespoons sugar
- 1 teaspoon salt
- 1/2 cup seasoned rice vinegar
- 1 package (ten 8" by 7" sheets) roasted seaweed for sushi (nori)

1. Assemble fillings: Place each filling in a small bowl. Cover bowls with plastic wrap and place in 15 1/2" by 10 1/2" jelly-roll pan for easy handling. Refrigerate fillings until ready to use.

2. Assemble Garnishes and Accompaniments: Place each garnish in a small bowl. Place each accompaniment in a small serving dish; cover. If not serving right away, refrigerate pickled ginger and wasabi.

3. Prepare sushi rice: In 3-quart saucepan, heat water, rice, sugar, and salt to boiling over high heat. Reduce heat to low; cover and simmer, without stirring or lifting lid, until rice is tender and liquid has been absorbed (rice will be sticky), about 25 minutes. Remove saucepan from heat; stir in vinegar. Cover and keep warm.

4. Make sushi rolls: Place 12-inch-long piece of plastic wrap on work surface. Place small bowl of water within reach of work area; it's easiest to handle sticky sushi rice with damp hands.

5. Place 1 nori sheet, shiny (smooth) side down, with a short side facing you, on plastic wrap; top with generous 1/2 cup rice. With small metal spatula and damp hands, spread and pat rice down to make an even layer over nori, leaving 1/4-inch border all around sheet. (To make an inside-out roll, flip rice-covered nori sheet over so that nori is on top.)

6. On top of rice (or nori), starting about 2 inches away from side facing you (see photo), arrange desired fillings crosswise in 1 1/2-inch-wide strip.

7. Using end of plastic wrap closest to you, lift edge of sushi, then firmly roll, jelly-roll fashion, away from you. Seal end of nori with water-dampened finger. (If making inside-out roll, coat outside of roll with 1 of the garnishes.) Place sushi roll on tray or platter.

8. Repeat steps 5 through 7 to make 10 sushi rolls in all, changing plastic wrap when necessary. Cover and refrigerate sushi rolls 30 minutes or up to 6 hours.

9. To serve, with serrated knife, slice off and discard ends from each roll. Slice each roll crosswise into ten 1/2-inch-thick slices. Arrange sliced rolls on platter. Serve with accompaniments. Makes about 100 pieces.

Each piece: About 25 calories (0 percent calories from fat), 1g protein, 4g carbohydrate, 0g total fat, 3mg cholesterol, 70mg sodium.

Shrimp Cocktail
Prep: 25 minutes plus chilling   Cook: 17 minutes

Everyone loves to nibble on shrimp before the main course. So, here's shrimp, boiled to perfection, and a zesty, Southwest-inspired sauce perfect for dipping.

 1 **lemon, thinly sliced**
 4 **bay leaves**
20 **whole black peppercorns**
10 **whole allspice berries**
 2 **teaspoons salt**
24 **extra-large shrimp (1 pound), shelled and deveined**
   Southwestern-Style Cocktail Sauce (below)
12 **small romaine lettuce leaves**
24 **(7-inch) bamboo skewers**

1. In 5-quart Dutch oven, combine 2 quarts water, lemon, bay leaves, peppercorns, allspice berries, and salt; heat to boiling. Cover and boil 15 minutes.

2. Add shrimp and cook just until opaque throughout, 1 to 2 minutes. Drain and rinse with cold running water to stop cooking. Cover and refrigerate shrimp up to 24 hours.

3. Prepare Southwestern-Style Cocktail Sauce.

4. Just before serving, place bowls of sauces in center of platter; arrange romaine leaves around bowls, leaf tips facing out. Thread each shrimp on a bamboo skewer and arrange skewers on romaine. Makes 8 first-course servings.

Each serving without sauce: About 51 calories (18 percent calories from fat), 10g protein, 1g carbohydrate, 1g total fat (0g saturated), 70mg cholesterol, 141mg sodium.

Southwestern-Style Cocktail Sauce

In bowl, stir 1 cup bottled cocktail sauce, 2 tablespoons chopped fresh cilantro, 2 teaspoons minced jalapeño chile, and 2 teaspoons fresh lime juice until well combined. Cover and refrigerate up to 24 hours. Makes about 1 cup.

Each tablespoon: About 18 calories (0 percent calories from fat), 0g protein, 4g carbohydrate, 0g total fat, 0mg cholesterol, 19mg sodium.

Pickled Shrimp

Prep: 20 minutes plus overnight to marinate Cook: 5 minutes

Long a favorite in the Good Housekeeping *dining room, this perfectly spiced appetizer is always made ahead: The shrimp are cooked the day before and marinated overnight. To keep them well chilled when served, set the bowl of shrimp in a larger bowl of crushed ice.*

1/4 **cup dry sherry**

3 **teaspoons salt**

1/4 **teaspoon whole black peppercorns**

1 **bay leaf**

3 **pounds large shrimp, shelled and deveined, leaving tail part of shell on, if desired**

2/3 **cup fresh lemon juice (about 3 large lemons)**

1/2 **cup distilled white vinegar**

1/2 **cup vegetable oil**

3 **tablespoons pickling spices, tied in cheesecloth bag**

2 **teaspoons sugar**

2 **dill sprigs**

1. In 4-quart saucepan combine 6 cups water, sherry, 2 teaspoons salt, peppercorns, and bay leaf; heat to boiling over high heat. Add shrimp; heat to boiling. Shrimp should be opaque throughout when water returns to boil; if not, cook about 1 minute longer. Drain.

2. In large bowl, combine lemon juice, vinegar, oil, pickling spices, sugar, dill, and remaining 1 teaspoon salt. Add shrimp and toss well to coat. Spoon into ziptight plastic bags, press out excess air, and seal. Refrigerate shrimp overnight to marinate, turning bags occasionally.

3. Remove shrimp from marinade and arrange in chilled bowl. Serve with cocktail picks. Makes 24 appetizer servings.

Each serving: About 69 calories (26 percent calories from fat), 9g protein, 1g carbohydrate, 2g total fat (0g saturated), 70mg cholesterol, 166mg sodium.

Gazpacho with Cilantro Yogurt,
page 31

Cream of Asparagus Soup

Prep: 5 minutes   Cook: 20 minutes

Start with a package of frozen vegetables, a can of broth, and seasonings—in 25 minutes you'll have a luscious, creamy, lower-fat soup.

- **1 tablespoon margarine or butter**
- **1 medium onion, finely chopped**
- **1 can (14^1/2 ounces) fat-free chicken broth**
- **1 package (10 ounces) frozen asparagus cuts or spears**
- **^{1}/4 teaspoon dried thyme**
- **^{1}/4 teaspoon dried tarragon**
- **^{1}/8 teaspoon salt**
- **^{1}/8 teaspoon ground black pepper**
- **1^1/2 cups fat-free (skim) milk**
- **2 teaspoons fresh lemon juice**
- **snipped fresh chives for garnish (optional)**

1. In 2-quart saucepan, melt margarine over medium heat. Add onion and cook, stirring occasionally, until tender, 5 minutes. Add broth, asparagus, thyme, tarragon, salt, and pepper; heat to boiling over high heat. Reduce heat to low and simmer 10 minutes.

2. Spoon one-fourth of mixture into blender; cover, with center part of cover removed to let steam escape, and puree until smooth. Pour puree into bowl. Repeat with remaining mixture.

3. Return soup to saucepan; stir in milk. Heat through over medium heat, stirring often (do not boil, or soup may curdle). Remove saucepan from heat; stir in lemon juice. Garnish with snipped chives, if you like. Makes about 3^3/4 cups or 4 first-course servings.

Each serving: About 115 calories, 8g protein, 11g carbohydrate, 3g total fat (1g saturated), 2mg cholesterol, 480mg sodium.

Cream of Lima Bean Soup

Prepare as directed but substitute 1 package (10 ounces) frozen lima beans for the asparagus. Delete the dried tarragon. If you like, garnish with chopped fresh thyme.

Each serving: About 155 calories, 9g protein, 20g carbohydrate, 3g total fat (1g saturated), 2mg cholesterol, 515mg sodium.

Cream of Kale Soup

Prepare as directed but substitute 1 package (10 ounces) frozen chopped kale for the asparagus. Add 1 garlic clove, minced, to the onions at the end of cooking time and cook 30 seconds longer. Omit the dried tarragon. Add the milk to the soup before pureeing. If you like, garnish with chopped fresh tomato.

Each serving: About 115 calories, 8g protein, 11g carbohydrate, 3g total fat (1g saturated), 2mg cholesterol, 480mg sodium.

Cream of Cauliflower Soup

Prepare as directed but substitute 1 package (10 ounces) frozen cauliflower florets for the asparagus and 1/2 teaspoon curry powder for the dried tarragon. If you like, garnish with chopped fresh apple.

Each serving: About 115 calories, 8g protein, 11g carbohydrate, 3g total fat (1g saturated), 2mg cholesterol, 480mg sodium.

The Skinny on Soup

Looking to lose a few pounds? Indulge in soup. Research shows that the best way to start a meal may be with water- or broth-based soup. It fills you up— even more so than other foods low in calorie density. You'll feel full faster and end up eating less at that sitting. Or make soup a meal in itself; with vegetable-based soups, you'll get plenty of fiber to keep you feeling full longer.

Cream of Corn Soup

Prepare as directed but substitute 1 package (10 ounces) frozen whole-kernel corn for the asparagus. Add 3/4 teaspoon chili powder to the onions at the end of cooking time and cook 30 seconds longer. Omit the dried tarragon. If you like, garnish with chopped fresh cilantro.

Each serving: About 155 calories (17 percent calories from fat), 9g protein, 20g carbohydrate, 3g total fat (1g saturated), 2mg cholesterol, 515mg sodium.

Cream of Squash Soup

Prepare as directed but substitute 1 package (10 ounces) frozen winter squash for the asparagus. Add 1/4 teaspoon pumpkin-pie spice to the onions at the end of cooking time and cook 30 seconds longer. Omit the dried tarragon. If you like, garnish with chopped tomato.

Each serving: About 115 calories (23 percent calories from fat), 8g protein, 11g carbohydrate, 3g total fat (1g saturated), 2mg cholesterol, 480mg sodium.

Cream of Pea Soup

Prepare as directed but substitute 1 package (10 ounces) frozen peas for the asparagus. Substitute 1/4 teaspoon dried mint for the dried tarragon. If you like, garnish with nonfat yogurt.

Each serving: About 155 calories, 9g protein, 20g carbohydrate, 3g total fat (1g saturated), 2mg cholesterol, 515mg sodium.

Gazpacho with Cilantro Yogurt

Prep: 30 minutes plus chilling

Based on the popular uncooked soup from southern Spain, our chunky garden-fresh version is a welcome lunch or supper on a hot day.

- 1   **pound cucumbers (2 medium), peeled**
- 1   **medium yellow pepper**
- 1/4   **small red onion**
- 2   **pounds ripe tomatoes (4 large), peeled, seeded, and cut into chunks**
- 1/2   **to 1 small jalapeño chile, seeded**
- 3   **tablespoons fresh lime juice**
- 1   **tablespoon extra virgin olive oil**
- 3/4   **plus 1/8 teaspoon salt**
- 1/4   **cup plain nonfat yogurt**
- 5   **teaspoons finely chopped fresh cilantro leaves**

1. Coarsely cut up half of 1 cucumber and half of the yellow pepper; slice all the red onion; set aside to stir into soup later. Cut remaining cucumbers and yellow pepper into chunks.

2. In food processor with knife blade attached, blend chunks of cucumber and yellow pepper, tomatoes, jalapeño, lime juice, olive oil, and 3/4 teaspoon salt until smooth. Pour into medium bowl; add cut-up cucumber, yellow pepper, and red onion. Cover and refrigerate until well chilled, at least 6 hours or overnight.

3. Meanwhile, prepare cilantro yogurt: In small bowl, mix yogurt, 4 teaspoons chopped cilantro, and remaining 1/8 teaspoon salt until smooth. Cover and refrigerate until ready to serve soup.

4. Serve cold soup with cilantro yogurt. Sprinkle with remaining 1 teaspoon chopped cilantro. Makes about 5 cups or 6 first-course servings.

Each serving: About 80 calories (22 percent calories from fat), 3g protein, 14g carbohydrate, 2g total fat (0g saturated), 1mg cholesterol, 335mg sodium.

Cool Cucumber Soup

Prep: 10 minutes

A blender whirls up this tangy no-cook soup in no time flat.

- **1 pound cucumbers (2 medium), peeled, seeded, and coarsely chopped**
- **1 container (16 ounces) plain lowfat yogurt**
- **1/2 cup cold water**
- **1 tablespoon fresh lemon juice**
- **3/4 teaspoon salt**
- **1/4 teaspoon coarsely ground black pepper**
- **1 cup ice cubes**
- **1/4 cup coarsely chopped fresh mint**

In blender, puree cucumbers, yogurt, water, lemon juice, salt, and pepper until almost smooth. With motor on and center part of cover removed, add ice cubes, one at a time. Add mint and process 5 seconds to blend. Makes about 4 cups or 4 first-course servings.

Each serving: About 91 calories (20 percent calories from fat), 7g protein, 12g carbohydrate, 2g total fat (1g saturated), 7mg cholesterol, 524mg sodium.

Carrot and Dill Soup

Prep: 25 minutes   Cook: 45 minutes

Combine sweet carrots with fresh orange, dill, and a touch of milk for a refreshing creamy soup without the cream.

- **1 tablespoon olive oil**
- **1 large onion, chopped**
- **1 medium stalk celery, chopped**
- **2 large oranges**
- **2 bags (16 ounces each) carrots, peeled and chopped**
- **1 can (14 1/2 ounces) chicken broth or 1 3/4 cup homemade**
- **1 tablespoon sugar**
- **3/4 teaspoon salt**
- **1/4 teaspoon coarsely ground black pepper**
- **1 cup milk**
- **1/4 cup chopped fresh dill**

1. In 5-quart Dutch oven, heat olive oil over medium-high heat. Add onion and celery and cook, stirring occasionally, until tender and golden, about 15 minutes.

2. Meanwhile, from 1 orange, with vegetable peeler, remove four 3" by 1" strips of peel; squeeze 1 cup juice from both oranges.

3. Add orange peel to Dutch oven and cook, stirring, 2 minutes longer. Add orange juice, carrots, water, broth, sugar, salt, and pepper; heat to boiling over high heat. Reduce heat to low; cover and simmer until carrots are very tender, about 25 minutes.

4. Remove and discard orange peel from soup. Spoon one-fourth of mixture into blender; cover, with center part of cover removed to let steam escape, and puree until smooth. Pour puree into bowl. Repeat with remaining mixture. Return soup to Dutch oven; stir in milk and chopped dill; heat just to simmering over medium heat. Makes about 10 1/2 cups or 10 first-course servings.

Each serving: About 95 calories (28 percent calories from fat), 3g protein, 16g carbohydrate, 3g total fat (1g saturated), 3mg cholesterol, 335mg sodium.

Chilled Buttermilk and Corn Soup

Prep: 20 minutes plus chilling

This refreshing refrigerator soup—with corn, tomatoes, cucumber, and basil—is both low-fat and satisfying.

- **1 quart buttermilk**
- **4 medium tomatoes (1¹/2 pounds), seeded and chopped**
- **1 small cucumber, peeled, seeded, and chopped**
- **2 cups corn kernels cut from cobs (about 4 ears)**
- **¹/2 teaspoon salt**
- **¹/4 teaspoon coarsely ground black pepper**
- **12 large fresh basil leaves**
- **6 small fresh basil sprigs**

1. In large bowl, combine buttermilk, tomatoes, cucumber, corn, salt, and pepper. Cover and refrigerate until very cold, at least 2 hours.

2. To serve, thinly slice large basil leaves. Spoon soup into 6 soup bowls; garnish with sliced basil and small basil sprigs. Makes about 4¹/2 cups or 6 first-course servings.

Each serving: About 135 calories (13 percent calories from fat), 8g protein, 24g carbohydrate, 2g total fat (1g saturated), 6mg cholesterol, 365mg sodium.

Leek Consommé with Herbs

Prep: 30 minutes   Cook: 25 minutes

A simple yet elegant clear soup for a light start to a hearty meal.

- **6 medium leeks (about 2 pounds)**
- **2 medium stalks celery**
- **4 medium carrots, peeled**
- **1 lemon**
- **3 cans (14¹/₂ ounces each) chicken or vegetable broth or 5¹/₄ cups homemade**
- **3 cups water**
- **¹/₈ teaspoon coarsely ground black pepper**
- **¹/₄ cup loosely packed fresh parsley leaves, chopped**
- **1 tablespoon coarsely chopped fresh dill lemon slices for garnish**

1. Cut root ends from leeks. Cut each leek crosswise to separate green tops from white bottoms, removing any tough outer leaves. Cut green tops crosswise into 1-inch pieces; place in large bowl of cold water. Use hands to swish leeks around to remove any grit or sand; repeat process, changing water several times. Drain well and place in 4-quart saucepan. Slice leek bottoms crosswise into thin slices; rinse thoroughly as with green tops and reserve separately.

2. Cut celery and 2 carrots crosswise into 1-inch chunks; thinly slice remaining 2 carrots crosswise on the diagonal. From lemon, with vegetable peeler, remove four 3" by 1" strips of peel; squeeze 1 tablespoon juice.

3. To saucepan with leek tops, add celery and carrot chunks, 2 strips lemon peel, broth, and water; heat to boiling over high heat. Reduce heat to low; cover and simmer 15 minutes.

4. Strain broth into 8-cup glass measuring cup or large bowl, pressing down on vegetables in strainer to extract as much broth as possible; discard vegetables. Return broth to saucepan.

5. Prepare consommé: Add pepper, lemon juice, leek bottoms, carrot slices, and remaining lemon peel to broth in saucepan; heat to boiling over high heat. Reduce heat to low; cover and simmer 10 minutes or just until vegetables are tender. Remove saucepan from heat; discard lemon peel. Stir in parsley and dill. Garnish each serving with a lemon slice. Makes about 10 cups or 10 first-course servings.

Each serving: About 45 calories (20 percent calories from fat), 3g protein, 6g carbohydrate, 1g total fat (0g saturated), 1mg cholesterol, 405mg sodium.

Tomato and Rice Soup

Prep: 20 minutes   Cook: 50 minutes

Serve this old-fashioned comfort food with crusty bread and a tossed salad for a satisfying winter meal. If you can't find either Wehani (an aromatic, reddish-brown rice that splits slightly when cooked and has a chewy texture) or black Japonica (a dark rice that tastes like a cross between basmati and wild rice), you can use long-grain brown rice.

- **¹/₂ cup Wehani, black Japonica, or long-grain brown rice**
- **1 tablespoon margarine or butter**
- **1 medium onion, finely chopped**
- **1 medium stalk celery, finely chopped**
- **1 medium carrot, peeled and finely chopped**
- **1 garlic clove, crushed with garlic press**
- **¹/₄ teaspoon dried thyme**
- **1 can (28 ounces) plum tomatoes**

1 can (14¹/2 ounces) chicken broth or 1³/4 cups homemade

1 cup water

¹/2 teaspoon salt

¹/4 teaspoon coarsely ground black pepper

1 bay leaf

¹/2 cup loosely packed fresh parsley leaves, chopped

1. Prepare rice as label directs but do not add salt, margarine, or butter; set rice aside.

2. Meanwhile, in 4-quart saucepan, melt margarine over medium heat. Add onion, celery, and carrot, and cook, stirring occasionally, until tender, about 10 minutes. Stir in garlic and thyme; cook 1 minute.

3. Add tomatoes with their juice, broth, water, salt, pepper, and bay leaf; heat to boiling over high heat, breaking up tomatoes with side of spoon. Reduce heat to medium-low and cook, covered, 30 minutes. Discard bay leaf.

4. Spoon one-fourth of mixture into blender; cover, with center part of cover removed to let steam escape, and puree until almost smooth. Pour puree into bowl. Repeat with remaining mixture. Return soup to saucepan; heat over high heat until hot. Remove pan from heat; add cooked rice and chopped parsley. Makes about 7¹/2 cups or 8 first-course or 4 main-dish servings.

Each first-course serving: About 95 calories (19 percent calories from fat), 3g protein, 16g carbohydrate, 2g total fat (1g saturated), 0mg cholesterol, 485mg sodium.

German Lentil Soup

Prep: 25 minutes   Cook: 1 hour 30 to 35 minutes

German cooks like to add a meaty ham hock and some chopped bacon to their lentil soups to lend a smoky note.

- **4** slices bacon, cut into 1/2-inch pieces
- **2** medium onions, chopped
- **2** carrots, peeled and chopped
- **1** large stalk celery, chopped
- **1** package (16 ounces) lentils, rinsed and picked through
- **1** smoked ham hock (1 pound)
- **8** cups water
- **1** bay leaf
- **1** teaspoon salt
- **1/2** teaspoon dried thyme
- **1/2** teaspoon ground black pepper
- **2** tablespoons fresh lemon juice

1. In 5-quart Dutch oven, cook bacon over medium-low heat until lightly browned. Add onions, carrots, and celery; cook over medium heat until vegetables are tender, 15 to 20 minutes. Add lentils, ham hock, water, bay leaf, salt, thyme, and pepper; heat to boiling over high heat. Reduce heat; cover and simmer until lentils are tender, 50 to 60 minutes. Remove and discard bay leaf.

2. Transfer ham hock to cutting board. Cut meat into bite-size pieces, discarding skin and bone. Return meat to soup. Heat through. Stir in lemon juice. Makes about 11 cups or 6 main-dish servings.

Each serving: About 390 calories (23 percent calories from fat), 25g protein, 52g carbohydrate, 10g total fat (3g saturated), 13mg cholesterol, 1,027mg sodium.

Hearty Mushroom-Barley Soup

Prep: 20 minutes   Cook: 1 hour

A real rib-sticker. Get a head start by cooking the barley the day before, then cool and refrigerate.

- **3/4** cup pearl barley
- **8** cups water
- **2** tablespoons olive oil
- **3** stalks celery, cut into 1/4-inch-thick slices
- **1** large onion (12 ounces), chopped
- **1 1/2** pounds mushrooms, trimmed and thickly sliced
- **2** tablespoons tomato paste
- **5** carrots, each peeled and cut lengthwise in half, then crosswise into 1/4-inch-thick slices
- **2** cans (14 1/2 ounces each) beef broth or 3 1/2 cups homemade
- **1/4** cup dry sherry
- **1 1/2** teaspoons salt

1. In 3-quart saucepan, combine barley and 4 cups water; heat to boiling over high heat. Reduce heat; cover and simmer 30 minutes. Drain.

2. Meanwhile, in 5-quart Dutch oven, heat oil over medium-high heat. Add celery and onion; cook, stirring, until golden, about 10 minutes. Increase heat to high; add mushrooms and cook, stirring occasionally, until liquid has evaporated and mushrooms are lightly browned, 10 to 12 minutes.

3. Reduce heat to medium-high; add tomato paste and cook, stirring, 2 minutes. Add barley, carrots, broth, sherry, salt, and remaining 4 cups water; heat to boiling. Reduce heat; cover and simmer until carrots and barley are tender, 20 to 25 minutes. Makes about 12 cups or 10 first-course servings.

Each serving: About 133 calories (27 percent calories from fat), 5g protein, 21g carbohydrate, 4g total fat (1g saturated), 1mg cholesterol, 684mg sodium.

Curried Sweet-Potato and Lentil Soup

Prep: 15 minutes   Cook: 1 hour 15 minutes

- 2 **tablespoons margarine or butter**
- 2 **medium sweet potatoes (1^1/$_2$ pounds), peeled and cut into ^{1}/$_2$-inch chunks**
- 2 **large stalks celery, finely chopped**
- 1 **large onion, finely chopped**
- 1 **garlic clove, finely chopped**
- 1 **tablespoon curry powder**
- 1 **tablespoon grated, peeled fresh ginger**
- 1 **teaspoon ground cumin**
- 1 **teaspoon ground coriander**
- 1 **teaspoon salt**
- ^{1}/$_8$ **teaspoon ground red pepper (cayenne)**
- 6 **cups water**
- 2 **cans (14^1/$_2$ ounces each) vegetable or chicken broth or 3^1/$_2$ cups homemade**
- 1 **package (16 ounces) dry lentils, rinsed and picked through**

garnishes: yogurt, toasted coconut, and lime wedges (optional)

1. In 6-quart Dutch oven, melt margarine over medium heat. Add sweet potatoes, celery, and onion, and cook until onion is tender, about 10 minutes, stirring occasionally. Add garlic, curry powder, ginger, cumin, coriander, salt, and ground red pepper; cook, stirring, 1 minute.

2. To vegetables in Dutch oven, add water, broth, and lentils; heat to boiling over high heat. Reduce heat to low; cover and simmer, stirring occasionally, until lentils are tender, 40 to 45 minutes. Serve soup with yogurt, toasted coconut, and lime wedges if you like. Makes about 14 cups or 8 main-dish servings.

Each serving without garnishes: About 295 calories (12 percent calories from fat), 15g protein, 51g carbohydrate, 4g total fat (1g saturated), 0mg cholesterol, 655mg sodium.

Spicy Black Bean Soup

Prep: 10 minutes   Cook: 30 minutes

Canned beans make this soup a snap to prepare, while just the right blend of spices gives it a Tex-Mex wallop of flavor.

- 1 **tablespoon vegetable oil**
- 1 **medium onion, chopped**
- 2 **garlic cloves, finely chopped**
- 2 **teaspoons chili powder**
- 1 **teaspoon ground cumin**
- ^{1}/$_2$ **teaspoon crushed red pepper**
- 2 **cans (15 to 19 ounces each) black beans, rinsed and drained**
- 2 **cups water**
- 1 **can (14^1/$_2$ ounces) chicken broth or 1^3/$_4$ cups homemade**
- ^{1}/$_4$ **cup coarsely chopped fresh cilantro**
  lime wedges

1. In 3-quart saucepan, heat oil over medium heat. Add onion and cook, stirring occasionally, until tender, 5 to 8 minutes. Stir in garlic, chili powder, cumin, and crushed red pepper; cook 30 seconds. Stir in beans, water, and broth; heat to boiling over high heat. Reduce heat and simmer 15 minutes.

2. Spoon one-fourth of mixture into blender; cover, with center part of cover removed to let steam escape, and puree until smooth. Pour puree into bowl. Repeat with remaining mixture. Sprinkle with cilantro and serve with wedges of lime. Makes about 6^2/$_3$ cups or 6 first-course servings.

Each serving: About 137 calories (26 percent calories from fat), 7g protein, 19g carbohydrate, 4g total fat (0g saturated), 0mg cholesterol, 563mg sodium.

Caribbean Black-Bean Soup

Prep: 45 minutes plus soaking beans   Cook: 2 hours 30 minutes

Our new take on black-bean soup is made with sweet potatoes and fresh cilantro for great flavor.

- 1   package (16 ounces) dry black beans
- 2   tablespoons vegetable oil
- 2   medium red onions, chopped
- 4   jalapeño chiles, seeded and minced
- 2   tablespoons minced, peeled fresh ginger
- 4   garlic cloves, finely chopped
- 1/2   teaspoon ground allspice
- 1/2   teaspoon dried thyme
- 8   cups water
- 1 1/2   pounds sweet potatoes (2 medium), peeled and cut into 3/4-inch chunks
- 1   tablespoon dark brown sugar
- 2   teaspoons salt
- 1   bunch green onions, thinly sliced
- 1   cup lightly packed fresh cilantro leaves, chopped
- 2   limes, cut into wedges (optional)

1. Rinse beans with cold running water and discard any stones or shriveled beans. In large bowl, place beans and enough water to cover by 2 inches. Cover and let stand at room temperature overnight. (Or, in 6-quart saucepot, place beans and enough water to cover by 2 inches. Heat to boiling over high heat; cook 2 minutes. Remove from heat; cover and let stand 1 hour.) Drain and rinse beans.

2. In 6-quart saucepot, heat vegetable oil over medium heat. Add onions and cook, stirring occasionally, until tender, about 10 minutes. Add jalapeño chiles, ginger, garlic, allspice, and thyme; cook, stirring, 3 minutes.

3. Add beans and water; heat to boiling over high heat. Reduce heat to low; cover and simmer 1 1/2 hours. Add sweet potatoes, brown sugar, and salt; heat to boiling over high heat. Reduce heat to low; cover and simmer until beans and sweet potatoes are tender, about 30 minutes longer.

4. Spoon 1 cup bean mixture to blender; cover, with center part of cover removed to let steam escape, and puree until smooth. Return to saucepot. Stir in green onions and cilantro. Serve with lime wedges, if you like. Makes about 13 cups or 6 main-dish servings.

Each serving: About 390 calories (14 percent calories from fat), 17g protein, 70g carbohydrate, 6g total fat (1g saturated), 0mg cholesterol, 705mg sodium.

Minestrone with Pesto

Prep: 20 minutes plus soaking beans   Cook: 1 hour

In Genoa, this hearty soup is traditionally topped with a dollop of pesto.

8   ounces dry Great Northern beans (about 1¹/3 cups)

2   tablespoons olive oil

3   medium carrots, peeled and sliced

2   stalks celery, sliced

1   large onion, finely chopped

2   ounces sliced pancetta or bacon, finely chopped

1   pound all-purpose potatoes (2 large), peeled and cut into ¹/2-inch cubes

1   pound zucchini (2 medium), quartered lengthwise then cut crosswise into ¹/4-inch pieces

4   cups sliced savoy cabbage (¹/2 medium head)

1   large garlic clove, crushed with garlic press

2   cans (14¹/2 ounces each) chicken broth or 3¹/2 cups homemade

1   can (14¹/2 ounces) diced tomatoes

1   cup water

¹/2   teaspoon salt

2   tablespoons pesto, homemade or store-bought

1. Rinse beans under cold running water and discard any stones or shriveled beans. In large bowl, place beans and enough water to cover by 2 inches. Cover and let stand at room temperature overnight. (Or, in 4-quart saucepan, place beans and enough water to cover by 2 inches. Heat to boiling over high heat; cook 2 minutes. Remove from heat; cover and let stand 1 hour.) Drain and rinse beans.

2. In 4-quart saucepan, combine beans and enough water to cover by 2 inches; heat to boiling over high heat. Reduce heat to low; cover and simmer, stirring occasionally, until beans are tender, 40 minutes to 1 hour. Drain beans.

3. Meanwhile, in 5-quart Dutch oven, heat olive oil over medium-high heat. Add carrots, celery, onion, and pancetta; cook, stirring occasionally, until onion begins to brown, 10 minutes. Add potatoes, zucchini, cabbage, and garlic; cook, stirring constantly, until cabbage wilts. Add broth, tomatoes with their juice, and water; heat to boiling over high heat. Reduce heat to low; cover and simmer until vegetables are tender, about 30 minutes.

4. Spoon ¹/2 cup beans and 1 cup soup into blender; cover, with center part of cover removed to let steam escape, and puree until smooth. Stir bean puree, remaining beans, and salt into soup; heat to boiling. Reduce heat to low; cover and simmer 10 minutes. Spoon soup into six soup bowls. Top each serving of soup with 1 teaspoon pesto. Makes 6 main-dish servings.

Each serving: About 360 calories (28 percent calories from fat), 16g protein, 52g carbohydrate, 11g total fat (3g saturated), 6mg cholesterol, 1,100mg sodium.

Italian White Bean and Spinach Soup

Prep: 20 minutes   Cook: 30 minutes

A touch of fresh lemon juice, stirred in just before serving, gives this robust soup a light citrus note.

- 1 **tablespoon vegetable oil**
- 1 **medium onion, chopped**
- 1 **stalk celery, chopped**
- 1 **garlic clove, finely chopped**
- 2 **cans (15 to 19 ounces each) white kidney beans (cannellini), rinsed and drained**
- 2 **cups water**
- 1 **can (14¹/₂ ounces) chicken broth or 1³/₄ cups homemade**
- ¹/₄ **teaspoon coarsely ground black pepper**
- ¹/₈ **teaspoon dried thyme**
- 1 **bunch (10 to 12 ounces) spinach, tough stems trimmed**
- 1 **tablespoon fresh lemon juice**
  freshly grated Parmesan cheese (optional)

1. In 3-quart saucepan, heat oil over medium heat. Add onion and celery; cook, stirring, until celery is tender, 5 to 8 minutes. Stir in garlic and cook 30 seconds. Add beans, water, broth, pepper, and thyme; heat to boiling over high heat. Reduce heat and simmer 15 minutes.

2. Roll up several spinach leaves together, cigar fashion, and thinly slice. Repeat with remaining spinach.

3. With slotted spoon, remove 2 cups beans from soup mixture and reserve. Spoon one-fourth of mixture into blender; cover, with center part of cover removed to let steam escape, and puree until smooth. Pour into bowl. Repeat with remaining mixture.

4. Return puree and reserved beans to saucepan; heat to boiling over medium-high heat. Stir in spinach and cook just until wilted, about 1 minute. Remove from heat and stir in lemon juice. Serve with Parmesan, if you like. Makes about 7¹/₂ cups or 6 first-course servings.

Each serving: About 170 calories (21 percent calories from fat), 11g protein, 24g carbohydrate, 4g total fat (1g saturated), 0mg cholesterol, 539mg sodium.

Asian Chicken-Noodle Soup

Prep: 15 minutes   Cook: 35 minutes

Ours tastes just as good as, if not better than, any noodle-shop version. Use chopsticks or a fork to pick up the long noodles.

- 4 **ounces rice noodles or linguine**
- 3 **cans (12 to 14 ounces each) chicken broth or 5¹/₄ cups homemade**
- ³/₄ **pound skinless boneless chicken breast halves**
- 4 **ounces shiitake mushrooms, stems removed and caps thinly sliced**
- 2 **tablespoons soy sauce**
- 1 **tablespoon grated, peeled fresh ginger**
- ³/₄ **teaspoon salt**
- ¹/₈ **teaspoon crushed red pepper**
- ¹/₄ **teaspoon Asian sesame oil**
- 1 **cup loosely packed fresh cilantro leaves**
- 2 **green onions, thinly sliced**

1. Prepare noodles as label directs; drain.

2. Meanwhile, in 4-quart saucepan, heat broth to boiling over high heat. Add the chicken and reduce heat to low. Simmer until chicken is cooked through, about 15

minutes. Remove chicken with a slotted spoon and set aside to cool.

3. Stir mushrooms, soy sauce, ginger, salt, and crushed red pepper into broth. Simmer, uncovered, 10 minutes.

4. Cut chicken into thin strips. Add chicken, sesame oil, and noodles to broth and heat through. Stir in cilantro and green onions. Makes about 7 cups or 4 main-dish servings.

Each serving: About 285 calories (16 percent calories from fat), 25g protein, 30g carbohydrate, 5g total fat (1g saturated), 58mg cholesterol, 1,050mg sodium.

Split Pea Soup with Ham

Prep: 10 minutes   Cook: 1 hour 15 minutes

On a wintry day, nothing satisfies more than an old-fashioned favorite like split pea soup.

- 2 **tablespoons vegetable oil**
- 2 **white turnips (6 ounces each), peeled and chopped (optional)**
- 2 **carrots, peeled and finely chopped**
- 2 **stalks celery, finely chopped**
- 1 **medium onion, finely chopped**
- 1 **package (16 ounces) dry split peas, rinsed and picked through**
- 2 **smoked ham hocks (1½ pounds)**
- 8 **cups water**
- 1 **bay leaf**
- 1 **teaspoon salt**
- ¼ **teaspoon ground allspice**

1. In 5-quart Dutch oven, heat oil over medium-high heat. Add turnips if using, carrots, celery, and onion; cook, stirring frequently, until carrots are tender-crisp, about 10 minutes. Add split peas, ham hocks, water, bay leaf, salt, and allspice; heat to boiling over high heat. Reduce heat; cover and simmer 45 minutes.

2. Discard bay leaf. Transfer ham hocks to cutting board; discard skin and bones. Finely chop meat, discarding skin and bones. Return meat to soup. Heat through. Makes 11 cups or 6 main-dish servings.

Each serving: About 343 calories (18 percent calories from fat), 21g protein, 52g carbohydrate, 7g total fat (1g saturated), 3mg cholesterol, 1,174mg sodium.

Beef-Vegetable Soup

Prep: 30 minutes plus soaking beans   Cook: 1 hour 45 minutes

An old-fashioned soup to feed a crowd. It can be made a day ahead, but for the most vibrant color, stir in the peas just before serving. You'll have plenty of soup here—the leftovers freeze well.

- 8 **ounces large dry lima beans**
- 1 **tablespoon vegetable oil**
- 2 **pounds bone-in beef shank cross cuts, each 2 inches thick, trimmed**
- 2 **medium onions, chopped**
- 3 **garlic cloves, finely chopped**
- ⅛ **teaspoon ground cloves**
- 4 **large carrots, peeled and chopped**
- 2 **stalks celery, chopped**
- ½ **small head green cabbage (8 ounces), cored and chopped (5 cups)**
- 4 **cups water**
- 1 **can (14½ ounces) beef broth or 1¾ cups homemade**
- 2 **teaspoons salt**
- ½ **teaspoon dried thyme**
- ½ **teaspoon ground black pepper**
- 1 **pound all-purpose potatoes (3 medium), peeled and cut into 1-inch pieces**
- 1 **can (14 to 16 ounces) tomatoes, chopped**
- 1 **cup frozen whole-kernel corn**
- 1 **cup frozen peas**
- ½ **cup chopped fresh parsley**

1. Rinse beans with cold running water and discard any stones or shriveled beans. In large bowl, place beans and enough water to cover by 2 inches. Cover and let stand at room temperature overnight. (Or, in 6-quart saucepot, place beans and enough water to cover by 2 inches. Heat to boiling over high heat; cook 2 minutes. Remove from heat; cover and let stand 1 hour.) Drain and rinse beans.

2. In nonreactive 8-quart saucepot, heat oil over medium-high heat until very hot. Add beef, in batches, and cook until well browned, transferring meat to bowl as it is browned. Reduce heat to medium; add onions and cook, stirring, until tender, about 5 minutes. Stir in garlic and cloves and cook 30 seconds. Return beef to saucepot; add carrots, celery, cabbage, water, broth, salt, thyme, and pepper; heat to boiling. Reduce heat; cover and simmer until beef is tender, about 1 hour.

3. Meanwhile, in 4-quart saucepan, combine beans and enough water to cover by 2 inches; heat to boiling over high heat. Reduce heat; cover and simmer until beans are just tender, about 30 minutes; drain.

4. Add potatoes and beans to saucepot; heat to boiling. Cover and simmer 5 minutes. Stir in tomatoes with their juice; cover and simmer until potatoes are tender, about 10 minutes longer.

5. With slotted spoon, transfer beef to cutting board. Cut beef into 1/2-inch pieces, discarding bones and gristle. Return beef to saucepot and add frozen corn and peas; heat through. Spoon into bowls and sprinkle with parsley. Makes about 15 1/2 cups or 8 main-dish servings.

Each serving: About 278 calories (19 percent calories from fat), 24g protein, 35g carbohydrate, 6g total fat (1g saturated), 30mg cholesterol, 955mg sodium.

Beef and Barley Soup
Prep: 45 minutes   Cook: 2 hours 30 minutes

One batch of this beef soup serves a party of eight. But we like to cook it over the weekend and freeze it in family-size portions for quick school-night dinners.

- **1   tablespoon plus 4 teaspoons vegetable oil**
- **3   medium stalks celery, finely chopped**
- **1   large onion, finely chopped**
- **1 1/2   pounds lean boneless beef chuck, trimmed and cut into 1/2-inch pieces**
- **1/2   teaspoon salt**
- **6   cups water**
- **2   cans (14 1/2 ounces each) beef broth or 3 1/2 cups homemade**
- **1   can (14 1/2 ounces) diced tomatoes**
- **1   cup pearl barley**
- **5   medium carrots (12 ounces), peeled and cut crosswise into 1/4-inch-thick slices**
- **5   medium parsnips (12 ounces), peeled and cut crosswise into 1/4-inch-thick slices**
- **2   medium turnips (8 ounces), peeled and finely chopped**
- **3   strips (3" by 1" each) orange peel**
- **pinch ground cloves**

1. In 8-quart Dutch oven, heat 1 tablespoon vegetable oil over medium-high heat. Add celery and onion and cook, stirring occasionally, until tender and golden, about 10 minutes; transfer vegetables to bowl.

2. Pat beef dry with paper towels. In same Dutch oven, heat 2 teaspoons oil over high heat until very hot. Add half of beef and cook until browned on all sides. Transfer to plate. Repeat with remaining 2 teaspoons oil and beef.

3. Return beef to Dutch oven. Stir in salt, celery mixture, water, broth and tomatoes with their juice; heat to boiling over high heat. Reduce heat to low; cover and simmer 1 hour.

4. Add barley, carrots, parsnips, turnips, orange peel, and cloves; heat to boiling over high heat. Reduce heat to low; cover and simmer until beef, barley, and vegetables are tender, 50 to 60 minutes. Makes about 16 cups or 8 main-dish servings.

Each serving: About 320 calories (25 percent calories from fat), 25g protein, 36g carbohydrate, 9g total fat (3g saturated), 41mg cholesterol, 740mg sodium.

Pear and Red Wine Soup

Prep: 10 minutes plus chilling   Cook: 20 to 25 minutes

Serve this chilled soup before a hearty main course. As with all fruit soups, make it with fully ripened fruit at its peak of flavor.

- **1 cup dry red wine**
- **1 cup water**
- **1/2 cup sugar**
- **1 lemon**
- **1 1/2 pounds ripe pears, peeled, cored, and cut into quarters**

1. In nonreactive 2-quart saucepan, combine wine, water, and sugar; heat to boiling over high heat, stirring frequently, until sugar has dissolved.

2. Meanwhile, from lemon, with vegetable peeler, remove two 3-inch strips peel; squeeze 1 tablespoon juice.

3. Add pears and lemon peel to saucepan; heat to boiling over high heat. Reduce heat and simmer until pears are very tender, 10 to 15 minutes.

4. Spoon one-fourth of pear mixture into blender. Cover, with center part of cover removed to let steam escape, and puree until smooth. Pour puree into bowl. Repeat with remaining mixture. Stir in lemon juice. Cover soup and refrigerate at least 4 hours or until very cold. Makes about 3 1/2 cups or 4 first-course servings.

Each serving: About 234 calories, 1g protein, 50g carbohydrate, 1g total fat (0g saturated), 0mg cholesterol, 3mg sodium.

3

Rice Noodles with Many Herbs,
page 48

Rice Noodles with Many Herbs

Prep: 20 minutes   Cook: 10 minutes

Whip up this light summer main dish or accompaniment with fast-cooking noodles, cucumber, carrots, herbs, and our delicious Asian dressing.

- **3 small carrots, peeled and cut into 2" by 1/4" matchstick strips (1 1/3 cups)**
- **1/3 cup seasoned rice vinegar**
- **1 package (16 ounces) 1/2-inch-wide flat rice noodles**
- **1/3 English (seedless) cucumber, unpeeled and cut into 2" by 1/4" matchstick-thin strips (1 cup)**
- **1 cup loosely packed fresh cilantro leaves**
- **1/2 cup loosely packed fresh mint leaves**
- **1/3 cup loosely packed small fresh basil leaves**
- **1/3 cup snipped fresh chives**
- **2 teaspoons Asian sesame oil**

1. In small bowl, stir carrots with rice vinegar. Let stand at room temperature while preparing noodles.

2. In 8-quart saucepot, heat 5 quarts water to boiling over high heat. Add noodles and cook 3 minutes or just until cooked through. Drain noodles; rinse under cold running water and drain again.

3. Transfer noodles to large shallow serving bowl. Add carrots with their liquid, cucumber, cilantro, mint, basil, chives, and sesame oil; toss to mix well. Makes 4 main-dish or 8 accompaniment servings.

Each main-dish serving: About 470 calories (6 percent calories from fat), 7g protein, 105g carbohydrate, 3g total fat (0g saturated), 0mg cholesterol, 550mg sodium.

Bow Ties with a Trio of Peas

Prep: 15 minutes   Cook: 25 minutes

Snow peas, sugar snap peas, and green peas are combined in a lemon broth to make this a simple yet elegant pasta dish.

- **1 package (16 ounces) bow ties or rotini**
- **1 tablespoon butter or margarine**
- **1 tablespoon olive oil**
- **4 ounces snow peas, strings removed**
- **4 ounces sugar snap peas, strings removed**
- **1 garlic clove, crushed with garlic press**
- **1 cup frozen baby peas**
- **1/2 cup low-sodium chicken or vegetable broth**
- **3/4 teaspoon salt**
- **1/4 teaspoon coarsely ground black pepper**
- **1/2 teaspoon freshly grated lemon peel**

1. In large saucepot, cook pasta as label directs. Drain and keep warm.

2. Meanwhile, in 10-inch skillet, melt butter with oil over medium-high heat. Add snow peas and sugar snap peas and cook, stirring, until tender-crisp, 1 to 2 minutes. Stir in garlic and cook 30 seconds. Add frozen baby peas, broth, salt, and pepper; heat to boiling. Stir in lemon peel. In warm serving bowl, toss pasta with vegetable mixture until combined. Makes 4 main-dish servings.

Each serving: About 536 calories (13 percent calories from fat), 19g protein, 95g carbohydrate, 8g total fat (3g saturated), 8mg cholesterol, 704mg sodium.

Bow Ties with Tomatoes and Lemon

Prep: 15 minutes plus standing   Cook: 25 minutes

A quick and easy summery sauce that "cooks" from the heat of the drained pasta. Here, mint provides a light, refreshing note.

  2 pounds ripe tomatoes (6 medium), chopped
1/4 cup loosely packed fresh mint leaves, chopped
1/4 cup loosely packed fresh basil leaves, chopped
  1 garlic clove, crushed with garlic press
  1 teaspoon freshly grated lemon peel
  2 tablespoons olive oil
  1 teaspoon salt
1/4 teaspoon ground black pepper
  1 package (16 ounces) bow-tie or ziti pasta

1. In serving bowl, combine tomatoes, mint, basil, garlic, lemon peel, oil, salt, and pepper. Let stand at least 15 minutes or up to 1 hour at room temperature to blend flavors.

2. Meanwhile, in large saucepot, cook pasta as label directs. Drain. Add pasta to tomato mixture and toss well. Makes 4 main-dish servings.

Each serving: About 536 calories (15 percent calories from fat), 17g protein, 97g carbohydrate, 9g total fat (1g saturated), 0mg cholesterol, 711mg sodium.

Penne with Spinach and Raisins

Prep: 15 minutes   Cook: 20 minutes

Golden raisins are a classic flavor addition to many Sicilian dishes, where they add an unexpected touch of sweetness.

  1 package (16 ounces) penne or bow ties
  3 tablespoons olive oil
  4 garlic cloves, crushed with side of chef's knife
  1 bunch (10 to 12 ounces) spinach, tough stems trimmed, washed and dried very well
  1 can (15 to 19 ounces) garbanzo beans, rinsed and drained
1/2 cup golden raisins
1/2 teaspoon salt
1/4 teaspoon crushed red pepper
1/2 cup chicken or vegetable broth

1. In large saucepot, cook pasta as label directs. Drain and keep warm.

2. Meanwhile, in 12-inch skillet, heat oil over medium heat. Add garlic and cook until golden. Increase heat to medium-high. Add spinach, beans, raisins, salt, and crushed red pepper; cook, stirring frequently, just until spinach wilts. Stir in broth and heat through.

3. In warm serving bowl, toss pasta with spinach mixture. Makes 6 main-dish servings.

Each serving: About 445 calories (20 percent calories from fat), 14g protein, 76g carbohydrate, 10g total fat (1g saturated), 0mg cholesterol, 466mg sodium.

Linguine with Fresh Tomato Sauce

Prep: 15 minutes   Cook: 30 minutes

If the ripe summer tomatoes you use taste a bit acidic, simply add one teaspoon sugar to the sauce. If using juicy beefsteak tomatoes instead of meaty plum tomatoes, simmer the sauce uncovered for about twenty minutes to allow the excess juices to evaporate.

> 1   tablespoon olive oil
>
> 1   small onion, chopped
>
> 2   pounds ripe plum tomatoes or beefsteak tomatoes, peeled and coarsely chopped
>
> 1/2 teaspoon salt
>
> 3   tablespoons butter, cut into pieces, or olive oil
>
> 2   tablespoons chopped fresh sage or 1/2 cup chopped fresh basil
>
> 1   package (16 ounces) linguine or penne

1. In nonstick 10-inch skillet, heat oil over medium heat. Add onion and cook until tender and golden, about 10 minutes. Add tomatoes and salt; heat to boiling over high heat. Reduce heat; cover and simmer, stirring and breaking up tomatoes with side of spoon, until sauce has thickened, 15 to 20 minutes. Stir in butter and sage.

2. Meanwhile, in large saucepot, cook pasta as label directs. Drain. In warm serving bowl, toss pasta with sauce. Makes 6 main-dish servings.

Each serving: About 388 calories (23 percent calories from fat), 11g protein, 65g carbohydrate, 10g total fat (4g saturated), 16mg cholesterol, 334mg sodium.

Pairing Pastas and Sauces

Not every pasta works with every sauce. Fragile angel hair can absorb a creamy sauce in the time it takes to turn around and get a serving spoon, and sturdy penne overpowers a delicate seafood sauce. Here's a general guide to using the most common shapes:

Long *(spaghetti, vermicelli, linguine, spaghetti, capellini [angel hair])*: Best with smooth tomato- and oil-based sauces; these varieties don't carry a chunky topping well once you lift the fork. Save ultra-thin capellini for light sauces or use in broths.

Long Straws *(perciatelli, bucatini)*: Ideal for pesto, cheese, or cream sauces because the pasta gets coated inside and out.

Short *(farfalle [bow ties], fusilli [corkscrews], orecchiette [little ears], shells, gemelli, radiatore)*: Serve with butter, cheese, tomato, meat, vegetable, and light oil-based sauces; they catch every drop.

Short Tubes *(penne, rigatoni, ziti)*: Bite for bite, the most suitable partner for meat, vegetable, and chunky tomato sauces.

Small *(pastina, ditalini, orzo, stelline, tubettini, farfalline)*: Use in broths or soups.

Wide *(tagliatelle, fettuccine, pappardelle, lasagna, mafalda)*: Substantial enough to support cream, cheese, and thick meat sauces.

Orzo "Risotto" with Mushrooms

Prep: 10 minutes   Cook: 20 minutes

  1 **package (16 ounces) orzo**

  1 **tablespoon olive oil**

  1 **medium onion, chopped**

  8 **ounces medium shiitake mushrooms, stems removed and caps cut into 1/4-inch-thick slices**

  8 **ounces medium white mushrooms, trimmed and cut into 1/4-inch-thick slices**

 1/2 **teaspoon salt**

 1/4 **cup dry white wine**

  2 **tablespoons cornstarch**

2 1/2 **cups low-fat milk (1%)**

 1/3 **cup grated Parmesan cheese**

  3 **tablespoons chopped fresh parsley leaves**

  1 **tablespoon margarine or butter**

1. In 5-quart saucepot, cook orzo as label directs; drain and keep warm.

2. Meanwhile, in nonstick 12-inch skillet, heat oil over medium heat. Add onion and cook 5 minutes. Increase heat to medium-high. Add shiitake and white mushrooms and 1/4 teaspoon salt; cook, stirring frequently, until mushrooms are tender and golden. Remove skillet from heat; stir in white wine.

3. In small bowl, mix cornstarch with milk. Add cornstarch mixture to same 5-quart saucepot. Heat to boiling over medium heat. Reduce heat to low; simmer 1 minute. Stir in orzo, mushroom mixture, grated Parmesan, parsley, margarine, and remaining 1/4 teaspoon salt; heat through. Serve "risotto" immediately while still creamy. Makes 6 main-dish servings.

Each serving: About 425 calories (17 percent calories from fat), 17g protein, 70g carbohydrate, 8g total fat (2g saturated), 8mg cholesterol, 615mg sodium.

Penne with Tomato Cream

Prep: 15 minutes   Cook: 30 minutes

This restaurant favorite is a cinch to prepare at home. Don't hesitate to add the vodka. You won't taste it: It just melds the flavors.

- **1 tablespoon olive oil**
- **1 small onion, chopped**
- **1 garlic clove, finely chopped**
- **1/8 to 1/4 teaspoon crushed red pepper**
- **1 can (28 ounces) tomatoes in puree, coarsely chopped**
- **3 tablespoons vodka (optional)**
- **1/2 teaspoon salt**
- **1/2 cup heavy or whipping cream**
- **1 cup frozen peas, thawed**
- **1 package (16 ounces) penne or rotini**
- **1/2 cup loosely packed fresh basil leaves, thinly sliced**

1. In nonstick 12-inch skillet, heat oil over medium heat. Add onion and cook until tender, about 5 minutes. Add garlic and crushed red pepper; cook until garlic is golden, about 30 seconds longer. Stir in tomatoes with their puree, vodka if using, and salt; heat to boiling over high heat. Reduce heat and simmer until sauce has thickened, 15 to 20 minutes. Stir in cream and peas; heat to boiling.

2. Meanwhile, in large saucepot, cook pasta as label directs. Drain. In warm serving bowl, toss pasta with sauce and sprinkle with basil. Makes 6 main-dish servings.

Each serving: About 434 calories (23 percent calories from fat), 13g protein, 71g carbohydrate, 11g total fat (5g saturated), 27mg cholesterol, 509mg sodium.

Spaghetti with Roasted Tomatoes

Prep: 10 minutes plus cooling   Roast/Cook: 1 hour

Oven-roasted tomatoes have a sweet, intense flavor that is hard to resist. They make a terrific pasta sauce.

- **2 tablespoons olive oil**
- **3 pounds ripe plum tomatoes (16 medium), cut lengthwise in half**
- **6 garlic cloves, not peeled**
- **1 package (16 ounces) spaghetti or linguine**
- **3/4 teaspoon salt**
- **1/4 teaspoon coarsely ground black pepper**
  freshly grated Pecorino Romano cheese (optional)

1. Preheat oven to 450°F. Brush jelly-roll pan with 1 tablespoon oil. Arrange tomatoes, cut side down, in pan; add garlic. Roast tomatoes and garlic until tomatoes are well browned and garlic has softened, 50 to 60 minutes.

2. When cool enough to handle, peel tomatoes over medium bowl to catch any juices. Place tomatoes in bowl; discard skins. Squeeze garlic to separate pulp from skins. Add garlic to tomatoes.

3. Meanwhile, in large saucepot, cook the pasta as label directs. Drain.

4. With back of spoon, crush tomatoes and garlic. Stir in salt, pepper, and remaining 1 tablespoon oil. Serve sauce at room temperature or transfer to saucepan and heat through over low heat. In warm serving bowl, toss pasta with sauce. Serve with Pecorino, if you like. Makes 4 main-dish servings.

Each serving: About 552 calories (16 percent calories from fat), 17g protein, 101g carbohydrate, 10g total fat (1g saturated), 0mg cholesterol, 570mg sodium.

Reduced-Fat Macaroni and Cheese

Prep: 20 minutes   Bake/Broil: 22 minutes

They'll never know we took out ten grams of fat per serving, because this macaroni and cheese is as good as—even better than—the old-fashioned recipe.

- **8 ounces elbow macaroni twists**
- **1 container (16 ounces) lowfat cottage cheese (1%)**
- **2 tablespoons all-purpose flour**
- **2 cups fat-free (skim) milk**
- **4 ounces sharp Cheddar cheese, shredded (1 cup)**
- **1 teaspoon salt**
- **1/4 teaspoon ground black pepper**
  pinch ground nutmeg
- **1/4 cup freshly grated Parmesan cheese**

1. Preheat oven to 375°F. Grease broiler-safe, shallow 2 1/2-quart casserole. In medium saucepot, cook macaroni as label directs, but do not add salt to water. Drain.

2. In food processor with knife blade attached, puree cottage cheese until smooth. (Or, in blender, puree cottage cheese with 1/4 cup of milk in recipe until smooth.)

3. In 2-quart saucepan, blend flour with 1/4 cup milk until smooth. With wire whisk, slowly stir in remaining milk until blended. Cook over medium heat, whisking, until mixture has thickened slightly and boils. Remove from heat; stir in cottage cheese, Cheddar, salt, pepper, and nutmeg.

4. Spoon macaroni into prepared casserole and cover with cheese sauce. Bake 20 minutes. Remove from oven; sprinkle with Parmesan. Turn oven control to broil.

5. Place casserole in broiler at closest position to heat source; broil until top is golden brown, 2 to 3 minutes. Makes 8 accompaniment or 4 main-dish servings.

Each accompaniment serving: About 251 calories (25 percent calories from fat), 18g protein, 28g carbohydrate, 7g total fat (4g saturated), 21mg cholesterol, 724mg sodium.

Bow Ties with Cannellini and Spinach

Prep: 10 minutes   Cook: 15 minutes

- **12 ounces bow-tie pasta**
- **2 bags (10 ounces each) prewashed spinach**
- **1 tablespoon olive oil**
- **1 jumbo onion (1 pound), thinly sliced**
- **3/4 cup chicken or vegetable broth**
- **1 teaspoon cornstarch**
- **1/2 teaspoon salt**
- **1/4 teaspoon crushed red pepper**
- **1 can (15 to 19 ounces) white kidney beans (cannellini), rinsed and drained**
- **2 tablespoons grated Pecorino Romano or Parmesan cheese**

1. In large saucepot, cook pasta as label directs. Just before draining pasta, stir spinach into water in saucepot; leave in only until it wilts. Drain pasta and spinach; return to saucepot and keep warm.

2. Meanwhile, in nonstick 12-inch skillet, heat oil over medium-high heat. Add onion and cook until golden brown, 10 to 12 minutes. In 1-cup glass measuring cup, mix broth, cornstarch, salt, and crushed red pepper. Add to skillet along with beans and cook over medium-high heat until sauce boils and thickens slightly, about 1 minute.

3. Add sauce to pasta and spinach in saucepot; toss to mix well. Sprinkle with Romano to serve. Makes 4 main-dish servings.

Each serving: About 545 calories (12 percent calories from fat), 24g protein, 99g carbohydrate, 7g total fat (1g saturated), 5mg cholesterol, 925mg sodium.

Penne with Yellow Peppers and Sweet Onion

Prep: 15 minutes   Cook: 15 minutes

1 package (16 ounces) penne rigate or elbow twist pasta

2 tablespoons olive oil

2 medium yellow peppers, thinly sliced

1 large sweet onion (12 ounces) such as Walla Walla or Vidalia, thinly sliced

1/2 teaspoon salt

1/4 teaspoon coarsely ground black pepper

1 tablespoon balsamic vinegar

1/2 cup chopped fresh basil leaves

1. In large saucepot, cook pasta as label directs. Drain, reserving 1/2 cup pasta cooking water; return pasta to saucepot and keep warm.

2. Meanwhile, in 12-inch skillet, heat oil over medium heat. Add yellow peppers, onion, salt, and black pepper; cook, stirring frequently, until vegetables are tender and golden, about 15 minutes. Remove skillet from heat; stir in balsamic vinegar and basil.

3. Add the reserved pasta cooking water and yellow-pepper mixture to pasta in saucepot; toss well. Makes 4 main-dish or 8 accompaniment servings.

Each main-dish serving: About 525 calories (15 percent calories from fat), 16g protein, 95g carbohydrate, 9g total fat (1g saturated), 0mg cholesterol, 455mg sodium.

Ziti with Roasted Asparagus

Prep: 15 minutes   Roast/Cook: 30 minutes

Toasted pecans make this easy dish luxurious.

- **2 tablespoons olive oil**
- **1/4 teaspoon dried rosemary**
- **2 pounds asparagus, trimmed and cut into 1-inch pieces (6 cups)**
- **1 package (16 ounces) ziti**
- **1 cup half-and-half or light cream**
- **3/4 teaspoon freshly grated lemon peel**
- **1/2 teaspoon salt**
- **1/4 teaspoon ground black pepper**
- **1/3 cup toasted pecans, coarsely chopped**

1. Preheat oven to 400°F. Combine oil and rosemary in 13" by 9" baking pan. Place pan in oven until oil is hot, about 4 minutes. Add asparagus; toss to coat with oil. Roast asparagus, tossing occasionally, until tender, about 15 minutes.

2. Meanwhile, in large saucepot, cook the pasta as label directs. Drain.

3. In 12-inch skillet, heat half-and-half to boiling over medium heat; cook 5 minutes. Stir in lemon peel, salt, and pepper. Add pasta and asparagus; toss to coat. Transfer to warm serving bowls and sprinkle with pecans. Makes 6 main-dish servings.

Each serving: About 410 calories (26 percent calories from fat), 15g protein, 63g carbohydrate, 12g total fat (4g saturated), 15mg cholesterol, 282mg sodium.

Bow Ties with Fennel and Leeks

Prep: 35 minutes   Bake: 20 minutes

The vegetables become sweet and tender when cooked in olive oil.

- **4** **medium leeks (1¹/₂ pounds)**
- **2** **tablespoons olive oil**
- **2** **medium fennel bulbs (1 pound each), trimmed and thinly sliced, feathery tops reserved**
- **2** **garlic cloves, finely chopped**
- **1** **tablespoon sugar**
- **1** **package (16 ounces) bow-tie or gemelli pasta**
- **1** **cup chicken or vegetable broth**
- **¹/₄** **cup heavy or whipping cream**
- **¹/₂** **cup grated Parmesan cheese**
- **¹/₂** **teaspoon salt**
- **¹/₄** **teaspoon coarsely ground black pepper**
- **1** **ripe, medium tomato, finely chopped**

1. Preheat oven to 400°F. Cut off root ends and tough green tops from leeks. Cut each leek lengthwise in half, then crosswise into ¹/₄-inch-wide slices. Place in large bowl of cold water. Use hands to swish leeks around to remove any grit or sand. Repeat process, changing water several times. Drain well.

2. In nonstick 12-inch skillet, heat 1 tablespoon oil over medium heat. Add leeks and cook, stirring frequently, until tender and golden, about 15 minutes. Add fennel, garlic, sugar, and remaining 1 tablespoon oil; cook, stirring frequently, until fennel is tender and light golden, about 20 minutes.

3. Meanwhile, cook pasta as label directs. Drain; return pasta to saucepot and keep warm.

4. When fennel is tender, add broth, cream, all but 2 tablespoons Parmesan, salt, and pepper; boil 1 minute.

5. Spoon pasta into deep 4-quart casserole. Add leek mixture and toss well. Sprinkle top with chopped tomato and remaining 2 tablespoons Parmesan. Cover and bake until hot and bubbly, about 20 minutes. Garnish with fennel tops to serve. Makes 6 main-dish servings.

Each serving: About 460 calories (22 percent calories from fat), 15g protein, 77g carbohydrate, 11g total fat (4g saturated), 17mg cholesterol, 560mg sodium.

Chili Lasagna

Prep: 15 minutes   Bake: 1 hou

- 2 **tablespoons vegetable oil**
- 1 **medium onion, chopped**
- 2 **tablespoons chili powder**
- 2¹/2 **cups water**
- 1 **can (28 ounces) tomatoes**
- 1 **can (15¹/4 to 19 ounces) red kidney beans, rinsed and drained**
- 3 **tablespoons tomato paste**
- 1 **teaspoon sugar**
- 1 **teaspoon salt**
- ¹/2 **teaspoon coarsely ground black pepper**
- 3 **medium zucchini (1¹/2 pounds), chopped**
- 18 **no-boil lasagna noodles (12 ounces)**
- 12 **ounces part-skim mozzarella cheese, shredded (3 cups)**

1. In 3-quart saucepan, heat 1 tablespoon oil over medium-high heat. Add onion and cook, stirring occasionally, until tender and lightly browned. Stir in chili powder; cook 1 minute.

2. Add water, tomatoes with their juice, kidney beans, tomato paste, sugar, salt, and pepper; heat to boiling over high heat. Reduce heat to low; simmer, stirring occasionally, 15 minutes.

3. In 10-inch skillet, heat remaining 1 tablespoon oil over medium-high heat. Add zucchini and cook until golden brown.

4. Preheat oven to 375°F. In 13" by 9" glass baking dish, evenly spoon one-third of sauce. Arrange half of no-boil lasagna noodles over sauce, overlapping to fit. Top with zucchini, half of mozzarella, and half of remaining sauce. Top with remaining no-boil noodles, then remaining sauce. Sprinkle remaining mozzarella over sauce.

5. Cover lasagna and bake 40 to 45 minutes; uncover and bake until hot and cheese is brown and bubbly, 15 minutes longer. Makes 12 main-dish servings.

Each serving: About 255 calories (28 percent calories from fat), 14g protein, 34g carbohydrate, 8g total fat (3g saturated), 17mg cholesterol, 530mg sodium.

Lasagna Roll-ups

Prep: 35 minutes   Bake: 35 to 40 minutes

1/2 **(16-ounce) package curly lasagna noodles (9 noodles)**

2 **cans (14 1/2 ounces each) stewed tomatoes**

1 **can (8 ounces) tomato sauce**

1 **container (15 ounces) part-skim ricotta cheese**

2 **ounces part-skim mozzarella cheese, shredded (1/2 cup)**

3 **tablespoons grated Parmesan cheese**

4 **tablespoons chopped fresh basil**

1/2 **teaspoon coarsely ground black pepper**

2 **teaspoons olive oil**

1 **small onion, chopped**

1 **small zucchini (4 ounces), finely chopped**

1 **small tomato, finely chopped**

1 **tablespoon capers, drained and chopped**

1. In large saucepot, cook lasagna noodles as label directs. Drain and rinse with cold running water. Return noodles to saucepot with cold water to cover. Meanwhile, in 3-quart glass or ceramic baking dish, combine stewed tomatoes and tomato sauce; break up tomatoes with side of spoon.

2. Prepare filling: In large bowl, mix ricotta, mozzarella, Parmesan, 3 tablespoons basil, and pepper.

3. Preheat oven to 375°F. Place lasagna noodles on clean kitchen towels. Spread about 1/4 cup filling on each lasagna noodle and roll up jelly-roll fashion. Slice each rolled noodle crosswise in half. Arrange lasagna rolls, cut side down, in sauce in baking dish; cover loosely with foil. Bake until heated through, 35 to 40 minutes.

4. Meanwhile, prepare topping: In nonstick 10-inch skillet, heat oil over medium heat. Add onion; cook until tender and browned. Stir in zucchini; cook until tender. Stir in finely chopped tomato, capers and remaining 1 tablespoon basil; heat through.

5. To serve, place sauce and lasagna rolls on 6 plates; spoon topping over lasagna rolls. Makes 6 main-dish servings.

Each serving: About 335 calories (30 percent calories from fat), 18g protein, 42g carbohydrate, 11g total fat (6g saturated), 30mg cholesterol, 725mg sodium.

Butternut Squash Lasagna

Prep: 1 hour 15 minutes   Bake: 40 minutes

An elegant party entrée—serve with crusty bread and red wine.

- **12** lasagna noodles
- **1** large butternut squash (3 pounds), peeled, seeded, and cut into 1-inch chunks
- **2** tablespoons olive oil
- **3/4** teaspoon salt
- **1** jumbo onion (1 pound), cut in half and thinly sliced
- **1** large bunch Swiss chard (1 1/2 pounds), coarsely chopped, with tough stems discarded

WHITE SAUCE:

- **2** tablespoons margarine or butter
- **1/3** cup all-purpose flour
- **1/4** teaspoon ground nutmeg
- **1/4** teaspoon dried thyme
- **1/4** teaspoon salt
- **1/4** teaspoon coarsely ground black pepper
- **4** cups low-fat milk (1%)
- **3/4** cup grated Parmesan cheese

1. In large saucepot, cook lasagna noodles as label directs. Drain and rinse with cold running water to stop cooking; drain again. Layer noodles between sheets of waxed paper.

Nutrition Spotlight: Winter Squash

Take your pick of acorn, banana, butternut, delicata, and hubbard squash, all at about 50 calories per half cup. Like its pumpkin cousin, squash is rich in the antioxidant beta-carotene, though the amount varies with the color of the flesh. (For the biggest nutritional punch, go with deep yellow and orange flesh varieties.)

2. Meanwhile, preheat oven to 450°F. In large bowl, toss butternut squash chunks with 1 tablespoon oil and 1/2 teaspoon salt. Place squash on 15 1/2" by 10 1/2" jelly-roll pan or large cookie sheet. Roast squash, stirring halfway through cooking, until fork-tender, 30 minutes. Remove from oven and, with potato masher or fork, mash squash until almost smooth; set aside. Turn oven control to 375°F.

3. Meanwhile, in 5-quart Dutch oven or saucepot, heat remaining 1 tablespoon oil over medium heat. Add onion and remaining 1/4 teaspoon salt; cook, stirring often, until golden, about 25 minutes. Add Swiss chard and cook until wilted and liquid evaporates, about 7 minutes. Remove Dutch oven from heat; set aside.

4. Prepare White Sauce: In 3-quart saucepan, melt margarine over medium heat. With wire whisk, stir in flour, nutmeg, thyme, salt, and pepper; cook, whisking constantly, 1 minute. Gradually whisk in milk until blended. Cook over medium-high heat, whisking frequently, until sauce has thickened slightly and boils. Boil, whisking, 1 minute. Whisk in all but 2 tablespoons Parmesan. Remove saucepan from heat.

5. In 13" by 9" glass baking dish, evenly spoon about 1/2 cup white sauce to cover bottom of dish. Arrange 4 lasagna noodles over sauce, overlapping to fit. Evenly spread all Swiss chard mixture over noodles and top with about 1 cup white sauce. Arrange 4 lasagna noodles on top, then about 1 cup white sauce and all the butternut squash. Top with remaining lasagna noodles and remaining white sauce. Sprinkle with remaining 2 tablespoons Parmesan.

6. Cover lasagna with foil and bake 30 minutes; remove foil and bake until hot and bubbly, 10 minutes longer. Let lasagna stand 10 minutes for easier serving. Makes 10 main-dish servings.

Each serving: About 315 calories (26 percent calories from fat), 13g protein, 47g carbohydrate, 9g total fat (3g saturated), 10mg cholesterol, 575mg sodium.

Linguine with Scallops and Saffron

Prep: 20 minutes   Cook: 15 minutes

We flavored the creamy sauce with orange peel and saffron threads.

- **1 package (16 ounces) linguine or spaghetti**
- **3 medium leeks (1 pound)**
- **1 pound sea scallops, cut horizontally in half**
- **2 tablespoons margarine or butter**
- **3/4 teaspoon salt**
- **1/4 teaspoon coarsely ground black pepper**
- **1/2 teaspoon grated orange peel**
- **large pinch saffron threads, crumbled**
- **1/4 cup dry white wine**
- **1 bottle (8 ounces) clam juice**
- **1/4 cup heavy or whipping cream**
- **1/2 cup loosely packed fresh parsley leaves**

1. In large saucepot, cook pasta as label directs. Drain; return pasta to saucepot and keep warm.

2. Meanwhile, cut off root ends and tough green tops from leeks. Cut each leek lengthwise in half, then crosswise into 1/2-inch-wide slices. Place in large bowl of cold water. Use hands to swish leeks around to remove any grit or sand; repeat process, changing water several times. Drain well. Pull off and discard tough crescent-shaped muscle from each scallop.

3. In 12-inch skillet, melt margarine over medium heat. Add leeks, salt, and pepper; cook, stirring frequently, until leeks are soft, about 8 minutes. Add orange peel and saffron and cook, stirring, 2 minutes. Add wine; cook 1 minute longer. Increase heat to medium-high. Add clam juice and heat to boiling. Add scallops and cook until just opaque throughout, 3 to 4 minutes. Stir in cream and heat through.

4. Add leek mixture to pasta in saucepot; toss well. Sprinkle with parsley leaves just before serving. Makes 6 main-dish servings.

Each serving: About 440 calories (18 percent calories from fat), 24g protein, 66g carbohydrate, 9g total fat (3g saturated), 40mg cholesterol, 635mg sodium.

Linguine with White Clam Sauce

Prep: 15 minutes   Cook: 30 minutes

Start with fresh clams and add a few ingredients to cook up one of the best of all pasta dishes. Don't overcook the clams or they will become tough.

- **1/2 cup dry white wine**
- **2 dozen littleneck clams, scrubbed**
- **1 package (16 ounces) linguine or spaghetti**
- **1/4 cup olive oil**
- **1 large garlic clove, finely chopped**
- **1/4 teaspoon crushed red pepper**
- **1/4 cup chopped fresh parsley**

1. In nonreactive 5-quart Dutch oven, heat wine to boiling over high heat. Add clams; reduce heat to medium. Cover and simmer until clams open, 5 to 10 minutes, transferring clams to bowl as they open. Discard any clams that do not open.

2. Strain clam broth through sieve lined with paper towels; set aside. When cool enough to handle, remove clams from shells and coarsely chop. Discard shells.

3. Meanwhile, in large saucepot, cook the pasta as label directs. Drain.

4. Add oil, garlic, and crushed red pepper to same clean Dutch oven. Cook over medium heat, stirring occasionally, just until garlic turns golden. Stir in parsley, clams, and clam broth; heat just to simmering. Add pasta to Dutch oven and toss until combined. Makes 6 main-dish servings.

Each serving: About 427 calories (23 percent calories from fat), 19g protein, 59g carbohydrate, 11g total fat (1g saturated), 24mg cholesterol, 111mg sodium.

Linguine with Broccoli and Clams

Prep: 30 minutes   Cook: 20 minutes

*Our lightened version of classic linguine with clam sauce
includes healthy broccoli flowerets.*

     salt
- **15 ounces broccoli flowerets (6 cups)**
- **1 package (1 pound) linguine or spaghetti**
- **1/2 cup dry white wine**
- **2 dozen littleneck or small cherrystone clams,
  well scrubbed**
- **1 tablespoon olive oil**
- **2 garlic cloves, finely chopped**
- **1/2 teaspoon coarsely ground black pepper**
- **1/8 to 1/4 teaspoon crushed red pepper**
- **1/4 cup loosely packed fresh parsley leaves, chopped**

1. In large saucepot of boiling salted water, cook broccoli until almost tender, 4 to 6 minutes. With slotted
spoon or metal strainer, transfer broccoli to bowl; do
not discard cooking water. Rinse broccoli with cold
running water to stop cooking.

2. In same saucepot of boiling water, cook pasta as
label directs. Drain.

3. Meanwhile, in deep 12-inch skillet, heat wine to boiling over high heat. Add clams and reduce heat to
medium. Cover and simmer until clams open, 7 to 10
minutes, transferring clams to large bowl as they open.
Discard any clams that do not open. Strain clam broth
through sieve lined with paper towels; add enough
water to clam broth to equal 1 1/2 cups. When cool
enough to handle, remove clams from shells and
coarsely chop, adding any clam juices to reserved
broth. (Reserve a few clams in the shell for garnish if
you like.).

4. Clean skillet and wipe dry. Heat oil over medium
heat. Add garlic and cook, stirring, 30 seconds. Add
broccoli flowerets, black pepper, red pepper, clams,
and reserved broth to skillet; cook, stirring gently, until
heated through.

5. In warm serving bowl, toss hot pasta with broccoli
mixture. Add reserved clams in shells and sprinkle
with parsley. Makes 4 main-dish servings.

Each serving: About 520 calories (10 percent calories from fat),
24g protein, 91g carbohydrate, 6g total fat (1g saturated), 18mg
cholesterol, 360mg sodium.

Seafood Fra Diavolo

Prep: 25 minutes   Cook: 1 hour

*Shrimp and mussels adorn this festive pasta, while rings of
tender squid provide extra flavor.*

- **8 ounces cleaned squid**
- **1 tablespoon olive oil**
- **1 large garlic clove, finely chopped**
- **1/4 teaspoon crushed red pepper**
- **1 can (28 ounces) plum tomatoes**
- **1/2 teaspoon salt**
- **1 dozen mussels, scrubbed and debearded**
- **8 ounces medium shrimp, shelled and deveined**

- **1 package (16 ounces) linguine or spaghetti**
- **1/4 cup chopped fresh parsley**

1. Rinse squid and pat dry with paper towels. Slice
squid bodies crosswise into 1/4-inch rings. Cut tentacles into several pieces if they are large.

2. In non-reactive 4-quart saucepan, heat oil over
medium heat. Add garlic and crushed red pepper;
cook just until fragrant, about 30 seconds. Stir in tomatoes with their juice and salt, breaking up tomatoes
with side of spoon. Heat to boiling over high heat. Add

squid and heat to boiling. Reduce heat; cover and simmer 30 minutes. Remove cover and simmer 15 minutes longer. Increase heat to high. Add mussels; cover and cook 3 minutes. Stir in shrimp; cover and cook until mussels open and shrimp are opaque throughout, about 2 minutes longer. Discard any mussels that do not open.

3. Meanwhile, in large saucepot, cook pasta as label directs. Drain. In warm serving bowl, toss pasta with seafood mixture and parsley. Makes 6 main-dish servings.

Each serving: About 410 calories (11 percent calories from fat), 25g protein, 65g carbohydrate, 5g total fat (1g saturated), 140mg cholesterol, 588mg sodium.

Thai Pasta with Shrimp

Prep: 15 minutes   Cook: 15 minutes

Delicate angel hair pasta absorbs sauce quickly, so put this on plates as soon as it's tossed. Serve with lime wedges if you like.

- **1   package (16 ounces) angel hair pasta**
- **2   teaspoons curry powder**
- **1   can (14 ounces) light coconut milk (not cream of coconut)**
- **1   teaspoon salt**
- **1/8 teaspoon coarsely ground black pepper**
- **1   pound medium shrimp, shelled and deveined, leaving tail part of shell on, if you like**
- **1   cup loosely packed fresh cilantro leaves**

1. In large saucepot, cook pasta as label directs. Drain.

2. Meanwhile, in 10-inch skillet, cook curry powder over medium heat, stirring frequently, 2 minutes. Stir in coconut milk, salt, and pepper until blended; heat to boiling over high heat. Add shrimp; reduce heat to medium. Cover and cook until shrimp just turn opaque throughout, 2 minutes.

3. In warm serving bowl, toss pasta with shrimp mixture and cilantro. Makes 6 main-dish servings.

Each serving: About 410 calories (18 percent calories from fat), 23g protein, 59g carbohydrate, 8g total fat (4g saturated), 95mg cholesterol, 550mg sodium.

Pad Thai

Prep: 25 minutes plus soaking noodles   Cook: 5 minutes

Authentic Pad Thai is made with rice noodles (use the 1/8-inch-wide ones) that are available at Asian markets. If you can't find them, use angel hair pasta or linguine (cooked according to the package directions). It will still be delicious.

- **1   package (7 to 8 ounces) rice stick noodles (rice vermicelli), or 8 ounces angel hair pasta**
- **1/4 cup fresh lime juice**
- **1/4 cup Asian fish sauce (nam pla)**
- **2   tablespoons sugar**
- **1   tablespoon vegetable oil**
- **8   ounces medium shrimp, shelled and deveined, then cut lengthwise in half**
- **2   garlic cloves, finely chopped**
- **1/4 teaspoon crushed red pepper**
- **3   large eggs, lightly beaten**
- **6   ounces bean sprouts (2 cups), rinsed and drained**
- **1/3 cup unsalted roasted peanuts, coarsely chopped**
- **3   green onions, thinly sliced**
- **1/2 cup loosely packed fresh cilantro leaves lime wedges**

1. In large bowl, soak rice stick noodles, if using, in enough hot water to cover for 20 minutes. Drain. With kitchen shears, cut noodles into 4-inch lengths. If using angel hair pasta, break in half, cook in large saucepot as label directs, drain, and rinse with cold running water.

2. Meanwhile, in small bowl, combine lime juice, fish sauce, and sugar. Assemble all remaining ingredients and place next to stove.

3. In 12-inch skillet, heat oil over high heat until hot. Add shrimp, garlic, and crushed red pepper; cook, stirring, 1 minute. Add eggs and cook, stirring, until just set, about 20 seconds. Add drained noodles and cook, stirring, 2 minutes. Add fish-sauce mixture, half of bean sprouts, half of peanuts, and half of green onions; cook, stirring, 1 minute.

4. Transfer Pad Thai to warm platter or serving bowl. Top with remaining bean sprouts and sprinkle with remaining peanuts, remaining green onions, and cilantro. Serve with lime wedges. Makes 4 main-dish servings.

Each serving: About 472 calories (30 percent calories from fat), 21g protein, 63g carbohydrate, 16g total fat (3g saturated), 230mg cholesterol, 811mg sodium.

Bow Ties with Shrimp and Fennel

Prep: 10 minutes   Cook: 15 minutes

The secrets to success here are a bag of frozen shrimp and a mixture of garlic and fennel seeds. If you don't have a mortar and pestle, crush garlic with a press and place the seeds in a sealed plastic bag, then mash with a rolling pin.

- **1 package (16 ounces) bow-tie pasta**
- **1 bag (16 ounces) frozen uncooked extralarge shrimp, shelled and deveined**
- **1 cup frozen peas**
- **1 small garlic clove**
- **1 teaspoon fennel seeds**
- **1/2 teaspoon salt**
- **1/4 teaspoon coarsely ground black pepper**
- **4 ripe medium tomatoes, finely chopped**
- **2 tablespoons olive oil**
- **2 ounces feta cheese, crumbled (1/2 cup)**

1. In large saucepot, cook pasta as label directs. After pasta has cooked 12 minutes, add frozen shrimp and peas to pasta cooking water and continue cooking until pasta is done and shrimp turn opaque throughout, about 3 minutes. Drain pasta and shrimp; return to saucepot and keep warm.

2. Meanwhile, in mortar with pestle, crush garlic with fennel seeds, salt, and pepper. Transfer mixture to medium bowl and stir in tomatoes and olive oil.

3. Add tomato mixture and feta cheese to pasta and shrimp in saucepot; toss well. Makes 6 main-dish servings.

Each serving: About 465 calories (17 percent calories from fat), 29g protein, 66g carbohydrate, 9g total fat (3g saturated), 125mg cholesterol, 520mg sodium.

Shells with Smoked Trout and Chives

Prep: 15 minutes   Cook: 15 minutes

The lemony cream sauce is a delicious complement to the smoky fish. The flavors in this simple pasta dish would also work well with other smoked fish. Since the saltiness of smoked fish can vary considerably, taste first before adding salt in Step 2. Although the chives are an important flavor component here, minced scallion greens are a fine substitute.

- **1 package (16 ounces) medium shell pasta or linguine**
- **12 ounces green beans, trimmed**
- **1 whole smoked trout (6 ounces)**
- **1/2 cup half-and-half or light cream**
- **1/2 teaspoon grated lemon peel**
- **4 tablespoons chopped fresh chives**
- **1/4 teaspoon salt**
- **1/4 teaspoon coarsely ground black pepper**

1. In large saucepot, cook pasta as label directs. If you like, cut green beans crosswise in half. After pasta has cooked 5 minutes, add green beans to pasta cooking water and continue cooking until pasta is done and beans are crisp-tender. Drain, reserving 1/2 cup pasta water. Return pasta and beans to saucepot and keep warm.

2. Meanwhile, remove head, tail, skin, and bones from trout and discard. Separate flesh into 1-inch pieces. In 2-quart saucepan, heat half-and-half, lemon peel, 1 tablespoon chopped chives, salt, and pepper over low heat to simmering. Remove saucepan from heat; cover and keep warm.

3. Add reserved pasta water, trout, half-and-half mixture, and remaining 3 tablespoons chopped chives to pasta and beans in saucepot; toss well. Makes 6 main-dish servings.

Each serving: About 350 calories (13 percent calories from fat), 15g protein, 62g carbohydrate, 5g total fat (2g saturated), 10mg cholesterol, 360mg sodium.

Penne with Salmon and Asparagus

Prep: 15 minutes   Cook: 30 minutes

A white-wine-and-tarragon-infused broth is a luscious match for the salmon in this ever-popular seafood-and-vegetable combination.

- **1 package (16 ounces) penne rigate or bow-tie pasta**
- **3 teaspoons olive oil**
- **1 pound asparagus, trimmed and cut into 2-inch pieces**
- **1/2 teaspoon salt**
- **1/4 teaspoon coarsely ground black pepper**
- **1 large shallot, finely chopped (1/4 cup)**
- **1/3 cup dry white wine**
- **1 cup low-sodium chicken broth**
- **1 skinless salmon fillet (1 pound), cut crosswise into thirds, then lengthwise into 1/4-inch-thick slices**
- **1 tablespoon chopped fresh tarragon**

1. In large saucepot, cook pasta as label directs. Drain.

2. Meanwhile, in nonstick 12-inch skillet, heat 2 teaspoons oil over medium-high heat. Add asparagus, salt, and pepper and cook until asparagus is almost

tender-crisp, about 5 minutes. Add shallot and remaining 1 teaspoon oil; cook, stirring constantly, 2 minutes longer. Add wine; heat to boiling over high heat. Stir in broth and heat to boiling. Arrange salmon slices in skillet; cover and cook until just opaque throughout, 2 to 3 minutes. Remove skillet from heat; stir in tarragon. In warm serving bowl, toss pasta with asparagus mixture. Makes 6 main-dish servings.

Each serving: About 470 calories (23 percent calories from fat), 27g protein, 60g carbohydrate, 12g total fat (2g saturated), 45mg cholesterol, 404mg sodium.

Nutrition Spotlight: Asparagus

Fresh asparagus is a springtime treat not to be missed. It's a great source of folic acid, which protects against birth defects (in women of childbearing years) and heart disease. Enjoy it with rich salmon, or steam up a big handful (it takes less than 10 minutes), sprinkle lightly with salt or a pinch of grated Parmesan cheese, and enjoy. At 3 calories a spear, you can afford to eat the whole bunch.

Pasta with Tuna Puttanesca
Prep: 15 minutes   Cook: 25 minutes

This tomato-less, no-cook version of puttanesca sauce is simply mouthwatering. The unusual mix of greens, shallots, capers, and lemon hits the spot. For the most authentic Italian flavor, use tuna packed in olive oil.

- **1 package (16 ounces) rotini or medium shells**
- **3 tablespoons capers, drained and chopped**
- **3 tablespoons finely chopped shallots**
- **1/2 teaspoon freshly grated lemon peel**
- **2 tablespoons red wine vinegar**
- **1 tablespoon olive oil**
- **1/2 teaspoon salt**
- **1/4 teaspoon coarsely ground black pepper**
- **1 can (6 ounces) light tuna in olive oil**
- **2 bunches watercress (4 to 6 ounces each), tough stems removed**
- **1/2 cup loosely packed fresh basil leaves, chopped**

1. In large saucepot, cook pasta as label directs. Drain, reserving 1/2 cup pasta water. Return pasta to saucepot and keep warm.

2. Meanwhile, in large bowl, with fork, mix capers, shallots, lemon peel, vinegar, oil, salt, and pepper until well combined. Add undrained tuna and watercress; toss.

3. Add tuna mixture, reserved pasta water, and basil to pasta in saucepot. Toss to combine. Makes 6 main-dish servings.

Each serving: About 374 calories (17 percent calories from fat), 18g protein, 59g carbohydrate, 7g total fat (1g saturated), 11mg cholesterol, 630mg sodium.

Radiatori with Arugula, Cherry Tomatoes, and Pancetta

Prep: 15 minutes   Cook: 9 to 11 minutes

No need to cook the arugula in this easy dish; it quickly wilts when tossed with the hot pasta and sauce.

- **1   package (16 ounces) radiatori or rotini**
- **4   ounces sliced pancetta or bacon, chopped**
- **1   garlic clove, crushed with garlic press**
- **1   pound cherry tomatoes, cut into quarters**
- **1/2   teaspoon salt**
- **1/4   teaspoon coarsely ground black pepper**
- **2   bunches arugula (10 ounces each), trimmed**
- **1/4   cup freshly grated Parmesan cheese**

1. In large saucepot, cook pasta as label directs. Drain and keep warm.

2. Meanwhile, in nonstick 10-inch skillet, cook pancetta over medium heat until lightly browned. (If cooking bacon, discard all but 1 tablespoon bacon drippings.) Add garlic and cook, stirring, 30 seconds. Add tomatoes, salt, and pepper and cook until tomatoes are warmed through, 1 to 2 minutes longer.

3. In warm serving bowl, toss pasta with pancetta mixture, arugula, and Parmesan. Makes 4 main-dish servings.

Each serving: About 557 calories (18 percent calories from fat), 22g protein, 93g carbohydrate, 11g total fat (4g saturated), 14mg cholesterol, 676mg sodium.

Ziti with Sausage and Zucchini

Prep: 10 minutes   Cook: 15 minutes

- **1   package (16 ounces) ziti rigate or wagon-wheel pasta**
- **12   ounces sweet Italian-sausage links, casings removed**
- **3   medium zucchini (8 ounces each), each cut length-wise in half, then cut crosswise into 1/4-inch-thick slices**
- **1/4   teaspoon salt**
- **1/4   teaspoon coarsely ground black pepper**
- **1   can (28 ounces) whole plum tomatoes**
- grated Parmesan cheese (optional)

1. In large saucepot, cook pasta as label directs. Drain; return pasta to saucepot and keep warm.

2. Meanwhile, heat nonstick 12-inch skillet over medium-high heat. Add sausage meat and cook, stirring frequently to break up sausage, until browned, about 5 minutes. Transfer sausage to bowl.

3. Discard all but 1 tablespoon sausage drippings from skillet. Add zucchini, salt, and pepper and cook, stirring occasionally, until zucchini is golden, about 5 minutes. Stir in tomatoes with their juice; heat to boiling, breaking up tomatoes with side of spoon. Return sausage to skillet. Reduce heat to low; cover and simmer 5 minutes longer.

4. Add sausage mixture to pasta in saucepot; toss well. Serve with grated Parmesan cheese, if you like. Makes 6 main-dish servings.

Each serving: About 475 calories (28 percent calories from fat), 21g protein, 66g carbohydrate, 15g total fat (5g saturated), 35mg cholesterol, 785mg sodium.

Sesame Noodles and Vegetables

Prep: 10 minutes   Cook: 20 minutes

If you have access to Asian ingredients, try this with fresh Chinese noodles. Cook the broccoli and carrots in the boiling water first, then add the fresh noodles for the last minute or so of cooking. They should cook in the time it takes the water to come back to boiling.

- 1 package (16 ounces) linguine or spaghetti
- 1 package (7 to 8 ounces) broccoli flowerets
- 3 medium carrots, peeled and shredded
- 1 cup hot water
- 1/2 cup reduced-fat smooth peanut butter
- 3 tablespoons seasoned rice vinegar
- 3 tablespoons soy sauce
- 1 tablespoon Asian sesame oil
- 2 teaspoons sugar
- 2 ounces sliced cooked ham, cut into thin slivers
- 2 green onions, thinly sliced

1. In large saucepot, cook linguine as label directs, but do not add salt to water. After linguine has cooked 4 minutes, add broccoli and carrots to pasta cooking water. Continue cooking until linguine is done and vegetables are tender-crisp, 5 to 10 minutes longer. Drain linguine and vegetables; return to saucepot and keep warm.

2. Meanwhile, in medium bowl, combine hot water, peanut butter, rice vinegar, soy sauce, sesame oil, and sugar until smooth.

3. Add peanut sauce and ham to linguine mixture in saucepot; toss well. Spoon into large bowl; sprinkle with sliced green onions. Makes 6 main-dish servings.

Each serving: About 490 calories (24 percent calories from fat), 19g protein, 76g carbohydrate, 13g total fat (2g saturated), 6mg cholesterol, 930mg sodium.

Fettuccine with Broccoli Rabe and Italian Sausage

Prep: 10 minutes   Cook: 30 minutes

- 1 package (16 ounces) fettuccine or linguine
- 1 bunch broccoli rabe (1 pound)
- 12 ounces sweet Italian-sausage links, casings removed
- 1 medium onion, finely chopped
- 1 jar (32 ounces) marinara sauce
- 1/4 cup chopped fresh basil leaves

1. In large saucepot, cook pasta as label directs, but do not add salt. Drain and keep warm.

2. Cut off tough stem ends and discard tough leaves from broccoli rabe. Cut broccoli rabe crosswise in half.

3. In nonstick 12-inch skillet, cook sausage over medium-high heat, stirring frequently with spoon to break up, until well browned. Transfer sausage meat to bowl. Discard all but 2 tablespoons drippings from skillet. Add onion and cook, stirring, until tender. Stir in broccoli rabe; continue cooking until broccoli rabe wilts.

4. Stir in sausage meat and marinara sauce; heat to boiling. Reduce heat to low; cover and simmer, stirring occasionally, 10 minutes. Stir in basil.

5. Place pasta in warm serving bowl; top with sauce. Toss before serving. Makes 6 main-dish servings.

Each serving: About 470 calories (29 percent calories from fat), 20g protein, 62g carbohydrate, 15g total fat (5g saturated), 35mg cholesterol, 420mg sodium.

Spaghetti with Bacon and Peas

Prep: 10 minutes   Cook: 10 minutes

"The peas cook along with the pasta, and the sauce is really easy to make with ricotta and Romano cheese," says GH Food Director Susan Westmoreland of her speedy weeknight pasta dinner. Along with the spaghetti dish, she serves a side of sliced tomatoes, and fresh figs for dessert. To optimize the time it takes to prepare the meal, put water on to boil for the pasta, and while it heats, cook the bacon and onion. Then, as the pasta cooks, slice the tomatoes.

  1 **pound thin spaghetti or vermicelli**
  1 **package (10 ounces) frozen peas**
  4 **slices bacon**
  1 **medium onion, finely chopped**
  1 **container (15 ounces) part-skim ricotta cheese**
1/2 **cup grated Pecorino Romano or Parmesan cheese**
1/2 **teaspoon salt**
1/4 **teaspoon coarsely ground black pepper**

1. In large saucepot, cook pasta as label directs. During last 2 minutes of pasta cooking, add frozen peas to pasta cooking water; continue cooking until pasta is done. Drain, reserving 1 cup pasta cooking water. Return pasta and peas to saucepot and keep warm.

2. Meanwhile, in 12-inch skillet, cook bacon over medium heat until browned. Transfer to paper towels to drain. Pour off all but 1 tablespoon bacon drippings from skillet. Add onion and cook until tender and golden, 8 to 10 minutes.

3. Add reserved pasta water, onion mixture, ricotta, Romano, salt, and pepper to pasta and peas in saucepot. Crumble in bacon and toss again. Makes 6 main-dish servings.

Each serving: About 497 calories (24 percent calories from fat), 25g protein, 69g carbohydrate, 13g total fat (7g saturated), 36mg cholesterol, 587mg sodium.

Rigatoni with Fennel-Beef Sauce

Prep: 5 minutes   Cook: 25 minutes

Extralean ground beef flavored with crushed fennel seeds makes a delicious—and low-fat—stand-in for Italian sausage.

- **12 ounces rigatoni or ziti pasta**
- **12 ounces extralean ground beef**
- **1 medium onion, finely chopped**
- **1 teaspoon fennel seeds, crushed**
- **1/2 teaspoon salt**
- **1/4 teaspoon crushed red pepper**
- **2 cans (14¹/2 ounces each) Italian-style stewed tomatoes**
  chopped fresh parsley leaves for garnish

1. In large saucepot, cook pasta as label directs. Drain and keep warm.

2. Meanwhile, in nonstick 12-inch skillet, cook ground beef, onion, fennel seeds, salt and crushed red pepper over medium-high heat, stirring occasionally, until all pan juices evaporate and meat is well browned.

3. Stir in stewed tomatoes; heat to boiling over high heat. Reduce heat to low; cover and simmer 10 minutes. Place pasta in warm serving bowl; spoon sauce over pasta and sprinkle with parsley. Makes 4 main-dish servings.

Each serving: About 585 calories (25 percent calories from fat), 29g protein, 79g carbohydrate, 16g total fat (6g saturated), 57mg cholesterol, 975mg sodium.

Bow Ties with Curry-Spiced Chicken

Prep: 15 minutes   Cook: 30 minutes

Fresh ginger underscores the curry spices in this pasta-and-chicken dish.

- 1¹/₂ **cups bow-tie pasta (3 ounces)**
- 2 **tablespoons margarine or butter**
- 4 **small skinless, boneless chicken-breast halves (1 pound), each cut crosswise into 2 or 3 pieces**
- ³/₄ **teaspoon salt**
- 3 **large carrots, peeled and cut into 1¹/₂" by ¹/₄" sticks**
- 1 **medium onion, chopped**
- 3 **tablespoons plus 1 cup water**
- 1¹/₂ **teaspoons curry powder**
- 1 **teaspoon grated, peeled fresh ginger**
- 1 **can (14¹/₂ ounces) diced tomatoes**
- 1 **cup frozen peas, thawed**
- ¹/₂ **teaspoon sugar**

1. In 2-quart saucepan, heat 4 cups water to boiling over high heat. Add pasta and cook until almost tender; drain and set aside.

2. In nonstick 12-inch skillet, heat 1 tablespoon margarine over medium-high heat. Add chicken and ¹/₄ teaspoon salt and cook, turning occasionally, until chicken is browned and loses its pink color throughout; transfer to plate.

3. In same skillet, heat remaining 1 tablespoon butter; add carrots and onion and cook, stirring, until browned. Reduce heat to medium. Add 3 tablespoons water; cover and cook until vegetables are tender, about 5 minutes longer.

4. Stir curry powder and ginger into vegetable mixture; cook 1 minute. Stir in pasta, chicken, tomatoes with their juice, peas, sugar, remaining ¹/₂ teaspoon salt, and remaining ¹/₂ cup water; heat to boiling over high heat. Reduce heat to low; simmer, uncovered, until pasta is tender and mixture is heated through, about 3 minutes. Makes 4 main-dish servings.

Each serving: About 355 calories (20 percent calories from fat), 33g protein, 38g carbohydrate, 8g total fat (1g saturated), 66mg cholesterol, 815mg sodium.

Spaghetti and Meatballs

Prep: 45 minutes   Cook: 45 minutes

A childhood favorite—with kids of all ages. Here, we've baked the meatballs for leaner results. To further cut back on calories, reduce pasta portions.

SPAGHETTI SAUCE:

- 1 **tablespoon olive oil**
- 1 **medium carrot, peeled and finely chopped**
- 1 **small onion, finely chopped**
- 1 **garlic clove, finely chopped**
- 1 **can (28 ounces) Italian-style tomatoes in puree**
- 1 **small bay leaf**
- ¹/₄ **teaspoon salt**
- ¹/₈ **teaspoon coarsely ground black pepper**

MEATBALLS:

- 2 **slices firm white bread, diced**
- 3 **tablespoons water**
- 1 **pound lean ground beef or lean ground turkey**
- 1 **large egg white**
- 2 **tablespoons grated Pecorino Romano or Parmesan cheese**
- 1 **tablespoon grated onion**
- 1 **tablespoon finely chopped fresh parsley leaves**
- 1 **small garlic clove, crushed with garlic press**
- ¹/₂ **teaspoon salt**
- 1 **package (16 ounces) spaghetti, cooked as label directs**

1. Prepare Spaghetti Sauce: In 3-quart saucepan, heat oil over medium heat. Add carrot and chopped onion and cook, stirring occasionally, until vegetables are very tender and golden, about 15 minutes. Add chopped garlic; cook, stirring, 1 minute.

2. Meanwhile, place tomatoes with their puree in bowl. With hands or slotted spoon, crush tomatoes well. Add tomatoes with their puree, bay leaf, salt and pepper to saucepan; heat to boiling over high heat. Reduce heat to low; cover and simmer 15 minutes. Uncover and simmer, stirring occasionally, 15 minutes longer. Discard bay leaf.

3. While sauce is cooking, prepare Meatballs: Preheat oven to 425°F. Line 13" by 9" metal baking pan with foil; spray foil with nonstick cooking spray.

4. In medium bowl, combine diced bread and water. With hand, mix until bread is evenly moistened. Add ground meat, egg white, Romano, grated onion, parsley, crushed garlic and salt. With hand, mix until well combined.

5. Shape meat mixture into twelve 2-inch meatballs. (For easier shaping, use slightly wet hands.) Place meatballs in pan and bake until cooked through and lightly browned, 15 to 20 minutes. Add meatballs to sauce.

6. Place pasta in a large warm serving bowl; spoon meatballs and sauce over pasta. Makes 6 main-dish servings.

Each serving: About 430 calories (17 percent calories from fat), 28g protein, 63g carbohydrate, 8g total fat (2g saturated), 144mg cholesterol, 520mg sodium.

Thai Curry Chicken and Noodles

Prep: 15 minutes   Cook: 30 minutes

8 ounces flat dried rice noodles* or linguine

1 stalk fresh lemongrass (optional)

4 large green onions

1 tablespoon vegetable oil

1 package (10 ounces) mushrooms, sliced

1 tablespoon minced, peeled fresh ginger

2 teaspoons red curry paste*

2 large skinless, boneless chicken-breast halves
   (1 pound), cut into 1-inch-wide strips

2 tablespoons soy sauce

1 can (10 to 14 ounces) light or regular coconut
   milk* (not cream of coconut)

1 cup water

1 medium red pepper

2 tablespoons chopped fresh cilantro leaves

1. Cook noodles as label directs; drain and keep warm. (If package has no directions, prepare as you would regular pasta but cook only until just tender, about 5 minutes.)

2. Meanwhile, remove outer leaf from stalk of lemongrass if using. From bulb end, trim and cut a 6-inch-long piece; discard top. Cut lemongrass stalk lengthwise in half. Slice 2 green onions into 1-inch pieces; reserve remaining 2 for garnish.

3. In nonstick 12-inch skillet, heat oil over medium-high heat. Add mushrooms and sliced green onions and cook until vegetables are golden brown. Transfer to small bowl.

4. To same skillet, add ginger and red curry paste; cook, stirring, 1 minute. Add lemongrass, chicken, soy sauce, coconut milk, and water; heat to boiling. Reduce heat to low; cover and simmer until chicken just loses its pink color throughout, about 10 minutes.

5. While chicken is cooking, cut red pepper and remaining green onions into 3-inch-long paper-thin strips.

6. Remove lemongrass from chicken mixture and discard. Stir in mushroom mixture and cilantro; heat through. Arrange noodles in large bowl; top with chicken mixture. Garnish with red-pepper and green-onion strips. Makes 4 main-dish servings.

*Rice noodles, curry paste, and coconut milk can be purchased in the Asian section of larger grocery stores. Red curry paste, used in Thai cooking, is a pungent blend of herbs and spices pulverized into paste form. Coconut milk is made by processing equal amounts of coconut meat and water to a paste and straining out the milky liquid; light coconut milk has a higher water content, so it's lower in fat.

Each serving: About 475 calories (27 percent calories from fat), 36g protein, 52g carbohydrate, 14g total fat (8g saturated), 66mg cholesterol, 650mg sodium.

Filet Mignon with Tomatoes and
Roquefort, page 77

Steak and Oven Fries

Prep: 15 minutes   Cook: 25 minutes

Oven Fries (recipe below)

- 1 **beef flank steak (1 pound)**
- 1/4 **teaspoon coarsely ground black pepper**
- 2 **teaspoons olive oil**
- 1 **large shallot, finely chopped**
- 1/2 **cup dry red wine**
- 1/2 **cup chicken broth**
- 2 **tablespoons chopped fresh parsley**

1. Prepare Oven Fries.

2. Meanwhile, pat steak dry with paper towels; sprinkle on both sides with pepper. Heat nonstick 12-inch skillet over medium-high heat until very hot. Add steak and cook 7 minutes per side, turning once, for medium-rare, or until desired doneness. Transfer steak to cutting board; keep warm.

3. To drippings in skillet, add olive oil; heat over medium heat. Add shallot and cook, stirring occasionally, until golden, about 2 minutes. Increase heat to medium-high. Add wine and broth; heat to boiling. Cook 3 to 4 minutes. Stir in parsley.

4. To serve, holding knife almost parallel to cutting surface, slice steak crosswise into thin slices. Spoon

red-wine sauce over steak slices and serve with Oven Fries. Makes 4 main-dish servings.

Each serving with oven fries: About 390 calories (25 percent calories from fat), 31g protein, 40g carbohydrate, 11g total fat (4g saturated), 46mg cholesterol, 455mg sodium.

Oven Fries

Preheat oven to 500°F. Spray two 15½" by 10½" jelly-roll pans or 2 large cookie sheets with nonstick cooking spray. Scrub 4 medium unpeeled baking potatoes (2 pounds) well but do not peel. Cut each potato length-wise in half. Holding each half flat side down, cut lengthwise into ¼-inch-thick slices, then cut each slice lengthwise into ¼-inch-wide sticks. Place potatoes in medium bowl and toss with ½ teaspoon salt and ¼ teaspoon pepper. Divide potato sticks evenly between pans. Place pans on 2 oven racks and bake potatoes 20 to 25 minutes, until tender and lightly browned, turning potatoes once with pancake turner and rotating pans between upper and lower racks halfway through baking time. Makes 4 servings.

Filet Mignon with Tomatoes and Roquefort

Prep: 15 minutes   Cook: 20 minutes

This elegant and sophisticated dish seems indulgent, but it won't blow your fat or calorie budget.

- **12 ounces French green beans (haricots verts) or green beans, trimmed**
- **3 teaspoons light corn-oil spread (56% to 60% fat)**
- **4 ounces oyster or regular mushrooms, trimmed and sliced**
- **2 teaspoons soy sauce**
- **½ cup water**
- **¾ teaspoon cornstarch**
- **½ teaspoon beef-flavor instant bouillon**
- **2 large tomatoes**
- **4 beef tenderloin steaks (filet mignon), each 1 inch thick (4 ounces each)**
- **½ teaspoon salt**
- **2 tablespoons white wine (optional)**
- **1 ounce Roquefort or blue cheese, crumbled (about ¼ cup)**
- **1 loaf French or Italian bread (8 ounces)**

1. In 4-quart saucepan, heat 1 inch water to boiling over high heat. Add green beans; heat to boiling. Reduce heat to low; cover and simmer until beans are tender-crisp, 5 to 8 minutes. Drain beans and place in bowl.

2. In same saucepan, heat 2 teaspoons corn-oil spread over medium-high heat. Add mushrooms; cook, stirring frequently, until golden. Stir green beans and soy sauce into saucepan with mushrooms; keep warm.

3. In cup, mix water, cornstarch and beef bouillon until blended. Set aside. Cut center part of each tomato into 2-inch-thick slices and set aside; reserve ends for another use.

4. In nonstick 10-inch skillet, heat remaining 1 teaspoon corn-oil spread over medium-high heat until hot. Add steaks and sprinkle with salt; cook 5 minutes per side, turning once, for medium-rare, or until desired doneness. Transfer steaks to plate; keep warm. In same skillet, cook tomatoes over medium-high heat, turning once, just until hot. Transfer to warm dinner plates.

5. If using wine, add to skillet; cook 30 seconds, stirring. Stir cornstarch mixture into skillet; cook until sauce thickens slightly, 1 minute. Top each tomato slice with a steak. Spoon sauce over steaks and sprinkle with crumbled Roquefort cheese. Serve steaks with green-bean mixture and bread. Makes 4 main-dish servings.

Each serving: About 415 calories (30 percent calories from fat), 33g protein, 38g carbohydrate, 14g total fat (5g saturated), 77mg cholesterol, 1,095mg sodium.

Orange-Glazed Steak

Prep: 5 minutes plus marinating   Grill: 25 minutes

We marinate round steak in a soy-and-garlic mixture, then brush it with orange marmalade for a tasty finish.

- 1/4 **cup soy sauce**
- 2 **garlic cloves, crushed with garlic press**
- 1 **teaspoon coarsely ground black pepper**
- 1 **beef top round steak, 1¹/4 inches thick (2 pounds), well trimmed**
- 1/3 **cup orange marmalade**

1. In 13" by 9" baking dish, combine soy sauce, garlic, and pepper. Add steak to soy-sauce mixture, turning to coat. Cover and refrigerate 30 minutes to marinate, turning once.

2. Prepare grill. Place steak on grill over medium heat and grill, brushing with orange marmalade during last 10 minutes of cooking and turning occasionally, 25 minutes for medium-rare or until desired doneness. Transfer steak to cutting board and let stand 10 minutes to set juices for easier slicing. Cut into thin slices across the grain. Makes 6 main-dish servings.

Each serving: About 202 calories (18 percent calories from fat), 28g protein, 12g carbohydrate, 4g total fat (1g saturated), 72mg cholesterol, 419mg sodium.

Korean Steak

Prep: 40 minutes plus marinating   Grill: 15 minutes

- 1/2 **cup reduced-sodium soy sauce**
- 2 **tablespoons sugar**
- 2 **tablespoons minced, peeled fresh ginger**
- 2 **tablespoons seasoned rice vinegar**
- 1 **tablespoon Asian sesame oil**
- 1/4 **teaspoon ground red pepper (cayenne)**
- 3 **garlic cloves, crushed with garlic press**
- 1 **beef top round steak, 1 inch thick (1¹/2 pounds), well trimmed**
- 1 **cup regular long-grain rice**
- 1/4 **cup water**
- 3 **green onions, thinly sliced**
- 1 **tablespoon sesame seeds, toasted**
- 1 **head romaine lettuce, separated into leaves**

1. In large ziptight plastic bag, combine soy sauce, sugar, ginger, vinegar, sesame oil, ground red pepper, and garlic; add steak, turning to coat. Seal bag, pressing out as much air as possible. Place bag on plate; refrigerate steak 1 to 4 hours to marinate, turning once.

2. Just before grilling steak, prepare rice as label directs; keep warm.

3. Prepare grill. Remove steak from bag; reserve marinade. Place steak on grill over medium heat and grill 7 minutes per side, turning once, for medium-rare, or until desired doneness. Transfer steak to cutting board and let stand 10 minutes to set juices for easier slicing.

4. In 1-quart saucepan, heat reserved marinade and water to boiling over high heat; boil 2 minutes.

5. To serve, thinly slice steak. Let each person place some steak slices, rice, green onions, and sesame seeds on a lettuce leaf, then drizzle with some cooked marinade. Fold sides of lettuce leaf over filling to make a package to eat out of hand. Makes 6 main-dish servings.

Each serving: About 345 calories (21 percent calories from fat), 30 protein, 37g carbohydrate, 8g total fat (2g saturated), 56mg cholesterol, 1,165mg sodium.

Chunky Beef Stew

Prep: 30 minutes   Cook: 1 hour

Lean beef, winter vegetables, and a richly flavored sauce make this a candidate for family suppers or casual entertaining.

   1 **pound lean beef for stew, trimmed and cut into 1-inch cubes**
   1 **tablespoon vegetable oil**
 1/2 **teaspoon salt**
   2 **large stalks celery, chopped**
   1 **large onion, chopped**
   1 **can (14 1/2 ounces) stewed tomatoes**
   1 **can (14 1/2 ounces) beef broth or 1 3/4 cups homemade**
   1 **cup plus 2 tablespoons water**
   3 **large potatoes (1 1/2 pounds), peeled and cut into 1 1/2-inch chunks**
   3 **medium carrots (1/2 pound), peeled and cut into 3/4-inch chunks**
   3 **medium turnips (3/4 pound), peeled and cut into 1 1/2-inch chunks**
   1 **tablespoon soy sauce**
   1 **teaspoon sugar**
 3/4 **teaspoon browning and seasoning sauce (optional)**
   2 **tablespoons all-purpose flour**
   1 **package (10 ounces) frozen peas**
   2 **tablespoons freshly grated lemon peel**

1. Pat beef dry with paper towels. In 5-quart Dutch oven, heat vegetable oil over medium-high heat until very hot. Add beef, sprinkle with salt, and cook, turning pieces occasionally, until beef is browned on all sides. Transfer beef to bowl.

2. Add celery and onion to drippings in Dutch oven and cook, stirring, until lightly browned. Return beef to Dutch oven; stir in stewed tomatoes, broth, and 1 cup water. Heat to boiling over high heat. Reduce heat to low; cover and simmer 25 minutes.

3. Add potatoes, carrots, turnips, soy sauce, sugar, and browning and seasoning sauce; heat to boiling over high heat. Reduce heat to low; cover and simmer until meat and vegetables are fork-tender, about 20 minutes longer.

4. In cup, with fork, mix flour and remaining 2 tablespoons water until blended. Stir flour mixture into meat mixture; cook over medium-high heat until mixture boils and thickens slightly. Stir in frozen peas; heat through. Sprinkle with lemon peel. Makes 6 main-dish servings.

Each serving: About 330 calories (19 percent calories from fat), 23g protein, 45g carbohydrate, 7g total fat (2g saturated), 53mg cholesterol, 905mg sodium.

Orange Beef and Peppers

Prep: 20 minutes   Cook: 20 minutes

        1   **beef top round steak, 3/4 inch thick (1 pound),**
            well trimmed
        2   **tablespoons soy sauce**
        3   **large oranges**
        2   **tablespoons margarine or butter**
        1   **large red pepper, cut into 1/4-inch-thick slices**
        1   **large yellow pepper, cut into 1/4-inch-thick slices**
        1   **bunch green onions, cut into 2-inch pieces**
    1 1/2   **teaspoons grated, peeled fresh ginger**
      3/4   **teaspoon cornstarch**
        2   **bunches arugula (8 ounces), stems trimmed**

1. Cut steak lengthwise in half. Holding knife almost parallel to cutting surface, slice steak crosswise into 1/8-inch-thick slices. In bowl, toss steak with soy sauce.

2. With a sharp paring knife, cut peel and white pith from 2 oranges; cut the oranges crosswise into 1/4-inch-thick slices, then cut each slice in half. From remaining orange, grate 1 teaspoon peel and squeeze 1/2 cup juice.

3. In nonstick 12-inch skillet, melt 2 teaspoons margarine over medium-high heat. Add red pepper and yellow pepper and cook, stirring frequently, until tender-crisp; transfer to bowl.

4. In same skillet, melt 1 teaspoon margarine; add green onions and cook, stirring frequently, until tender-crisp; transfer to bowl with peppers.

5. In small bowl, mix grated orange peel, orange juice, ginger, and cornstarch until blended; set aside.

6. In same skillet, melt remaining 1 tablespoon margarine. Add half of beef mixture and cook, stirring quickly and constantly, just until beef loses its pink color; transfer to bowl with vegetables. In drippings in skillet, repeat with remaining beef mixture. Return vegetables and meat to skillet. Stir in orange-juice mixture and sliced oranges; cook until liquid boils and thickens slightly and mixture is heated through.

7. Serve beef mixture with arugula. Makes 4 main-dish servings.

Each serving: About 270 calories (30 percent calories from fat), 29 g protein, 19 g carbohydrate, 9 g total fat (2 g saturated), 65 mg cholesterol, 625 mg sodium.

Lean Beef Stroganoff

Prep: 20 minutes   Cook: 30 minutes

      1   **boneless beef top sirloin steak, 3/4 inch thick**
          (1 pound), well trimmed
          olive-oil nonstick cooking spray
      3   **teaspoons olive oil**
      1   **pound medium mushrooms, trimmed and**
          thickly sliced
      1   **medium onion, chopped**
      1   **teaspoon cornstarch**
      1   **cup beef broth**
    1/2   **cup chili sauce**
      2   **tablespoons spicy brown mustard**
      2   **tablespoons plus 1/4 cup water**
     12   **ounces sugar snap peas or snow peas, strings**
          removed
      2   **bags (6 ounces each) radishes, halved if large**
    1/2   **teaspoon salt**
      1   **package (12 ounces) extrawide curly noodles,**
          cooked as label directs
      6   **tablespoons nonfat sour cream**
      2   **tablespoons chopped fresh parsley leaves**

1. Holding knife almost parallel to cutting surface, slice steak crosswise into very thin slices.

2. Spray nonstick 12-inch skillet lightly with olive-oil nonstick cooking spray. Place skillet over medium-high heat and heat. Add half of meat and cook, stirring quickly and constantly, until meat loses its pink color, about 2 minutes. Transfer to bowl. Repeat with remaining meat but do not use nonstick spray again.

3. In same skillet, heat 2 teaspoons olive oil over medium-high heat. Add mushrooms and onion and cook, stirring, until tender. In cup, mix cornstarch and beef broth; stir into mushroom mixture with chili sauce and mustard. Cook, stirring, until mixture boils and thickens slightly. Return beef to skillet; heat through.

4. Meanwhile, in nonstick 10-inch skillet, heat remaining 1 teaspoon olive oil and 2 tablespoons water over medium-high heat until hot. Add sugar snap peas and cook until tender-crisp, 5 to 7 minutes. Transfer to bowl. In same skillet, cook radishes and 1/4 cup water over medium-high heat, until tender-crisp, 5 to 7 minutes. Add sugar snap peas and salt to radishes; heat through.

5. Spoon noodles onto 6 dinner plates. Spoon beef mixture over noodles; top each serving with 1 tablespoon sour cream and sprinkle with parsley. Serve with sugar snap peas and radishes. Makes 6 main-dish servings.

Each serving: About 430 calories (19 percent calories from fat), 30g protein, 58g carbohydrate, 9g total fat (2g saturated), 90mg cholesterol, 740mg sodium.

Easy Beef Teriyaki Stir-Fry

Prep: 20 minutes   Cook: 20 minutes

Quickly made with deli roast beef, this is a great last-minute dinner.

1	**cup regular long-grain rice.**
2	**tablespoons vegetable oil**
1	**garlic clove, crushed with side of chef's knife**
1	**piece (1" by 3/4") fresh ginger, peeled and minced**
1	**bunch green onions, cut into 1-inch pieces**
1	**pound carrots, peeled and thinly sliced**
8	**ounces snow peas, strings removed, halved lengthwise**
1	**medium red pepper, thinly sliced**
1/2	**cup teriyaki sauce**
2	**teaspoons cornstarch**
3/4	**cup water**
8	**ounces cooked roast beef, in one piece, cut into paper-thin slices (about 3" by 1")**
1	**can (5 ounces, drained weight) water chestnuts, drained**

1. In 2-quart saucepan, prepare rice as label directs.

2. In 10-inch skillet, heat vegetable oil over medium-high heat. Add garlic and cook until golden; discard garlic. Add ginger and green onions; cook, stirring occasionally, until green onions are golden. Add carrots; cook, stirring occasionally, 3 minutes. Add snow peas and red pepper; cook, stirring occasionally, until vegetables are tender-crisp.

3. In cup, stir together teriyaki sauce and cornstarch. Add teriyaki mixture and water to vegetables in skillet. Heat to boiling over high heat. Reduce heat to low; simmer until sauce is thickened slightly, 1 minute. Add beef and water chestnuts; heat through. Serve beef mixture over rice. Makes 6 main-dish servings.

Each serving: About 500 calories (27 percent calories from fat), 24g protein, 66g carbohydrate, 15g total fat (4g saturated), 47mg cholesterol, 1,465mg sodium.

Steak and Pepper Fajitas

Prep: 10 minutes   Cook: 20 minutes

Arrange the meat and condiments in pretty dishes and let everyone make his own.

- **1 beef top round steak, 1 inch thick (3/4 pound), well trimmed**
- **1 bottle (8 ounces) medium-hot chunky salsa**
- **1 tablespoon light corn-oil spread (56% to 60% fat)**
- **1 medium red onion, thinly sliced**
- **1 medium green pepper, thinly sliced**
- **1 medium red pepper, thinly sliced**
- **2 tablespoons chopped fresh cilantro leaves**
- **8 (6-inch) low-fat flour tortillas, warmed as label directs**
- **1 container (8 ounces) fat-free sour cream**
- **8 ounces fat-free sharp Cheddar cheese, shredded chile peppers, lime wedges, and cilantro sprigs for garnish**

1. Preheat broiler. Place steak on rack in broiling pan; spread 1/4 cup salsa on top. Place pan in broiler at closest position to source of heat; broil steak 8 minutes. Turn steak over and spread 1/4 cup salsa on top; broil

8 minutes longer for medium-rare or until desired doneness.

2. Meanwhile, in nonstick 12-inch skillet, melt corn-oil spread over medium-high heat. Add red onion, green pepper, and red pepper; cook until vegetables are tender-crisp. Stir in chopped cilantro. Spoon mixture into serving bowl.

3. To serve, place steak on cutting board; holding knife almost parallel to cutting surface, slice steak crosswise into thin slices. Serve sliced steak with pepper mixture, tortillas, sour cream, shredded cheese, and remaining salsa. Garnish with chile peppers, lime wedges, and cilantro. Makes 4 main-dish servings.

Each serving: About 450 calories (14 percent calories from fat), 45g protein, 55g carbohydrate, 7g total fat (1g saturated), 51mg cholesterol, 1,060mg sodium.

Braised Veal Chops with Tomatoes and Peas

Prep: 10 minutes   Cook: 1 hour 15 minutes

The bones in the shoulder chops contribute extra flavor and body to the sauce. Two large chops will easily feed four people.

- **1 slice bacon, chopped**
- **2 veal shoulder blade chops, 1-inch-thick (1 pound each)**
- **1/4 teaspoon salt**
- **1/8 teaspoon ground black pepper**
- **1 medium onion, chopped**
- **2 garlic cloves, finely chopped**
- **1 can (14 1/2 ounces) tomatoes in puree**
- **1 cup chicken broth**
- **1/2 cup dry white wine**
- **1/4 teaspoon dried sage, crumbled**
- **1 cup frozen peas**

1. In nonstick 12-inch skillet, cook bacon over medium-high heat until browned. With slotted spoon, transfer bacon to paper towels to drain; reserve. Pat veal dry with paper towels. Sprinkle chops with salt and pepper.

Cook chops in drippings in skillet over medium-high heat until browned, about 5 minutes per side. Transfer veal to plate.

2. Add onion to skillet and cook over medium heat, stirring occasionally, until lightly browned, about 5 minutes. Stir in garlic and cook 1 minute longer. Stir in tomatoes with their puree, broth, wine, and sage and heat to boiling, breaking up tomatoes with side of spoon.

3. Return chops to skillet; cover and simmer over medium-low heat until veal is tender, about 45 minutes. Transfer to platter; keep warm. Add peas to skillet and cook 5 minutes. To serve, cut veal into serving portions, spoon sauce over veal, and sprinkle bacon on top. Makes 4 main-dish servings.

Each serving: About 289 calories (28 percent calories from fat), 35g protein, 16g carbohydrate, 9g total fat (3g saturated), 139mg cholesterol, 782mg sodium.

Osso Buco with Gremolata

Prep: 40 minutes   Bake: 2 hours

Long cooking brings out the flavors of his aromatic recipe from Northern Italy.

- **4 meaty veal shank cross cuts (osso buco), each about 2 inches thick (1 pound each)**
- **1/2 teaspoon salt**
- **1/4 teaspoon ground black pepper**
- **1 tablespoon olive oil**
- **2 medium onions, chopped**
- **3 carrots, peeled and chopped**
- **2 stalks celery, chopped**
- **4 garlic cloves, finely chopped**
- **1 can (14 1/2) tomatoes in puree**
- **1 cup dry white wine**
- **1 cup chicken broth**
- **1 bay leaf**
- **2 tablespoons chopped fresh parsley**
- **1/2 teaspoon freshly grated lemon peel**

1. Preheat oven to 350°F. Pat shanks dry with paper towels. Sprinkle shanks with salt and pepper. In nonreactive 5-quart Dutch oven, heat oil over medium-high heat until very hot. Add shanks and cook until browned, about 10 minutes, transferring shanks to plate as they are browned. Add onions to Dutch oven and cook over medium heat, stirring occasionally, until slightly browned, about 5 minutes. Add carrots, celery, and three-fourths of garlic; cook 2 minutes longer.

2. Return veal to Dutch oven. Stir in tomatoes with their puree, wine, broth, and bay leaf. Heat to boiling over high heat. Cover and place in oven. Bake until veal is tender when pierced with fork, about 2 hours.

3. Meanwhile, prepare gremolata: In small bowl, mix parsley, lemon peel, and remaining garlic. Cover and refrigerate until ready to serve.

4. Transfer veal to platter. Heat sauce in Dutch oven to boiling over high heat; boil until it has reduced to 4 cups, about 10 minutes. Pour sauce over veal and sprinkle with gremolata. Makes 4 main-dish servings.

Each serving: About 374 calories (19 percent calories from fat), 53g protein, 20g carbohydrate, 8g total fat (2g saturated), 183mg cholesterol, 874mg sodium.

Brazilian Pork

Prep: 15 minutes   Cook: 15 minutes

Serve these bold chops with a mixed green salad.

- **4 boneless pork loin chops, 3/4 inch thick (5 ounces each), well trimmed**
- **1/2 teaspoon ground cumin**
- **1/2 teaspoon ground coriander**
- **1/4 teaspoon dried thyme**
- **1/8 teaspoon ground allspice**
- **1/2 teaspoon salt**
- **1 teaspoon olive oil**
- **1 medium onion, chopped**
- **3 garlic cloves, crushed with garlic press**
- **1 can (15 to 19 ounces) black beans, rinsed and drained**
- **1/2 cup chicken broth**
- **1 tablespoon fresh lime juice**
- **1/4 teaspoon coarsely ground black pepper**
- **1/4 cup packed fresh cilantro, chopped fresh orange wedges (optional)**

1. Pat pork chops dry with paper towels. In cup, mix cumin, coriander, thyme, allspice, and 1/4 teaspoon salt. Rub spice mixture on pork chops.

2. Heat nonstick 12-inch skillet over medium-high heat until very hot. Add pork chops and cook 4 minutes; turn chops over and cook until lightly browned on the outside and still slightly pink on the inside, 3 to 4 minutes longer. Transfer pork to platter; cover with foil to keep warm.

3. In same skillet, heat oil over medium heat. Add onion and cook, stirring frequently, until golden, about 5 minutes. Add garlic and cook, stirring, 1 minute longer. Stir in beans, broth, lime juice, pepper, and remaining 1/4 teaspoon salt; heat through.

4. To serve, spoon bean mixture over pork; sprinkle with cilantro. Serve with orange wedges if you like. Makes 4 main-dish servings.

Each serving: About 340 calories (29 percent calories from fat), 42g protein, 25g carbohydrate, 11g total fat (3g saturated), 76mg cholesterol, 760mg sodium.

Cabbage-Wrapped Pork Roast

Prep: 30 minutes   Roast: 1 hour

Pork and cabbage, a traditional pairing, is recast: the cabbage wrapping helps to keep today's leaner pork moist while it cooks.

- **1   large head green cabbage (3 pounds)**
- **1   bunch green onions**
- **1   tablespoon finely chopped fresh thyme leaves or 1/2 teaspoon dried thyme**
- **1/4   teaspoon ground black pepper**
- **1 1/2   teaspoons salt**
- **1   boneless pork loin roast (3 pounds), trimmed**
- **1   envelope chicken-flavor bouillon dissolved in 2 cups hot water**
- **8   medium red potatoes (2 1/2 pounds)**
- **1   tablespoon vegetable oil**
- **1   teaspoon caraway seeds, crushed**
- **1   pint cherry tomatoes**
- **2   teaspoons cornstarch**
- **2   tablespoons water**

1. Remove 6 large outer leaves from cabbage; trim tough ribs from leaves. Reserve remaining cabbage. Cut off root ends of green onions.

2. In 5-quart Dutch oven or saucepot, heat 3 quarts water to boiling over high heat. Add cabbage leaves and cook, pressing leaves under water with tongs, until leaves are pliable, 3 to 5 minutes. With slotted spoon, transfer leaves to colander to drain. Add green onions to boiling water; blanch until just wilted, 10 seconds. Drain and pat dry with paper towels.

3. Preheat oven to 350°F. In cup, mix thyme, black pepper, and 1 teaspoon salt. Rub thyme mixture on pork roast. Wrap roast in wilted cabbage leaves; secure leaves with blanched green onions (you will probably have to tie 2 green onion leaves together so strand is long enough to wrap around the roast).

4. Place pork loin in 14" by 10" roasting pan. Pour bouillon mixture into pan. Roast pork, basting occasionally with pan juices, until meat thermometer inserted in center registers 155°F., about 1 hour (internal temperature will rise to about 160°F. upon standing).

5. Meanwhile, in 4-quart saucepan, heat potatoes and enough water to cover to boiling over high heat. Reduce heat to low; cover and simmer until potatoes are tender, about 20 minutes. Drain well and cut into 1/2-inch cubes.

6. Coarsely slice remaining cabbage. In nonstick 5-quart Dutch oven, heat oil over medium-high heat. Add cabbage, caraway seeds, and remaining 1/2 teaspoon salt; cook, stirring frequently, until cabbage is tender-crisp. Add potato cubes; heat through. Spoon cabbage mixture onto large warm platter.

7. In same Dutch oven, heat cherry tomatoes over medium-high heat until heated through.

8. When pork loin is done, place on platter with cabbage mixture. In cup, mix cornstarch with water. Stir cornstarch mixture into drippings in roasting pan. Place roasting pan over high heat; heat to boiling and boil 1 minute. Skim fat from pan sauce. Spoon sauce over pork and cabbage and serve with cherry tomatoes. Makes 12 main-dish servings.

Each serving: About 325 calories (30 percent calories from fat), 30g protein, 24g carbohydrate, 11g total fat (4g saturated), 50mg cholesterol, 435mg sodium.

Smoked Pork Chop Dinner

Prep: 10 minutes   Cook: 1 hour

A fruit compote, such as Autumn Fruit Compote (page 274), is the perfect dessert for this hearty German favorite.

- **1 tablespoon vegetable oil**
- **4 smoked pork loin or rib chops, each 3/4 inch thick (7 ounces each), well trimmed**
- **1 medium Granny Smith or Rome Beauty apple, cut in half and cored**
- **1 bag (1 ounces) carrots, peeled and cut into bite-size chunks**
- **11/2 pounds sauerkraut, rinsed and drained**
- **1 can or bottle (12 ounces) beer or nonalcoholic beer**
- **1/2 cup water**
- **1/4 cup packed light or dark brown sugar**
- **2 teaspoons caraway or fennel seeds, crushed**

1. Pat pork chops dry with paper towels. In 12-inch skillet, heat oil over high heat until very hot. Add pork chops and cook until browned on both sides. Meanwhile, coarsely grate 1/2 of unpeeled apple.

2. To pork chops in skillet, add grated apple, carrots, sauerkraut, beer, water, brown sugar, and caraway seeds. Heat to boiling over high heat. Reduce heat to low; cover and simmer 35 minutes.

3. Cut remaining half apple into wedges; add to mixture in skillet. Cook, occasionally spooning liquid in skillet over pork chops, until carrots and pork chops are fork-tender, 10 minutes longer. Makes 4 main-dish servings.

Each serving: About 380 calories (28 percent calories from fat), 32g protein, 36g carbohydrate, 12g total fat (3g saturated), 82mg cholesterol, 500mg sodium.

Gingered Pork and Vegetable Stir-Fry

Prep: 15 minutes   Cook: 15 minutes

- **1 pork tenderloin (12 ounces), thinly sliced**
- **2 tablespoons grated, peeled fresh ginger**
- **1 cup chicken broth**
- **2 tablespoons teriyaki sauce**
- **2 teaspoons cornstarch**
- **2 teaspoons vegetable oil**
- **8 ounces snow peas, strings removed**
- **1 medium zucchini (8 ounces), halved lengthwise and thinly sliced**
- **3 green onions, cut into 3-inch pieces**

1. In medium bowl, toss pork and fresh ginger. In cup, mix broth, teriyaki sauce, and cornstarch.

2. In nonstick 12-inch skillet, heat 1 teaspoon oil over medium-high heat until hot. Add snow peas, zucchini, and green onions and cook, stirring frequently (stir-frying), until lightly browned and tender-crisp, about 5 minutes. Transfer to bowl.

3. In same skillet, heat remaining 1 teaspoon oil; add pork mixture and stir-fry until pork just loses its pink color. Transfer pork to bowl with vegetables. Stir cornstarch mixture; add to skillet and heat to boiling. Boil until sauce thickens, 1 minute. Stir in pork and vegetables; heat through. Makes 4 main-dish servings.

Each serving: About 170 calories (26 percent calories from fat), 21g protein, 10g carbohydrate, 5g total fat (1g saturated), 51mg cholesterol, 550mg sodium.

Glazed Pork with Pear Chutney

Prep: 10 minutes   Broil: 20 minutes

PORK TENDERLOINS:

- 1/4 **cup packed brown sugar**
- 1 **tablespoon cider vinegar**
- 1 **teaspoon Dijon mustard**
- 2 **pork tenderloins (12 ounces each), trimmed**
- 1/4 **teaspoon salt**
- 1/4 **teaspoon coarsely ground black pepper**

PEAR CHUTNEY:

- 1 **can (28 ounces) pear halves in heavy syrup**
- 1/3 **cup pickled sweet red peppers, drained and chopped**
- 1/4 **cup dark seedless raisins**
- 2 **teaspoons cider vinegar**
- 1 **teaspoon brown sugar**
- 1/4 **teaspoon ground ginger**
- 1/4 **teaspoon salt**
- 1/8 **teaspoon coarsely ground black pepper**
- 1 **green onion, chopped**

1. Prepare Pork Tenderloins: Preheat broiler. In small bowl, mix brown sugar, vinegar, and mustard; set aside. Rub tenderloins with salt and black pepper; place on rack in broiling pan. Place pan in broiler 5 to 7 inches from heat source. Broil tenderloins 8 minutes. Brush with some brown-sugar glaze and broil 2 minutes longer. Turn tenderloins and broil 8 minutes. Brush with remaining brown-sugar glaze and broil until tenderloins are still slightly pink in center, about 2 minutes longer (internal temperature of meat should be 160°F. on meat thermometer).

2. Meanwhile, prepare Pear Chutney: Drain all but 1/2 cup syrup from canned pears and reserve; cut pears into 1/2-inch chunks. In 2-quart saucepan, heat red peppers, raisins, vinegar, brown sugar, ginger, salt, black pepper, and reserved pear syrup to boiling over high heat. Reduce heat to medium and cook 5 minutes. Reduce heat to low; stir in pears and green onion and cook, covered, 5 minutes longer. Makes about 2 1/2 cups chutney.

3. Place tenderloins on cutting board. Holding knife at an angle, thinly slice tenderloins. Spoon warm chutney over pork slices to serve. Makes 6 main-dish servings.

Each serving: About 350 calories (26 percent calories from fat), 28g protein, 39g carbohydrate, 10g total fat (3g saturated), 70mg cholesterol, 410mg sodium.

Chinese-Style Pork and Baby Peas

Prep: 10 minutes   Cook: 10 minutes

Serve this one-skillet dinner with basmati rice—a long-grain variety that cooks in twenty minutes—for a well-rounded meal.

- 2 **teaspoons vegetable oil**
- 1 **pork tenderloin (1 pound), trimmed and cut into 1/4-inch-thick slices**
- 2 **garlic cloves, crushed with garlic press**
- 1 **package (10 ounces) frozen baby peas**
- 3 **tablespoons reduced-sodium soy sauce**
- 2 **tablespoons seasoned rice vinegar**
- 1 **tablespoon grated, peeled fresh ginger**
- 1 **tablespoon light (mild) molasses**
- 1/4 **teaspoon crushed red pepper**

1. In nonstick 12-inch skillet, heat oil over medium-high heat. Add pork slices and garlic and cook, stirring occasionally, until pork slices are browned on the outside and just lose their pink color on the inside, about 6 minutes. Transfer pork to plate.

2. To same skillet, add peas, soy sauce, rice vinegar, ginger, molasses, and crushed red pepper; cook until peas are heated through, about 4 minutes. Return pork to skillet; toss to coat. To serve, spoon over rice. Makes 4 main-dish servings.

Each serving: About 230 calories (23 percent calories from fat), 28g protein, 19g carbohydrate, 6g total fat (1g saturated), 64mg cholesterol, 840mg sodium.

Latin American Pork Stew

Prep: 30 minutes   Bake: about 1 hour 30 minutes

Pork, black beans, cilantro, and sweet potatoes give this dish authentic Latin flavor.

- 2 **teaspoons olive oil**
- 2 **pounds boneless pork loin, cut into 1-inch pieces**
- 1 **large onion, chopped**
- 4 **garlic cloves, finely chopped**
- 2 **cups water**
- 1 **can (14 1/2 ounces) diced tomatoes**
- 1 **cup loosely packed fresh cilantro leaves and stems, chopped**
- 1 **teaspoon ground cumin**
- 3/4 **teaspoon salt**
- 1/2 **teaspoon ground coriander**
- 1/4 **teaspoon ground red pepper (cayenne)**
- 3 **medium sweet potatoes (1 1/2 pounds), peeled and cut into 1/2-inch chunks**
- 2 **cans (15 to 19 ounces each) black beans, rinsed and drained**

1. Preheat oven to 350°F. Pat pork dry with paper towels. In nonstick 5-quart Dutch oven, heat oil over medium-high heat until very hot. Add half of pork and cook, turning pieces, until lightly browned; transfer pork to a bowl as it is browned. Repeat with remaining pork.

2. Reduce heat to medium. To drippings in Dutch oven, add onion and cook, stirring frequently, until tender, about 10 minutes. Add garlic and cook 1 minute longer.

3. Add water, tomatoes with their juice, cilantro, cumin, salt, coriander, and ground red pepper; heat to boiling over high heat. Stir in pork; cover Dutch oven and bake 30 minutes.

4. Stir in sweet potatoes; cover and bake until meat and potatoes are very tender, about 40 minutes. Stir in black beans; cover and bake until heated through, 15 minutes longer. Makes about 10 cups or 8 main-dish servings.

Each serving: About 340 calories (24 percent calories from fat), 36g protein, 36g carbohydrate, 9g total fat (3g saturated), 58mg cholesterol, 735mg sodium.

Sesame Pork Stir-Fry

Prep: 20 minutes   Cook: 20 minutes

So gingery good—and this one-dish meal is only 375 calories per serving.

   Aromatic Rice (page 212)

 1 **cup loosely packed watercress leaves, coarsely chopped**

 1 **pork tenderloin (12 ounces), trimmed and thinly sliced**

 2 **tablespoons soy sauce**

 1 **tablespoon minced, peeled fresh ginger**

 1 **teaspoon Asian sesame oil**

 1 **garlic clove, crushed with garlic press**

 3/4 **cup chicken broth**

 1 1/4 **teaspoons cornstarch**

 2 **teaspoons olive oil**

 3 **medium carrots, peeled and cut into 2" by 1/4" matchstick strips**

 1 **medium red pepper, cut into 1/4-inch-wide strips**

 1 **tablespoon water**

 1 **medium zucchini (about 8 ounces), cut into 2" by 1/4" matchstick strips**

1. Prepare Aromatic Rice. Stir in watercress and keep warm.

2. Meanwhile, in medium bowl, toss pork, soy sauce, ginger, sesame oil, and garlic. In cup, mix broth and cornstarch.

3. In nonstick 12-inch skillet, heat 1 teaspoon oil over medium-high heat until hot. Add carrots and red pepper; cook, stirring frequently (stir-frying), until lightly browned, about 5 minutes. Add water and stir-fry until vegetables are tender-crisp, 3 to 5 minutes longer. Transfer to bowl.

4. In same skillet, heat remaining 1 teaspoon olive oil. Add zucchini; stir-fry until tender-crisp, about 3 minutes. Transfer zucchini to bowl with other vegetables.

5. In same skillet, add pork mixture and stir-fry until pork just loses its pink color. Stir cornstarch mixture; add to pork. Stir in vegetables; heat to boiling. Boil until sauce thickens, 1 minute. Serve pork stir-fry with watercress rice. Makes 4 main-dish servings.

Each serving: About 375 calories (24 percent calories from fat), 23g protein, 48g carbohydrate, 10g total fat (2g saturated), 56mg cholesterol, 975mg sodium.

Sweet and Savory Pork

Prep: 15 minutes   Cook: 10 minutes

Salty olives and capers interplay with sweet prunes to make the mouthwatering sauce for pork tenderloin slices.

 1 **pork tenderloin (1 pound), trimmed and cut crosswise into 1-inch-thick slices**

 2 **tablespoons brown sugar**

 3 **garlic cloves, crushed with garlic press**

 3/4 **teaspoon salt**

 1/4 **teaspoon ground black pepper**

 2 **teaspoons olive oil**

 1/2 **cup dry white wine**

 2 **tablespoons red wine vinegar**

 1 **teaspoon cornstarch**

 1/4 **teaspoon dried oregano**

 1/2 **cup pitted prunes, coarsely chopped**

 1/4 **cup pitted green olives, coarsely chopped**

 2 **tablespoons capers, drained**

1. Pat pork dry with paper towels. On waxed paper, combine brown sugar, garlic, salt, and pepper; use to coat pork.

2. In nonstick 12-inch skillet, heat oil over medium-high heat until very hot. Add pork and cook until slices are lightly browned and lose their pink color throughout, about 3 minutes per side. Transfer pork to plate.

3. In 1-cup measuring cup, blend wine, vinegar, cornstarch, and oregano until combined. Stir cornstarch mixture into skillet. Heat to boiling, stirring constantly. Return pork to skillet. Add prunes, olives, and capers; heat through. Makes 4 main-dish servings.

Each serving: About 270 calories (23 percent calories from fat), 25g protein, 22g carbohydrate, 7g total fat (2g saturated), 74mg cholesterol, 892mg sodium.

Ham Steak with Apple Chutney

Prep: 10 minutes   Cook: 35 minutes

This freshly made chutney is perfect with ham steak. You can also serve the chutney with grilled pork or chicken.

- **2 teaspoons vegetable oil**
- **1 medium onion, chopped**
- **2 Golden Delicious apples, peeled, cored, and chopped**
- **1 teaspoon minced, peeled fresh ginger**
- **3/4 cup apple juice**
- **1 tablespoon cider vinegar**
- **1/4 cup golden raisins**
- **1/2 teaspoon freshly grated orange peel**
- **1/4 teaspoon salt**
- **1 fully cooked smoked-ham center slice, 1 inch thick (2 pounds)**

1. In 2-quart saucepan, heat oil over medium heat. Add onion and cook, stirring occasionally, 5 minutes. Stir in apples and ginger and cook 3 minutes longer. Stir in apple juice, vinegar, raisins, orange peel, and salt; heat to boiling. Reduce heat and simmer 10 minutes. (Makes 2 2/3 cups chutney.)

2. Meanwhile, heat 10-inch skillet over medium heat until hot. Add ham steak and cook until heated through and lightly browned, 8 to 10 minutes per side. Serve with chutney. Makes 6 main-dish servings.

Each serving: About 257 calories (28 percent calories from fat), 29g protein, 17g carbohydrate, 8g total fat (2g saturated), 65mg cholesterol, 1,922mg sodium.

Whole Smithfield Ham

Prep: 10 minutes plus 24 to 36 hours soaking and cooling   Cook/Bake: 4 hours 30 minutes

To qualify as a "genuine" Smithfield ham, the ham must be dry salt–cured and aged for a minimum of six months. Generic country hams are generally aged for about three months, resulting in a milder-tasting ham.

- **1 cook-before-eating Smithfield or country-style ham (15 pounds)**
- **1/2 cup dark corn syrup**

1. Prepare ham as label directs, or prepare as follows: Place ham, skin side down, in saucepot large enough to hold whole ham; add enough water to cover ham completely. Let ham soak in water in cool place at least 24 hours or up to 36 hours, changing water frequently.

2. About 6 hours before serving or early in day, drain ham. With vegetable brush, scrub and rinse ham well with cool running water.

3. In same saucepot, cover ham with water; heat to boiling over high heat. Reduce heat; cover and simmer until bone on small end of ham (shank bone) pokes out about 1 inch and feels loose, about 3 hours 30 minutes.

4. Transfer ham to rack in large roasting pan (17" by 11 1/2"); cool until easy to handle.

5. Preheat oven to 325°F. With sharp knife, remove skin and trim fat from ham, leaving about 1/4-inch layer of fat. Brush ham with corn syrup. Bake until well glazed, about 15 minutes. Serve ham warm, or refrigerate to serve cold later. Cut into very thin slices. Makes about 35 main-dish servings.

Each serving: About 117 calories (23 percent calories from fat), 14g protein, 5g carbohydrate, 3g total fat (2g saturated), 45mg cholesterol, 1,639mg sodium.

Pork Tenderloin Cutlets with Plum Glaze

Prep: 10 minutes Grill: 6 minutes

The cutlets and glaze can be prepped in advance—up to several hours ahead. The grilling takes only minutes.

- **1 pork tenderloin (1 pound), trimmed**
- **3/4 teaspoon salt**
- **1/4 teaspoon coarsely ground black pepper**
- **1/2 cup plum jam or preserves**
- **1 tablespoon brown sugar**
- **1 tablespoon grated, peeled fresh ginger**
- **2 garlic cloves, crushed with garlic press**
- **1 tablespoon fresh lemon juice**
- **1/2 teaspoon ground cinnamon**
- **4 large plums (1 pound), each pitted and cut in half**

1. Prepare grill. Using sharp knife, cut tenderloin lengthwise almost in half, being careful not to cut all the way through. Open and spread flat like a book. With meat mallet or between two sheets of plastic wrap or waxed paper with rolling pin, pound meat to 1/4-inch thickness. Cut crosswise into 4 equal pieces; sprinkle cutlets with salt and pepper.

2. In small bowl, combine plum jam, brown sugar, ginger, garlic, lemon juice, and cinnamon. Brush one side of each cutlet and cut side of each plum half with plum glaze. Place cutlets and plums on grill over medium heat, glaze side down, and grill 3 minutes. Brush cutlets and plums with remaining plum glaze; turn pork and plums over and grill until cutlets are lightly browned on both sides and just lose their pink color throughout and plums are hot, about 3 minutes longer. Makes 4 main-dish servings.

Each serving: About 333 calories (16 percent calories from fat), 27g protein, 44g carbohydrate, 6g total fat (2g saturated), 80mg cholesterol, 509mg sodium.

Nutrition Spotlight: Plums

Colorful plums are an excellent source of vitamin C, plus they offer fiber and potassium. Try them split, pitted, and grilled; their natural sugars caramelize, boosting their sweetness without adding one extra calorie.

Pork Tenderloin with Plum Kabobs

Prep: 20 minutes plus marinating   Grill: 20 minutes

When you want a spontaneous—and sophisticated—summer supper, this easy recipe perfectly fits the bill.

-   8 (12-inch) bamboo skewers
-   2 tablespoons fresh lemon juice
-   1/2 teaspoon salt
-   1/4 teaspoon coarsely ground black pepper
-   2 tablespoons finely chopped fresh parsley leaves
-   1 pork tenderloin (1 pound), trimmed
-   1 teaspoon freshly grated lemon peel
-   1 garlic clove, chopped
-   1/4 teaspoon fresh thyme leaves
-   4 ripe medium purple, red, and/or green plums, each cut into quarters
-   3 green onions, cut into 1 1/2-inch pieces

1. Soak bamboo skewers in water 20 minutes.

2. Meanwhile, in large ziptight plastic bag, combine lemon juice, salt, pepper, and 1 tablespoon parsley; add tenderloin, turning to coat. Seal bag, pressing out as much air as possible. Place on a plate and let tenderloin marinate, turning occasionally, at room temperature 15 minutes or in the refrigerator 30 minutes.

3. Prepare grill. On cutting board, finely chop together lemon peel, garlic, thyme, and remaining 1 tablespoon parsley. Transfer to small bowl; set aside.

4. On each skewer, alternately thread 1 plum quarter, 2 green-onion pieces, another plum quarter, and 2 more green-onion pieces.

5. Remove tenderloin from plastic bag. Place tenderloin on grill over medium heat and grill, turning occasionally, until browned on the outside and still slightly pink on the inside, 18 to 20 minutes (internal temperature of pork should be 160°F. on a meat thermometer).

6. After tenderloin has cooked 10 minutes, place skewers with plums and green onions on grill and grill, turning once, until plums are hot and lightly browned, 6 to 8 minutes.

7. Holding knife at an angle, thinly slice pork and place on 4 dinner plates. Arrange 2 plum skewers on each plate. Sprinkle pork and skewers with parsley-lemon mixture. Makes 4 main-dish servings.

Each serving: About 275 calories (29 percent calories from fat), 28g protein, 10g carbohydrate, 9g total fat (3g saturated), 71mg cholesterol, 335mg sodium.

Roast Chicken with 40 Cloves of Garlic

Prep: 15 minutes   Roast: 1 hour

The garlic cooks in the same pan as the chicken, until the cloves are soft and golden. Some of the garlic is then mashed into the pan juices; save the rest to spread on crusty bread.

- 1 chicken (3¹/2 pounds)
- 6 fresh thyme sprigs
- 1/2 teaspoon salt
- 1/4 teaspoon coarsely ground black pepper
- 40 garlic cloves (about 2 heads), unpeeled, with loose papery skin discarded
- 1 cup chicken broth

1. Preheat oven to 450°F. Remove giblets and neck from chicken; refrigerate for another use. Rinse chicken with cold running water and drain well; pat dry with paper towels.

2. With fingertips, gently separate skin from meat on chicken breast. Place 4 thyme sprigs under skin of chicken breast. Place remaining thyme sprigs inside cavity of chicken. Sprinkle outside of chicken with salt and pepper.

Nutrition Spotlight: Garlic

Garlic brings a vivid flavor to lower-fat dishes, but its benefits extend far beyond taste. The latest research suggests that garlic is rich in plant chemicals that help lower "bad" (LDL) cholesterol.

3. With breast side up, lift wings up toward neck, then fold wing tips under back of chicken so wings stay in place. With string, tie legs together. Place chicken, breast side up, on rack in medium roasting pan (14" by 10").

4. Roast chicken 30 minutes. Add garlic cloves to pan and roast about 30 minutes longer. Chicken is done when temperature on meat thermometer inserted in thickest part of thigh reaches 175° to 180°F. and juices run clear when thigh is pierced with tip of knife.

5. Place chicken on warm platter; let stand 10 minutes to set juices for easier carving.

6. Meanwhile, remove rack from roasting pan. With slotted spoon, transfer garlic cloves to small bowl. Skim and discard fat from drippings in pan. Discard skin from 6 garlic cloves; add garlic to roasting pan with broth. Heat broth mixture to boiling over medium heat, stirring to loosen brown bits and mashing garlic with spoon until well blended.

7. Serve chicken with pan juices and remaining garlic cloves. Remove skin from chicken before eating if you like. Makes 4 main-dish servings.

Each serving without skin: About 330 calories (30 percent calories from fat), 45g protein, 10g carbohydrate, 11g total fat (3g saturated), 129mg cholesterol, 590mg sodium.

The Skinny on Poultry

The breast is the most tender part of the bird— and also the leanest. A 3¹/2-ounce portion of breast meat without skin has about 4 grams of fat. The same amount of skinless dark meat has about 10 grams of fat. And keep in mind that removing poultry skin slashes the amount of fat almost in half. You may prefer, however, to cook poultry with the skin on to keep the moisture in. Then simply remove the skin before eating. The fat reduction is practically the same.

Rosemary-Apricot Chicken

Prep: 20 minutes plus marinating   Roast: 45 minutes

A great buffet dish that is hard to beat. Served hot or cold, it has a delicious, tangy-sweet flavor that everyone will love.

- **4 garlic cloves, crushed with garlic press**
- **2 teaspoons salt**
- **1 teaspoon dried rosemary, crumbled**
- **1/2 teaspoon ground black pepper**
- **3 chickens (3 pounds each), each cut into quarters and skin removed from all but wings**
- **1/2 cup apricot preserves**
- **2 tablespoons fresh lemon juice**
- **2 teaspoons Dijon mustard**

1. In cup, combine garlic, salt, rosemary, and pepper; rub mixture on chicken. Place chicken in large bowl or ziptight plastic bags; cover bowl or seal bags and refrigerate chicken 2 hours to marinate.

2. Preheat oven to 350°F. Arrange chicken, skinned side up, in 2 large roasting pans (17" by 11½") or 2 jelly-roll pans (15½" by 10½"). Roast chicken 25 minutes, rotating pans between upper and lower oven racks halfway through roasting.

3. Meanwhile, in small bowl, with fork, mix apricot preserves, lemon juice, and mustard. Brush apricot mixture over chicken. Continue roasting, rotating pans after 10 minutes, until juices run clear when thickest part of chicken is pierced with tip of knife, about 20 minutes longer. Serve chicken hot, or cover and refrigerate to serve cold. Makes 12 main-dish servings.

Each serving: About 267 calories (30 percent calories from fat), 35g protein, 9g carbohydrate, 9g total fat (2g saturated), 108mg cholesterol, 519mg sodium.

Irish Chicken Dinner

Prep: 20 minutes   Cook: 50 minutes

Here's an interesting rendition of what New Englanders fondly call a boiled dinner, with chicken standing in for the traditional corned beef.

- **1 chicken (3½ pounds), cut into 8 pieces and skin removed from all but wings**
- **1 tablespoon vegetable oil**
- **1 small head green cabbage (2 pounds), cut into 8 wedges**
- **1 large onion, cut into 8 wedges**
- **8 ounces carrots, peeled and cut into 2½-inch pieces**
- **2 small turnips (8 ounces), peeled and cut into 1-inch-wide wedges**
- **1 cup water**
- **1 cup chicken broth**
- **10 whole black peppercorns**
- **3 whole cloves**
- **1 large bay leaf**
- **1 cup loosely packed spinach leaves, cut into 1/4-inch-wide strips**

1. Cut each chicken breast half in half.

2. In 8-quart Dutch oven, heat oil over medium-high heat. Add cabbage and onion wedges and cook until lightly browned.

3. Add chicken, carrots, turnips, water, broth, peppercorns, cloves, and bay leaf to Dutch oven; heat to

boiling over high heat. Reduce heat to low; cover and simmer, gently stirring occasionally, until chicken loses its pink color throughout and vegetables are tender, about 40 minutes.

4. With slotted spoon, transfer chicken and vegetables to 4 large soup bowls; top with spinach. Strain cooking broth through sieve into medium bowl; discard spices and bay leaf. Spoon hot broth over chicken and vegetables in soup bowls. Makes 4 main-dish servings.

Each serving: About 380 calories (24 percent calories from fat), 46g protein, 27g carbohydrate, 10g total fat (2g saturated), 134mg cholesterol, 515mg sodium.

Thyme-Roasted Chicken and Vegetables

Prep: 20 minutes   Roast: 50 minutes

In just over an hour, you can have a one-dish meal of roasted chicken with fennel, potatoes, and onion ready to serve.

- 1 **chicken (3¹/2 pounds), cut into 8 pieces and skin removed from all but wings**
- 1 **pound all-purpose potatoes (3 medium), not peeled, cut into 2-inch pieces**
- 1 **large fennel bulb (1¹/2 pounds), trimmed and cut into 8 wedges**
- 1 **large red onion, cut into 8 wedges**
- 1 **tablespoon chopped fresh thyme or 1 teaspoon dried thyme**
- 1 **teaspoon salt**
- ¹/2 **teaspoon ground black pepper**
- 2 **tablespoons olive oil**
- ¹/3 **cup water**

1. Preheat oven to 450°F. In large roasting pan (17" by 11¹/2"), arrange chicken pieces, skinned side up, and place potatoes, fennel, and onion around them.

Sprinkle chicken with thyme, salt, and pepper. Drizzle oil over chicken and vegetables.

2. Roast chicken and vegetables 20 minutes; baste with drippings in pan. Roast, basting once more, until juices run clear when chicken breasts are pierced with tip of knife, about 20 minutes longer. Transfer chicken breasts to platter; keep warm.

3. Continue roasting remaining chicken pieces until juices run clear when thickest part of chicken is pierced with tip of knife and vegetables are fork-tender, about 10 minutes longer. Transfer chicken and vegetables to platter with breasts; keep warm.

4. Skim and discard fat from drippings in pan. To drippings, add water; heat to boiling over medium heat, stirring until brown bits are loosened from bottom. Spoon pan juices over chicken and vegetables. Makes 4 main-dish servings.

Each serving: About 401 calories (29 percent calories from fat), 43g protein, 28g carbohydrate, 13g total fat (2g saturated), 124mg cholesterol, 870mg sodium.

Caribbean Roast Chicken
Prep: 25 minutes   Roast: 40 minutes

Our new take on basic roast chicken calls for flavorful spices, citrus juices, brown sugar, and pineapple to turn mealtime into a tropical feast.

- **2 limes**
- **1 orange**
- **2 garlic cloves, crushed with garlic press**
- **2 tablespoons light brown sugar**
- **1 tablespoon vegetable oil**
- **1 teaspoon salt**
- **1/2 teaspoon dried thyme**
- **1/4 teaspoon ground red pepper (cayenne)**
- **1/4 teaspoon ground allspice**
- **1 chicken (31/2 pounds), cut into 8 pieces and skin removed from all but wings**
- **2 small onions, each cut into 6 wedges**
- **1 medium pineapple, cored and cut into 8 wedges**

1. Preheat oven to 450°F. From limes, grate 1/2 teaspoon peel and squeeze 2 tablespoons juice. From orange, grate 1/2 teaspoon peel and squeeze 4 tablespoons juice.

2. In cup, with fork, mix lime peel, 1 tablespoon lime juice, orange peel, 2 tablespoons orange juice, garlic, brown sugar, oil, salt, thyme, ground red pepper and allspice until blended.

3. In large roasting pan (17" by 111/2"), toss chicken, onions, and pineapple with juice mixture until evenly coated. Roast, tossing mixture once during cooking, until juices run clear when thickest parts of chicken pieces are pierced with tip of knife, 35 to 40 minutes. Transfer chicken, onions, and pineapple to platter; cover and keep warm.

4. Add remaining 1 tablespoon lime juice and remaining 2 tablespoons orange juice to drippings in roasting pan; heat to boiling over medium heat, stirring until brown bits are loosened from bottom. Spoon pan juices over chicken, onions, and pineapple. Makes 4 main-dish servings.

Each serving: About 325 calories (25 percent calories from fat), 34g protein, 28g carbohydrate, 9g total fat (2g saturated), 109mg cholesterol, 660mg sodium.

Lemony Roast Chicken with Artichokes

Prep: 30 minutes   Roast: 40 minutes

Cook plump thighs and drumsticks with spring artichokes and baby red potatoes for a delectable dinner. Make sure to use a large roasting pan; otherwise ingredients will steam, not brown.

2	**large lemons**
3	**garlic cloves, crushed with garlic press**
3	**tablespoons olive oil**
1¹/₂	**teaspoons salt**
1	**teaspoon dried oregano**
¹/₂	**teaspoon coarsely ground black pepper**
6	**medium bone-in chicken thighs (1³/4 pounds), skin removed**
6	**medium chicken drumsticks (1¹/2 pounds), skin removed**
2	**pounds baby red potatoes, each cut in half**
4	**medium or 16 baby artichokes**

1. Preheat oven to 450°F. From lemons, grate 2 teaspoons peel and squeeze ¹/2 cup juice.

2. In cup, mix lemon peel, garlic, oil, salt, oregano, and pepper. In large roasting pan (17" by 11¹/2"), toss chicken thighs, drumsticks, and potatoes with oil mixture. Roast 20 minutes.

3. While chicken is roasting, prepare medium artichokes*: With serrated knife, cut 1 inch straight across top of medium artichoke. Cut off stem; peel. Pull dark outer leaves from artichoke bottom. With kitchen shears, trim thorny tips of remaining leaves. Cut artichoke lengthwise into quarters. Scrape out choke, removing center petals and fuzzy center portion; discard. Repeat with remaining artichokes. Rinse artichokes well.

4. In 5-quart saucepot, heat 1 tablespoon lemon juice and 1 inch water to boiling over medium-high heat. Add artichokes and stems, cover and cook until fork-tender, about 10 minutes. Drain well on paper towels.

5. Add artichokes to roasting pan with chicken; roast until juices run clear when thickest part of chicken is pierced with tip of knife and potatoes are tender, about 20 minutes longer..

6. Pour remaining 7 tablespoons lemon juice over chicken and vegetables and toss to mix. Transfer chicken and vegetables to serving bowl. Makes 6 main-dish servings.

*To prepare baby artichokes: Bend back green outer leaves and snap them off at base until remaining leaves are half green (at the top) and half yellow (at the bottom). Cut off stem and top of each artichoke at point where yellow meets green. Cut each artichoke lengthwise in half. Do not discard center portion; baby artichokes are completely edible.

Each serving: About 385 calories (28 percent calories from fat), 34g protein, 36g carbohydrate, 12g total fat (2g saturated), 111mg cholesterol, 740mg sodium.

Roasted Tandoori-Style Chicken Breasts

Prep: 10 minutes plus marinating   Roast: 30 minutes

Plain yogurt tenderizes the chicken, while the exotic spices add plenty of flavor.

2	limes
1	container (8 ounces) plain low-fat yogurt
1/2	small onion, chopped
1	tablespoon minced, peeled fresh ginger
1	tablespoon paprika
1	teaspoon ground cumin
1	teaspoon ground coriander
3/4	teaspoon salt
1/4	teaspoon ground red pepper (cayenne)
	pinch ground cloves
6	medium bone-in chicken breast halves (3 pounds), skin removed

1. From 1 lime, squeeze 2 tablespoons juice. Cut remaining lime into 6 wedges; set aside for garnish. In blender, puree yogurt, onion, ginger, paprika, cumin, coriander, salt, ground red pepper, and cloves until smooth. Place chicken and yogurt marinade in medium bowl or in ziptight plastic bag, turning to coat chicken. Cover bowl or seal bag and refrigerate chicken 30 minutes to marinate.

2. Preheat oven to 450°F. Arrange chicken on rack in medium roasting pan (14" by 10"). Spoon half of marinade over chicken; discard remaining marinade.

3. Roast chicken until juices run clear when thickest part of chicken is pierced with tip of knife, about 30 minutes.

4. Transfer chicken to warm platter; garnish with lime wedges to serve. Makes 6 main-dish servings.

Each serving: About 197 calories (14 percent calories from fat), 36g protein, 5g carbohydrate, 3g total fat (1g saturated), 88mg cholesterol, 415mg sodium.

Sticky Drumsticks

Prep: 20 minutes   Bake: 35 minutes

Have lots of napkins on hand for these delicious oven-barbe-cued drumsticks—guaranteed to be a favorite with the kids in your family.

1/2	cup apricot preserves
1/4	cup teriyaki sauce
1	tablespoon dark brown sugar
1	teaspoon cornstarch
1	teaspoon cider vinegar
1/4	teaspoon salt
12	medium chicken drumsticks (3 pounds), skin removed

1. Preheat oven to 425°F. In large bowl, with wire whisk, mix apricot preserves, teriyaki sauce, brown sugar, cornstarch, vinegar, and salt until blended. Add chicken, tossing to coat.

2. Spoon chicken and sauce into 15 1/2" by 10 1/2" jelly-roll pan. Bake 15 minutes. Remove chicken from oven; with pastry brush, brush chicken with sauce in pan. Continue baking, brushing with sauce every 5 minutes, until juices run clear when drumsticks are pierced with tip of knife, 15 to 20 minutes longer.

3. Remove chicken from oven; brush with sauce. Let chicken cool on jelly-roll pan 10 minutes. Transfer chicken to serving dish and spoon sauce over chicken. Makes 6 main-dish servings.

Each serving: About 240 calories (15 percent calories from fat), 26g protein, 24g carbohydrate, 4g total fat (2g saturated), 96mg cholesterol, 660mg sodium.

Chicken Marianne

Prep: 15 minutes   Bake: 50 minutes

8 **medium bone-in chicken thighs (2 pounds), skin removed**

1/2 **teaspoon dried oregano leaves**

3/4 **teaspoon salt**

1/2 **teaspoon coarsely ground black pepper**

1 **medium onion, thinly sliced**

3 **small plum tomatoes, cut crosswise into 1/4-inch-thick slices**

3 **strips (3" by 1" each) lemon peel**

2 **tablespoons margarine or butter**

1 1/4 **pounds carrots, peeled and cut into 2-inch pieces**

1 1/4 **pounds parsnips, peeled and cut into 2-inch pieces**

1. Preheat oven to 400°F. Place chicken in 13" by 9" metal baking pan. Sprinkle chicken with oregano, 1/2 teaspoon salt, and pepper. Arrange onion, tomatoes, and lemon peel in pan with chicken.

2. Place margarine in 15 1/2" by 10 1/2" jelly-roll pan. Place pan in oven just long enough to melt margarine. Toss carrots, parsnips, and remaining 1/4 teaspoon salt with melted margarine in jelly-roll pan.

3. Place chicken and vegetables on 2 oven racks. Bake, rotating pans between upper and lower oven racks halfway through baking, basting chicken occasionally with pan juices, and turning vegetables twice with metal spatula. Chicken and vegetables are done when juices run clear when thickest part of chicken is pierced with tip of knife and vegetables are fork-tender and nicely browned, 45 to 50 minutes.

4. Arrange chicken and vegetables on large platter. Spoon vegetables from pan over chicken. Makes 4 main-dish servings.

Each serving: About 380 calories (28 percent calories from fat), 29g protein, 40g carbohydrate, 12g total fat (2g saturated), 107mg cholesterol, 675mg sodium.

Baked "Fried" Chicken

Prep: 15 minutes   Bake: 35 minutes

For this healthier version of fried chicken, skinless chicken pieces are dipped in a spicy bread-crumb coating and baked until crispy and golden brown. You won't miss the calories.

olive oil nonstick cooking spray

1/2 **cup plain dried bread crumbs**

1/4 **cup freshly grated Parmesan cheese**

2 **tablespoons cornmeal**

1/2 **teaspoon ground red pepper (cayenne)**

1 **large egg white**

1/2 **teaspoon salt**

1 **chicken (3 1/2 pounds), cut into 8 pieces and skin removed from all but wings**

1. Preheat oven to 425°F. Grease 15 1/2" by 10 1/2" jelly-roll pan with cooking spray.

2. On waxed paper, combine bread crumbs, Parmesan, cornmeal, and ground red pepper. In pie plate, beat egg white and salt.

3. Dip each piece of chicken in egg-white mixture, then coat with crumb mixture, firmly pressing so mixture adheres. Arrange chicken in prepared pan; lightly coat chicken with cooking spray.

4. Bake chicken until coating is crisp and golden brown and juices run clear when thickest part of chicken is pierced with tip of knife, about 35 minutes. Makes 4 main-dish servings.

Each serving: About 329 calories (25 percent calories from fat), 46g protein, 14g carbohydrate, 9g fat (3g saturated), 137mg cholesterol, 660mg sodium.

Chicken Breasts in Orange Sauce

Prep: 15 minutes   Cook: 30 minutes

Use sweet seedless oranges for this flavorful entrée.

- **4 large navel oranges**
- **4 medium bone-in chicken breast halves (2 1/2 pounds), skin removed**
- **1/2 teaspoon salt**
- **1/2 teaspoon coarsely ground black pepper**
- **1/4 teaspoon dried thyme leaves**
- **1 tablespoon olive oil**
- **1/2 cup chicken broth**
- **1/4 cup orange marmalade**
- **1 teaspoon cornstarch**

1. From 1 orange, with vegetable peeler, remove four 3-inch-long strips of peel (each about 3/4 inch wide). Cut peel lengthwise into very thin slivers. Squeeze enough juice from the peeled orange and 1 other orange to equal 2/3 cup. Cut peel and white pith from

Nutrition Spotlight: Citrus

Looking for some vitamin C? Head to the citrus section! On average, a single piece of citrus fruit has 3 grams of fiber and only about 50 calories. Look for the diminutive clementines, garnet-fleshed blood oranges, funny-looking ugli fruit, bite-size kumquats, generous-size yellow and pink grapefruit— and, of course, the fragrant and flavorful traditional orange. And while a glass of fresh-squeezed OJ is pretty sweet to wake up to, you'll miss out on all that good fiber.

remaining 2 oranges. Cut each orange in half from stem to blossom end, then cut each half crosswise into 1/4-inch-thick slices; set aside.

2. Rub chicken breasts with salt, pepper, and thyme. In nonstick 12-inch skillet, heat oil over medium-high heat until very hot. Add chicken breasts and cook until golden brown, about 3 minutes per side. Add orange-peel strips, orange juice, and broth; heat to boiling. Reduce heat to low; cover and simmer until juices run clear when thickest part of chicken is pierced with tip of knife, about 20 minutes. Transfer chicken to warm platter; keep warm.

3. In cup, mix orange marmalade and cornstarch until blended. Add marmalade mixture to skillet; heat to boiling. Cook, stirring constantly, until sauce thickens slightly, 1 minute. Stir in orange slices; heat through. Spoon sauce over chicken on platter. Makes 4 main-dish servings.

Each serving: About 305 calories (18 percent calories from fat), 35g protein, 29g carbohydrate, 6g total fat (1g saturated), 82mg cholesterol, 460mg sodium.

Apricot-Glazed Chicken

Prep: 5 minutes   Bake: 25 minutes

A quick and easy four-ingredient glaze is how we season up this winning recipe.

- 1/3 **cup apricot preserves**
- 1 **tablespoon chili sauce**
- 2 **teaspoons Dijon mustard**
- 1/2 **teaspoon salt**
- 4 **large bone-in chicken breast halves (2¹/2 pounds), skin removed**

1. Preheat oven to 425°F. In a small bowl, combine apricot preserves, chili sauce, mustard, and salt. Arrange chicken in 13" by 9" baking dish; brush with apricot glaze.

2. Bake, brushing occasionally with glaze, until juices run clear when thickest part of chicken is pierced with tip of knife, 25 to 30 minutes. Transfer to warm platter. Makes 4 main-dish servings.

Each serving: About 338 calories (5 percent calories from fat), 43g protein, 35g carbohydrate, 2g total fat (1g saturated), 107mg cholesterol, 548mg sodium.

Chicken Provençal

Prep: 30 minutes   Cook: 1 hour

A melt-in-your-mouth stew flavored with orange peel and fennel seed.

- 2 **teaspoons olive oil**
- 2 **pounds skinless, boneless chicken thighs, cut into quarters**
- 3/4 **teaspoon salt**
- 2 **medium red peppers, cut into ¹/4-inch-thick slices**
- 1 **medium yellow pepper, cut into ¹/4-inch-thick slices**
- 1 **jumbo onion (1 pound), thinly sliced**
- 3 **garlic cloves, crushed with garlic press**
- 1 **can (28 ounces) Italian-style plum tomatoes**
- 1/4 **teaspoon dried thyme leaves**
- 1/4 **teaspoon fennel seeds, crushed**
- 3 **strips (3" by 1" each) orange peel**
- 1/2 **cup loosely packed fresh basil leaves, chopped**

1. In nonstick 5-quart Dutch oven, heat 1 teaspoon oil over medium-high heat until very hot. Add half of chicken and ¹/4 teaspoon salt; cook, turning the pieces, until lightly browned on all sides, about 10 minutes. Transfer chicken to plate. Repeat with remaining oil, chicken, and ¹/4 teaspoon salt.

2. To drippings in Dutch oven, add red peppers, yellow peppers, onion, and remaining ¹/4 teaspoon salt; cook, stirring frequently, until vegetables are tender and lightly browned, about 20 minutes. Add garlic; cook 1 minute.

3. Return chicken to Dutch oven. Add tomatoes with their juice, thyme, fennel seeds, and orange peel, breaking up tomatoes with side of spoon; heat to boiling. Reduce heat to low; cover and simmer until chicken loses its pink color throughout, about 15 minutes. Sprinkle with basil to serve. Makes 8 main-dish servings.

Each serving: About 200 calories (27 percent calories from fat), 25g protein, 13g carbohydrate, 6g total fat (1g saturated), 94mg cholesterol, 460mg sodium.

Baked Honey-Mustard Chicken and Vegetables

Prep: 10 minutes   Bake: 50 minutes

The beauty of this flavor-packed dinner? It all cooks in the oven at the same time.

1¹/₂   **pounds small red potatoes, quartered**
1   **jumbo onion (1 pound), cut into eighths**
6   **teaspoons olive oil**
³/₄   **teaspoon salt**
¹/₄   **teaspoon coarsely ground black pepper**
4   **medium bone-in chicken breast halves (2¹/₂ pounds), skin removed**
2   **tablespoons honey mustard**

1. Preheat oven to 450°F. In 13" by 9" metal baking pan, toss potatoes and onion with 4 teaspoons oil, salt, and pepper. Place pan in oven on middle rack and bake 25 minutes.

2. Meanwhile, place chicken breasts in small roasting pan and coat with 1 teaspoon oil. In cup, mix remaining 1 teaspoon oil with honey mustard; set aside.

3. After vegetables have baked 25 minutes, remove pan from oven and carefully turn vegetables with metal spatula. Return vegetables to oven, placing pan on lower oven rack. Place chicken on upper rack. Bake 10 minutes.

4. Remove chicken from oven and brush with honey-mustard mixture. Return to oven and bake until juices run clear when thickest part of chicken is pierced with tip of knife and vegetables are golden, 12 to 15 minutes longer. Serve chicken with vegetables. Makes 4 main-dish servings.

Each serving: About 380 calories (24 percent calories from fat), 31g protein, 44g carbohydrate, 10g total fat (1g saturated), 66mg cholesterol, 630mg sodium.

Poulé au Pot with Tarragon

Prep: 15 minutes　Cook: 1 hour

Stewed chicken and vegetables is a favorite Sunday supper in France. Use the leftover broth as the base for a soup.

- **3　medium leeks (1 pound)**
- **1　chicken (3¹/2 pounds), cut into 8 pieces**
- **1　pound small red potatoes**
- **1　bag (16 ounces) carrots, peeled and cut into 3-inch pieces**
- **4　cups water**
- **1　can (14¹/2 ounces) chicken broth or 1³/4 cups homemade**
- **¹/2　teaspoon salt**
- **¹/4　teaspoon dried thyme**
- **¹/4　teaspoon ground black pepper**
- **1　large sprig plus 1 tablespoon chopped fresh tarragon**

1. Cut off roots and trim dark green tops from leeks; cut each leek lengthwise in half, then crosswise into 3-inch pieces. Rinse in large bowl of cold water, swishing to remove sand; transfer to colander to drain, leaving sand in bottom of bowl.

2. In 6- to 8-quart Dutch oven, combine leeks, chicken, potatoes, carrots, water, broth, salt, thyme, pepper, and tarragon sprig. Heat to boiling over high heat. Reduce heat; cover and simmer until chicken loses its pink color throughout, about 45 minutes.

3. With slotted spoon, transfer chicken and vegetables to serving bowl. Remove and discard skin from chicken. Skim and discard fat from broth. Pour 1 cup broth over chicken (refrigerate remaining broth for another use). To serve, sprinkle chopped tarragon on top. Makes 4 main-dish servings.

Each serving: About 472 calories (21 percent calories from fat), 47g protein, 44g carbohydrate, 11g total fat (3g saturated), 127mg cholesterol, 859mg sodium.

Chicken and Leek Casserole

Prep: 40 minutes　Bake: 1 hour 15 minutes

- **1　tablespoon vegetable oil**
- **6　large chicken legs (4¹/2 pounds), skin removed**
- **¹/2　cup water**
- **1　tablespoon all-purpose flour**
- **6　medium leeks (2¹/2 pounds), rinsed and cut crosswise into 2-inch pieces**
- **1 ¹/2　pounds medium red potatoes, quartered**
- **1　pound carrots, peeled and cut into 2¹/2" by ¹/2" pieces**
- **1　can (14¹/2 ounces) chicken broth or 1³/4 cups homemade**
- **³/4　teaspoon salt**

1. Preheat oven to 375°F. In 8-quart Dutch oven, heat oil over medium-high heat until very hot. Add 3 chicken legs and cook until golden brown on all sides; transfer to plate. Repeat with remaining chicken legs.

2. In cup, stir water and flour. Return chicken to Dutch oven; stir in leeks, potatoes, carrots, broth, salt, and flour mixture. Heat to boiling over high heat. Cover Dutch oven and bake until chicken loses its pink color throughout, about 1¹/4 hours.

3. Spoon 1¹/2 cups vegetables and ¹/4 cup liquid from Dutch oven into blender. Cover, with center part of cover removed to let steam escape, and puree at low speed until very smooth. Stir pureed vegetables into Dutch oven. Makes 6 main-dish servings.

Each serving: About 440 calories (23 percent calories from fat), 44g protein, 41g carbohydrate, 11g total fat (2g saturated), 156mg cholesterol, 810mg sodium.

Country Captain Casserole

Prep: 30 minutes   Bake: 1 hour

Though the exact origin of this well-known dish is often debated, its great flavor is never in dispute.

- **2 tablespoons plus 1 teaspoon vegetable oil**
- **2 chickens (3¹/2 pounds each), each cut into 8 pieces and skin removed from all but wings**
- **2 medium onions, chopped**
- **1 large Granny Smith apple, peeled, cored, and chopped**
- **1 large green pepper, chopped**
- **3 large garlic cloves, finely chopped**
- **1 tablespoon grated, peeled fresh ginger**
- **3 tablespoons curry powder**
- **¹/2 teaspoon coarsely ground black pepper**
- **¹/4 teaspoon ground cumin**
- **1 can (28 ounces) plum tomatoes in puree**
- **1 can (14¹/2 ounces) chicken broth or 1³/4 cups homemade**
- **¹/2 cup dark seedless raisins**
- **1 teaspoon salt**
- **¹/4 cup chopped fresh parsley**

1. In nonreactive 8-quart Dutch oven, heat 2 tablespoons oil over medium-high heat until very hot. Add chicken, in batches, and cook until golden brown, about 5 minutes per side. Transfer chicken pieces to bowl as they are browned.

2. Preheat oven to 350°F. In same Dutch oven, heat remaining 1 teaspoon oil over medium-high heat. Add onions, apple, green pepper, garlic, and ginger; cook, stirring frequently, 2 minutes. Reduce heat to medium; cover and cook 5 minutes longer.

3. Stir in curry powder, black pepper, and cumin; cook 1 minute. Add tomatoes with their puree, broth, raisins, salt, and chicken pieces. Heat to boiling over high heat; boil 1 minute. Cover and place in oven. Bake 1 hour. Sprinkle with parsley. Makes 8 main-dish servings.

Each serving: About 347 calories (29 percent calories from fat), 43g protein, 19g carbohydrate, 11g total fat (2g saturated), 133mg cholesterol, 825mg sodium.

Chicken Gumbo Casserole

Prep: 45 minutes   Bake: 45 minutes

Most gumbos—a Creole specialty from New Orleans—are a bit indulgent, but we created a lighter version and baked it, casserole-style.

- 1/4 **cup all-purpose flour**
- 1 **tablespoon vegetable oil**
- 4 **medium bone-in chicken thighs (1¹/4 pounds), skin removed**
- 2 **ounces low-fat kielbasa (smoked Polish sausage), finely chopped (¹/2 cup)**
- 1 **can (14¹/2 ounces) chicken broth or 1³/4 cup homemade**
- 1 **can (14¹/2 ounces) diced tomatoes**
- 1/4 **cup tomato paste**
- 1 **medium red pepper, chopped**
- 1 **medium onion, thinly sliced**
- 1 **large stalk celery, sliced**
- 1 **garlic clove, finely chopped**
- 1 **bay leaf**
- 1/2 **teaspoon salt**
- 1/4 **teaspoon dried thyme**
- 1/4 **teaspoon ground red pepper (cayenne)**
- 1/4 **teaspoon ground allspice**
- 1 **package (10 ounces) frozen cut okra**
- 1 **cup regular long-grain rice**

1. Preheat oven to 375°F. In 5-quart Dutch oven, toast flour over low heat until pale golden, 10 to 15 minutes, stirring frequently. Transfer flour to cup; set aside.

2. In same Dutch oven, heat oil over medium-high heat until very hot. Add chicken and cook until golden brown, about 5 minutes per side; transfer to plate. Reduce heat to medium; add kielbasa and cook, stirring, until lightly browned, 1 minute. Transfer kielbasa to plate with chicken. Stir ¹/4 cup broth into flour in cup until blended; add to Dutch oven and cook 1 minute, stirring. Gradually stir in remaining broth.

3. Return chicken and kielbasa to Dutch oven. Stir in tomatoes, tomato paste, red pepper, onion, celery, garlic, bay leaf, salt, thyme, ground red pepper, and allspice; heat to boiling over high heat. Add okra; cover and bake until chicken loses its pink color throughout and vegetables are tender, about 45 minutes.

4. Meanwhile, in 2-quart saucepan, prepare rice as label directs, but do not add salt, margarine, or butter.

5. Discard bay leaf and serve gumbo over rice. Makes 4 main-dish servings.

Each serving: About 435 calories (21 percent calories from fat), 25g protein, 61g carbohydrate, 10g total fat (1g saturated), 57mg cholesterol, 845mg sodium.

Chicken with Rosemary Dumplings

Prep: 15 minutes   Cook: 1 hour

It doesn't take hours to make a stew when you're using chicken breasts. And the tender dumplings will melt in your mouth.

- 2 **tablespoons vegetable oil**
- 6 **large bone-in chicken breast halves (3¹/4 pounds), skin removed**
- 4 **large carrots, peeled and cut into 1-inch pieces**
- 2 **large stalks celery, cut into ¹/4-inch-thick slices**
- 1 **medium onion, finely chopped**
- 1 **cup plus 2 tablespoons all-purpose flour**
- 2 **teaspoons baking powder**
- 1¹/2 **teaspoons chopped fresh rosemary or ¹/2 teaspoon dried rosemary, crumbled**
- 1 **teaspoon salt**
- 1 **large egg**
- 1¹/2 **cups milk**
- 2 **cups water**
- 1 **can (14¹/2 ounces) low-sodium chicken broth or 1³/4 cups homemade**
- 1/4 **teaspoon ground black pepper**
- 1 **package (10 ounces) frozen peas**

1. In 8-quart Dutch oven, heat 1 tablespoon oil over medium-high heat until very hot. Add 3 chicken breast halves; cook until golden brown, about 5 minutes per side. Transfer to bowl. Repeat with remaining chicken.

2. Add remaining 1 tablespoon oil to drippings in Dutch oven. Add carrots, celery, and onion and cook, stirring frequently, until vegetables are golden brown and tender, about 10 minutes.

3. Meanwhile, prepare dumplings: In small bowl, combine 1 cup flour, baking powder, rosemary, and 1/2 teaspoon salt. In cup, with fork, beat egg with 1/2 cup milk. Stir egg mixture into flour mixture until just blended.

4. Return chicken to Dutch oven; add water, broth, pepper, and remaining 1/2 teaspoon salt. Heat to boiling over high heat. Drop dumpling mixture by rounded tablespoons on top of chicken and vegetables to make 12 dumplings. Reduce heat; cover and simmer 15 minutes.

5. With slotted spoon, transfer dumplings, chicken, and vegetables to serving bowl; keep warm. Reserve broth in Dutch oven.

6. In cup, blend remaining 2 tablespoons flour with remaining 1 cup milk until smooth; stir into broth mixture. Heat to boiling over high heat; boil 1 minute to thicken slightly. Add peas and heat through. Pour sauce over chicken and dumplings. Makes 6 main-dish servings.

Each serving: About 437 calories (21 percent calories from fat), 46g protein, 38g carbohydrate, 10g total fat (3g saturated), 137mg cholesterol, 951mg sodium.

Arroz con Pollo

Prep: 15 minutes   Cook: 40 minutes

From Santiago to Miami to Madrid, different versions of this comforting chicken-and-rice dish are served almost anywhere Spanish is spoken.

- 1 **tablespoon vegetable oil**
- 6 **medium bone-in chicken thighs (11/2 pounds), skin and fat removed**
- 1 **medium onion, finely chopped**
- 1 **red pepper, chopped**
- 1 **garlic clove, finely chopped**
- 1/8 **teaspoon ground red pepper (cayenne)**
- 1 **cup regular long-grain rice**
- 1 **can (141/2 ounces) chicken broth or 13/4 cups homemade**
- 1/4 **cup water**
- 1 **strip (3" by 1/2") lemon peel**
- 1/4 **teaspoon dried oregano**
- 1/4 **teaspoon salt**
- 1 **cup frozen peas**
- 1/4 **cup chopped pimiento-stuffed olives (salad olives)**
- 1/4 **cup chopped fresh cilantro**
- **lemon wedges**

1. In 5-quart Dutch oven, heat oil over medium-high heat until very hot. Add chicken, in batches, and cook until golden brown, about 5 minutes per side. Transfer chicken pieces to bowl as they are browned.

2. Reduce heat to medium. Add onion and red pepper to Dutch oven and cook until tender, about 5 minutes. Stir in garlic and ground red pepper and cook 30 seconds. Add rice and cook, stirring, 1 minute. Stir in broth, water, lemon peel, oregano, salt, and chicken; heat to boiling. Reduce heat; cover and simmer until juices run clear when thickest part of chicken is pierced with tip of knife, about 20 minutes.

3. Stir in peas; cover and heat through. Remove from heat and let stand 5 minutes. Sprinkle with olives and cilantro; serve with lemon wedges. Makes 4 main-dish servings.

Each serving: About 387 calories (21 percent calories from fat), 26g protein, 48g carbohydrate, 9g total fat (2g saturated), 81mg cholesterol, 927mg sodium.

Chicken and Sweet-Potato Stew

Prep: 20 minutes   Cook: 45 minutes

Coat chicken thighs with an exotic mix of cumin and cinnamon, then simmer with beta-carotene-rich sweet potatoes in a creamy peanut-butter sauce. Delectable over brown rice.

4 medium bone-in chicken thighs (1¹/2 pounds), skin removed

1 teaspoon ground cumin

¹/4 teaspoon ground cinnamon

1 tablespoon olive oil

1¹/2 pounds sweet potatoes (3 medium), peeled and cut into ¹/2-inch chunks

1 medium onion, sliced

1 can (28 ounces) whole tomatoes in juice

3 tablespoons natural peanut butter

¹/2 teaspoon salt

¹/4 teaspoon crushed red pepper

2 garlic cloves, peeled

¹/4 cup packed fresh cilantro leaves plus 2 tablespoons chopped cilantro leaves

1. Rub chicken thighs with cumin and cinnamon; set aside.

2. In nonstick 12-inch skillet, heat oil over medium heat. Add sweet potatoes and onion; cook, stirring occasionally, until onion is tender, 12 to 15 minutes. Transfer to plate.

3. Increase heat to medium-high. Add seasoned chicken to skillet and cook until lightly browned, about 3 minutes per side.

4. Meanwhile, drain tomatoes, reserving juice. Coarsely chop tomatoes and set aside. In blender at high speed or in food processor with knife blade attached, puree tomato juice, peanut butter, salt, crushed red pepper, garlic, and ¹/4 cup cilantro leaves until smooth.

5. Add sweet-potato mixture, chopped tomatoes, and peanut-butter sauce to skillet with chicken; heat to boiling over high heat. Reduce heat to low; cover and simmer until chicken loses its pink color throughout, about 25 minutes. To serve, sprinkle with chopped cilantro. Makes 4 main-dish servings.

Each serving: About 410 calories (26 percent calories from fat), 26g protein, 50g carbohydrate, 12g total fat (2g saturated), 76mg cholesterol, 725mg sodium.

Chicken Bouillabaisse

Prep: 1 hour   Bake: 30 minutes

Don't miss this tasty non-seafood version of the Mediterranean favorite.

1 tablespoon olive oil

8 medium bone-in chicken thighs (2¹/2 pounds), skin removed

2 large carrots, peeled and finely chopped

1 medium onion, finely chopped

1 medium fennel bulb (1¹/4 pounds), sliced

¹/2 cup water

3 garlic cloves, finely chopped

1 can (14¹/2 ounces) diced tomatoes

1 can (14¹/2 ounces) chicken broth or 1³/4 cups homemade

¹/2 cup dry white wine

2 tablespoons anise-flavor liquor (optional)

¹/2 teaspoon salt

¹/4 teaspoon dried thyme leaves

¹/8 teaspoon ground red pepper (cayenne)

1 bay leaf
    pinch saffron threads

1. In 5-quart Dutch oven, heat oil over medium-high heat until very hot. Add 4 chicken thighs and cook until golden brown, about 6 minutes per side. Transfer to bowl. Repeat with remaining chicken.

2. Add carrots and onion to Dutch oven and reduce heat to medium. Cook, stirring occasionally, until vegetables are tender and golden, about 10 minutes. Transfer to bowl with chicken thighs.

3. Preheat oven to 350°F. Add fennel and water to Dutch oven, stirring to loosen brown bits. Cook, stirring occasionally, until fennel is tender and browned, about 7 minutes. Add garlic and cook 3 minutes longer.

4. Return chicken and carrot mixture to Dutch oven; add tomatoes with their juice, broth, wine, anise liquor, salt, thyme, ground red pepper, bay leaf, and saffron. Heat to boiling over high heat. Cover and bake until chicken loses its pink color throughout, about 30 minutes. Discard bay leaf before serving. Makes 4 main-dish servings.

Each serving: About 310 calories (29 percent calories from fat), 32g protein, 24g carbohydrate, 10g total fat (2g saturated), 119mg cholesterol, 935mg sodium.

Spicy Moroccan Stew

Prep: 30 minutes   Cook: 40 minutes

This dish is delicious alone, or served the way we like it best, with piping hot couscous.

- **8 ounces peeled baby carrots (half 16-ounce package)**
- **2 tablespoons all-purpose flour**
- **1 teaspoon ground cumin**
- **1/2 teaspoon ground coriander**
- **1/4 teaspoon ground red pepper (cayenne)**
- **1/4 teaspoon coarsely ground black pepper**
- **1/8 teaspoon ground cinnamon**
- **3/4 teaspoon salt**
- **8 medium bone-in chicken thighs (2 pounds), skin removed**
- **1 tablespoon vegetable oil**
- **1 medium onion, sliced**
- **1 pound zucchini (2 medium), cut lengthwise in half, then crosswise into 1/4-inch-thick slices**
- **1/4 cup water**
- **1 can (28 ounces) tomatoes in puree**
- **1 can (15 to 19 ounces) garbanzo beans, rinsed and drained**
- **1 package (10 ounces) couscous (Moroccan pasta)**
- **1 cup packed fresh cilantro leaves, chopped**

1. In 10-inch skillet, heat 1 inch water to boiling over high heat. Add carrots; heat to boiling. Reduce heat to low; cover and simmer until carrots are just tender-crisp, 5 minutes. Drain carrots; set aside.

2. Meanwhile, in large ziptight plastic bag, combine flour, cumin, coriander, ground red pepper, black pepper, cinnamon, and 1/2 teaspoon salt. Add chicken and toss with flour mixture until coated.

3. In nonstick 12-inch skillet, heat oil over medium-high heat until very hot. Add chicken and cook until golden brown, about 5 minutes per side. Transfer to large bowl.

4. Reduce heat to medium. Add onion, zucchini, and remaining 1/4 teaspoon salt to skillet; cook, stirring occasionally, until onion is lightly browned, 8 to 10 minutes. Add carrots and water, and cook 5 minutes longer.

5. Add tomatoes with puree, garbanzo beans, and chicken to skillet; heat to boiling over medium-high heat, stirring and breaking up tomatoes with side of spoon. Reduce heat to medium-low; cover and simmer until chicken loses its pink color throughout, 10 minutes.

6. Meanwhile, prepare couscous as label directs.

7. To serve, spoon couscous onto large platter; top with chicken mixture. Sprinkle with cilantro leaves. Makes 4 main-dish servings.

Each serving: About 465 calories (23 percent calories from fat), 38g protein, 53g carbohydrate, 12g total fat (2g saturated), 1,110mg cholesterol, 1,540mg sodium.

Paella

Prep: 1 hour   Cook: 50 minutes

The quintessential Spanish dish is traditionally cooked in a paella pan over an open fire of vine cuttings, and may include a range of ingredients, from seafood to rabbit. But the crucial part—in the classic pan or in a skillet—is rice, preferably short-grain white.

1 1/2 **pounds skinless, boneless chicken thighs, cut into 2-inch pieces**

1 **package (3 1/2 ounces) cooked chorizo sausage, thinly sliced**

1 **medium onion, finely chopped**

1 **medium red pepper, finely chopped**

2 **garlic cloves, finely chopped**

1/4 **teaspoon ground red pepper (cayenne)**

1/2 **cup dry white wine**

3 **cups water**

1 **can (14 1/2 ounces) chicken broth or 1 3/4 cups homemade**

2 **cups short-grain white rice**

4 **ounces green beans, trimmed and cut into 1-inch pieces**

2 **tablespoons tomato paste**

1 1/2 **teaspoons salt**

1/4 **teaspoon loosely packed saffron threads, crumbled**

1/8 **teaspoon dried thyme**

1 **bay leaf**

1 **pound mussels, scrubbed and debearded**

3/4 **pound large shrimp, shelled and deveined**

1 **large plum tomato, chopped**

1/2 **cup loosely packed fresh parsley leaves, chopped lemon wedges (optional)**

1. Heat deep nonstick 12-inch skillet over medium-high heat until very hot. Add chicken and chorizo, and cook, stirring frequently, until golden brown all over, about 5 minutes. Transfer chicken and chorizo to plate.

2. Reduce heat to medium; add onion and red pepper to skillet, and cook until tender, about 5 minutes. Stir in garlic and ground red pepper; cook 30 seconds. Add wine; heat to boiling over medium-high heat. Continue cooking, stirring frequently, until mixture is very dry.

3. Stir in water, broth, and rice; add the chicken and chorizo, green beans, tomato paste, salt, saffron, thyme, and bay leaf. Heat to boiling over medium-high heat. Reduce heat to low; cover and simmer 15 minutes.

4. Tuck mussels into rice mixture; cover and cook 5 minutes. Tuck in shrimp; cover and cook just until mussels open and shrimp are opaque throughout, 8 minutes longer. Remove skillet from heat and let paella stand 5 minutes. Discard any mussels that have not opened.

5. Discard bay leaf. Sprinkle paella with chopped tomato and parsley. Serve with lemon wedges if you like. Makes 8 main-dish servings.

Each serving: About 410 calories (20 percent calories from fat), 36g protein, 44g carbohydrate, 9g total fat (2g saturated), 2g fiber, 153mg cholesterol, 1,010mg sodium.

Chicken Breasts with Six Quick Sauces

Prep: 2 minutes plus making sauce   Cook: 10 minutes

Simply sauté boneless chicken breasts, then take your pick from these easy sauces.

> **1 teaspoon vegetable oil**
>
> **4 small skinless, boneless chicken breast halves (1 pound)**
>
> **choice of sauce (below)**

1. In nonstick 12-inch skillet, heat oil over medium-high heat until very hot. Add chicken and cook until chicken is golden brown and loses its pink color throughout, 4 to 5 minutes per side. Transfer chicken to platter; keep warm.

2. Prepare sauce and serve. Makes 4 main-dish servings.

Apple-Curry Sauce

After removing chicken, reduce heat to medium. Add 2 teaspoons vegetable oil to skillet. Add 1 Golden Delicious apple, peeled, cored, and chopped, and 1 small onion, chopped. Cook, stirring, until tender. Stir in 1 1/2 teaspoons curry powder and 1/4 teaspoon salt; cook 1 minute. Stir in 1/2 cup mango chutney, 1/2 cup frozen peas, and 1/2 cup water. Heat to boiling; boil 1 minute. Spoon over chicken.

Each serving with chicken: About 352 calories (13 percent calories from fat), 34g protein, 38g carbohydrate, 5g total fat (1g saturated), 82mg cholesterol, 596mg sodium.

Black Bean Salsa

After removing chicken, reduce heat to medium. Add 1 can (15 to 19 ounces) black beans, rinsed and drained, 1 jar (10 ounces) thick-and-chunky salsa, 1 can (8 3/4 ounces) whole-kernel corn, drained, 1/4 cup water, and 2 tablespoons chopped fresh cilantro to skillet. Cook, stirring, until heated through, about 1 minute. Spoon over chicken.

Each serving with chicken: About 282 calories (13 percent calories from fat), 38g protein, 22g carbohydrate, 4g total fat (1g saturated), 82mg cholesterol, 1,086mg sodium.

Chinese Ginger Sauce

After removing chicken, reduce heat to medium. Add 1 teaspoon vegetable oil to skillet. Add 1 red pepper, thinly sliced, and cook until tender-crisp. Add 1/2 cup water, 2 tablespoons soy sauce, 2 tablespoons seasoned rice vinegar, and 1 tablespoon grated, peeled fresh ginger. Heat to boiling; boil 1 minute. Spoon over chicken and sprinkle with 2 green onions, chopped.

Each serving with chicken: About 195 calories (18 percent calories from fat), 34g protein, 4g carbohydrate, 4g total fat (1g saturated), 82mg cholesterol, 757mg sodium.

Chicken-Breast Savvy

The demand for chicken breasts has increased with consumers' growing commitment to cut back on fat. Now, companies market several variations of this popular choice. For example, skinless, boneless breast halves may be labeled exactly that, or they may say skinless, boneless split breasts or portions. If the label doesn't indicate that the breast is cut into two pieces—the clues to look for are halves, split, or portions—it could be whole and would have to be halved.

Companies also package tenderloins (the narrow pieces of chicken from the underside of the breast). These could be labeled tenders or fillets—any which way, they're boneless, very tender, and perfect for chicken fingers, stir-fries, and salads. Thin-sliced chicken-breast cutlets are breast halves cut horizontally in half for quicker cooking (about 5 minutes). They're great in place of pounded chicken breasts, or instead of veal in veal scalloppine.

Provençal Sauce

After removing chicken, reduce heat to medium. Add 1 teaspoon olive or vegetable oil to skillet. Add 1 medium onion, chopped, and cook, stirring, until tender. Stir in 1 can (14 1/2 ounces) Italian-style stewed tomatoes, 1/2 cup pitted ripe olives, each cut in half, 1 tablespoon drained capers, and 1/4 cup water. Cook, stirring, until heated through, about 1 minute. Spoon over chicken.

Each serving with chicken: About 253 calories (25 percent calories from fat), 35g protein, 11g carbohydrate, 7g total fat (1g saturated), 82mg cholesterol, 785mg sodium.

Creamy Mushroom Sauce

After removing chicken, add 1 teaspoon vegetable oil to skillet. Add 10 ounces mushrooms, trimmed and sliced, 1 medium onion, thinly sliced, and 3/4 teaspoon salt. Cook, stirring, until vegetables are golden brown and tender. Reduce heat to low; stir in 1/2 cup light sour cream and 1/4 cup water; heat through (do not boil). Spoon over chicken.

Each serving with chicken: About 260 calories (28 percent calories from fat), 37g protein, 9g carbohydrate, 8g total fat (3g saturated), 92mg cholesterol, 548mg sodium.

Dijon Sauce

After removing chicken, add 1/2 cup half-and-half or light cream, 2 tablespoons Dijon mustard with seeds, and 3/4 cup seedless red or green grapes, each cut in half, to skillet. Cook over low heat, stirring to blend flavors, until sauce has thickened, about 1 minute. Spoon over chicken.

Each serving with chicken: About 234 calories (27 percent calories from fat), 34g protein, 7g carbohydrate, 7g total fat (3g saturated), 93mg cholesterol, 285mg sodium.

Chicken Breasts with Vegetable Ribbons

Prep: 15 minutes   Cook: 25 minutes

A quick sprinkle of lemon peel, garlic, and parsley adds a burst of flavor and an elegant touch.

   4 **medium skinless, boneless chicken breast halves (1 1/4 pounds)**
 1/2 **teaspoon salt**
 1/4 **teaspoon coarsely ground black pepper**
   2 **garlic cloves, finely chopped**
   2 **teaspoons freshly grated lemon peel**
   1 **tablespoon olive oil**
   3 **medium carrots, peeled**
   2 **medium zucchini (1 pound)**
 3/4 **cup chicken broth**
 1/2 **cup water**
   1 **cup loosely packed fresh parsley leaves, chopped**

1. Sprinkle chicken with 1/4 teaspoon salt and the pepper. In cup, mix garlic, lemon peel, and remaining 1/4 teaspoon salt; set aside.

2. In nonstick 12-inch skillet, heat oil over medium-high heat until very hot. Add chicken and cook 6 minutes. Reduce heat to medium; turn chicken over and cook until chicken is golden brown and loses its pink color throughout, 6 to 8 minutes longer. Transfer chicken to platter; sprinkle with garlic mixture and keep warm.

3. Meanwhile, with sharp vegetable peeler, peel carrots lengthwise into wide, thin strips. Repeat with zucchini.

4. In same skillet, heat broth and water to boiling over high heat. Reduce heat to medium-low and add carrots; cover and cook 3 minutes. Add zucchini; cover and cook until vegetables are just tender, 5 to 7 minutes longer. Stir in all but 1 tablespoon parsley.

5. To serve, spoon vegetable ribbons and broth onto 4 dinner plates; top with chicken. Sprinkle with remaining parsley. Makes 4 main-dish servings.

Each serving: About 240 calories (23 percent calories from fat), 36g protein, 10g carbohydrate, 6g total fat (1g saturated), 82mg cholesterol, 530mg sodium.

Balsamic Chicken and Pears

Prep: 10 minutes   Cook: 20 minutes

Balsamic vinegar has a unique sweet-and-sour flavor; use sparingly. Look for the word "tradizionale" on the label.

- **2 teaspoons vegetable oil**
- **4 small skinless, boneless chicken breast halves (1 pound)**
- **2 Bosc pears, not peeled, each cut in half, cored, and cut into 8 wedges**
- **1 cup chicken broth**
- **3 tablespoons balsamic vinegar**
- **2 teaspoons cornstarch**
- **1 1/2 teaspoons sugar**
- **1/4 cup dried cherries or raisins**

1. In nonstick 12-inch skillet, heat 1 teaspoon oil over medium-high heat until very hot. Add chicken and cook until chicken is golden brown and loses its pink color throughout, 4 to 5 minutes per side. Transfer chicken to plate; keep warm.

2. In same skillet, heat remaining 1 teaspoon oil. Add pears and cook until tender and golden brown.

3. In cup, with fork, blend broth, vinegar, cornstarch, and sugar. Stir broth mixture and dried cherries into

skillet with pears. Heat to boiling, stirring; boil 1 minute. Return chicken to skillet; heat through. Makes 4 main-dish servings.

Each serving: About 235 calories (15 percent calories from fat), 27g protein, 22g carbohydrate, 4g total fat (1g saturated), 66mg cholesterol, 325mg sodium.

Peachy Chicken with Basil

Prep: 20 minutes   Cook: 15 minutes

Combine fragrant basil and juicy fruit slices in a perfect sauce for sautéed chicken breasts. Spoon over noodles or rice, so you get every drop.

- **3 tablespoons all-purpose flour**
- **1/2 teaspoon salt**
- **1/2 teaspoon coarsely ground black pepper**
- **4 medium skinless, boneless chicken breast halves (1 1/4 pounds)**

- **2 tablespoons margarine or butter**
- **3/4 cup chicken broth**
- **3 medium peaches (1 pound), peeled and sliced**
- **1 small red onion, thinly sliced**
- **1/4 teaspoon freshly grated lemon peel**
- **8 large basil leaves, thinly sliced**

1. On waxed paper, mix flour, salt, and pepper; use to coat chicken breasts.

2. In nonstick 12-inch skillet, melt margarine over medium heat. Add chicken and cook 6 minutes. Turn chicken over and cook until chicken is golden brown and loses its pink color throughout, 6 to 8 minutes longer. Transfer chicken to platter and keep warm.

3. Add broth to skillet; heat to boiling over high heat. Add peaches, red onion, and lemon peel. Cook, stirring frequently, until peaches are softened and sauce is slightly thickened, about 3 minutes. Stir sliced basil into skillet. Spoon sauce over chicken to serve. Makes 4 main-dish servings.

Each serving: About 280 calories (26 percent calories from fat), 35g protein, 16g carbohydrate, 8g total fat (2g saturated), 82mg cholesterol, 580mg sodium.

Tarragon and Grape Chicken

Prep: 15 minutes   Cook: about 20 minutes

Serve with steamed broccoli and orzo.

- **4 medium skinless, boneless chicken breast halves (1 1/4 pounds)**
- **1/2 teaspoon salt**
- **1/4 teaspoon coarsely ground black pepper**
- **1 teaspoon olive oil**
- **2 teaspoons margarine or butter**
- **3 medium shallots, finely chopped (1/3 cup)**
- **1/4 cup dry white wine**
- **1/4 cup chicken broth**
- **1/4 cup half-and-half or light cream**
- **1 cup seedless red and/or green grapes, each cut in half**
- **1 tablespoon chopped fresh tarragon**

1. Sprinkle chicken with 1/4 teaspoon salt and the pepper.

2. In nonstick 12-inch skillet, heat oil over medium-high heat until hot. Add chicken and cook 6 minutes. Reduce heat to medium; turn chicken over and cook until chicken is golden brown and loses its pink color throughout, 6 to 8 minutes longer. Transfer chicken to platter and keep warm.

3. In same skillet, melt margarine over medium-low heat. Add shallots and remaining 1/4 teaspoon salt; cook, stirring, until tender and golden, 3 to 5 minutes. Stir in wine; cook 30 seconds. Stir in broth, half-and-half, grapes, and tarragon. Return chicken to skillet; heat through. Makes 4 main-dish servings.

Each serving: About 255 calories (28 percent calories from fat), 34g protein, 10g carbohydrate, 8g total fat (2g saturated), 87mg cholesterol, 455mg sodium.

Chicken Breasts with Green Peppercorns

Prep: 10 minutes   Cook: 10 minute

Green peppercorns have a mild bite that adds a moderate level of heat. Refrigerate leftover peppercorns for up to one week.

- **4 medium skinless, boneless chicken breast halves (1¼ pounds)**
- **2 tablespoons all-purpose flour**
- **2 tablespoons butter or margarine**
- **1 green onion, finely chopped**
- **½ cup water**
- **¼ cup dry white wine**
- **1 tablespoon water-packed green peppercorns, drained**
- **2 teaspoons Dijon mustard**
- **½ teaspoon sugar**
- **½ teaspoon salt**

1. With meat mallet, or between 2 sheets of plastic wrap or waxed paper with rolling pin, pound chicken breast halves to ¼-inch thickness. Place flour on waxed paper; use to coat chicken, shaking off excess.

2. In 12-inch skillet, melt butter over medium-high heat. Add chicken and cook until chicken is golden brown and loses its pink color throughout, 1 to 1½ minutes per side. Transfer to platter; keep warm.

3. Reduce heat to medium. To drippings in skillet, add green onion and cook, stirring occasionally, until tender, about 1 minute. Add water, wine, green peppercorns, mustard, sugar, and salt, stirring until browned bits are loosened from bottom of skillet. Heat to boiling over high heat; immediately remove from heat. Spoon sauce over chicken. Makes 4 main-dish servings.

Each serving: About 237 calories (30 percent calories from fat), 33g protein, 4g carbohydrate, 8g total fat (4g saturated), 98mg cholesterol, 577mg sodium.

Skillet Lemon Chicken

Prep: 15 minutes   Cook: 10 minutes

Impressive enough to serve to guests. Steam up a bunch of fresh spring asparagus to serve alongside.

- **4 medium skinless, boneless chicken breast halves (1¼ pounds)**
- **½ teaspoon salt**
- **2 teaspoons olive oil**
- **3 garlic cloves, crushed with side of chef's knife**
- **½ cup fat-free chicken broth**
- **¼ cup dry white wine**
- **2 tablespoons fresh lemon juice**
- **1½ teaspoons all-purpose flour**
- **2 teaspoons margarine or butter**
- **½ lemon, thinly sliced**

1. With meat mallet, or between 2 sheets of plastic wrap or waxed paper with rolling pin, pound chicken breast halves to ¼-inch thickness. Sprinkle with salt.

2. In nonstick 12-inch skillet, heat oil over medium-high heat until very hot. Add chicken; cook 6 minutes. Reduce heat to medium; turn chicken over and cook until chicken is golden brown and loses its pink color throughout, 5 to 8 minutes longer. Transfer chicken to platter and keep warm.

3. Add garlic to skillet; cook until golden. In cup, with fork, mix broth, wine, lemon juice, and flour until smooth; stir into mixture in skillet and heat to boiling. Boil 1 minute. Stir in margarine. Discard garlic. Pour sauce over chicken and top with lemon slices. Makes 4 main-dish servings.

Each serving: About 205 calories (26 percent calories from fat), 33g protein, 2g carbohydrate, 6g total fat (1g saturated), 82mg cholesterol, 480mg sodium.

Chicken Cordon Bleu

Prep: 10 minutes   Cook: 15 minutes

An elegant entrée made more healthful—and easier. Sautéed chicken breasts are topped with sliced ham and mozzarella and served on a bed of baby spinach.

- **1 teaspoon margarine or butter**
- **4 small skinless, boneless chicken breast halves (1 pound)**
- **1/2 cup fat-free chicken broth**
- **2 tablespoons balsamic vinegar**
- **1/8 teaspoon coarsely ground black pepper**
- **4 thin slices cooked ham (2 ounces)**
- **4 thin slices part-skim mozzarella cheese (2 ounces)**
- **1 bag (5 to 6 ounces) prewashed baby spinach**

1. In nonstick 12-inch skillet, melt magarine over medium-high heat until hot. Add chicken and cook 5 minutes. Reduce heat to medium and turn chicken over; cover and cook until chicken is golden brown and just loses its pink color throughout, about 5 minutes longer.

2. Increase heat to medium-high. Stir in broth, vinegar, and pepper; cook, uncovered, 1 minute. Remove skillet from heat; top each chicken breast with a slice of ham, then a slice of cheese. Cover skillet until cheese melts, about 3 minutes.

3. Arrange spinach on large platter; top with chicken breasts and drizzle with pan sauce. Makes 4 main-dish servings.

Each serving: About 210 calories (26 percent calories from fat), 34g protein, 5g carbohydrate, 6g total fat (3g saturated), 82mg cholesterol, 560mg sodium.

Chicken with Asparagus and Mushrooms

Prep: 20 minutes   Cook: 25 minutes

Serve alongside couscous flecked with chopped tomato.

- **4 medium skinless, boneless chicken breast halves (1¹/4 pounds)**
- **3/4 teaspoon salt**
- **1/4 teaspoon coarsely ground black pepper**
- **3 teaspoons olive oil**
- **1 medium onion, chopped**
- **1/4 pound shiitake mushrooms, thinly sliced and stems discarded**
- **1/4 pound white mushrooms, thinly sliced**
- **1/4 cup water**
- **1¹/2 pounds asparagus, trimmed and cut into 2-inch pieces**
- **1/2 cup half-and-half or light cream**

1. Sprinkle chicken with 1/4 teaspoon salt and the pepper.

2. In nonstick 12-inch skillet, heat 1 teaspoon oil over medium-high heat until hot. Add chicken and cook 6 minutes. Reduce heat to medium; turn chicken over and cook until chicken is golden brown and loses its pink color throughout, 6 to 8 minutes longer. Transfer chicken to platter and keep warm.

3. In same skillet, heat remaining 2 teaspoons olive oil over medium heat. Add onion and mushrooms and cook, stirring frequently, until vegetables are tender and liquid evaporates, about 5 minutes.

4. Add asparagus, water, and remaining 1/2 teaspoon salt to mushroom mixture; heat to boiling. Cook, stirring often, until asparagus is tender-crisp, about 5 minutes. Stir in half-and-half; heat through.

5. To serve, spoon asparagus mixture over chicken. Makes 4 main-dish servings.

Each serving: About 270 calories (30 percent calories from fat), 38g protein, 11g carbohydrate, 9g total fat (3g saturated), 92mg cholesterol, 510mg sodium.

Jamaican Jerk Chicken Kabobs

Prep: 15 minutes plus marinating   Broil: 10 minutes

Originally, jerk seasoning was only used to season pork shoulder, which was "jerked" apart into shreds before serving. Nowadays, this very popular power-packed seasoning rub is enjoyed on fish and chicken as well.

- **2 green onions, chopped**
- **1 jalapeño chile, seeded and finely chopped**
- **1 tablespoon minced, peeled fresh ginger**
- **2 tablespoons white wine vinegar**
- **2 tablespoons Worcestershire sauce**
- **3 teaspoons vegetable oil**
- **1 teaspoon ground allspice**
- **1 teaspoon dried thyme**
- **1/2 teaspoon plus 1/8 teaspoon salt**

- **1 pound skinless, boneless chicken breast halves, cut into 12 pieces**
- **1 red pepper, cut into 1-inch pieces**
- **1 green pepper, cut into 1-inch pieces**
- **4 metal skewers**

1. In blender or in food processor with knife blade attached, process green onions, jalapeño, ginger, vinegar, Worcestershire, 2 teaspoons oil, allspice, thyme, and 1/2 teaspoon salt until paste forms.

2. Place chicken in small bowl or in ziptight plastic bag and add green-onion mixture, turning to coat chicken. Cover bowl or seal bag and refrigerate chicken 1 hour to marinate.

3. Meanwhile, in small bowl, toss red and green peppers with remaining 1 teaspoon oil and remaining 1/8 teaspoon salt.

4. Preheat broiler. Alternately thread chicken and pepper pieces onto skewers.

5. Place kabobs on rack in broiling pan. Brush kabobs with any remaining marinade. Place pan in broiler at closest position to heat source. Broil kabobs 5 minutes; turn and broil until chicken loses its pink color throughout, about 5 minutes longer. Makes 4 main-dish servings.

Each serving: About 181 calories (25 percent calories from fat), 27g protein, 6g carbohydrate, 5g total fat (1g saturated), 66mg cholesterol, 525mg sodium.

Asian Stir-Fry with Spring Peas
Prep: 20 minutes   Cook: 20 minutes

Serve over fluffy white rice for a simple any-day supper.

- **1 pound chicken tenders**
- **1/2 teaspoon Chinese five-spice powder**
- **1/4 teaspoon salt**
- **3 teaspoons vegetable oil**
- **8 ounces snow peas and/or sugar snap peas, strings removed**
- **1 medium red pepper, thinly sliced**
- **2 tablespoons water**
- **1 cup chicken broth**
- **1 tablespoon dark brown sugar**
- **1 tablespoon soy sauce**
- **2 teaspoons cornstarch**
- **2 green onions, trimmed and cut into 1/2-inch pieces**
- **1 tablespoon grated, peeled fresh ginger**
- **2 garlic cloves, crushed with garlic press**

1. Sprinkle chicken with Chinese five-spice powder and salt. In nonstick 12-inch skillet, heat 1 teaspoon oil over medium-high heat until very hot. Add chicken tenders and cook, turning once, until they lose their pink color throughout, 6 to 7 minutes. Transfer to plate; set aside.

2. To same skillet, add remaining 2 teaspoons oil. Add peas and red pepper and cook, stirring occasionally, until golden, about 5 minutes. Add water and cover; cook, stirring occasionally, until vegetables are tender-crisp, 3 minutes.

3. Meanwhile, in cup, with fork, mix broth, brown sugar, soy sauce, and cornstarch.

4. Add green onions, ginger, and garlic to skillet; cook, stirring, 1 minute. Stir broth mixture, then add to skillet; heat to boiling. Boil 30 seconds. Return chicken to skillet and heat through. Makes 4 main-dish servings.

Each serving: About 220 calories (20 percent calories from fat), 30g protein, 12g carbohydrate, 5g total fat (1g saturated), 66mg cholesterol, 665mg sodium.

Thai Chicken with Basil

Prep: 20 minutes plus marinating   Cook: 10 minutes

The essence of Thai cooking, the blending of cool and hot flavors, such as cilantro, basil, ginger, garlic, and chiles, lends an exotic touch to this stir-fry.

- **1   pound skinless, boneless chicken breast halves**
- **3   tablespoons Asian fish sauce (nuoc nam)**
- **1   tablespoon soy sauce**
- **1   tablespoon brown sugar**
- **2   teaspoons vegetable oil**
- **1   large onion (12 ounces), cut into 1/4-inch-thick slices**
- **2   red or green chiles (serrano or jalapeño), seeded and cut into matchstick strips**
- **2   teaspoons minced, peeled fresh ginger**
- **2   garlic cloves, crushed with garlic press**
- **11/2 cups loosely packed fresh basil leaves**

1. Holding knife almost parallel to cutting surface, cut each chicken breast half crosswise into 1/4-inch-thick slices. In medium bowl, combine fish sauce, soy sauce, and brown sugar; add chicken slices, tossing to coat. Let marinate 5 minutes.

2. In nonstick 12-inch skillet, heat oil over medium-high heat until very hot. Add chicken with marinade and cook, stirring frequently (stir-frying), until chicken loses its pink color throughout, 3 to 4 minutes. With slotted spoon, transfer chicken to bowl.

3. Add onion to marinade remaining in skillet and cook, stir-frying, until tender-crisp, about 4 minutes. Stir in chiles, ginger, and garlic; cook 1 minute longer.

4. Return chicken to skillet; heat through. Stir in basil leaves just before serving. Makes 4 main-dish servings.

Each serving: About 238 calories (19 percent calories from fat), 3g protein, 16g carbohydrate, 5g total fat (1g saturated), 66mg cholesterol, 784mg sodium.

Mock Buffalo Wings

Prep: 8 minutes   Cook: 8 minutes

Our version is remarkably similar to the popular red-hot deep-fried chicken wings that originated in Buffalo, New York—except it has less fat and can be whipped up in minutes! Serve with carrot and celery sticks and a tangy lower-fat blue-cheese dip.

- **1   pound chicken tenders**
- **1/2   cup reduced-fat sour cream**
- **1/4   cup crumbled blue cheese (1 ounce)**
- **2   tablespoons light mayonnaise**
- **2   tablespoons fat-free (skim) milk**
- **1/2   teaspoon Worcestershire sauce**
- **1/4   teaspoon coarsely ground black pepper**
- **1/4   cup cayenne pepper sauce***
- **1   tablespoon water**
- **1   tablespoon lower-fat margarine (40% fat)**
- **1   bag (12 ounces) precut carrot sticks**
- **1   bag (12 ounces) precut celery sticks**

1. Heat nonstick skillet over medium-high heat until hot. Add chicken tenders and cook, turning once, until they lose their pink color throughout, 6 to 7 minutes. Transfer to small platter.

2. Meanwhile, prepare the blue-cheese dip: In small bowl, with fork, mix sour cream, blue cheese, mayonnaise, milk, Worcestershire, and black pepper until blended.

3. Add cayenne pepper sauce and water to skillet; heat to boiling. Remove skillet from heat; stir in margarine until blended. Pour sauce over chicken.

4. Serve chicken with blue-cheese dip and carrot and celery sticks. Makes 4 main-dish servings.

*Cayenne pepper sauce is a milder variety of hot pepper sauce that adds tang and flavor, not just heat.

Each serving: About 270 calories (27 percent calories from fat), 31g protein, 17g carbohydrate, 8g total fat (2g saturated), 81mg cholesterol, 1180mg sodium.

Tortilla Chicken Tenders with Easy Corn Salsa

Prep: 15 minutes   Bake: 10 minutes

- **2   ounces baked tortilla chips**
- **2   teaspoons chili powder**
- **1/4   teaspoon salt**
- **   olive oil nonstick cooking spray**
- **1   pound chicken tenders**
- **2   ears corn, husks and silk removed**
- **1   jar (11 to 12 ounces) mild salsa**
- **1/4   cup loosely packed fresh cilantro leaves, chopped**
- **   lime wedges**

1. Place tortilla chips in ziptight plastic bag. Crush tortilla chips with rolling pin to fine crumbs (you should have about 1/2 cup crumbs). On waxed paper, combine tortilla-chip crumbs, chili powder, and salt; set aside.

2. Preheat oven to 450°F. Spray 151/2" by 101/2" jelly-roll pan with olive oil spray. Place chicken tenders in medium bowl; spray with olive oil spray, tossing to coat well. Roll chicken in tortilla crumbs to coat; place in jelly-roll pan and spray again.

3. Bake chicken until it loses its pink color throughout, about 10 minutes.

4. Meanwhile, prepare corn salsa: Cut corn kernels from cobs; place in small bowl. Stir in salsa and cilantro until blended.

5. Serve chicken with corn salsa and lime wedges. Makes 4 main-dish servings.

Each serving: About 245 calories (11 percent calories from fat), 30g protein, 24g carbohydrate, 3g total fat (0g saturated), 66mg cholesterol, 685mg sodium.

Skillet Arroz con Pollo

Prep: 15 minutes   Cook: 40 minutes

This dish, popular in Spain and Mexico, simply means rice with chicken. We call for chicken tenders instead of bone-in pieces to shorten cooking time.

- **1 tablespoon olive oil**
- **1 medium onion, finely chopped**
- **1 medium red pepper, cut into 1/2-inch pieces**
- **1 cup long-grain white rice**
- **1 garlic clove, finely chopped**
- **1/8 teaspoon ground red pepper (cayenne)**
- **1 can (14 1/2 ounces) chicken broth or 1 3/4 cups homemade**
- **1/4 cup dry sherry or water**
- **1 strip (3" by 1/2") fresh lemon peel**
- **1/4 teaspoon salt**
- **1 pound chicken tenders, cut into 2-inch pieces**
- **1 cup frozen peas**
- **1/4 cup drained chopped pimiento-stuffed olives (salad olives)**
- **1/2 cup loosely packed fresh cilantro leaves or parsley leaves, chopped**
  lemon wedges

1. In nonstick 12-inch skillet, heat oil over medium heat. Add onion and red pepper; cook, stirring occasionally, until tender, about 12 minutes. Stir in rice, garlic, and ground red pepper; cook 2 minutes. Stir in broth, sherry, lemon peel, and salt; heat to boiling over medium-high heat. Reduce heat to low; cover and simmer 13 minutes.

2. Stir in chicken tenders; cover and simmer, stirring once halfway through cooking time, until chicken loses its pink color throughout and rice is tender, 13 minutes longer. Stir in frozen peas; cover and heat through. Remove skillet from heat; let stand 5 minutes.

3. To serve, stir in olives and sprinkle with cilantro. Pass lemon wedges to squeeze over each serving. Makes 4 main-dish servings.

Each serving: About 410 calories (15 percent calories from fat), 34g protein, 49g carbohydrate, 7g total fat (2g saturated), 66mg cholesterol, 925mg sodium.

Indian Chicken and Rice Casserole

Prep: 30 minutes   Bake: 35 minutes

This elaborate feast dish is usually made with lamb; our lighter recipe calls for skinless, boneless chicken breast.

- **1 can (14 1/2 ounces) chicken broth or 1 3/4 cups homemade**
- **1 cup basmati rice**
- **3 garlic cloves, peeled**
- **1 piece (1" by 1/2") fresh ginger, peeled and coarsely chopped**
- **1/4 cup sweetened flaked coconut**
- **1 large onion, cut lengthwise in half and thinly sliced**
- **3 teaspoons vegetable oil**
- **1 small red pepper, cut into 1/2-inch pieces**
- **1 pound skinless, boneless chicken breast halves, cut into 1/2-inch pieces**
- **3/4 teaspoon ground cumin**
- **3/4 teaspoon ground coriander**
- **1/2 teaspoon salt**
- **1/8 teaspoon ground red pepper (cayenne)**
- **2 cups cauliflower flowerets (about 1/2 medium head), cut into 1/2-inch pieces**
- **3/4 cup water**
- **1 package (10 ounces) frozen peas and carrots**
- **1 can (14 1/2 ounces) diced tomatoes**
- **1 container (8 ounces) plain nonfat yogurt raisins, toasted sliced almonds, and toasted sweetened flaked coconut for garnish (optional)**

1. Preheat oven to 350°F. In 2-cup measuring cup, add enough water to broth to equal 2 cups liquid. In 2-quart saucepan, heat broth mixture to boiling over high heat. Place rice in shallow 2¹⁄₂-quart casserole; stir in boiling broth mixture. Cover casserole tightly and bake until rice is tender and all liquid has been absorbed, 20 minutes. Remove casserole from oven; set aside.

2. Meanwhile, in food processor with knife blade attached, or in blender at medium speed, process garlic, ginger, coconut, and half of onion slices until a paste forms; set aside.

3. In nonstick 12-inch skillet, heat 2 teaspoons vegetable oil over medium heat. Add remaining onion slices and red pepper; cook until golden, about 10 minutes. With slotted spoon, transfer vegetables to large bowl.

4. Add garlic mixture to same skillet and cook until golden, 8 to 10 minutes. Add chicken pieces and remaining 1 teaspoon oil and cook, stirring occasionally, until chicken is lightly browned and just loses its pink color throughout. Add cumin, coriander, salt, and ground red pepper and cook 2 minutes longer. Transfer chicken mixture to bowl with vegetables.

5. To same skillet, add cauliflower and water; heat to boiling over high heat. Reduce heat to low; cover and simmer 6 minutes. Add frozen peas and carrots and tomatoes with their juice; heat to boiling over high heat. Reduce heat to low; uncover and cook until cauliflower is tender and peas and carrots are heated through, 2 minutes longer. Transfer cauliflower mixture to bowl with chicken. Stir in yogurt until well mixed.

6. With fork, fluff rice in casserole. Top cooked rice with chicken mixture. Bake, uncovered, until heated through, 15 minutes longer. Serve garnished with raisins, toasted almonds, and toasted coconut if you like. Makes 6 main-dish servings.

Each serving without garnishes: About 335 calories (16 percent calories from fat), 28g protein, 45g carbohydrate, 6g total fat (2g saturated), 45mg cholesterol, 760mg sodium.

French Chicken Stew

Prep: 15 minutes   Cook: 40 minutes

3 teaspoons olive oil

1 pound skinless, boneless chicken breast halves, cut into 2-inch chunks

4 medium carrots, peeled and cut into 1¹/₂-inch pieces

³/₄ pound potatoes (2 medium), peeled and cut into 2 inch chunks

1 medium onion, coarsely chopped

¹/₄ cup dry red wine

1 can (14¹/₂ to 16 ounces) stewed tomatoes

1¹/₄ cups chicken broth

1 teaspoon fresh thyme or ¹/₄ teaspoon dried

2 tablespoons water

1 tablespoon all-purpose flour

1 package (10 ounces) frozen peas, thawed

1. In nonstick 12-inch skillet, heat 2 teaspoons olive oil over medium-high heat. Add chicken tenders and cook, turning once, until they lose their pink color throughout, 6 to 7 minutes. Transfer to bowl; set aside.

2. To drippings in skillet, add remaining 1 teaspoon olive oil and heat until hot. Add carrots, potatoes, and onion; cook until browned. Stir in wine; cook 1 minute. Stir in stewed tomatoes, broth, and thyme; heat to boiling over high heat. Reduce heat to low; cover and simmer until vegetables are tender, 25 minutes.

3. In cup, with fork, mix water and flour and stir into skillet. Add peas and chicken and heat to boiling over high heat. Boil until mixture thickens slightly and is heated through, 1 minute. Makes 4 main-dish servings.

Each serving: About 350 calories (15 percent calories from fat), 34g protein, 41g carbohydrate, 6g total fat (1g saturated), 66mg cholesterol, 785mg sodium.

Chicken Potpie with Corn-Bread Crust

Prep: 45 minutes   Bake: 35 minutes

Our healthy down-home potpie is made with low-fat milk, extra veggies, and a tender country-style topping instead of the usual pastry crust. To reduce prep time, buy a rotisserie chicken at your market to shred (without skin) for the filling.

CHICKEN FILLING:

1 tablespoon margarine or butter

2 medium carrots, cut into ¹/₂-inch pieces

1 medium onion, cut into ¹/₄-inch pieces

1 can (14¹/₂ ounces) chicken broth

³/₄ teaspoon salt

¹/₄ teaspoon coarsely ground black pepper

¹/₄ teaspoon dried thyme

3 tablespoons cornstarch

1¹/₂ cups low-fat milk (1%)

12 ounces shredded cooked chicken, without skin (3 cups)

1 package (10 ounces) frozen whole-kernel corn, thawed

1 package (10 ounces) frozen lima beans, thawed

CORN-BREAD CRUST:

¹/₂ cup all-purpose flour

¹/₂ cup yellow cornmeal

1 tablespoon sugar

1¹/₂ teaspoons baking powder

¹/₂ teaspoon salt

2 tablespoons cold margarine or butter

³/₄ cup low-fat milk (1%)

1. Preheat oven to 375°F. Prepare chicken filling: In 3-quart saucepan, melt margarine over medium-low heat. Add carrots and onion, and cook, stirring occasionally, 5 minutes. Add broth, salt, pepper, and thyme; heat to boiling over high heat. Reduce heat to low; cover and simmer until vegetables are tender, 10 minutes.

2. Meanwhile, in small bowl, with wire whisk, mix cornstarch and 1/2 cup milk until blended. Stir cornstarch mixture and remaining 1 cup milk into saucepan with carrots; heat to boiling over high heat. Boil, stirring, 1 minute. Stir in chicken, corn, and lima beans. Transfer mixture to shallow 2 1/2-quart casserole.

3. Prepare corn-bread crust: In medium bowl, with fork, stir flour, cornmeal, sugar, baking powder, and salt. With pastry blender or two knives used scissor-fashion, cut in margarine until mixture resembles coarse crumbs. Stir in milk until blended and mixture thickens slightly. Pour mixture over filling; spread to form an even layer. Bake, uncovered, until filling is bubbling and top is golden, 35 minutes. Makes 6 main-dish servings.

Each serving: About 440 calories (27 percent calories from fat), 32g protein, 51g carbohydrate, 13g total fat (3g saturated), 67mg cholesterol, 960mg sodium.

Spicy Buttermilk-Grilled Chicken

Prep: 5 minutes plus marinating   Grill: 20 minutes

Buttermilk is a welcome addition to marinades. Its natural acidity tenderizes and adds tangy flavor to meat and poultry. Best of all, it turns grilled food a luscious golden brown.

- 1/2 **cup buttermilk**
- 1 **tablespoon hot pepper sauce**
- 1 **teaspoon paprika**
- 1/2 **teaspoon salt**
- 1 **chicken (3 1/2 pounds), cut into 8 pieces and skin removed from all but wings**

1. In ziptight plastic bag, combine buttermilk, hot pepper sauce, paprika, and salt. Add chicken, turning to coat. Seal bag, pressing out as much air as possible. Refrigerate chicken 1 hour to marinate, turning once.

2. Prepare grill. Remove chicken from bag; discard marinade. Place chicken on grill over medium heat and grill, turning occasionally, until juices run clear when thickest part of chicken is pierced with tip of knife, 20 to 25 minutes. Makes 4 main-dish servings.

Each serving: About 222 calories (24 percent calories from fat), 39g protein, 1g carbohydrate, 6g total fat (2g saturated), 125mg cholesterol, 454mg sodium.

Tandoori-Style Grilled Chicken

Prep: 10 minutes plus marinating   Grill: 20 minutes

The appealingly spicy yogurt marinade keeps skinless chicken moist and succulent and provides lots of flavor without extra fat.

- **1   tablespoon paprika, preferably sweet Hungarian**
- **1/2 teaspoon ground cinnamon**
- **1/2 teaspoon ground coriander**
- **1/2 teaspoon ground cumin**
- **1/4 teaspoon ground cardamom**
- **1   container (8 ounces) plain low-fat yogurt**
- **2   tablespoons fresh lemon juice**
- **1   tablespoon olive oil**
- **1/2 small onion, cut into quarters**
- **2   garlic cloves**
- **1   tablespoon sliced pickled jalapeño chile or finely chopped fresh jalapeño chile with seeds**
- **1   tablespoon sliced, peeled fresh ginger**
- **1/2 teaspoon salt**
- **1   chicken (3 1/2 pounds), cut into 8 pieces and skin removed from all but wings**
- **lemon wedges (optional)**

1. In 6-inch skillet, heat paprika, cinnamon, coriander, cumin, and cardamom over low heat until very fragrant, about 3 minutes. Transfer to blender with yogurt, lemon juice, oil, onion, garlic, jalapeño, ginger, and salt; puree until smooth.

2. Make several 1/4-inch-deep slashes in each chicken piece. Place chicken in ziptight plastic bag, pour in yogurt mixture and turn to coat the chicken. Seal bag, pressing out as much air as possible. Refrigerate chicken 1 to 3 hours to marinate, turning once or twice.

3. Lightly grease grill rack. Prepare grill. Place chicken on grill over medium heat and grill, turning chicken every 5 minutes, until juices run clear when thickest part of chicken is pierced with tip of knife, 20 to 25 minutes. Transfer to warm platter and serve with lemon wedges, if desired. Makes 4 main-dish servings.

Each serving: About 301 calories (30 percent calories from fat), 44g protein, 7g carbohydrate, 10g total fat (2g saturated), 136mg cholesterol, 466mg sodium.

Grilled Chicken Breasts Saltimbocca

Prep: 5 minutes   Grill: 10 minutes

In Italian, saltimbocca means "jump in your mouth" and these irresistible prosciutto-and-sage-topped chicken breasts will do just that. One note of caution: Don't slice the prosciutto paper-thin, or it could burn.

> **4** medium skinless, boneless chicken breast halves (1¹/₄ pounds)
>
> ¹/₈ teaspoon salt
>
> ¹/₈ teaspoon ground black pepper
>
> **12** fresh sage leaves
>
> **4** large slices prosciutto (4 ounces)

1. Prepare grill. Sprinkle chicken with salt and pepper. Place 3 sage leaves on each breast half. Place 1 prosciutto slice on top of each breast half, tucking in edges if necessary; secure with toothpicks.

2. Place chicken, prosciutto side down, on grill over medium heat and grill 5 to 6 minutes. Turn and grill until chicken loses its pink color throughout, 5 to 6 minutes longer. Makes 4 main-dish servings.

Each serving: About 223 calories (24 percent calories from fat), 41g protein, 0g carbohydrate, 6g total fat (1g saturated), 105mg cholesterol, 690mg sodium.

Chicken Breasts with Cumin, Coriander and Lime

Prep: 10 minutes   Cook: 10 to 12 minutes

An exotic blend of spices and lime juice adds instant flavor to boneless chicken breasts.

- **3 tablespoons fresh lime juice (about 2 limes)**
- **1 teaspoon ground cumin**
- **1 teaspoon ground coriander**
- **1 teaspoon sugar**
- **1 teaspoon salt**
- **1/8 teaspoon ground red pepper (cayenne)**
- **4 small skinless, boneless chicken breast halves (1 pound)**
- **1 tablespoon chopped fresh cilantro leaves**

1. In large bowl, mix lime juice, cumin, coriander, sugar, salt, and ground red pepper; add chicken, tossing to coat.

2. Spray grill pan or cast-iron skillet with nonstick cooking spray; heat over medium-high heat until hot but not smoking. Add chicken and cook until chicken loses its pink color throughout, 5 to 6 minutes per side. Turn chicken once and brush with any remaining cumin mixture halfway through cooking. Place chicken breasts on platter; sprinkle with cilantro. Makes 4 main-dish servings.

Each serving: About 150 calories (18 percent calories from fat), 27g protein, 3g carbohydrate, 3g total fat (1g saturated), 72mg cholesterol, 600mg sodium.

Lemon-Rosemary Chicken Breasts

Prep: 10 minutes   Grill: 10 minutes

This quick, lowfat grilled chicken has plenty of flavor. Grill some zucchini, onions, and red peppers alongside, if desired.

- **2 lemons**
- **1 tablespoon chopped fresh rosemary or**
  1/2 teaspoon dried rosemary
- **1 garlic clove, finely chopped**
- **2 teaspoons olive oil**
- **1/2 teaspoon salt**
- **1/4 teaspoon coarsely ground black pepper**
- **4 small skinless, boneless chicken breast halves (1 pound)**

1. Prepare grill. From 1 lemon, grate 2 teaspoons peel. From 1/2 lemon, cut thin slices; reserve for garnish.

Squeeze juice from remaining 3 lemon halves into medium bowl. Stir in lemon peel, rosemary, garlic, oil, salt, and pepper.

2. Add chicken breast halves to bowl, turning to coat with lemon-juice mixture.

3. Place chicken on grill over medium heat and grill, brushing with remaining lemon-juice mixture in bowl, 5 minutes. Turn chicken and grill until chicken loses its pink color throughout, about 5 minutes longer. Garnish with lemon slices. Makes 4 main-dish servings.

Each serving: About 153 calories (24 percent calories from fat), 26g protein, 3g carbohydrate, 4g total fat (1g saturated), 66mg cholesterol, 364mg sodium.

Chutney Chicken Breasts

Prep: 15 minutes   Grill: 12 minutes

For a refreshing and flavorful accompaniment, grill thick slices of pineapple when you grill the chicken.

**4   large skinless, boneless chicken breast halves
    (1½ pounds)**

**1   jar (8½ ounces) mango chutney, coarsely
    chopped**

1   can (8 to 8¼ ounces) crushed pineapple, drained

1   tablespoon curry powder

1   tablespoon fresh lime or lemon juice

**1   tablespoon vegetable oil
    lime slices for garnish**

1. Prepare grill. With tip of knife, cut a horizontal slit in thickest part of each chicken breast half to form a pocket.

2. In medium bowl, mix chutney, pineapple, curry powder, and lime juice. Transfer half of chutney mixture to bowl to serve with chicken later.

3. Stir oil into remaining chutney mixture. Place 1 tablespoon chutney-oil mixture in each chicken breast pocket. Coat chicken breasts with remaining chutney-oil mixture.

4. Place chicken on grill over medium heat and grill, turning occasionally, until chicken loses its pink color throughout, 10 to 12 minutes.

5. Arrange chicken on 4 dinner plates. Garnish with lime slices and serve with reserved chutney mixture. Makes 4 main-dish servings.

Each serving: About 450 calories (12 percent calories from fat), 40g protein, 55g carbohydrate, 6g total fat (1g saturated), 99mg cholesterol, 650mg sodium.

Grilled Chicken Breasts with Plum Salsa

Prep: 20 minutes plus marinating   Grill: 10 to 12 minutes

Here's a quick dish that turns ordinary chicken into the specialty of the house. (The plum salsa can also be used to spice up plain fish and seafood dishes.)

2   tablespoons seasoned rice vinegar

1/2   teaspoon salt

1/8   teaspoon coarsely ground black pepper

4   medium skinless, boneless chicken breast halves (1¹/4 pounds)

1   pound ripe purple and/or green plums (4 medium), chopped

1/4   cup finely chopped red onion

1/4   cup finely chopped yellow pepper

1/4   cup loosely packed fresh cilantro leaves, finely chopped

1   jalapeño chile, seeded and finely chopped mixed baby greens (optional)

1. In pie plate, with wire whisk or fork, combine vinegar, salt, and black pepper. Spoon half of vinegar mixture into medium bowl. Add chicken breasts to mixture in pie plate, turning to coat. Cover and refrigerate 30 minutes to marinate, turning occasionally.

2. Meanwhile, prepare grill and spray grill rack (away from heat source) with nonstick cooking spray. Prepare the plum salsa: Stir plums, red onion, yellow pepper, cilantro, and jalapeño into vinegar mixture left in bowl. Set plum salsa aside.

3. Place chicken breasts on grill over medium heat; discard marinade in pie plate. Grill chicken, turning once, until chicken loses its pink color throughout, 10 to 12 minutes. (If using a grill pan, spray pan with nonstick cooking spray and heat over medium heat until hot but not smoking. Add chicken breasts and cook, turning once, until chicken loses its pink color throughout, 10 to 12 minutes.)

4. To serve, place chicken on a bed of mixed baby greens if you like, and spoon plum salsa on top. Makes 4 main-dish servings.

Each serving: About 245 calories (15 percent calories from fat), 36g protein, 14g carbohydrate, 4g total fat (1g saturated), 96mg cholesterol, 550mg sodium.

Rosemary Roast Turkey Breast

Prep: 20 minutes   Roast: 2 hours 15 to 30 minutes

When a whole turkey is too much, just use the breast. It will make white-meat fans very happy.

- **1 bone-in turkey breast (6 to 7 pounds)**
- **1 1/2 teaspoons dried rosemary, crumbled**
- **1 teaspoon salt**
- **3/4 teaspoon coarsely ground black pepper**
- **1 cup chicken broth**

1. Preheat oven to 350°F. Rinse turkey breast with cold running water and drain well; pat dry with paper towels. In cup, combine rosemary, salt, and pepper. Rub rosemary mixture on inside and outside of turkey breast.

2. Place turkey, skin side up, on rack in small roasting pan (13" by 9"). Cover turkey with loose tent of foil.

3. Roast turkey 1 hour 30 minutes. Remove foil. Roast 45 to 60 minutes longer, occasionally basting with pan drippings. Start checking for doneness during last 30 minutes of cooking. Turkey breast is done when temperature on meat thermometer inserted into thickest part of breast (not touching bone) reaches 170°F. and juices run clear when thickest part of breast is pierced with tip of knife.

4. Transfer turkey to warm platter. Let stand 15 minutes to set juices for easier carving.

5. Meanwhile, pour broth into drippings in hot roasting pan. Heat to boiling over medium-high heat, stirring until browned bits are loosened from bottom of pan. Strain pan-juice mixture through sieve into 1-quart saucepan; let stand 1 minute. Skim and discard fat. Heat pan-juice mixture over medium heat until hot; serve with turkey. Remove skin before eating. Makes 10 main-dish servings.

Each serving without skin and with pan juices: About 251 calories (7 percent calories from fat), 55g protein, 0g carbohydrate, 2g total fat (0g saturated), 152mg cholesterol, 428mg sodium.

Turkey Thighs Osso Buco–Style

Prep: 20 minutes   Bake: 1 hour 30 minutes

Cooked in a manner usually reserved for veal shanks, turkey thighs make an excellent stew. Serve with soft polenta or rice pilaf.

- 1/4 **teaspoon salt**
- 1/4 **teaspoon ground black pepper**
- 2 **turkey thighs (1¼ pounds each), skin removed**
- 2 **teaspoons vegetable oil**
- 2 **medium onions, finely chopped**
- 4 **carrots, peeled and cut into 3/4-inch pieces**
- 2 **stalks celery, cut into 1/2-inch pieces**
- 4 **garlic cloves, finely chopped**
- 1 **can (14½ ounces) tomatoes in puree**
- 1/2 **cup dry red wine**
- 1 **bay leaf**
- 1/4 **teaspoon dried thyme**

1. Preheat oven to 350°F. Sprinkle salt and pepper on turkey. In nonreactive 5-quart Dutch oven, heat oil over medium-high heat until very hot. Add 1 turkey thigh and cook, turning occasionally, until golden brown, about 5 minutes. Transfer thigh to plate; repeat with second thigh. Discard all but 1 tablespoon fat from Dutch oven.

2. Reduce heat to medium. Add onions to Dutch oven and cook, stirring occasionally, 5 minutes. Add carrots, celery, and garlic; cook, stirring frequently, 2 minutes longer.

3. Stir in tomatoes with puree, wine, bay leaf, and thyme, breaking up tomatoes with side of spoon. Heat to boiling; add browned turkey. Cover and place in oven. Bake until turkey is tender, about 1 hour 30 minutes. Discard bay leaf. Remove turkey meat from bones and cut into bite-size pieces; return meat to Dutch oven and stir well. Makes 4 main-dish servings.

Each serving: About 323 calories (25 percent calories from fat), 36g protein, 24g carbohydrate, 9g total fat (3g saturated), 122mg cholesterol, 483mg sodium.

Sautéed Turkey Cutlets

Prep: 15 minutes plus making sauce   Cook: 15 minutes

Tender turkey cutlets cook in just minutes. Take your pick of the three easy, delicious sauces for spooning over the top.

- 1 **pound turkey cutlets**
- 1/4 **teaspoon salt**
- 1/4 **teaspoon coarsely ground black pepper**
- 2 **teaspoons olive oil**
  choice of sauce (below)

1. With meat mallet, or between two sheets of plastic wrap or waxed paper with rolling pin, pound turkey cutlets to 1/4-inch thickness. Sprinkle salt and pepper on cutlets. In nonstick 12-inch skillet, heat oil over medium-high heat until very hot. Add turkey cutlets, a few at a time, and cook until cutlets are golden brown and lose their pink color throughout, about 2 minutes per side. Transfer cutlets to platter as they are done; keep warm.

2. In same skillet, prepare one of the sauces. Spoon sauce over turkey cutlets. Makes 4 main-dish servings.

Tomato-Olive Sauce

To drippings in skillet, add 2 teaspoons olive oil and 1 small onion, finely chopped; cook over medium heat until tender, about 5 minutes. Add 1 garlic clove, finely chopped; cook 1 minute. Stir in 1 can (14¹/2 ounces) diced tomatoes with their juice. Sprinkle with 2 tablespoons coarsely chopped pitted Kalamata olives.

Each serving with turkey: About 211 calories (30 percent calories from fat), 29g protein, 8g carbohydrate, 7g total fat (1g saturated), 70mg cholesterol, 443mg sodium.

Mushroom Sauce

To drippings in skillet, add 2 teaspoons olive oil and 1 garlic clove, crushed with garlic press; cook over medium heat 10 seconds. Add 1 pound mushrooms, trimmed and sliced, and ¹/4 teaspoon dried thyme; cook until mushrooms are golden brown and liquid has evaporated, about 10 minutes. In cup, blend 1 cup chicken broth and 1 teaspoon cornstarch until smooth. Stir broth mixture into skillet; heat to boiling, stirring. Boil 1 minute.

Each serving with turkey: About 206 calories (26 percent calories from fat), 31g protein, 6g carbohydrate, 6g total fat (1g saturated), 70mg cholesterol, 453mg sodium.

Curry-Apricot Sauce

To drippings in skillet, add 2 teaspoons olive oil and 1 small onion, chopped; cook over medium heat, stirring occasionally, until onion is golden and tender, 6 to 8 minutes. Increase heat to medium-high. Add 1 teaspoon curry powder and ¹/2 teaspoon ground coriander; cook, stirring, 1 minute. In cup, blend 1 cup chicken broth and 1 teaspoon cornstarch until smooth. Stir broth mixture and ¹/2 cup dried apricots, coarsely chopped, into skillet; heat to boiling, stirring. Boil 1 minute.

Each serving with turkey: About 259 calories (21 percent calories from fat), 36g protein, 13g carbohydrate, 6g total fat (0g saturated), 88mg cholesterol, 465mg sodium.

Rolled Turkey Breast with Basil Mayonnaise

Prep: 45 minutes   Roast: 1 hour 15 minutes

Here's a dramatic-looking party entrée that takes very little effort.

- **1 boneless turkey breast (4¹/₂ to 5 pounds), cut in half**
- **2 teaspoons salt**
- **1 teaspoon coarsely ground black pepper**
- **1 jar (12 ounces) roasted red peppers, drained**
- **1¹/₂ cups loosely packed fresh basil leaves plus additional sprigs**
- **1 tablespoon olive oil**
   Basil Mayonnaise (below)

1. To butterfly breast halves, place 1 breast half, skinned side up, on cutting board. With sharp knife held parallel to surface, and starting at one long side, horizontally cut turkey breast half three-quarters of the way through and open like a book. With meat mallet, or between two sheets of plastic wrap or waxed paper with rolling pin, pound turkey breast half to about ¹/₄-inch thickness. Repeat with second breast half.

2. Preheat oven to 350°F. Sprinkle ¹/₂ teaspoon salt and ¹/₄ teaspoon black pepper on each breast half. Arrange roasted red peppers evenly over breast halves, leaving 2-inch border around edges; top with basil leaves. Starting at one narrow end, roll each breast half jelly-roll fashion. Tie each turkey roll with string at 2-inch intervals; brush with oil and sprinkle with remaining 1 teaspoon salt and remaining ¹/₂ teaspoon pepper.

3. Place turkey rolls, seam side down, on rack in large roasting pan (17" by 11¹/₂"). Roast turkey rolls about

1 hour 15 minutes. Turkey is done when temperature on meat thermometer inserted in center of roll reaches 160°F. Internal temperature of turkey will rise to 165°F upon standing.

4. When turkey rolls are done, place on warm platter. Let stand 10 minutes to set juices for easier slicing if serving warm. If not serving right away, cool turkey 1 hour; wrap in plastic wrap and refrigerate up to 24 hours to serve cold later.

5. To serve, remove strings. Thinly slice turkey, garnish with basil sprigs, and serve with Basil Mayonnaise. Makes 10 main-dish servings.

Each serving with 1 tablespoon Basil Mayonnaise: About 308 calories (20 percent calories from fat), 54g protein, 6g carbohydrate, 7g total fat (2g saturated), 138mg cholesterol, 718mg sodium.

Basil Mayonnaise

In blender or in food processor with knife blade attached, puree 2 cups loosely packed fresh basil leaves, 1 cup light mayonnaise, 1 cup reduced-fat sour cream, 2 teaspoons fresh lemon juice, and 1/4 teaspoon salt until smooth. Cover and refrigerate until ready to use. Makes 2 cups mayonnaise.

Each tablespoon: About 40 calories (90 percent calories from fat), 1g protein, 1g carbohydrate, 4g total fat (1g saturated), 5mg cholesterol, 80mg sodium.

Turkey Burgers and Coleslaw

Prep: 15 minutes   Cook: 20 minutes

Moist, juicy, and mildly spiced, these turkey burgers will satisfy any fast-food diehard. Paired with our sweet-and-tangy slaw, they make a great family dinner. Also great cold—for lunch-box sandwiches.

BURGERS:

- 1 teaspoon olive oil
- 1 small onion, finely chopped
- 1 garlic clove, crushed with garlic press
- 3 tablespoons water
- 1 pound ground turkey breast
- 1 large egg
- 1 slice firm white bread, crumbled
- 3 tablespoons mango chutney, chopped
- 1/2 teaspoon salt
- 1/4 teaspoon rubbed sage

COLESLAW:

- 1 can (8 ounces) crushed pineapple in unsweetened juice
- 3 tablespoons chili sauce
- 1/2 teaspoon salt
- 1/8 teaspoon coarsely ground black pepper
- 1 bag (16 ounces) shredded cabbage mix for coleslaw

1. Prepare burgers: In nonstick 12-inch skillet, heat oil over medium heat. Add onion, garlic, and 1 tablespoon water and cook, stirring often, until onion is tender, 5 minutes. Transfer mixture to large bowl; set skillet aside.

2. Add remaining 2 tablespoons water, ground turkey, egg, bread, chutney, salt, and sage to onion mixture and mix well. With wet hands, shape mixture into four 1-inch-thick round patties.

3. Heat same skillet over medium heat until hot. Add patties and cook, turning once, until browned on both sides and cooked through, about 12 minutes.

4. Meanwhile, prepare coleslaw: In large bowl, stir pineapple with its juice, chili sauce, salt, and pepper until blended. Add cabbage mix and toss to coat. Serve burgers with coleslaw. Makes 4 main-dish servings.

Each serving Burger: About 210 calories (17 percent calories from fat), 28g protein, 13g carbohydrate, 4g total fat (1g saturated), 112mg cholesterol, 375mg sodium.

Each serving Coleslaw: About 75 calories (0 percent calories from fat), 2g protein, 18g carbohydrate, 0g total fat, 0mg cholesterol, 460mg sodium.

Turkey Meat Loaf

Prep: 20 minutes   Bake: 1 hour

- **1 tablespoon olive oil**
- **2 medium stalks celery, finely chopped**
- **1 small onion, finely chopped**
- **2 garlic cloves, finely chopped**
- **3/4 teaspoon ground cumin**
- **1 1/2 pounds ground turkey breast**
- **1/3 cup fresh bread crumbs**
- **1/3 cup fat-free (skim) milk**
- **1/3 cup bottled salsa**
- **1 large egg white**
- **1/2 teaspoon salt**
- **1/2 teaspoon coarsely ground black pepper**
- **1/4 cup ketchup**
- **1 teaspoon Dijon mustard**

1. In nonstick 10-inch skillet, heat oil over medium heat. Add celery and onion; cook, stirring often, until vegetables are tender, 10 minutes. Add garlic and cumin; cook, stirring, 30 seconds. Set vegetable mixture aside to cool slightly.

2. Preheat oven to 350°F. In large bowl, with hands, mix vegetable mixture, ground turkey, bread crumbs, milk, salsa, egg white, salt, and pepper until well combined but not overmixed.

3. In small bowl, mix ketchup and mustard; set aside.

4. In 13" by 9" metal baking pan, shape meat mixture into 9" by 5" loaf. Spread ketchup mixture over top of loaf. Bake meat loaf until meat thermometer inserted in center registers 160°F., about an hour (temperature will rise to 165°F. upon standing). Let meat loaf stand 10 minutes before removing from pan and slicing. Makes 8 main-dish servings.

Each serving: About 145 calories (25 percent calories from fat), 20g protein, 5g carbohydrate, 4g total fat (1g saturated), 45mg cholesterol, 400mg sodium.

Turkey Stir-Fry

Prep: 20 minutes   Cook: 12 minutes

Toss bite-size pieces of turkey meat with broccoli, red pepper, mushrooms, and a tasty ginger-and-garlic sauce. Serve with rice or curly egg noodles.

- 2 tablespoons soy sauce
- 2 tablespoons seasoned rice vinegar
- 1 tablespoon grated, peeled fresh ginger
- 1 teaspoon sugar
- 1/4 teaspoon crushed red pepper
- 2 garlic cloves, crushed with garlic press
- 3/4 cup chicken broth
- 1 teaspoon cornstarch
- 1 tablespoon olive oil
- 4 cups broccoli flowerets
- 1 medium red pepper, thinly sliced
- 8 ounces white mushrooms, thinly sliced
- 8 ounces bite-size pieces cooked turkey meat (2 cups)

1. In small bowl, combine soy sauce, vinegar, ginger, sugar, crushed red pepper, and garlic. In cup, with fork, mix broth and cornstarch.

2. In nonstick 12-inch skillet, heat oil over medium-high heat until very hot. Add broccoli, red pepper, and mushrooms; cook, stirring frequently (stir-frying), 5 minutes. Stir in soy-sauce mixture and stir-fry until vegetables are lightly browned and tender-crisp, 3 to 5 minutes longer.

3. Stir broth mixture, then add to skillet with turkey; heat to boiling, stirring. Cook, stirring, until turkey is heated through, 1 minute. Makes 4 main-dish servings.

Each serving: About 210 calories (30 percent calories from fat), 22g protein, 16g carbohydrate, 7g total fat (2g saturated), 44mg cholesterol, 930mg sodium.

Moo Shu Turkey

Prep: 20 minutes   Cook: 15 minutes

The Rosemary Roast Turkey (page 135) adds an especially nice and unexpected flavor to this Asian-inspired dish. However, any leftover skinless roast-turkey meat would be fine.

  8   **(6-inch) low-fat flour tortillas**
  3   **tablespoons hoisin sauce**
  2   **tablespoons soy sauce**
3/4   **teaspoon Asian sesame oil**
  3   **teaspoons olive oil**
  1   **package (8 ounces) sliced mushrooms**
  1   **package (16 ounces) shredded cabbage mix**
      for coleslaw
1/2   **medium red pepper, thinly sliced**
  3   **green onions, thinly sliced**
  1   **garlic clove, crushed with garlic press**
  2   **teaspoons grated, peeled fresh ginger**
12   **ounces cooked turkey breast, pulled into shreds**
      (3 cups)

1. Warm tortillas as label directs; keep warm

2. Meanwhile, in small bowl, mix hoisin sauce, soy sauce, and sesame oil until smooth; set aside.

3. In nonstick 12-inch skillet, heat 1 teaspoon oil over medium-high heat. Add mushrooms and cook until all liquid evaporates and mushrooms are browned, about 8 minutes; transfer mushrooms to bowl.

4. In same skillet, heat remaining 2 teaspoons oil. Add cabbage mix, red pepper, and green onions and cook, stirring constantly, 3 minutes. Add garlic and ginger; cook, stirring constantly, 1 minute. Stir in hoisin-sauce mixture, mushrooms, and turkey; heat through.

5. To serve, spoon turkey mixture onto warm tortillas and roll up. Makes 4 main-dish servings.

Each serving: About 405 calories (16 percent calories from fat), 35g protein, 53g carbohydrate, 7g total fat (1g saturated), 71mg cholesterol, 1,140mg sodium.

Turkey Chili

Prep: 20 minutes   Cook: 20 minutes

This spicy potful is made with limas and white beans—it's just right for a simple Sunday-evening supper. Serve with tortilla chips or corn bread.

   1   **tablespoon olive oil**
   1   **medium onion, chopped**
   3   **garlic cloves, finely chopped**
11/2   **teaspoons chili powder**
   1   **teaspoon ground cumin**
   1   **teaspoon ground coriander**
1/4   **teaspoon salt**
1/4   **teaspoon coarsely ground black pepper**
   1   **can (15 to 16 ounces) Great Northern or small**
       white beans, rinsed and drained
   1   **can (14 1/2 ounces) reduced-sodium chicken**
       broth or 13/4 cups homemade
   1   **package (10 ounces) frozen lima beans**
   1   **can (4 to 41/2 ounces) chopped mild green chiles**
   8   **ounces bite-size pieces cooked turkey meat**
       (2 cups)
   1   **cup loosely packed fresh cilantro leaves, chopped**
   2   **tablespoons fresh lime juice**
       lime wedges (optional)

1. In 5-quart Dutch oven, heat oil over medium heat. Add onion and cook, stirring often, until tender, about 5 minutes. Add garlic and cook 30 seconds. Stir in chili powder, cumin, coriander, salt, and pepper; cook 1 minute longer.

2. Meanwhile, in small bowl, mash half of beans.

3. Add mashed beans and unmashed beans, broth, frozen lima beans, green chiles, and turkey to Dutch oven. Heat to boiling over medium-high heat. Reduce heat to low; cover and simmer 5 minutes to blend fla-vors. Remove Dutch oven from heat; stir in cilantro and lime juice. Serve with lime wedges if you like. Makes 4 main-dish servings.

Each serving: About 380 calories (19 percent calories from fat), 33g protein, 45g carbohydrate, 8g total fat (2g saturated), 44mg cholesterol, 995mg sodium.

Turkey Shepherd's Pies

Prep: 30 minutes   Bake: 30 minutes

Here's a good way to use up those Thanksgiving leftovers: A turkey-meat filling is topped with leftover mashed potatoes. Our Mashed Potatoes with Horseradish Cream (page 206) make an especially good topping for these individual shepherd's pies, but any other mashed spuds will be delicious as well. Although the canned chicken broth called for here works well, we recommend using the turkey carcass to make a flavorful homemade turkey broth.

  1 **tablespoon olive oil**

  2 **medium carrots, finely chopped**

  1 **medium onion, finely chopped**

  1 **medium celery stalk, finely chopped**

  2 **cups mashed potatoes**

3/4 **cup milk**

  2 **tablespoons all-purpose flour**

  1 **cup chicken broth or turkey broth**

  8 **ounces bite-size pieces cooked turkey meat (2 cups)**

  1 **cup frozen peas**

1/4 **teaspoon salt**

1/8 **teaspoon coarsely ground black pepper**

    pinch dried thyme

1. In 5- to 6-quart Dutch oven, heat oil over medium heat. Add carrots, onion, and celery; cook until vegetables are tender and lightly browned, about 15 minutes.

2. Meanwhile, in small bowl, stir mashed potatoes with 1/4 cup milk until combined.

3. Preheat oven to 450°F. In cup, with fork, mix flour with broth and remaining 1/2 cup milk until blended. Pour broth mixture into Dutch oven with vegetables. Cook over high heat, stirring often, until mixture boils and thickens slightly. Boil 1 minute. Reduce heat to medium; add turkey, frozen peas, salt, pepper, and thyme; heat through.

4. Place four 1 1/2-cup ramekins or soufflé dishes on 15 1/2" by 10 1/2" jelly-roll pan for easier handling. Spoon warm turkey mixture into ramekins; top with potato mixture. Bake until hot and bubbly and potatoes are lightly browned, 30 minutes. Makes 4 main-dish servings.

Each serving: About 320 calories (28 percent calories from fat), 25g protein, 33g carbohydrate, 10g total fat (3g saturated), 54mg cholesterol, 615mg sodium.

Moules à la Marinière

Prep: 20 minutes   Cook: 15 minutes

This is the way French cooks like to serve mussels. Use a crisp white wine, such as sauvignon blanc or dry vermouth, which adds extra flavor because of the herbs used in the distillation process.

1¹/2   **cups dry white wine or dry vermouth**
  ¹/3   **cup finely chopped shallots or red onion**
    2   **garlic cloves, finely chopped**
    1   **tablespoon butter or olive oil**
  ¹/2   **teaspoon salt**
         pinch ground black pepper
    4   **pounds mussels, preferably cultivated, scrubbed and debearded**
  ¹/4   **cup chopped fresh parsley**

1. In nonreactive 5-quart Dutch oven, combine wine, shallots, garlic, butter, salt, and pepper; heat to boiling over high heat. Boil 2 minutes.

2. Add mussels; heat to boiling. Reduce heat; cover and simmer until mussels open, about 5 minutes, transferring mussels to large bowl as they open. Discard any mussels that do not open. Pour mussel broth over mussels and sprinkle with parsley. Makes 4 main-dish servings.

Each serving: About 212 calories (25 percent calories from fat), 16g protein, 9g carbohydrate, 6g total fat (2g saturated), 45mg cholesterol, 703mg sodium.

Crab Boil

Prep: 5 minutes   Cook: 40 minutes

A big pot of spiced boiled crabs, a Chesapeake Bay tradition, is a delicious but messy affair. Cover the table with newspaper and have lots of large napkins on hand. Serve with coleslaw and rolls. (If you want to cook crab so you can pick the meat for another recipe, omit the crab boil seasoning and red pepper.)

    2   **medium onions, coarsely chopped**
    1   **carrot, peeled and coarsely chopped**
    1   **stalk celery, coarsely chopped**
    1   **lemon, sliced**
  ¹/2   **cup crab boil seasoning**
    1   **tablespoon crushed red pepper**
    1   **tablespoon salt**
    1   **gallon (16 cups) water**
    1   **can or bottle (12 ounces) beer**
    2   **dozen live hard-shell blue crabs, rinsed**

1. In 12-quart stockpot, combine onions, carrot, celery, lemon, crab boil seasoning, crushed red pepper, salt, water, and beer. Heat to boiling over high heat; cook 15 minutes.

2. Using tongs, transfer crabs to stockpot. Cover and heat to boiling. Boil 5 minutes (crabs will turn red). With tongs, transfer crabs to colander to drain, then place on platter.

3. To eat crab, twist off claws and legs, then crack shell to remove meat. Break off flat pointed apron from underside of crab; remove top shell. Discard feathery gills. With kitchen shears or hands, break body in half down center. With fingers or lobster pick, remove meat. Makes 4 main-dish servings.

Each serving: About 123 calories (15 percent calories from fat), 24g protein, 0g carbohydrate, 2g total fat (0g saturated), 119mg cholesterol, 1,410mg sodium.

Chili Scallops with Black Bean Salsa

Prep: 15 minutes   Cook: 5 minutes

Silky, sweet scallops contrast perfectly with the bright and spicy salsa flavors.

- 1 can (15 to 19 ounces) black beans, rinsed and drained
- 1 can (15¼ to 16 ounces) whole-kernel corn, drained
- ¼ cup finely chopped red onion
- ¼ cup loosely packed fresh cilantro leaves, chopped
- 2 tablespoons fresh lime juice
- ½ teaspoon salt
- 1 pound sea scallops
- 1 tablespoon chili powder
- 1 teaspoon sugar
- 2 teaspoons vegetable oil
- fresh cilantro leaves and hot red chiles for garnish

1. Prepare black bean salsa: In large bowl, mix black beans, corn, onion, chopped cilantro, lime juice, and ¼ teaspoon salt. Set aside.

2. Pat scallops dry with paper towels. Pull off and discard tough crescent-shaped muscle from each scallop. In medium bowl, mix chili powder, sugar, and remaining ¼ teaspoon salt; add scallops, tossing to coat.

3. In nonstick 12-inch skillet, heat oil over medium-high heat until very hot. Add scallops and cook, turning once, until scallops are lightly browned on the outside and just opaque throughout, 3 to 6 minutes.

4. Arrange black bean salsa and scallops on 4 dinner plates; garnish with cilantro leaves and red chiles. Makes 4 main-dish servings.

Each serving: About 290 calories (16 percent calories from fat), 31g protein, 40g carbohydrate, 5g total fat (1g saturated), 38mg cholesterol, 1,005mg sodium.

Pan-Seared Scallops with Lemon Couscous

Prep: 20 minutes   Cook: 25 minutes

- 4 teaspoons vegetable oil
- 1 large red pepper, thinly sliced
- 1 medium onion, thinly sliced
- 12 ounces medium mushrooms, trimmed and quartered
- 1¾ cups water
- 8 ounces sugar snap peas, strings removed
- 1 medium lemon
- 1 cup couscous (Moroccan pasta)
- ¾ teaspoon salt
- 1 pound sea scallops
- 2 tablespoons soy sauce
- 2 bunches arugula (8 ounces), stems trimmed

1. In nonstick 12-inch skillet, heat 2 teaspoons oil over medium-high heat until hot. Add red pepper and onion and cook, stirring occasionally, until golden brown. Transfer red-pepper mixture to plate. In same skillet, heat 1 teaspoon oil; add mushrooms and cook until golden brown. Transfer mushrooms to plate with red-pepper mixture. Add 1/4 cup water to same skillet; heat to boiling. Add sugar snap peas and cook until tender-crisp, 3 to 4 minutes. Drain and set aside.

2. Meanwhile, from lemon, grate 1/2 teaspoon peel and squeeze 1 1/2 teaspoons juice. In 2-quart saucepan, heat lemon juice and remaining 1 1/2 cups water to boiling over high heat. Stir in couscous and salt. Cover saucepan and remove from heat. Let stand 5 minutes; stir in lemon peel. Keep warm.

3. Pull off and discard tough crescent-shaped muscle from each scallop. Pat scallops dry with paper towels. Wipe skillet dry and heat remaining 1 teaspoon oil over medium-high heat until hot. Add scallops and cook, turning once, until lightly browned on the outside and just opaque throughout, 3 to 4 minutes.

4. Return mushroom-pepper mixture to skillet; stir in soy sauce. Cook mixture over medium-high heat until heated through. Stir in sugar snap peas. Arrange arugula on plates. Top with couscous and scallop mixture. Makes 6 main-dish servings.

Each serving: About 263 calories (14 percent calories from fat), 20g protein, 36g carbohydrate, 4g total fat (1g saturated), 25mg cholesterol, 770mg sodium.

Shrimp and Scallop Kabobs

Prep: 20 minutes   Grill: 6 minutes

One word of advice: Don't soak the shellfish in the soy and rice vinegar mixture. The vinegar will firm and "cook" the flesh.

- **12 ounces large sea scallops**
- **1 pound large shrimp, shelled and deveined, leaving tail part of shell on, if you like**
- **3 tablespoons soy sauce**
- **3 tablespoons seasoned rice vinegar**
- **1 tablespoon Asian sesame oil**
- **2 tablespoons grated, peeled fresh ginger**
- **2 garlic cloves, crushed with garlic press**
- **1 tablespoon brown sugar**
- **1 bunch green onions, cut on diagonal into 3-inch pieces**
- **12 cherry tomatoes**
- **6 long metal skewers**

1. Prepare grill. Pull off and discard tough crescent-shaped muscle from each scallop. Pat shrimp and scallops dry with paper towels.

2. In large bowl, combine soy sauce, vinegar, sesame oil, ginger, garlic, and brown sugar. Add shrimp and scallops, tossing to coat.

3. Alternately thread shrimp, scallops, green-onion pieces, and cherry tomatoes onto skewers. Place skewers on grill over medium heat and grill, turning skewers occasionally and brushing shrimp and scallops with any remaining soy-sauce mixture during first half of cooking, until shrimp and scallops are just opaque throughout, 6 to 8 minutes. Makes 6 main-dish servings.

Each serving: About 168 calories (21 percent calories from fat), 23g protein, 9g carbohydrate, 4g total fat (1g saturated), 112mg cholesterol, 851mg sodium.

Shrimp Curry and Rice

Prep: 10 minutes   Cook: 20 minutes

This tastes as good as classic slow-cooking curry, but is ready in a flash. Serve with crisp flatbreads such as pappadams.

- **1 cup regular long-grain rice**
- **2 teaspoons olive oil**
- **1 medium onion, finely chopped**
- **1 tablespoon curry powder**
- **1 teaspoon mustard seeds**
- **1 pound large shrimp, shelled and deveined, leaving tail part of shell on, if you like**
- **1/2 cup light coconut milk (not cream of coconut)**
- **3/4 cup frozen peas, thawed**
- **1 cup frozen whole baby carrots, thawed**
- **1/2 teaspoon salt**
- **chopped fresh cilantro leaves (optional)**

1. Prepare rice as label directs but do not add margarine or butter.

2. Meanwhile, in nonstick 12-inch skillet, heat 1 teaspoon oil over medium-high heat. Reduce heat to medium; add onion and cook until tender, 8 minutes. Add curry powder and cook, stirring, 1 minute. Transfer onion mixture to medium bowl.

3. Increase heat to medium-high. In same skillet, heat remaining 1 teaspoon oil. Add mustard seeds; cook, stirring, 30 seconds. Add shrimp and cook, stirring frequently, until opaque throughout, 4 minutes.

4. Return onion mixture to skillet; stir in coconut milk, peas, carrots, and salt; heat through. Serve over rice. Sprinkle with cilantro if you like. Makes 4 main-dish servings.

Each serving: About 390 calories (18 percent calories from fat), 30g protein, 49g carbohydrate, 8g total fat (2g saturated), 175mg cholesterol, 490mg sodium.

Shrimp Risotto with Baby Peas

Prep: 35 minutes   Cook: 55 minutes

Making a quick stock with the shrimp shells gives this pretty risotto a complex shellfish flavor.

- **4 cups water**
- **1 can (14¹/2 ounces) chicken or vegetable broth or 1³/4 cups homemade**
- **1 pound medium shrimp, shelled and deveined, shells reserved**
- **1 tablespoon butter or margarine**
- **1¹/2 teaspoons salt**
- **¹/8 teaspoon ground black pepper**
- **1 tablespoon olive oil**
- **1 small onion, finely chopped**
- **2 cups Arborio rice (Italian short-grain rice) or medium-grain rice**
- **¹/2 cup dry white wine**
- **1 cup frozen baby peas**
- **¹/4 cup chopped fresh parsley**

1. In 3-quart saucepan, combine water, broth, and shrimp shells. Heat to boiling over high heat. Reduce heat; simmer 20 minutes. Strain broth through sieve into bowl and measure. If needed, add water to equal 5¹/2 cups. Return broth to same clean saucepan; heat to boiling. Reduce heat to maintain simmer; cover.

2. In 4-quart saucepan, melt butter over medium-high heat. Add shrimp, ¹/2 teaspoon salt, and pepper; cook, stirring, just until shrimp are opaque throughout, about 2 minutes. Transfer to bowl.

3. In same saucepan, heat oil over medium heat. Add onion and cook until tender, about 5 minutes. Add rice and remaining 1 teaspoon salt; cook, stirring frequently, until rice grains are opaque. Add wine; cook until wine has been absorbed. Add about ¹/2 cup simmering broth to rice, stirring until liquid has been absorbed. Continue cooking, adding remaining broth ¹/2 cup at a time and stirring after each addition, until all liquid has been absorbed and rice is tender but still firm, about 25 minutes (risotto should have a creamy consistency). Stir in frozen peas and shrimp and heat through. Stir in parsley. Makes 4 main-dish servings.

Each serving: About 511 calories (18 percent calories from fat), 28g protein, 76g carbohydrate, 10g total fat (3g saturated), 148mg cholesterol, 1,532mg sodium.

Frozen Shrimp

Flavorful shrimp, with just under two grams of fat in a four-ounce serving, is a savvy dieter's favorite seafood. Keep some on hand in the freezer and it's a snap to whip up low-fat meals without a special trip to the supermarket. And even better: Frozen shrimp, available at wholesale food clubs and larger supermarkets, is a bargain!

The shrimp is either individually frozen and sold in bags or (more often) sold in blocks. Put the individually frozen shrimp in a colander and place under cold running water until thawed. For block-frozen shrimp, place under cold running water, and pull off the amount of shrimp you need as they thaw; return the remaining block of shrimp to the freezer.

Asian-Style Flounder Baked in Parchment

Prep: 15 minutes   Bake: 8 minutes

Baking in parchment packets seals in the juices and the flavor. Substitute foil for the parchment paper, if necessary.

- **2 large green onions**
- **2 tablespoons soy sauce**
- **2 tablespoons seasoned rice vinegar**
- **4 flounder fillets (6 ounces each)**
- **4 sheets (12" by 15" each) cooking parchment or foil**
- **2 teaspoons grated, peeled fresh ginger**

1. Cut green onion tops into 2" by 1/4" matchstick strips; reserve for garnish. Thinly slice white part of green onions.

2. In small bowl, combine soy sauce and vinegar.

3. Preheat oven to 425°F. Place 1 flounder fillet on one half of each parchment sheet. Sprinkle with ginger and sliced green onions; drizzle with soy-sauce mixture. Fold unfilled half of parchment over fish. To seal packets, beginning at a corner where parchment is folded, make small 1/2-inch-wide folds, with each new fold overlapping previous one, until packet is completely sealed. Packet will resemble half-circle. Place packets in jelly-roll pan. Bake 8 minutes (packets will puff up and brown).

4. To serve, cut packets open and garnish fish with reserved green-onion strips. Makes 4 main-dish servings.

Each serving: About 170 calories (11 percent calories from fat), 33g protein, 3g carbohydrate, 2g total fat (0g saturated), 82mg cholesterol, 802mg sodium.

Grilled Thai Snapper Packets

Prep: 25 minutes   Grill: 8 minutes

Grilling snapper fillets in foil packets keeps the meat intact, and Thai seasonings give the fish a distinctive Asian flavor.

- **3 tablespoons fresh lime juice**
- **1 tablespoon Asian fish sauce (nuoc nam)**
- **1 tablespoon olive oil**
- **1 teaspoon grated, peeled fresh ginger**
- **1 small garlic clove, finely chopped**
- **1/2 teaspoon sugar**
- **4 red snapper fillets (6 ounces each)**
- **1 large carrot, peeled and cut into 2 1/4" by 1/4" matchstick strips**
- **1 large green onion, thinly sliced**
- **1/4 cup tightly packed fresh cilantro**

1. Prepare grill. In small bowl, with wire whisk, whisk lime juice, fish sauce, oil, ginger, garlic, and sugar. With tweezers, remove any bones from snapper fillets.

2. From roll of foil, cut four 16" by 12" sheets. Fold each sheet crosswise in half, then open up like a book.

3. Place 1 snapper fillet, skin side down, on one half of each piece of foil. Evenly sprinkle fillets with carrot, green onion, and cilantro; drizzle with lime-juice mixture. Fold unfilled half of foil over fish. To seal, fold and crimp edges of foil all around.

4. Place packets on grill over medium heat; grill 8 minutes. To serve, cut packets open. Makes 4 main-dish servings.

Each serving: About 228 calories (24 percent calories from fat), 36g protein, 5g carbohydrate, 6g total fat (1g saturated), 63mg cholesterol, 268mg sodium.

Jamaican Jerk Snapper with Grilled Pineapple

Prep: 15 minutes   Grill: 10 minutes

Other fish fillets like sole and flounder would also work well with these zesty flavors.

- 2 **green onions, chopped**
- 1 **jalapeño chile, seeded and chopped**
- 2 **tablespoons white wine vinegar**
- 2 **tablespoons Worcestershire sauce**
- 1 **tablespoon minced, peeled fresh ginger**
- 1 **tablespoon vegetable oil**
- 1¼ **teaspoons dried thyme**
- 1 **teaspoon ground allspice**
- ¼ **teaspoon salt**
- 4 **red snapper fillets (5 ounces each)**
- 1 **small pineapple, cut lengthwise into 4 wedges or crosswise into ¹/2-inch-thick slices**
- 2 **tablespoons brown sugar**

1. Prepare grill. In medium bowl, mix green onions, jalapeño chile, vinegar, Worcestershire, ginger, oil, thyme, allspice, and salt until combined. Add snapper fillets to bowl, turning to coat; let stand 5 minutes.

2. Meanwhile, rub pineapple wedges or slices with brown sugar.

3. Place pineapple and snapper on grill over medium heat. Spoon half of jerk mixture remaining in bowl on snapper. Grill pineapple and snapper 5 minutes, then turn over. Spoon remaining jerk mixture on fish and grill until fish is just opaque throughout and pineapple is golden brown, 5 to 7 minutes longer. Makes 4 main-dish servings.

Each serving: About 280 calories (26 percent calories from fat), 24g protein, 25g carbohydrate, 8g total fat (1g saturated), 52mg cholesterol, 305mg sodium.

Grilled Tuna with Tuscan White Beans

Prep: 35 minutes   Grill/Broil: 4 minutes

Serve tuna slices on a bed of warm cannellini beans seasoned with lemon, garlic, and sage. With two cans of beans, a pound of tuna stretches nicely to six servings.

- **1 lemon**
- **1 tablespoon plus 3 teaspoons extravirgin olive oil**
- **1 medium onion, chopped**
- **1 medium stalk celery, finely chopped**
- **2 garlic cloves, crushed with garlic press**
- **6 large fresh sage leaves, thinly sliced**
- **2 cans (15 to 19 ounces each) white kidney beans (cannellini), rinsed and drained**
- **1 teaspoon salt**
- **1/2 teaspoon coarsely ground black pepper**
- **1 tuna steak, 1 inch thick (1 pound), cut into 1/2-inch-thick slices**
- **2 medium plum tomatoes, finely chopped**
- **1 tablespoon chopped fresh parsley leaves for garnish**

1. From lemon, grate 1/2 teaspoon peel and squeeze 2 tablespoons juice.

2. In 3-quart saucepan, heat 1 tablespoon plus 1 teaspoon oil over medium heat. Add onion and celery; cook, stirring occasionally, until tender, about 12 minutes. Add garlic, sage, and lemon peel; cook, stirring, 1 minute. Add beans, lemon juice, 1/2 teaspoon salt, and 1/4 teaspoon pepper; cook, stirring gently, until heated through.

3. Meanwhile, brush both sides of tuna with remaining 2 teaspoons oil and sprinkle with remaining 1/2 teaspoon salt and 1/4 teaspoon pepper.

4. Heat grill pan over medium-high heat until hot. Add tuna and cook, turning once, until just opaque throughout, 3 to 4 minutes. (Or, preheat broiler. Place tuna on rack in broiling pan; place pan in broiler at closest position to heat source; broil tuna 3 to 4 minutes.)

5. Place warm bean mixture on platter and top with tuna. Sprinkle with diced tomatoes and chopped parsley. Makes 6 main-dish servings.

Each serving: About 275 calories (20 percent calories from fat), 27g protein, 30g carbohydrate, 6g total fat (1g saturated), 33mg cholesterol, 745mg sodium.

Baked Scrod with Fennel and Potatoes

Prep: 15 minutes   Bake: 55 minutes

A simple dish that only needs a green salad to be a complete meal.

- **11/2 pounds red potatoes (4 large), thinly sliced**
- **1 medium fennel bulb (1 pound), trimmed and thinly sliced, feathery tops reserved**
- **1 garlic clove, finely chopped**
- **2 tablespoons olive oil**
- **3/4 plus 1/8 teaspoon salt**
- **1/2 teaspoon coarsely ground black pepper**
- **4 pieces scrod fillet (5 ounces each)**
- **1 large ripe tomato (8 ounces), seeded and chopped**

1. Preheat oven to 425°F. In shallow 21/2-quart baking dish, toss potatoes, fennel, garlic, oil, 3/4 teaspoon salt, and 1/4 teaspoon pepper until well combined; spread evenly in baking dish. Bake, stirring once, until vegetables are tender and lightly browned, about 45 minutes.

2. With tweezers, remove any bones from scrod. Sprinkle scrod with remaining 1/8 teaspoon salt and remaining 1/4 teaspoon pepper. Arrange on top of potato mixture. Bake until fish is just opaque throughout, 10 to 15 minutes. Sprinkle with tomato and garnish with reserved fennel tops. Makes 4 main-dish servings.

Each serving: About 335 calories (21 percent calories from fat), 30g protein, 35g carbohydrate, 8g total fat (1g saturated), 61mg cholesterol, 679mg sodium.

Roasted Scrod with Tomato Relish

Prep: 15 minutes   Cook/Roast: 40 minutes

A sweet-and-sour relish is just the thing to perk up scrod fillets.

- **1 can (28 ounces) plum tomatoes**
- **3 teaspoons vegetable oil**
- **1 small onion, chopped**
- **2 tablespoons water**
- **1/4 cup red wine vinegar**
- **2 tablespoons brown sugar**
- **1/2 teaspoon salt**
- **4 pieces scrod fillet (6 ounces each)**
- **1/4 teaspoon coarsely ground black pepper**

1. Preheat oven to 450°F. Drain tomatoes; cut each tomato into quarters.

2. In 2-quart saucepan, heat 2 teaspoons oil over medium heat. Add onion and water and cook until tender and golden, about 10 minutes. Stir in tomatoes, vinegar, brown sugar, and 1/4 teaspoon salt; heat to boiling over high heat. Continue cooking over high heat, stirring frequently, until relish has thickened, about 15 minutes.

3. Meanwhile, with tweezers, remove any bones from scrod. Arrange fillets in 9-inch square baking dish; sprinkle with remaining 1 teaspoon oil, remaining 1/4 teaspoon salt, and pepper. Roast scrod until just opaque throughout, 12 to 15 minutes. To serve, transfer fish to plates and spoon tomato relish on top. Makes 4 main-dish servings.

Each serving: About 248 calories (18 percent calories from fat), 32g protein, 18g carbohydrate, 5g total fat (1g saturated), 73mg cholesterol, 708mg sodium.

Snapper Livornese

Prep: 10 minutes   Cook: 25 minutes

Vibrant with olives, capers, and basil, this preparation works beautifully with any lean white fish.

- **1 tablespoon olive oil**
- **1 garlic clove, finely chopped**
- **1 can (14 to 16 ounces) tomatoes**
- **1/8 teaspoon salt**
- **1/8 teaspoon ground black pepper**
- **4 red snapper fillets (6 ounces each)**
- **1/4 cup chopped fresh basil**
- **1/4 cup Kalamata or Gaeta olives, pitted and chopped**
- **2 teaspoons capers, drained**

1. In nonstick 10-inch skillet, heat oil over medium heat. Add garlic and cook just until very fragrant, about 30 seconds. Stir in tomatoes with their juice, salt, and pepper, breaking up tomatoes with side of spoon. Heat to boiling; reduce heat and simmer 10 minutes.

2. With tweezers, remove any bones from snapper fillets. Place fillets, skin side down, in skillet. Cover and simmer until fish is just opaque throughout, about 10 minutes. With wide slotted spatula, transfer fish to warm platter. Stir basil, olives, and capers into tomato sauce and spoon over snapper. Makes 4 main-dish servings.

Each serving: About 250 calories (29 percent calories from fat), 36g protein, 6g carbohydrate, 8g total fat (1g saturated), 63mg cholesterol, 571mg sodium.

Lentils and Cod

Prep: 40 minutes   Bake: 25 minutes

The fennel and orange in this recipe bring home the flavors of Provence.

- 8 ounces lentils (1 cup)
- 1 tablespoon olive oil
- 2 medium carrots, finely chopped
- 1 medium onion, finely chopped
- 1 large stalk celery, finely chopped
- 1/2 teaspoon herbes de Provence*
- 1/4 teaspoon fennel seeds
- 3 strips (3" by 1" each) orange peel
- 3 garlic cloves, crushed with garlic press
- 2 cups water
- 1 can (14 1/2 ounces) reduced-sodium chicken broth or 1 3/4 cup homemade
- 1 can (14 1/2 ounces) tomatoes in puree
- 3/4 teaspoon salt
- 1/2 teaspoon coarsely ground black pepper
- 4 pieces cod fillet (6 ounces each)

1. Preheat oven to 400°F. Rinse lentils with cold running water and discard any stones or shriveled lentils. Set aside.

2. In 4-quart saucepan, heat oil over medium-high heat. Add carrots, onion, and celery; cook, stirring occasionally, until lightly browned, about 10 minutes. Add herbes de Provence, fennel seeds, orange peel, and garlic; cook, stirring, 2 minutes.

3. Add lentils, water, and broth; heat to boiling over high heat. Reduce heat to low; cover and simmer, stirring occasionally, 20 minutes. Add tomatoes with their puree, 1/2 teaspoon salt, and 1/4 teaspoon pepper, stirring and breaking up tomatoes with side of spoon. Heat to boiling over high heat. Reduce heat to low; cover and simmer 5 minutes longer.

4. Transfer lentil mixture to shallow 2 1/2-quart casserole. Place cod fillets on top of lentil mixture; sprinkle cod with remaining 1/4 teaspoon salt and 1/4 teaspoon pepper. Cover and bake until fish is just opaque throughout and lentil mixture is heated through, 20 to 25 minutes. Discard orange peel. Makes 6 main-dish servings.

*If you can't find herbes de Provence, substitute 1/4 teaspoon each dried thyme and rosemary, crushed, and increase fennel seeds to 1/2 teaspoon.

Each serving: About 325 calories (11 percent calories from fat), 32g protein, 40g carbohydrate, 4g total fat (1g saturated), 49mg cholesterol, 760mg sodium.

Miso-Glazed Salmon

Prep: 10 minutes   Broil: 10 minutes

Brian Hagiwara, one of Good Housekeeping's *favorite food photographers, shared this special recipe. We love the taste of the rich salmon with the sweet and savory glaze. Serve with a side of steamed Aromatic Rice (page 212).*

- 1/4 cup white miso
- 5 teaspoons sugar
- 4 teaspoons seasoned rice vinegar
- 3 teaspoons water
- 2 teaspoons minced, peeled fresh ginger
- 4 salmon steaks, 1 inch thick (6 ounces each)
- 1 green onion, thinly sliced diagonally

1. Preheat broiler. Lightly spray rack in broiling pan with nonstick cooking spray.

2. In small bowl, mix miso, sugar, vinegar, water, and ginger; set aside.

3. Place salmon steaks on rack in broiling pan. Place pan in broiler at closest position to heat source; broil salmon 5 minutes. Remove pan from broiler and spread half of miso mixture on salmon; broil 1 minute longer.

4. Remove pan from broiler; turn salmon over and top with remaining miso mixture. Broil salmon until miso mixture is bubbly and salmon is opaque throughout, 3 to 4 minutes longer. Sprinkle with green onion before serving. Makes 4 main-dish servings.

Each serving: About 260 calories (24 percent calories from fat), 35g protein, 13g carbohydrate, 7g total fat (1g saturated), 86mg cholesterol, 870mg sodium.

Mustard-Dill Salmon with Herbed Potatoes

Prep: 20 minutes   Broil: 8 to 10 minutes

A light and creamy sauce adds piquant flavor to succulent salmon. After you make the sauce, sauté snow peas in a nonstick skillet with a teaspoon of vegetable oil for a healthy side dish.

- **12 ounces small red potatoes, cut into 1-inch chunks**
- **12 ounces small white potatoes, cut into 1-inch chunks**
- **1 1/2 teaspoons salt**
- **3 tablespoons chopped fresh dill**
- **1/2 teaspoon coarsely ground black pepper**
- **4 pieces salmon fillet (6 ounces each)**
- **2 tablespoons light mayonnaise**
- **1 tablespoon white wine vinegar**
- **2 teaspoons Dijon mustard**
- **3/4 teaspoon sugar**

1. In 3-quart saucepan, heat potatoes, 1 teaspoon salt, and enough water to cover to boiling over high heat. Reduce heat to low; cover and simmer until potatoes are fork-tender, about 15 minutes. Drain potatoes and toss with 1 tablespoon dill, 1/4 teaspoon salt, and 1/4 teaspoon coarsely ground black pepper; keep the potatoes warm.

2. Meanwhile, preheat broiler. Grease rack in broiling pan. Place salmon on rack; sprinkle with 1/8 teaspoon salt and 1/8 teaspoon coarsely ground black pepper. Place broiling pan at closest position to heat source. Broil until salmon is just opaque throughout, 8 to 10 minutes.

3. While salmon is broiling, prepare sauce: In small bowl, mix mayonnaise, vinegar, mustard, sugar, remaining 2 tablespoons dill, 1/8 teaspoon salt, and 1/8 teaspoon black pepper.

4. Serve salmon with sauce and potatoes. Makes 4 main-dish servings.

Each serving: About 335 calories (19 percent calories from fat), 37g protein, 31g carbohydrate, 7g total fat (1g saturated), 86mg cholesterol, 655mg sodium.

Kedgeree

Prep: 30 minutes   Bake: 15 minutes

A spiced East Indian dish made with flaked smoked haddock (known as finnan haddie), hard-cooked eggs, and rice, Kedgeree makes a delicious brunch or supper main dish that can be prepared a day ahead.

- **1 tablespoon margarine or butter**
- **1 small onion, finely chopped**
- **3/4 teaspoon curry powder**
- **1 1/2 cups long-grain white rice**
- **3 cups water**
- **1 teaspoon salt**
- **1/4 teaspoon coarsely ground black pepper**
- **1 pound smoked haddock fillets (finnan haddie) or 12 ounces smoked trout fillets***
- **2 lemons**
- **4 large hard-cooked eggs, coarsely chopped**
- **1/2 cup loosely packed fresh parsley leaves, chopped**
- **1/2 cup half-and-half or light cream**

1. In 2-quart saucepan, melt margarine over medium heat. Add onion and cook, stirring occasionally, until tender, about 5 minutes. Stir in curry powder, then rice; cook 1 minute. Add water, salt, and pepper; heat to boiling over high heat. Reduce heat to low; cover and

simmer, without stirring or lifting lid, until rice is tender and all liquid has been absorbed, 15 to 18 minutes. Transfer rice to large bowl.

2. Meanwhile, in 10-inch skillet, cover smoked haddock with enough water to cover; heat to boiling over high heat. Reduce heat to low; simmer 5 minutes. Drain.

3. Preheat oven to 350°F. From 1 lemon, grate 1/2 teaspoon peel and squeeze 1 tablespoon juice; add to cooked rice, fluffing with fork. Flake haddock, discarding any skin and bones. Add haddock, eggs, and all but 1 tablespoon parsley to rice, toss gently.

4. Spoon rice mixture evenly into 13" by 9" glass baking dish; drizzle half-and-half evenly over top. Cover with foil and bake until heated through, 15 minutes. (If making ahead and refrigerating, bake 30 minutes.) Spoon Kedgeree into serving bowl and sprinkle with remaining 1 tablespoon parsley. Cut remaining lemon into 6 wedges and serve with Kedgeree. Makes 6 main-dish servings.

*If smoked haddock or trout fillets are unavailable, you can substitute smoked white fish.

Each serving: About 355 calories (23 percent calories from fat), 27g protein, 40g carbohydrate, 9g total fat (3g saturated), 206mg cholesterol, 1,010mg sodium.

Roasted Striped Bass

Prep: 5 minutes   Roast: 30 minutes

Serve this dramatic-looking entrée with a vibrant sauce such as Sweet Red Pepper Chutney (page 230), Olive and Lemon Salsa (page 228) or Tomato Salsa (page 228), or with lemon wedges.

- **1 whole striped bass (2¹/4 pounds), cleaned and scaled**
- **3 thin slices lemon**
- **3 rosemary sprigs (optional)**

1. Preheat oven to 450°F. Rinse bass inside and out with cold running water; pat dry with paper towels. Place lemon slices and rosemary, if using, in cavity. Make diagonal slashes on each side of fish at 1-inch intervals, about ¹/4 inch deep. Place bass in medium roasting pan (14" by 10"). Roast until fish is just opaque throughout when knife is inserted at backbone, about 30 minutes.

2. To serve, slide cake server under front section of top fillet and lift off fillet; transfer to platter. Slide server under backbone and lift it away from bottom fillet; discard. Slide cake server between bottom fillet and skin and transfer fillet to platter. Makes 4 main-dish servings.

Each serving: About 117 calories (31 percent calories from fat), 20g protein, 0g carbohydrate, 4g total fat (1g saturated), 88mg cholesterol, 76mg sodium.

Salt-Baked Fish

Prep: 5 minutes   Bake: 30 minutes

Baking a whole fish in a crust of kosher salt seals in the juices and guarantees exquisitely moist (and surprisingly unsalty) flesh.

- **4 cups kosher salt**
- **1 whole red snapper, striped bass, or porgy (1¹/2 pounds), cleaned and scaled**
- **1 lemon**
- **3 rosemary or thyme sprigs**

1. Preheat oven to 450°F. Line 13" by 9" baking pan with foil; spread 2 cups salt in bottom of pan.

2. Rinse snapper inside and out with cold running water; pat dry with paper towels. From lemon, cut 3 slices. Cut remaining lemon into wedges. Place lemon slices and rosemary in cavity of fish. Place snapper on bed of salt; cover with remaining 2 cups salt. Bake until fish is just opaque throughout when knife is inserted at backbone, about 30 minutes.

3. To serve, tap salt crust to release from top of fish; discard. Slide cake server under front section of top fillet and lift off fillet; transfer to platter. Slide server under backbone and lift it away from bottom fillet; discard. Slide cake server between bottom fillet and skin and transfer fillet to platter. Serve with reserved lemon wedges. Makes 2 main-dish servings.

Each serving: About 188 calories (14 percent calories from fat), 37g protein, 6g carbohydrate, 3g total fat (1g saturated), 66mg cholesterol, 800mg sodium.

Grilled Whole Flounder

Prep: 5 minutes Grill: 14 minutes

Make sure your grill is good and hot when you cook this deliciously simple fish. It's a perfect quick dinner for two. If you have a hinged fish grilling basket, use it here. Simply oil the basket before enclosing the fish.

- 1 **whole flounder (1¹/₂ pounds), cleaned and scaled**
- 1 **teaspoon vegetable oil**
- ¹/₂ **teaspoon salt**
  lemon wedges

1. Prepare grill. Rinse flounder inside and out with cold running water; pat dry with paper towels. Rub oil all over flounder; sprinkle with salt. Place flounder on grill over medium-high heat and grill until just opaque throughout when knife is inserted at backbone, about 7 minutes per side.

2. To serve, slide cake server under front section of top fillet and lift off fillet; transfer to platter. Slide server under backbone and lift it away from bottom fillet; discard. Slide cake server between bottom fillet and skin and transfer fillet to platter. Serve with lemon wedges. Makes 2 main-dish servings.

Each serving: About 161 calories (22 percent calories from fat), 29g protein, 0g carbohydrate, 4g total fat (1g saturated), 74mg cholesterol, 704mg sodium.

Quick Seafood Stew

Prep: 10 minutes Cook: 20 minutes

- 1¹/₄ **pounds all-purpose potatoes, peeled and cut into ¹/₂-inch pieces**
- 1 **can (14¹/₂ ounces) chunky tomatoes with olive oil, garlic, and spices**
- 1 **can (14¹/₂ ounces) chicken broth or 1³/₄ cups homemade**
- ¹/₃ **cup dry white wine**
- 16 **large mussels, scrubbed and debearded**
- 16 **large shrimp, shelled and deveined, with tail part of shell left on, if you like**
- 1 **piece cod fillet (12 ounces), cut into 2-inch pieces**
- 1 **tablespoon chopped fresh parsley leaves**

1. In 2-quart saucepan, heat potatoes and enough water to cover to boiling over high heat. Reduce heat to low; cover and simmer until potatoes are tender, 5 to 8 minutes; drain.

2. Meanwhile, in 5-quart Dutch oven, heat tomatoes with their liquid, broth, and wine to boiling over high heat. Add mussels; reduce heat to medium. Cover and simmer until mussels open, 3 to 5 minutes, transferring mussels to bowl as they open. Discard any mussels that do not open.

3. Add shrimp and cod to Dutch oven; cover and cook until shrimp and cod are just opaque throughout, 3 to 5 minutes. Add potatoes and mussels; heat through. Sprinkle with parsley. Makes 4 main-dish servings.

Each serving: About 305 calories (15 percent calories from fat), 35g protein, 28g carbohydrate, 5g total fat (0g saturated), 136mg cholesterol, 965mg sodium.

Seafood Paella

Prep: 30 minutes   Cook: 1 hour 45 minutes

This festive dish is party fare at its finest. You can prepare the shrimp stock in advance and cook the paella through Step 2. If you purchase already-cleaned shrimp, substitute chicken broth for the shrimp stock and reduce the salt. Try to use medium-grain rice: It will give the paella an authentic, slightly sticky texture.

- 1 **pound medium shrimp, shelled and deveined, shells reserved**
- 4 **cups water**
- 1 **pound cleaned squid**
- 2 **tablespoons olive oil**
- 1 **medium onion, chopped**
- 3 **garlic cloves, thinly sliced**
- 1 **red pepper, cut into thin strips**
- 1 **cup canned tomatoes, with their juice, chopped**
- 1 1/2 **teaspoons salt**
- 2 **cups medium-grain rice**
- 1/8 **teaspoon ground saffron**
- 1 **pound sea scallops**
- 1 **cup frozen peas**

1. Prepare shrimp stock: In 3-quart saucepan, combine shrimp shells and water. Heat to boiling; reduce heat, partially cover, and simmer 30 minutes. Strain broth through sieve; discard shells. There should be about 3 cups shrimp stock.

2. Rinse squid with cold running water and pat dry with paper towels. Slice squid bodies crosswise into 1/2-inch rings. Cut tentacles into 1-inch pieces. In deep nonstick 12-inch skillet, heat oil over medium-low heat. Add onion and garlic and cook, stirring frequently, until onion is tender, about 7 minutes. Add red pepper and cook 4 minutes. Add squid and cook 2 minutes.

3. Add tomatoes with their juice, 1/2 cup shrimp broth, and 1/4 teaspoon salt; heat to boiling. Reduce heat; cover and simmer 30 minutes. Stir in rice, saffron, remaining 2 1/2 cups shrimp stock, and remaining 1 1/4 teaspoons salt. Heat to boiling over high heat. Reduce heat; cover and simmer until squid is tender and rice is cooked through, about 20 minutes.

4. Pull off and discard tough crescent-shaped muscle from each scallop. Cut scallops horizontally in half if large. Stir scallops, shrimp, and frozen peas into rice mixture in skillet; cover and cook until scallops and shrimp are just opaque throughout, about 9 minutes longer. Makes 6 main-dish servings.

Each serving: About 518 calories (14 percent calories from fat), 43g protein, 65g carbohydrate, 8g total fat (1g saturated), 294mg cholesterol, 921mg sodium.

Peruvian Seafood Soup

Prep: 30 minutes   Cook: 25 minutes

This cilantro and lime scented soup is an opportunity to enjoy one of the classic dishes of Peru.

- 1 **tablespoon vegetable oil**
- 1 **medium onion, chopped**
- 2 **garlic cloves, finely chopped**
- 2 **serrano or jalapeño chiles, seeded and finely chopped**
- 1 **pound red potatoes, cut into 3/4-inch pieces**
- 3 **bottles (8 ounces each) clam juice**
- 2 **cups water**
- 3/4 **teaspoon salt**
- 1/8 **teaspoon dried thyme**
- 1 **lime**
- 1 **pound monkfish, dark membrane removed, cut into 1-inch pieces**
- 1 **pound medium shrimp, shelled and deveined, leaving tail part of shell on, if you like**
- 1/4 **cup chopped fresh cilantro**

1. In 4-quart saucepan, heat oil over medium heat. Add onion and cook, stirring frequently, until tender and golden, about 10 minutes. Stir in garlic and chiles and cook 30 seconds. Add potatoes, clam juice, water, salt, and thyme; heat to boiling over high heat. Reduce heat to medium; cook until potatoes are just tender, about 10 minutes.

2. Cut lime in half; cut one half into wedges and set aside. Add remaining lime half and monkfish to soup; cover and cook 5 minutes. Stir in shrimp and cook until shrimp are just opaque throughout and monkfish is tender, 3 to 5 minutes.

3. With tongs, remove lime half, squeezing juice into soup. Sprinkle soup with cilantro and serve with lime wedges. Makes about 11 cups or 6 main-dish servings.

Each serving: About 222 calories (20 percent calories from fat), 26g protein, 18g carbohydrate, 5g total fat (0g saturated), 112mg cholesterol, 660mg sodium.

Stuffed Cabbage

Prep: 1 hour 10 minutes   Bake: 40 minutes

We filled large cabbage leaves with a medley of veggies, flavorful seasonings, and textured vegetable protein (TVP), a soy product that can be used in place of ground meat in many recipes.

1 cup textured vegetable protein (TVP)

1 medium head savoy cabbage (2¹/4 pounds)

1 tablespoon olive oil

2 medium carrots, peeled and chopped

2 medium stalks celery, chopped

1 medium red pepper, chopped

3 garlic cloves, finely chopped

3 green onions, sliced

2 tablespoons minced, peeled fresh ginger

¹/4 cup water

2 tablespoons plus 1 teaspoon reduced-sodium soy sauce

2 tablespoons seasoned rice vinegar

1 can (14¹/2 ounces) diced tomatoes

1 tablespoon light brown sugar

2 tablespoons chopped fresh parsley leaves for garnish

1. Rehydrate TVP: In 1-quart saucepan, heat 1 cup water to boiling over high heat. Remove saucepan from heat; stir in TVP and set aside.

2. Carefully remove 10 large outer leaves from cabbage (more, if leaves are small) and set aside; finely chop remaining cabbage.

3. In nonstick 5-quart saucepot, heat 3 quarts water to boiling over high heat. Add whole cabbage leaves and cook, pressing leaves under water with tongs, until leaves are pliable, 3 to 5 minutes. Drain leaves in colander; set aside. Discard water and wipe saucepot dry.

4. In same saucepot, heat oil over medium heat. Add carrots, celery, and red pepper; cook, stirring occasionally, until vegetables are tender-crisp, 10 to 12 minutes. Increase heat to medium-high; add chopped cabbage and cook, stirring, until cabbage wilts, 5 minutes. Add garlic, green onions, and ginger, and cook, stirring, 2 minutes longer.

5. Stir in water. Reduce heat to low; cover and simmer until vegetables are very tender, 8 minutes. Remove from heat; stir in rehydrated TVP, 2 tablespoons soy sauce, and 1 tablespoon rice vinegar.

6. In small bowl, combine tomatoes with their juice, brown sugar, remaining 1 teaspoon soy sauce, and remaining 1 tablespoon rice vinegar.

7. Preheat oven to 350°F. With paper towel, pat cabbage leaves dry. With sharp knife, trim thick center ribs. With stem end toward you, place heaping ¹/2 cup TVP mixture in center of bottom half of 1 leaf. Fold in sides of leaf and roll up. Place roll, seam side down, in shallow 2¹/2-quart casserole or baking dish. Repeat with remaining cabbage leaves and TVP mixture, overlapping 2 smaller leaves to make 1 roll if necessary.

8. Spoon tomato mixture over cabbage rolls. Cover casserole and bake until rolls are hot and sauce is bubbly, about 40 minutes. Sprinkle with parsley before serving. Makes 10 rolls or 5 main-dish servings.

Each serving: About 240 calories (15 percent calories from fat), 19g protein, 41g carbohydrate, 4g total fat (1g saturated), 0mg cholesterol, 1,115mg sodium.

Easy Barbecued Beans and Rice

Prep: 15 minutes   Cook: 25 minutes

This vegetarian skillet dinner is especially good with a rich, smoky barbecue sauce.

3/4 **cup regular long-grain rice**

1 **tablespoon vegetable oil**

1 **medium green pepper, cut into 1/2-inch pieces**

1 **medium red pepper, cut into 1/2-inch pieces**

1 **medium onion, chopped**

1 **can (15 to 19 ounces) black beans, rinsed and drained**

1 **can (15 to 19 ounces) red kidney beans, rinsed and drained**

1 **can (15 to 19 ounces) garbanzo beans, rinsed and drained**

1 **can (15 to 16 ounces) pink beans, rinsed and drained**

1 **can (14 1/2 ounces) no-salt-added stewed tomatoes**

1 **cup water**

1/2 **cup bottled barbecue sauce**

1. In 2-quart saucepan, prepare rice as label directs but do not add butter or margarine.

2. Meanwhile, in 12-inch skillet, heat oil over medium heat until hot. Add peppers and onion and cook, stirring, until tender. Add black beans, red kidney beans, garbanzo beans, pink beans, stewed tomatoes, water, and barbecue sauce; heat to boiling over high heat. Reduce heat to low; cover and simmer 15 minutes.

3. Spoon rice into center of beans. Before serving, stir to combine rice and bean mixture. Makes 6 main-dish servings.

Each serving: About 355 calories (13 percent calories from fat), 16g protein, 61g carbohydrate, 5g total fat (1g saturated), 0mg cholesterol, 790mg sodium.

Three-Bean Vegetarian Chili

Prep: 25 minutes plus soaking beans   Cook: 1 hour 45 minutes

Hearty and colorful, this chili gets an extra wallop of flavor from a chipotle (smoked jalapeño) chile. If you can't find chipotles, add one or two additional fresh jalapeños with seeds for more heat. Vary the beans according to what you have on hand.

- 1 **cup dry white kidney beans (cannellini)**
- 1 **cup dry red kidney beans**
- 1 **cup dry black beans**
- 1 **tablespoon olive or vegetable oil**
- 2 **medium onions, chopped**
- 3 **carrots, peeled and chopped**
- 1 **stalk celery, chopped**
- 1 **red pepper, chopped**
- 3 **garlic cloves, finely chopped**
- 1 **jalapeño chile, finely chopped**
- 2 **teaspoons ground cumin**
- 1/2 **teaspoon ground coriander**
- 1/8 **teaspoon ground cinnamon**
- 1/8 **teaspoon ground red pepper (cayenne)**
- 1 **can (28 ounces) tomatoes in puree**
- 1 **chipotle chile in adobo, finely chopped**
- 2 **teaspoons salt**
- 1/4 **teaspoon dried oregano**
- 2 **cups water**
- 1 **package (10 ounces) frozen whole-kernel corn, thawed**
- 1/2 **cup chopped fresh cilantro**

1. Rinse white kidney beans, red kidney beans, and black beans with cold running water and discard any stones or shriveled beans. In large bowl, place beans and enough water to cover by 2 inches. Cover and let stand at room temperature overnight. (Or, in 6-quart saucepot, place beans and enough water to cover by 2 inches. Heat to boiling over high heat; cook 2 minutes. Remove from heat; cover and let stand 1 hour.) Drain and rinse beans.

2. In nonreactive 5-quart Dutch oven, combine beans with enough water to cover by 2 inches; heat to boiling over high heat. Reduce heat; cover and simmer until beans are tender, about 1 hour. Drain beans and return to Dutch oven.

3. Meanwhile, in nonstick 10-inch skillet, heat oil over medium heat. Add onions, carrots, celery, and red pepper. Cook, stirring frequently, until carrots are tender, about 10 minutes. Stir in garlic, jalapeño, cumin, coriander, cinnamon, and ground red pepper; cook 30 seconds. Stir in tomatoes with their puree, chipotle chile, salt, and oregano, breaking up tomatoes with side of spoon. Heat to boiling; reduce heat and simmer 10 minutes, stirring several times.

4. Add tomato mixture and water to beans in Dutch oven; heat to boiling over medium-high heat. Reduce heat; cover and simmer, stirring occasionally, 15 minutes. Stir in corn and cook 5 minutes longer. Remove from heat and stir in 1/4 cup cilantro. Spoon into bowls and sprinkle with remaining 1/4 cup cilantro. Makes about 10 cups or 6 main-dish servings.

Each serving: About 461 calories (8 percent calories from fat), 25g protein, 86g carbohydrate, 4g total fat (1g saturated), 0mg cholesterol, 1,048mg sodium.

Curried Vegetable Stew

Prep: 15 minutes   Cook: 25 minutes

Serve over rice for a healthful vegetarian meal.

>   2 **teaspoons olive oil**
>   1 **large sweet potato (12 ounces), peeled and cut into 1/2-inch pieces**
>   1 **medium onion, cut into 1/2-inch pieces**
>   1 **medium zucchini (8 ounces), cut into 1-inch pieces**
>   1 **small green pepper, cut into 3/4-inch pieces**
> 1 1/2 **teaspoons curry powder**
>   1 **teaspoon ground cumin**
>   1 **can (15 to 19 ounces) garbanzo beans, rinsed and drained**
>   1 **can (14 1/2 ounces) diced tomatoes**
> 3/4 **cup vegetable broth**
> 1/2 **teaspoon salt**

1. In deep nonstick 12-inch skillet, heat oil over medium-high heat. Add sweet potato, onion, zucchini, and green pepper; cook, stirring, until vegetables are tender, 8 to 10 minutes. Add curry powder and cumin; cook 1 minute.

2. Add garbanzo beans, tomatoes with their juice, broth, and salt; heat to boiling over high heat. Reduce heat to medium-low; cover and simmer until vegetables are very tender but still hold their shape, about 10 minutes longer. Makes 4 main-dish servings.

Each serving: About 223 calories (20 percent calories from fat), 8g protein, 39g carbohydrate, 5g total fat (0g saturated), 0mg cholesterol, 790mg sodium.

Winter Vegetable Chili

Prep: 15 minutes   Cook: 1 hour 15 minutes

Serve this black-bean chili with a stack of warmed tortillas.

- **4 teaspoons olive oil**
- **1 medium butternut squash (1³/4 pounds), peeled and cut into ³/4-inch pieces**
- **2 carrots, peeled and chopped**
- **1 medium onion, chopped**
- **3 tablespoons chili powder**
- **1 can (28 ounces) plum tomatoes**
- **1 can (4 to 4¹/2 ounces) chopped mild green chiles**
- **1 cup vegetable broth**
- **¹/4 teaspoon salt**
- **2 cans (15 to 19 ounces each) black beans, rinsed and drained**
- **¹/4 cup chopped fresh cilantro sour cream or yogurt (optional)**

1. In nonreactive 5-quart Dutch oven, heat 2 teaspoons oil over medium-high heat. Add squash; cook until golden. Transfer to bowl.

2. In same Dutch oven, heat remaining 2 teaspoons oil. Add carrots and onion; cook, stirring occasionally, until well browned. Stir in chili powder; cook, stirring, 1 minute. Add tomatoes with their juice, chiles with their liquid, broth, and salt. Heat to boiling over high heat, breaking up tomatoes with side of spoon. Reduce heat; cover and simmer 30 minutes.

3. Stir in beans and squash; heat to boiling over high heat. Reduce heat; cover and simmer until squash is tender and chili has thickened, about 15 minutes. Stir in cilantro. Serve with sour cream, if you like. Makes 9 cups or 6 main-dish servings.

Each serving: About 233 calories (19 percent calories from fat), 9g protein, 42g carbohydrate, 5g total fat (1g saturated), 0mg cholesterol, 911mg sodium.

Polenta with Garlicky Greens

Prep: 30 minutes   Cook: 20 minutes

A nutritious vegetarian meal of soft cornmeal, with a tasty topping of sautéed Swiss chard, raisins, and pine nuts. We simplified and reduced the total prep time by microwaving the polenta. (Stir just once instead of constantly.)

- **2 large bunches Swiss chard (3¹/2 pounds)**
- **1 tablespoon olive oil**
- **3 garlic cloves, thinly sliced**
- **¹/4 teaspoon crushed red pepper**
- **1¹/4 teaspoons salt**
- **¹/3 plus 4¹/2 cups water**
- **¹/4 cup golden raisins**
- **1¹/2 cups yellow cornmeal**
- **2 cups fat-free (skim) milk**
- **2 tablespoons grated Parmesan or Pecorino Romano cheese**
- **1 tablespoon pine nuts (pignoli), toasted and chopped**

1. Cut off and discard bottom 3 inches of Swiss-chard stems. Cut remaining stems into ¹/2-inch-thick slices; coarsely chop leaves. Rinse and dry stems and leaves separately; place in separate bowls.

2. In nonstick 12-inch skillet, heat oil over medium heat. Add garlic and crushed red pepper and cook, stirring occasionally, until garlic is lightly golden, about 2 minutes.

3. Increase heat to medium-high; add sliced chard stems to skillet and cook, stirring occasionally, 8 minutes. Gradually add chard leaves and 1/2 teaspoon salt, stirring until leaves wilt. Stir in 1/3 cup water. Cover skillet and simmer until stems and leaves are tender, 5 minutes. Stir in raisins and set aside.

4. Meanwhile, prepare polenta in microwave oven:* In 4-quart microwave-safe bowl or casserole, combine remaining 41/2 cups water, cornmeal, milk, and remaining 3/4 teaspoon salt. Cover and cook on High, stirring once, until thickened, 12 to 15 minutes.

5. To serve, stir Parmesan into polenta. Spoon polenta onto platter; top with Swiss-chard mixture and sprinkle with pine nuts. Makes 4 main-dish servings.

*If you like, polenta can be prepared on top of range: In 4-quart saucepan, stir 1 teaspoon salt with 2 cups cold milk. Gradually whisk in cornmeal until blended, then whisk in 41/2 cups boiling water. Heat to boiling over high heat, stirring occasionally. Reduce heat to medium-low and cook, partially covered and stirring frequently, 20 minutes.

Each serving: About 375 calories (14 percent calories from fat), 16g protein, 66g carbohydrate, 6g total fat (1g saturated), 5mg cholesterol, 1,265mg sodium.

Moroccan Vegetable Stew

Prep: 15 minutes   Cook: 40 minutes

Spiced with cinnamon and crushed pepper, sweetened with prunes, and served over couscous, this Moroccan stew is richly flavored and satisfying.

- 1 **tablespoon olive oil**
- 1 **medium butternut squash (2 pounds), peeled and cut into 1-inch pieces**
- 2 **carrots, peeled and cut into 1/4-inch-thick slices**
- 1 **medium onion, chopped**
- 1 **can (15 to 19 ounces) garbanzo beans, rinsed and drained**
- 1 **can (141/2 ounces) stewed tomatoes**
- 1/2 **cup pitted prunes, chopped**
- 1/2 **teaspoon ground cinnamon**
- 1/2 **teaspoon salt**
- 1/8 **to 1/4 teaspoon crushed red pepper**
- 11/2 **cups water**
- 1 **cup couscous (Moroccan pasta)**
- 11/4 **cups vegetable or chicken broth**
- 2 **tablespoons chopped fresh cilantro or parsley**

1. In nonstick 12-inch skillet, heat oil over medium-high heat. Add squash, carrots, and onion and cook, stirring frequently, until onion is tender and golden, about 10 minutes.

2. Stir in garbanzo beans, tomatoes, prunes, cinnamon, salt, crushed red pepper, and water; heat to boiling. Reduce heat; cover and simmer until all vegetables are tender, about 30 minutes.

3. Meanwhile, prepare couscous as label directs, but use broth in place of water.

4. To serve, stir cilantro into stew and spoon over couscous. Makes 4 main-dish servings.

Each serving: About 474 calories (11 percent calories from fat), 14g protein, 95g carbohydrate, 6g total fat (1g saturated), 0mg cholesterol, 1,022mg sodium.

Skillet Vegetable Curry

Prep: 15 minutes Cook: 20 minutes

A package of precut cauliflower shortens prep time. As vegetables simmer, toast some pita bread to serve alongside.

- 12 **ounces cauliflower flowerets**
- 1 **large all-purpose potato (8 ounces), peeled and cut into 1-inch chunks**
- 1 **large sweet potato (12 ounces), peeled and cut into 1-inch chunks**
- 2 **tablespoons lightly packed flaked sweetened coconut**
- 2 **teaspoons olive oil**
- 1 **medium onion, finely chopped**
- 1 **teaspoon mustard seeds**
- 1¹/₂ **teaspoons ground cumin**
- 1¹/₂ **teaspoons ground coriander**
- ¹/₈ **teaspoon ground red pepper (cayenne)**
- 2 **medium tomatoes, finely chopped**
- 1 **cup frozen peas, thawed**
- 1¹/₄ **teaspoons salt**
- ¹/₂ **cup loosely packed fresh cilantro leaves, chopped**

1. In 4-quart saucepan, heat cauliflower, potato, sweet potato, and enough water to cover to boiling over high heat. Reduce heat to low; cover and simmer until vegetables are tender, 8 to 10 minutes. Drain well, reserving ³/₄ cup cooking water.

2. Meanwhile, in nonstick 12-inch skillet, cook coconut over medium heat, stirring constantly, until lightly browned, about 3 minutes; transfer to small bowl.

3. In same skillet, heat oil over medium heat; add onion and cook 5 minutes. Add mustard seeds, cumin, coriander, and ground red pepper; cover and cook, shaking skillet frequently, until onion is tender and lightly browned and seeds start to pop, 5 minutes longer.

4. Spoon cauliflower mixture into skillet; add reserved cooking water, toasted coconut, tomatoes, peas, and salt; heat through. Sprinkle with cilantro to serve. Makes about 8 cups or 4 main-dish servings.

Each serving: About 230 calories (16 percent calories from fat), 8g protein, 43g carbohydrate, 4g total fat (1g saturated), 0mg cholesterol, 735mg sodium.

Vegetable Omelet

Prep: 30 minutes Bake/Broil: 12 minutes

More vegetables and fewer whole eggs make this a great healthy choice.

- 8 **ounces red potatoes, cut into ¹/₂-inch pieces**
- 1 **medium onion, finely chopped**
- 1 **medium red pepper, cut into ¹/₂-inch pieces**
- 1 **medium green pepper, cut into ¹/₂-inch pieces**
- 1 **small zucchini (8 ounces), cut into ¹/₂-inch pieces**
- 1 **teaspoon sugar**
- ³/₄ **teaspoon salt**
- ¹/₄ **teaspoon coarsely ground black pepper**
- ¹/₄ **cup water**
- 4 **tablespoons chopped fresh basil leaves**
- 6 **large egg whites**
- 2 **large eggs**
- ¹/₂ **cup crumbled feta cheese (2 ounces)**

1. In small saucepan, heat potatoes and enough water to cover to boiling over high heat. Reduce heat to low; cover and simmer until tender, about 10 minutes. Drain.

2. Spray nonstick 12-inch skillet with nonstick cooking spray. Add onion and cook over medium-high heat until golden. Add red pepper, green pepper, zucchini, sugar, salt, and black pepper and cook, stirring frequently, until vegetables are tender-crisp. Stir in water and heat to boiling. Reduce heat to low; cover and simmer until vegetables are tender, 10 minutes. Remove skillet from heat; stir in potatoes and 1 tablespoon basil.

3. Preheat oven to 375°F. In medium bowl, with wire whisk or fork, mix egg whites, eggs, 1/4 cup crumbled feta, and remaining 3 tablespoons basil.

4. Spray oven-safe 10-inch skillet with nonstick cooking spray. Pour egg mixture into pan and cook over medium-high heat until egg mixture begins to set, 1 to 2 minutes. Remove skillet from heat. With slotted spoon, spread vegetable mixture over egg mixture in skillet; sprinkle with remaining 1/4 cup crumbled feta. Bake omelet until set, 10 minutes. (Wrap handle of skillet with double layer of foil if handle is not oven-safe.) If you like, broil 1 to 2 minutes to brown top of omelet. Makes 4 main-dish servings.

Each serving: About 185 calories (29 percent calories from fat), 13g protein, 20g carbohydrate, 6g total fat (3g saturated), 119mg cholesterol, 860mg sodium.

California Frittata

Prep: 30 minutes   Cook: 35 minutes

Mexican-style salsa, crisp jicama, and tortillas contribute as much to the California flavor of this robust frittata as does the medley of fresh vegetables. An egg substitute may be used instead of the eggs.

2	to 3 small red potatoes (6 1/2 ounces)
1	tablespoon olive oil
1 1/2	cups thinly sliced onions
1	zucchini (6 ounces), thinly sliced
1	cup thinly sliced cremini mushrooms
2	plum tomatoes (6 1/2 ounces), cored, halved, and thinly sliced
1/2	teaspoon kosher salt (optional)
1/2	teaspoon freshly ground black pepper
1	cup shredded spinach or Swiss chard
1	tablespoon slivered fresh basil leaves (optional)
2	large eggs
3	large egg whites
3	tablespoons crumbled feta cheese (optional)
2	tablespoons chopped fresh flat-leaf parsley
3/4	cup bottled salsa
4	(6-inch) corn tortillas
1/2	jicama (8 ounces), peeled and cut into 2" by 1/4" matchstick strips
2	teaspoons fresh lime juice

1. Preheat oven to 350°F. In saucepan, heat potatoes and enough water to cover to a boil over high heat. Reduce heat to low; cover and simmer until fork-tender, 15 to 20 minutes. Drain and cool. Cut into 1/4-inch-thick slices.

2. In nonstick 10-inch oven-safe skillet, heat oil over medium heat. Add onions and cook until softened, about 5 minutes. Add potatoes, zucchini, mushrooms, and tomatoes; cook, stirring gently, until zucchini begins to soften, 2 to 3 minutes. Season with salt, if using, and pepper. Add spinach and basil, if using, and cook until spinach wilts, 1 to 2 minutes.

3. In medium bowl with wire whisk or fork, mix eggs and egg whites. With spatula, stir vegetables while pouring eggs into skillet. Transfer skillet to oven and bake until eggs are set, 3 to 5 minutes. (Wrap handle of skillet with double layer of foil if handle is not oven-safe.)

4. Sprinkle frittata with feta cheese, if using, and parsley. Cut frittata into 4 pieces and serve with salsa, tortillas, and jicama sticks sprinkled with lime juice. Makes 4 main-dish servings.

Each serving: About 265 calories (24 percent calories from fat), 11g protein, 38g carbohydrate, 7g total fat (1g saturated), 106mg cholesterol, 140mg sodium.

Mushroom and Gruyère Rösti

Prep: 15 minutes   Cook: 40 minutes

This Swiss favorite is typically made with shredded potatoes that are formed into a pancake and cooked until golden and crisp on both sides. But we used two layers of white rice (short grain is best because it holds together so well), with a layer of melted cheese and mushrooms in between.

2²/3   **cups water**

1¹/3   **cups short-grain white rice**

1   **teaspoon salt**

4   **teaspoons margarine or butter**

1   **large onion, finely chopped**

2   **ounces Gruyère cheese, shredded (¹/2 cup)**

8   **ounces cremini and/or oyster mushrooms, trimmed and thinly sliced**

8   **ounces shiitake mushrooms, stems removed and caps thinly sliced**

1   **garlic clove, finely chopped**

¹/4   **teaspoon dried thyme**

¹/4   **teaspoon coarsely ground black pepper**

¹/2   **cup loosely packed fresh parsley leaves, chopped**

3   **teaspoons vegetable oil**

1. In 2-quart saucepan, heat water, rice, and ³/4 teaspoon salt to boiling over high heat. Reduce heat to low; cover and simmer, without stirring or lifting lid, until rice is just tender and liquid has been absorbed, 15 minutes.

2. Meanwhile, in nonstick 10-inch skillet, melt 2 teaspoons margarine over medium heat. Add onion and cook, stirring occasionally, until tender, 15 minutes. Transfer onion to medium bowl. Stir half of cooked onion and ¹/4 cup cheese into cooked rice; set aside.

3. In same skillet, melt remaining 2 teaspoons margarine over medium-high heat. Add mushrooms and cook, stirring occasionally, until tender and golden, 6 to 8 minutes. Add remaining cooked onion, garlic, thyme, pepper, and remaining ¹/4 teaspoon salt; cook, stirring, 1 minute. Transfer mushroom mixture to medium bowl; stir in parsley. Reserve ¹/4 cup mushroom mixture for garnish. Stir remaining ¹/4 cup cheese into mushrooms in bowl.

4. In same skillet, heat 1¹/2 teaspoons oil over medium-high heat until hot; remove skillet from heat. Add half of rice mixture to skillet and, with wide metal spatula, spread and press to form an even layer covering bottom of skillet (rice may be sticky). Top with mushroom mixture from bowl, leaving ¹/2-inch border of rice. Spoon remaining rice mixture over mushroom layer; press to seal rice edges together.

5. Cook rösti over medium-high heat 5 minutes; invert onto large plate (if rösti cracks or sticks to pan, press pieces back together). Add remaining 1¹/2 teaspoons oil to skillet; slide rösti back into skillet and cook until golden and heated through, 5 minutes longer. To serve, slide rösti onto platter and top with reserved mushroom mixture. Cut into wedges. Makes 6 main-dish servings.

Each serving: About 270 calories (27 percent calories from fat), 7g protein, 42g carbohydrate, 8g total fat (3g saturated), 10mg cholesterol, 430mg sodium.

Vegetarian Tortilla Pie

Prep: 8 minutes   Bake: 12 minutes

This dish can be assembled in a jiffy, thanks to its no-cook filling of canned black beans and corn, prepared salsa, and pre-shredded Monterey Jack cheese.

- **1 jar (12 ounces) medium salsa**
- **1 can (8 ounces) no-salt-added tomato sauce**
- **1 can (15 to 16 ounces) no-salt-added black beans, rinsed and drained**
- **1 can (15 1/4 ounces) no-salt-added whole-kernel corn, drained**
- **1/2 cup packed fresh cilantro leaves**
- **4 (10-inch) low-fat flour tortillas**
- **6 ounces reduced-fat Monterey Jack cheese, shredded (1 1/2 cups)**
- **reduced-fat sour cream (optional)**

1. Preheat oven to 500°F. Spray 15 1/2" by 10 1/2" jelly-roll pan with nonstick cooking spray.

2. In small bowl, mix salsa and tomato sauce. In medium bowl, mix black beans, corn, and cilantro.

3. Place 1 tortilla in prepared jelly-roll pan. Spread one-third of salsa mixture over tortilla. Top with one-third of bean mixture and one-third of cheese. Repeat layering 2 more times, ending with last tortilla.

4. Bake pie until cheese melts and filling is heated through, 10 to 12 minutes. Serve with reduced-fat sour cream if you like. Makes 4 main-dish servings.

Each serving without sour cream: About 440 calories (23 percent calories from fat), 25g protein, 65g carbohydrate, 11g total fat (5g saturated), 30mg cholesterol, 820mg sodium.

Veggie Enchiladas

Prep: 25 minutes   Bake: 20 minutes

- 2 teaspoons olive oil
- 1 small zucchini (8 ounces), cut into $1/2$-inch pieces
- 1 medium onion, chopped
- 1 medium red pepper, chopped
- 2 cans (15 to 19 ounces each) no-salt-added white kidney beans (cannellini), rinsed and drained
- $1/2$ cup vegetable or chicken broth
- 2 garlic cloves, finely chopped
- 1 can ($15 1/4$ ounces) no-salt-added whole-kernel corn, drained
- 2 pickled jalapeño chiles, finely chopped, with seeds
- 1 cup loosely packed fresh cilantro leaves and stems, chopped
- 6 (8-inch) flour tortillas
- 1 jar ($15 1/2$ ounces) mild salsa
- $1/3$ cup shredded Monterey Jack cheese
  lime wedges for garnish

1. In nonstick 12-inch skillet, heat oil over medium heat. Add zucchini, onion, and red pepper; cook, stirring frequently, until vegetables are tender and golden, 10 to 15 minutes.

2. Meanwhile, in food processor with knife blade attached or in blender at medium speed, puree half of white kidney beans with broth until almost smooth. Transfer bean mixture to large bowl; stir in remaining beans and set aside.

3. To vegetables in skillet, add garlic and cook 1 minute longer. Stir in corn and pickled jalapeños; cook 2 minutes. Transfer vegetable mixture to bowl with beans; stir in cilantro until mixed.

4. Preheat oven to 375°F. Spoon about $3/4$ cup bean mixture along center of each tortilla. Fold sides of tortilla over filling, overlapping slightly.

5. Spoon $1/2$ cup salsa into bottom of 13" by 9" glass or ceramic baking dish. Place enchiladas, seam side down, on top of salsa. Spoon remaining salsa over enchiladas; sprinkle with cheese. Bake until heated through, 20 minutes. Serve with lime wedges. Makes 6 main-dish servings.

Each serving: About 415 calories (17 percent calories from fat), 17g protein, 70g carbohydrate, 8g total fat (2g saturated), 6mg cholesterol, 700mg sodium.

Southwestern Black-Bean Burgers

Prep: 10 minutes   Cook: 6 minutes

To have handy for another meal, make a double batch and freeze the uncooked patties. Defrost for 10 minutes, then cook burgers, turning once, until heated through, about 12 minutes.

- **1 can (15 to 19 ounces) black beans, rinsed and drained**
- **2 tablespoons light mayonnaise**
- **1/4 cup packed fresh cilantro leaves, chopped**
- **1 tablespoon plain dried bread crumbs**
- **1/2 teaspoon ground cumin**
- **1/2 teaspoon hot pepper sauce**
  nonstick cooking spray
- **1 cup loosely packed sliced lettuce**
- **4 mini (4-inch) whole wheat pitas, warmed**
- **1/2 cup bottled mild salsa**

1. In large bowl, with potato masher or fork, mash beans with mayonnaise until almost smooth (some lumps of beans should remain). Stir in cilantro, bread crumbs, cumin, and pepper sauce until combined. With lightly floured hands, shape bean mixture into four 3-inch round patties. Spray both sides of each patty lightly with nonstick cooking spray.

2. Heat nonstick 12-inch skillet over medium heat. Add patties and cook until lightly browned, about 3 minutes. With wide metal spatula, turn patties over and cook until heated through, 3 minutes longer.

3. Arrange lettuce on pitas; top with burgers, then salsa. Makes 4 main-dish servings.

Each serving: About 210 calories (13 percent calories from fat), 13g protein, 42g carbohydrate, 3g total fat (0g saturated), 0mg cholesterol, 715mg sodium.

Vegetarian Bean Burritos

Prep: 10 minutes   Cook: 8 minutes

"I love bold, assertive flavors. This is a quick version of the burritos my favorite restaurant serves," says GH test kitchen associate, Mary Ann Svec.

- **4 (10-inch) flour tortillas**
- **2 teaspoons vegetable oil**
- **4 medium zucchini (5 ounces each), each cut lengthwise in half, then sliced crosswise**
- **1/4 teaspoon ground cinnamon**
- **1/4 teaspoon salt**
- **1 can (15 ounces) Spanish-style red kidney beans**
- **1 can (15 to 19 ounces) black beans, rinsed and drained**
- **4 ounces Monterey Jack cheese, shredded (1 cup)**
- **1/2 cup loosely packed fresh cilantro leaves**
- **1 jar (16 ounces) chunky-style salsa**

1. Warm tortillas as label directs; keep warm.

2. In nonstick 12-inch skillet, heat oil over medium-high heat. Add zucchini, cinnamon, and salt; cook until zucchini is tender-crisp, about 5 minutes.

3. Meanwhile, in 2-quart saucepan, heat kidney beans with their sauce and black beans just to simmering over medium heat; keep warm.

4. To serve, allow each person to assemble a burrito as desired, using a warm flour tortilla, zucchini, bean mixture, cheese, and cilantro. Pass salsa to serve with burritos. Makes 4 main-dish servings.

Each serving: About 550 calories (28 percent calories from fat), 29g protein, 77g carbohydrate, 17g total fat (1g saturated), 25mg cholesterol, 1,943mg sodium.

Watermelon and Jicama Salad,
page 178

Watermelon and Jicama Salad

Prep: 25 minutes plus chilling

Jicama is a slightly flattened round root vegetable with a thin brown skin and crunchy white flesh.

- **2 medium jicama (12 ounces each), peeled and cut into 3/4-inch cubes**
- **1/4 cup fresh lime juice (about 2 limes)**
- **1/2 teaspoon salt**
- **1 piece watermelon (2 1/2 pounds)**
- **1/2 cup loosely packed fresh cilantro leaves, chopped**
- **1/8 teaspoon ground red pepper (cayenne) lime slices for garnish**

1. In large bowl, toss jicama with lime juice and salt; cover and refrigerate 30 minutes.

2. Meanwhile, cut rind from watermelon and discard. Cut flesh into 1/2-inch cubes to equal 4 cups; discard seeds.

3. Add watermelon, cilantro, and ground red pepper to jicama in bowl; toss well. Cover and refrigerate 15 minutes to allow flavors to blend. Garnish with lime slices. Makes about 8 cups or 12 accompaniment servings.

Each serving: About 40 calories (0 percent calories from fat), 1g protein, 9g carbohydrate, 0g total fat, 0mg cholesterol, 90mg sodium.

Peaches and Greens

Prep: 25 minutes

A cool, refreshing alternative to a classic green salad.

- **1 large lime**
- **2 tablespoons honey**
- **1 tablespoon olive oil**
- **1 tablespoon chopped fresh mint leaves**
- **1/2 teaspoon Dijon mustard**
- **1/4 teaspoon salt**
- **1/4 teaspoon coarsely ground black pepper**
- **2 bunches watercress (4 ounces each), tough stems discarded**
- **2 pounds ripe peaches (6 medium), peeled and cut into wedges**
- **1 large jicama (1 1/4 pounds), peeled and cut into 1 1/2" by 1/4" sticks**

1. From lime, grate 1/4 teaspoon peel and squeeze 2 tablespoons juice. Prepare dressing: In large bowl, with wire whisk, mix lime peel, lime juice, honey, oil, mint, Dijon mustard, salt, and pepper.

2. Just before serving, add watercress, peaches, and jicama to dressing in bowl; toss to coat. Makes 12 accompaniment servings.

Each serving: About 55 calories (16 percent calories from fat), 1g protein, 11g carbohydrate, 1g total fat (0g saturated), 0mg cholesterol, 55mg sodium.

Crunchy Carrot Coleslaw

Prep: 10 minutes

1/3 **cup fresh orange juice**

1/4 **cup cider vinegar**

2 **tablespoons sugar**

2 **tablespoons Dijon mustard**

1 **tablespoon vegetable oil**

1 **teaspoon salt**

1/4 **teaspoon dried mint**

1/8 **teaspoon ground red pepper (cayenne)**

1 **bag (16 ounces) shredded cabbage (for coleslaw)**

1 **bag (10 ounces) shredded carrots**

In large bowl, with wire whisk, mix orange juice, vinegar, sugar, mustard, oil, salt, mint, and ground red pepper until blended. Add cabbage and carrots; toss well. Serve slaw at room temperature, or cover and refrigerate until ready to serve. Makes about 10 cups or 8 accompaniment servings.

Each serving: About 65 calories (28 percent calories from fat), 1g protein, 12g carbohydrate, 2g total fat (0g saturated), 0mg cholesterol, 385mg sodium.

Asian Cucumber Salad

Prep: 15 minutes plus standing and chilling   Cook: 3 minutes

An easy salad that goes well with spicy food.

2 **English (seedless) cucumbers**

1 **teaspoon salt**

1/4 **cup seasoned rice vinegar**

4 **teaspoons sugar**

1. With vegetable peeler, remove 4 evenly spaced lengthwise strips of peel from each cucumber. Thinly slice cucumbers. In colander set over large bowl, toss cucumbers and 1/2 teaspoon salt; let stand 30 minutes at room temperature. Discard liquid in bowl. Pat cucumbers dry with paper towels.

2. In 6-inch skillet, combine vinegar and sugar; heat to boiling over high heat. Cook until sugar has dissolved. Transfer to same clean bowl and stir in remaining 1/2 teaspoon salt. Add cucumbers and toss to coat. Refrigerate to blend flavors, 1 hour or up to 4 hours. Makes 8 accompaniment servings.

Each serving: About 27 calories (0 percent calories from fat), 1g protein, 6g carbohydrate, 0g total fat, 0mg cholesterol, 332mg sodium.

Black-Eyed Pea Salad

Prep: 15 minutes   Cook: 30 minutes

Black-eyed peas, also called cowpeas, are actually beans. Unlike most dried beans, they don't need to be soaked. Their short cooking time makes them a natural for summer salads.

- 1 **package (16 ounces) dry black-eyed peas**
- 1/3 **cup cider vinegar**
- 2 **tablespoons olive oil**
- 1 **tablespoon cayenne pepper sauce***
- 2 **teaspoons sugar**
- 1 1/2 **teaspoons salt**
- 2 **medium stalks celery, finely chopped**
- 1 **medium red onion, finely chopped**
- 1 **package (10 ounces) frozen peas, thawed**

1. Rinse black-eyed peas with cold running water and discard any stones or shriveled peas. In 8-quart Dutch oven, heat black-eyed peas and 3 quarts water to boiling over high heat. Reduce heat to low; cover and simmer until peas are just tender, 25 to 30 minutes.

2. Meanwhile, prepare dressing: In large bowl, with wire whisk, mix vinegar, oil, pepper sauce, sugar, and salt until blended.

3. Drain black-eyed peas and rinse well. Add warm black-eyed peas to dressing in bowl and toss gently. Stir in celery, onion, and peas. Serve salad at room temperature or cover and refrigerate until ready to serve. Makes 12 accompaniment servings.

*Cayenne pepper sauce is a milder variety of hot pepper sauce that adds tang and flavor, not just heat. It can be found in the condiment section of the supermarket.

Each serving: About 135 calories (20 percent calories from fat), 8g protein, 21g carbohydrate, 3g total fat (1g saturated), 0mg cholesterol, 360mg sodium.

Tomato and Melon Salad

Prep: 15 minutes

- 1 **pint cherry tomatoes**
- 1 **large honeydew melon (4 1/2 pounds)**
- 1 **large cantaloupe (3 pounds)**
- 1/4 **cup red currant or apple jelly**
- 1/2 **teaspoon salt**
- 1 **teaspoon coarsely ground black pepper**
- 1 **bunch spinach, tough stems trimmed and washed and dried well**

1. Cut small "x" in stem end of each cherry tomato. Add tomatoes to large saucepot of boiling water; cook 5 seconds. Drain; rinse tomatoes with cold running water to stop cooking. With fingers, slip tomatoes from their skins; place in colander to drain off excess liquid.

2. Cut each melon in half; discard seeds. With melon baller, scoop melons into balls; reserve any remaining melon for another use. Place melon balls in colander with cherry tomatoes. Cover colander, place on a plate to catch drips, and refrigerate if not serving right away.

3. To serve, in a large bowl, with wire whisk, stir jelly, salt, and pepper until smooth. Finely chop enough spinach to equal 1/4 cup. Add chopped spinach and melon-tomato mixture to bowl with jelly mixture; toss to coat. Arrange remaining spinach leaves on platter; spoon melon-tomato mixture over spinach leaves. Toss to serve. Makes 8 accompaniment servings.

Each serving: About 110 calories (8 percent calories from fat), 2g protein, 27g carbohydrate, 1g total fat (0g saturated), 0mg cholesterol, 190mg sodium.

Summer Corn Salad

Prep: 30 minutes   Cook: 10 minutes

A colorful salad created from farmstand-fresh summer vegetables.

- **12 ears corn, husks and silk removed**
- **12 ounces green beans, trimmed and cut into 1/4-inch pieces**
- **1/2 cup cider vinegar**
- **1/4 cup olive oil**
- **1/4 cup chopped fresh parsley**
- **1 teaspoon salt**
- **1/2 teaspoon coarsely ground black pepper**
- **1 red pepper, finely chopped**
- **1 small sweet onion, such as Vidalia or Walla Walla, finely chopped**

1. In 8-quart saucepot, heat 2 inches water to boiling over high heat; add corn. Heat to boiling. Reduce heat; cover and simmer 5 minutes. Drain. When cool enough to handle, cut kernels from corncobs.

2. Meanwhile, in 2-quart saucepan, heat 1 inch water to boiling over high heat; add green beans and heat to boiling. Reduce heat; simmer until tender-crisp, 3 to 5 minutes. Drain green beans. Rinse with cold running water; drain.

3. Prepare dressing: In large bowl, with wire whisk, mix vinegar, oil, parsley, salt, and black pepper until blended.

4. Add corn, green beans, red pepper, and onion to dressing in bowl; toss to coat. Serve at room temperature or cover and refrigerate up to 2 hours. Makes 12 accompaniment servings.

Each serving: About 179 calories (30 percent calories from fat), 5g protein, 31g carbohydrate, 6g total fat (1g saturated), 0mg cholesterol, 219mg sodium.

Moroccan Carrot Salad

Prep: 20 minutes

A simple go-along dish spiced with coriander, cilantro, and cumin for a Middle Eastern twist.

- **1 bag (16 ounces) carrots, peeled and coarsely shredded**
- **2 teaspoons extra virgin olive oil**
- **2 teaspoons fresh lemon juice**
- **1/4 teaspoon ground coriander**
- **1/4 teaspoon ground cumin**
- **1/4 teaspoon salt**
- **1/8 teaspoon ground black pepper**
- **2 tablespoons chopped fresh cilantro leaves**

In medium bowl, combine carrots, oil, lemon juice, coriander, cumin, salt, and pepper. Cover and refrigerate until ready to serve. Stir in cilantro just before serving. Makes about 2 1/2 cups or 4 accompaniment servings.

Each serving: About 70 calories (26 percent calories from fat), 1g protein, 11g carbohydrate, 2g total fat (1g saturated), 0mg cholesterol, 170mg sodium.

Cranberry-Orange Mold

Prep: 15 minutes plus chilling and overnight to set

For many families, a cranberry mold is an essential partner to the holiday turkey. This recipe, chock-full of cranberries and flavored with orange juice, is one of our favorites.

      3 **envelopes unflavored gelatin**
      3 **cups cold water**
      1 **package (8 servings) cranberry- or strawberry-flavored gelatin**
      2 **cups orange juice**
      1 **package (12 ounces) fresh cranberries**
  11/4 **cups sugar**
         lettuce leaves (optional)

1. In 4-quart saucepan, evenly sprinkle unflavored gelatin over 2 cups cold water; let stand 2 minutes to soften gelatin slightly. Cook over medium heat, stirring frequently, until gelatin has completely dissolved (do not boil). Remove saucepan from heat; add cranberry-flavored gelatin, stirring until it has completely dissolved. Stir in orange juice and remaining 1 cup cold water. Refrigerate until mixture mounds slightly when dropped from spoon, about 1 hour.

2. Meanwhile, in food processor with knife blade attached, combine cranberries and sugar; process until cranberries are finely chopped. Fold cranberry mixture into thickened gelatin. Pour into 10-inch Bundt pan or nonreactive 12-cup mold. Cover and refrigerate overnight.

3. To unmold, dip pan in large bowl of hot water for 10 seconds and invert onto platter lined with lettuce leaves, if desired. Makes 16 accompaniment servings.

Each serving: About 130 calories (0 percent calories from fat), 2g protein, 31g carbohydrate, 0g total fat, 0mg cholesterol, 30mg sodium.

Thai Squid Salad

Prep: 30 minutes   Cook: 12 minutes

An abundance of fresh herbs and a sweet, pungent dressing contribute glorious flavor to this lively first course—but with a minimum of fat and calories.

  21/4 **teaspoons salt**
      3 **tablespoons Asian fish sauce (nuoc nam)**
      3 **tablespoons fresh lime juice**
      1 **tablespoon sugar**
    1/4 **teaspoon crushed red pepper**
    1/2 **small sweet onion, such as Vidalia or Walla Walla, very thinly sliced**
      1 **carrot, peeled and shredded**
      1 **pound cleaned squid**
      1 **large head Boston lettuce, torn into bite-size pieces**
    1/2 **cup loosely packed fresh mint leaves**
    1/2 **cup loosely packed fresh cilantro leaves**

1. In 4-quart saucepan, combine 3 quarts water and 2 teaspoons salt; heat to boiling over high heat.

2. Meanwhile, prepare dressing: In large bowl, with wire whisk, combine fish sauce, lime juice, sugar, crushed red pepper, and remaining 1/4 teaspoon salt; stir until sugar has dissolved. Stir in onion and carrot.

3. Rinse squid under cold running water. Slice squid bodies crosswise into very thin rings. Cut tentacles into several pieces if large. Add to boiling water and cook until tender and opaque, 30 seconds to 1 minute. Drain and add to dressing in bowl. Add lettuce, mint, and cilantro; toss until mixed and coated with dressing. Makes 4 first-course servings.

Each serving: About 185 calories (15 percent calories from fat), 22g protein, 18g carbohydrate, 3g total fat (1g saturated), 264mg cholesterol, 954mg sodium.

Cool Rice Bowl with Radishes

Prep: 20 minutes plus cooling   Cook: 20 minutes

This test kitchen favorite, a refreshing mixture of aromatic rice, sweet peas, crunchy radishes, and toasted almonds, is tossed in a light vinaigrette.

- 1 **package (14 ounces) Texmati rice (2 cups)**
- 3¹/2 **cups water**
- ¹/3 **cup seasoned rice vinegar**
- 2 **tablespoons vegetable oil**
- 2 **teaspoons grated, peeled fresh ginger**
- 1¹/2 **teaspoons sugar**
- 1 **teaspoon salt**
- ¹/4 **teaspoon coarsely ground black pepper**
- ¹/4 **teaspoon Asian sesame oil**
- 1 **package (10 ounces) frozen peas**
- 2 **bunches radishes (15), each cut in half and thinly sliced**
- 2 **green onions, thinly sliced**
- ¹/2 **cup slivered blanched almonds, toasted**

1. In 3-quart saucepan, combine rice and water; heat to boiling over high heat. Reduce heat to low; cover and simmer, without stirring or lifting lid, until rice is tender and all liquid has been absorbed, 15 to 20 minutes.

Nutrition Spotlight: Radishes

Radishes, one of the cruciferous family members that have shown to be potent cancer fighters, are delicious raw in salads and as crudités. At only 10 calories a dozen, they're a noble, and spicy, alternative to the pedestrian carrot-sticks snack.

2. Meanwhile, prepare dressing: In large bowl, with wire whisk, mix vinegar, vegetable oil, ginger, sugar, salt, pepper, and sesame oil.

3. Add hot rice and frozen peas to dressing in bowl; set aside to cool slightly, about 10 minutes.

4. Serve salad at room temperature, or cover and refrigerate up to 4 hours. Toss with radishes, green onions, and almonds just before serving. Makes about 12 cups or 16 accompaniment servings.

Each serving: About 155 calories (23 percent calories from fat), 4g protein, 26g carbohydrate, 4g total fat (0g saturated), 0mg cholesterol, 285mg sodium.

Japanese Rice Salad

Prep: 20 minutes plus cooling   Cook: 30 minutes

Seasoned rice vinegar gives this salad its distinctive flavor.

- 1¹/2 **cups regular long-grain rice**
- 2 **teaspoons salt**
- 3 **tablespoons seasoned rice vinegar**
- 2 **tablespoons vegetable oil**
- 1 **teaspoon grated, peeled fresh ginger**
- ¹/4 **teaspoon ground black pepper**
- 4 **ounces green beans, trimmed and cut into ¹/4-inch pieces**
- 2 **carrots, peeled and shredded**
- 3 **green onions, thinly sliced**

1. Cook rice as label directs, using ¹/2 teaspoon salt. Prepare dressing: In large bowl, with wire whisk, mix vinegar, oil, ginger, ¹/2 teaspoon salt, and pepper. Add

rice and toss to coat. Let cool, tossing occasionally with fork, 30 minutes.

2. Meanwhile, in 2-quart saucepan, heat 2 cups water and remaining 1 teaspoon salt to boiling over high heat. Add green beans and cook until tender-crisp, 3 to 5 minutes. Drain and rinse with cold running water; drain.

3. Add green beans, carrots, and green onions to rice in bowl; toss until mixed and coated with dressing. Makes 8 accompaniment servings.

Each serving: About 175 calories (21 percent calories from fat), 3g protein, 32g carbohydrate, 4g total fat (0g saturated), 0mg cholesterol, 484mg sodium.

Barley Salad with Nectarines

Prep: 30 minutes   Cook: 55 minutes

Barley is another grain that makes a flavorful salad. You can use mangoes or peaches instead of the nectarines, if you prefer.

- 1 **package (16 ounces) pearl barley**
- 2³/4 **teaspoons salt**
- 4 **limes**
- 1/3 **cup olive oil**
- 1 **tablespoon sugar**
- 3/4 **teaspoon coarsely ground black pepper**
- 1¹/2 **pounds nectarines (4 medium), cut into 1/2-inch pieces**
- 1 **pound ripe tomatoes (2 large), seeded and cut into 1/2-inch pieces**
- 4 **green onions, thinly sliced**
- 1/2 **cup chopped fresh mint**

1. In 4-quart saucepan, heat 6 cups water to boiling over high heat. Add barley and 1¹/2 teaspoons salt; heat to boiling. Reduce heat; cover and simmer until barley is tender and liquid has been absorbed, about 45 minutes. (Barley will have creamy consistency.)

2. Meanwhile, from limes, grate 1 tablespoon peel and squeeze 1/2 cup juice. Prepare dressing: In large bowl, with wire whisk, mix lime peel, lime juice, oil, sugar, pepper, and remaining 1¹/4 teaspoons salt until blended.

3. Rinse barley with cold running water; drain. Add barley, nectarines, tomatoes, green onions, and mint to dressing in bowl; stir gently until mixed and coated with dressing. Serve at room temperature or cover and refrigerate up to 1 hour. Makes 16 accompaniment servings.

Each serving: About 172 calories (26 percent calories from fat), 4g protein, 30g carbohydrate, 5g total fat (1g saturated), 0mg cholesterol, 333mg sodium.

Tomato and Mint Tabbouleh

Prep: 20 minutes plus standing and chilling

Tabbouleh, the popular bulgur wheat and vegetable salad, is one of the best ways to enjoy tomatoes, cucumbers, and herbs.

1¹/2	**cups boiling water**
1¹/2	**cups bulgur (cracked wheat)**
¹/4	**cup fresh lemon juice**
1	**pound ripe tomatoes (3 medium), cut into ¹/2-inch pieces**
1	**medium cucumber (8 ounces), peeled and cut into ¹/2-inch pieces**
3	**green onions, chopped**
³/4	**cup loosely packed fresh flat-leaf parsley leaves, chopped**
¹/2	**cup loosely packed fresh mint leaves, chopped**
1	**tablespoon olive oil**
³/4	**teaspoon salt**
¹/4	**teaspoon coarsely ground black pepper**

1. In medium bowl, combine water, bulgur, and lemon juice, stirring to mix. Let stand until liquid has been absorbed, about 30 minutes.

2. To bulgur mixture, add tomatoes, cucumber, green onions, parsley, mint, oil, salt, and pepper, stirring to mix. Cover and refrigerate to blend flavors, at least 1 hour or up to 4 hours. Makes 12 accompaniment servings.

Each serving: About 87 calories (21 percent calories from fat), 3g protein, 17g carbohydrate, 2g total fat (0g saturated), 0mg cholesterol, 157mg sodium.

Warm Caesar Potato Salad

Prep: 5 minutes   Cook: 15 minutes

1¹/4	**pounds red potatoes, cut into ³/4-inch chunks**
2	**tablespoons light mayonnaise**
1	**tablespoon grated Parmesan cheese**
2	**teaspoons cider vinegar**
1	**teaspoon Dijon mustard**
¹/2	**teaspoon salt**
¹/4	**teaspoon coarsely ground black pepper**
¹/8	**teaspoon anchovy paste**
1	**green onion, sliced**

1. In 3-quart saucepan, heat potatoes and enough water to cover to boiling over high heat. Reduce heat to low, cover, and simmer until potatoes are fork-tender, about 15 minutes. Drain.

2. Meanwhile, prepare dressing: In large bowl, with wire whisk, mix mayonnaise, Parmesan, vinegar, mustard, salt, pepper and anchovy paste until blended.

3. Add potatoes to dressing in bowl and toss gently. Sprinkle with green onions. Makes 4 accompaniment servings.

Each serving: About 125 calories (7 percent calories from fat), 4g protein, 26g carbohydrate, 1g total fat (0g saturated), 2mg cholesterol, 415mg sodium.

Red Potato Salad

Prep: 25 minutes plus cooling   Cook: 30 minutes

In France, potato salad is prepared with a shallot vinaigrette and the freshest, smallest red potatoes available. A bit of crumbled bacon over the top makes it even better.

4   pounds small red potatoes, not peeled, each cut into quarters or eighths if large

3¹/₂   teaspoons salt

4   slices bacon

3   large shallots, chopped (³/₄ cup)

¹/₃   cup cider vinegar

¹/₄   cup olive oil

2   teaspoons sugar

2   teaspoons Dijon mustard

¹/₄   teaspoon coarsely ground black pepper

2   green onions, chopped

1. In 5-quart saucepot, combine potatoes, enough water to cover, and 2 teaspoons salt; heat to boiling over high heat. Reduce heat; cover and simmer until tender, 10 to 12 minutes.

2. Meanwhile, in 10-inch skillet, cook bacon over medium-low heat until browned. With slotted spoon, transfer to paper towels to drain; crumble. Discard all but 1 teaspoon bacon drippings from skillet. Reduce heat to low. Add shallots and cook, stirring, until tender, about 5 minutes. Remove from heat.

3. Prepare dressing: In large bowl, with wire whisk, mix shallots, vinegar, oil, sugar, mustard, remaining 1¹/₂ teaspoons salt, and pepper until blended.

4. Drain potatoes. Add hot potatoes to dressing in bowl. With rubber spatula, stir gently until potatoes absorb dressing. Let potatoes cool 30 minutes at room temperature, stirring occasionally. Stir in green onions.

5. Serve salad at room temperature or cover and refrigerate up to 4 hours. If chilled, let stand 30 minutes at room temperature before serving. To serve, sprinkle with crumbled bacon. Makes 12 accompaniment servings.

Each serving: About 185 calories (29 percent calories from fat), 4g protein, 29g carbohydrate, 6g total fat (1g saturated), 2mg cholesterol, 456mg sodium.

Roasted Potato Salad

Prep: 25 minutes   Roast: 45 minutes

Potatoes and shallots, roasted until tender and caramelized, become a spectacular salad when tossed with a lemon-Dijon dressing.

> 2   **pounds red potatoes (12 medium), not peeled, cut into 1¹/₂-inch pieces**
> 16   **small shallots, peeled, or 2 medium red onions, each cut into 8 wedges**
> 1   **teaspoon salt**
> ¹/₄   **teaspoon ground black pepper**
> 2   **tablespoons olive or vegetable oil**
> 8   **ounces French green beans (haricots verts) or regular green beans, trimmed**
> 1   **tablespoon fresh lemon juice**
> 1   **teaspoon Dijon mustard**

1. Preheat oven to 425°F. In large roasting pan (17" by 11¹/₂"), sprinkle potatoes and shallots with salt and pepper. Drizzle with 1 tablespoon oil and toss. Roast 30 minutes.

2. After vegetables have roasted 30 minutes, stir in green beans. Roast, stirring occasionally, until all vegetables are tender, about 15 minutes longer.

3. Meanwhile, prepare dressing: In large bowl, with wire whisk, mix lemon juice, remaining 1 tablespoon oil, and mustard until blended and smooth.

4. Add vegetables to dressing in bowl and toss to coat. Serve warm or at room temperature. Makes 6 accompaniment servings.

Each serving: About 212 calories (21 percent calories from fat), 5g protein, 39g carbohydrate, 5g total fat (1g saturated), 0mg cholesterol, 428mg sodium.

Tubetti Macaroni Salad

Prep: 25 minutes   Cook: 25 minutes

Carrots and celery add crunch to this lemon-scented salad. If the salad appears dry after chilling, stir in a touch of milk.

   1 **package (16 ounces) tubetti or ditalini pasta**
2 3/4 **teaspoons salt**
   4 **carrots, peeled and cut into 2" by 1/4" matchstick strips**
   1 **to 2 lemons**
 2/3 **cup light mayonnaise**
 1/3 **cup milk**
   2 **stalks celery, cut into 2" by 1/4" matchstick strips**
   2 **green onions, thinly sliced**

1. In large saucepot, cook pasta as label directs, using 2 teaspoons salt. After pasta has cooked 10 minutes, add carrots to pasta water and cook until carrots are just tender-crisp and pasta is done, 1 to 2 minutes longer.

2. Meanwhile, from lemon, grate 1 teaspoon peel and squeeze 3 tablespoons juice. Prepare dressing: In large bowl, with wire whisk, mix lemon peel, lemon juice, mayonnaise, milk, and remaining 3/4 teaspoon salt until blended.

3. Drain pasta and carrots; add to dressing in bowl, along with celery and green onions; toss until mixed and coated with dressing. Serve at room temperature or cover and refrigerate up to 4 hours. Makes 12 accompaniment servings.

Each serving: About 202 calories (22 percent calories from fat), 5g protein, 33g carbohydrate, 5g total fat (1g saturated), 5mg cholesterol, 463mg sodium.

Orzo Salad with Sun-Dried Tomatoes

Prep: 10 minutes plus cooling   Cook: 15 minutes

We used the tiny rice-shaped pasta to create an Italian summer salad.

   1 **package (16 ounces) orzo**
   2 **green onions, chopped**
 1/2 **cup drained oil-packed sun-dried tomatoes with herbs, coarsely chopped, with 1 tablespoon oil from tomatoes reserved**
   2 **tablespoons red wine vinegar**
   2 **teaspoons Dijon mustard**
 1/2 **teaspoon salt**
 1/4 **teaspoon coarsely ground black pepper**
 1/2 **cup loosely packed fresh basil leaves, cut into thin strips**

1. In large saucepot, cook orzo as label directs.

2. Meanwhile, in large bowl, combine green onions, tomatoes, reserved oil from tomatoes, vinegar, mustard, salt, and pepper.

3. Drain orzo. Add warm orzo to green-onion mixture in bowl, stirring to coat. Let orzo mixture cool slightly, then stir in basil. Serve at room temperature or cover and refrigerate until ready to serve. Makes about 7 cups or 8 accompaniment servings.

Each serving: About 240 calories (15 percent calories from fat), 8g protein, 44g carbohydrate, 4g total fat (0g saturated), 0mg cholesterol, 220mg sodium.

Tex-Mex Cobb Salad

Prep: 30 minutes

Warm Southwestern accents give this classic a new attitude.

- 1/4 **cup fresh lime juice**
- 2 **tablespoons chopped fresh cilantro leaves**
- 4 **teaspoons olive oil**
- 1 **teaspoon sugar**
- 1/4 **teaspoon ground cumin**
- 1/4 **teaspoon salt**
- 1/4 **teaspoon coarsely ground black pepper**
- 1 **medium head romaine lettuce (1 1/4 pounds), trimmed and leaves cut into 1/2-inch-wide strips**
- 1 **pint cherry tomatoes, each cut into quarters**
- 12 **ounces cooked skinless roast turkey meat, cut into 1/2-inch pieces (2 cups)**
- 1 **can (15 to 19 ounces) black beans, rinsed and drained**
- 2 **small cucumbers (6 ounces each), peeled, seeded, and sliced 1/2 inch thick**

1. Prepare dressing: In small bowl, with wire whisk, combine lime juice, cilantro, oil, sugar, cumin, salt, and pepper.

2. Place lettuce in large serving bowl. Arrange tomatoes, turkey, black beans, and cucumbers in rows over lettuce. Just before serving, toss salad with dressing. Makes 4 main-dish servings.

Each serving: About 310 calories (20 percent calories from fat), 39g protein, 32g carbohydrate, 7g total fat (1g saturated), 71mg cholesterol, 505mg sodium.

Rice Salad with Black Beans

Prep: 10 minutes   Cook: 20 minutes

A satisfying meal in one, this zesty salad is packed with the bright flavors of citrus, salsa, and cilantro.

- 3/4 **cup regular long-grain rice**
- 2 **large limes**
- 2 **cans (15 to 19 ounces each) black beans, rinsed and drained**
- 1 **bunch watercress, tough stems discarded**
- 1/2 **cup bottled salsa**
- 1 **cup corn kernels from cobs (about 2 ears)**
- 1/4 **cup packed fresh cilantro leaves, chopped**
- 1 **tablespoon olive oil**
- 1/2 **teaspoon salt**
- 1/4 **teaspoon coarsely ground black pepper**

1. Prepare rice as label directs. Meanwhile, from limes, grate 1/2 teaspoon peel and squeeze 3 tablespoons juice.

2. In large bowl, mix rice, lime peel, lime juice, beans, watercress, salsa, corn, cilantro, oil, salt, and pepper; toss well. Serve at room temperature or cover and refrigerate until ready to serve. Makes about 7 cups or 4 main-dish servings.

Each serving: About 405 calories (13 percent calories from fat), 24g protein, 81g carbohydrate, 6g total fat (1g saturated), 0mg cholesterol, 1125mg sodium.

Sesame Noodle and Chicken Salad

Prep: 25 minutes   Cook: 15 minutes

A great dish to make when you have leftover chicken.

- 12 **ounces linguine or spaghetti**
- 6 **ounces snow peas, strings removed and cut crosswise into thirds**
- 3/4 **cup very hot water**
- 1/4 **cup creamy peanut butter**
- 3 **tablespoons seasoned rice vinegar**
- 3 **tablespoons soy sauce**
- 1 **tablespoon light brown sugar**
- 1 **tablespoon minced, peeled fresh ginger**
- 1 **tablespoon Asian sesame oil**
- 1/4 **teaspoon ground red pepper (cayenne)**
- 1 **small garlic clove, crushed with garlic press**
- 2 **medium carrots, peeled and shredded**
- 3 **cups thinly sliced red cabbage (1/2 small head)**
- 12 **ounces boneless, roasted chicken, pulled into thin strips**

1. In large saucepot, cook pasta as label directs. During last minute of pasta cooking, add snow peas. Continue cooking until pasta is done. Drain linguine and snow peas. Rinse under cold running water to cool; drain again and set aside.

2. Meanwhile, prepare dressing: In large bowl, with wire whisk, mix hot water, peanut butter, rice vinegar, soy sauce, brown sugar, ginger, sesame oil, ground red pepper, and garlic until blended.

3. Add pasta, snow peas, carrots, red cabbage, and chicken to dressing in bowl; toss to blend. Makes 6 main-dish servings .

Each serving: About 460 calories (25 percent calories from fat), 28g protein, 58g carbohydrate, 13g total fat (3g saturated), 51mg cholesterol, 880mg sodium.

Curried Chicken-Mango Salad

Prep: 20 minutes

Precooked chicken from the deli or supermarket makes our salad a cinch. The recipe can easily be doubled if you need to feed a crowd.

1   **store-bought rotisserie chicken (2 pounds)**

1/4   **cup plain low-fat yogurt**

1/4   **cup light mayonnaise**

2   **tablespoons mango chutney, chopped**

1   **tablespoon fresh lime juice**

1   **teaspoon curry powder**

1   **large ripe mango, peeled and finely chopped**

1   **medium stalk celery, finely chopped**

1   **medium Granny Smith apple, cored and finely chopped**

1/2   **cup loosely packed fresh cilantro leaves, chopped**

1   **head leaf lettuce, separated and rinsed**

1. Remove skin from chicken; discard. With fingers, pull chicken meat into 1-inch pieces.

2. In large bowl, with wire whisk, mix yogurt, mayonnaise, chutney, lime juice, and curry powder until combined. Stir in chicken, mango, celery, apple, and cilantro until well coated. Serve salad on bed of lettuce leaves. Makes 4 main-dish servings.

Each serving: About 310 calories (26 percent calories from fat), 32g protein, 25g carbohydrate, 9g total fat (2g saturated), 95mg cholesterol, 255mg sodium.

Couscous and Smoked-Turkey Salad

Prep: 10 minutes   Cook: 5 minutes

If you see plums, peaches, or apricots at the farmers' market, try using them instead of the nectarines.

- **1   teaspoon ground cumin**
- **1   package (10 ounces) couscous (Moroccan pasta)**
- **1/3   cup dried tart cherries**
- **3   tablespoons fresh lemon juice**
- **2   tablespoons olive oil**
- **1   tablespoon Dijon mustard**
- **3/4   teaspoon salt**
- **1/4   teaspoon coarsely ground black pepper**
- **3   ripe medium nectarines, finely chopped**
- **4   ounces smoked turkey breast (in 1 piece), cut into 1/4-inch pieces**
- **Boston lettuce leaves**

1. In 3-quart saucepan, heat cumin over medium-high heat until fragrant, 1 to 3 minutes. In saucepan with cumin, prepare couscous as label directs, adding cherries but no salt or butter.

2. Meanwhile, prepare dressing: In large bowl, with wire whisk or fork, mix lemon juice, oil, mustard, salt, and pepper until blended.

3. Add warm couscous mixture, finely chopped nectarines, and turkey to dressing in bowl. Spoon salad onto large platter lined with Boston lettuce leaves. Makes about 7 1/2 cups or 6 main-dish servings.

Each serving: About 300 calories (18 percent calories from fat), 11g protein, 51g carbohydrate, 6g total fat (1g saturated), 3mg cholesterol, 470mg sodium.

Warm Pork Tenderloin Salad with Dijon Dressing

Prep: 20 minutes   Cook: 5 minutes

1   pork tenderloin (12 ounces), well trimmed

2   tablespoons dry sherry

1   tablespoon plus 1 1/2 teaspoons soy sauce

2   teaspoons grated, peeled fresh ginger

2   tablespoons light mayonnaise

2   tablespoons balsamic vinegar

1   tablespoon water

1   tablespoon Dijon mustard with seeds

1   teaspoon sugar

1/4 teaspoon coarsely ground black pepper

2   large heads Belgian endive, cut crosswise into
     1-inch-thick slices

1   small head radicchio, thinly sliced

2   bunches arugula (8 ounces), stems trimmed
     nonstick cooking spray

1   package (10 ounces) frozen peas, thawed

1. Holding knife almost parallel to the cutting surface, slice pork crosswise into very thin slices. In bowl, mix pork, sherry, soy sauce, and ginger; set aside.

2. In large bowl, with wire whisk, stir mayonnaise, vinegar, water, mustard, sugar, and pepper until blended. Add endive, radicchio, and arugula; toss well.

3. Spray nonstick 12-inch skillet lightly with nonstick cooking spray. Heat skillet over medium-high heat. Add pork mixture to skillet and cook, stirring quickly and constantly, until pork just loses its pink color, about 2 minutes.

4. Add pork and peas to salad; toss well. Makes 4 main-dish servings.

Each serving: About 230 calories (27 percent calories from fat), 24g protein, 17g carbohydrate, 7g total fat (2g saturated), 45mg cholesterol, 270mg sodium.

Side Dishes

6

Charred Peppers with Peaches,
page 196

Charred Peppers with Peaches

Prep: 30 minutes plus standing   Broil: 10 minutes

A welcome first course or side dish on its own, or as salad, served on a bed of Boston or Bibb lettuce.

- **1 large yellow pepper**
- **1 large red pepper**
- **1 tablespoon olive oil**
- **2 teaspoons fresh lemon juice**
- **1/2 teaspoon ground cumin**
- **1/4 teaspoon salt**
- **1/8 teaspoon ground red pepper (cayenne)**
- **3 large ripe peaches**

1. Preheat broiler. Line broiling pan (without rack) with foil. Cut each pepper lengthwise in half; discard stem and seeds. Arrange peppers, cut side down, in broiling pan. With hand, flatten each pepper half. Place pan in broiler 5 to 6 inches from source of heat and broil peppers until skins are charred and blistered, about 10 minutes. Wrap foil around peppers and allow to steam at room temperature 15 minutes or until cool enough to handle.

2. Remove peppers from foil. Peel off skins and discard. Cut peppers lengthwise into 1/2-inch-wide strips. Pat dry with paper towels.

3. In bowl, mix peppers with olive oil, lemon juice, cumin, salt, and ground red pepper. Cover and refrigerate if not serving right away.

4. To serve, peel, pit, and slice peaches; stir into pepper mixture. Serve at room temperature. Makes about 3 cups or 4 accompaniment or first-course servings.

Each serving: About 100 calories (27 percent calories from fat), 2g protein, 17g carbohydrate, 3g total fat (1g saturated), 0mg cholesterol, 135mg sodium.

Sesame Green Beans

Prep: 15 minutes   Cook: 20 minutes

These Asian-inspired green beans are served hot, but they are also delicious at room temperature.

- **1 teaspoon salt**
- **1 pound green beans, trimmed**
- **1 tablespoon soy sauce**
- **1/2 teaspoon Asian sesame oil**
- **1 1/2 teaspoons minced, peeled fresh ginger or**
  - **3/4 teaspoon ground ginger**
- **1 1/2 teaspoons sesame seeds, toasted**

1. In 4-quart saucepan, combine 7 cups water and salt; heat to boiling over high heat. Add green beans; heat to boiling. Cover and cook until just tender-crisp, 6 to 8 minutes. Drain; return green beans to saucepan.

2. Add soy sauce, sesame oil, and ginger to green beans in saucepan. Cook over low heat, stirring occasionally, until flavors have blended, about 3 minutes. Transfer to serving bowl and sprinkle with sesame seeds. Makes 4 accompaniment servings.

Each serving: About 45 calories (20 percent calories from fat), 2g protein, 8g carbohydrate, 1g total fat (0g saturated), 0mg cholesterol, 553mg sodium.

Sautéed Cabbage with Peas

Prep: 10 minutes   Cook: 25 minutes

Onion, sautéed until golden, adds wonderful nutty flavor to this simple side dish.

- **2 tablespoons margarine or butter**
- **1 medium onion, thinly sliced**
- **1 small head savoy cabbage (2 pounds), tough outer leaves discarded, cored, and cut into 1/2-inch-thick slices**
- **3/4 teaspoon salt**
- **1/2 teaspoon sugar**
- **1/4 teaspoon coarsely ground black pepper**
- **1/2 cup chicken broth**
- **1 package (10 ounces) frozen baby peas**
- **1/4 cup chopped fresh dill**

1. In 12-inch skillet, melt margarine over medium heat. Add onion and cook, stirring often, until tender and golden, about 8 minutes.

2. Add cabbage, salt, sugar, and pepper; cook, stirring often, until cabbage is tender-crisp, about 5 minutes. Stir in broth, and cook until cabbage is tender, about 10 minutes.

3. Add frozen peas and dill. Cook over medium heat, stirring frequently, until heated through, about 5 minutes. Makes about 6 cups or 8 accompaniment servings.

Each serving: About 90 calories (30 percent calories from fat), 4g protein, 13g carbohydrate, 3g total fat (1g saturated), 0mg cholesterol, 345mg sodium.

Microwave-Steamed Vegetables

Want fast, tasty vegetables? Follow these simple instructions and use the chart below to microwave-steam perfect veggies every time. And be sure to check out "12 Lowfat Ways to Dress Your Veggies" (page 201) for great sauces and flavor-boosters.

In a casserole dish, cook 1 pound vegetables (unless otherwise specified) with 1/4 cup water, covered, on high until tender, stirring halfway through cooking. Serve immediately.

VEGETABLE	MINUTES TO COOK
Asparagus	4 to 6
Beans, green or yellow wax	4 to 7
Beets, whole	10 to 14
Broccoli spears	5 to 6
Carrots, sliced	5 to 8
Cauliflower flowerets	5 to 6
Peas, shelled (1 cup)	4 to 5
Peppers, cut into strips	5 to 7
Spinach (10 ounces)	30 to 90 seconds
Vidalia onions (2), cut in half crosswise	7 to 8
Zucchini or yellow squash, sliced	4 to 7

Roasted Chestnuts

Prep: 30 minutes   Roast: 20 minutes

Chestnuts are an integral part of cold-weather cooking and can be presented in many guises; in almost any stuffing, added to your favorite vegetable medley, or pureed with sugar and vanilla and served with softly whipped cream for a special dessert.

1   pound fresh chestnuts

1. Preheat oven to 400°F. With sharp knife, cut an "x" in flat side of shell of each chestnut. Place in jelly-roll pan and roast chestnuts until shells open, about 20 minutes.

2. Cover chestnuts. When cool enough to handle, with paring knife, peel hot chestnuts, keeping unpeeled chestnuts warm for easier peeling. Makes 2 cups.

Each 1/2 cup: About 179 calories (10 percent calories from fat), 2g protein, 38g carbohydrate, 2g total fat (0g saturated), 0mg cholesterol, 3mg sodium.

Succotash

Prep: 10 minutes   Cook: 25 minutes

Corn and lima beans, two staples of Native American cooking, are combined to make this simple dish. The name succotash comes from the Narraganset word for "ear of corn."

5   slices bacon

3   stalks celery, cut into 1/4-inch-thick slices

1   medium onion, chopped

2   cans (151/4 to 16 ounces each) whole-kernel corn, drained

2   packages (10 ounces each) frozen baby lima beans

1/2   cup chicken broth

3/4   teaspoon salt

1/4   teaspoon coarsely ground black pepper

2   tablespoons chopped fresh parsley

1. In 12-inch skillet, cook bacon over medium-low heat until browned. With slotted spoon, transfer to paper towels to drain; crumble.

2. Discard all but 2 tablespoons bacon drippings from skillet. Add celery and onion and cook over medium heat, stirring, until vegetables are tender and golden, about 15 minutes. Stir in corn, frozen lima beans, broth, salt, and pepper; heat to boiling over high heat. Reduce heat; cover and simmer until heated through, 5 to 10 minutes longer. Stir in parsley and sprinkle with bacon. Makes 10 accompaniment servings.

Each serving: About 171 calories (26 percent calories from fat), 7g protein, 27g carbohydrate, 5g total fat (1g saturated), 5mg cholesterol, 458mg sodium.

Mixed Pea Pod Stir-Fry

Prep: 15 minutes   Cook: 16 minutes

This sweet and tender-crisp medley celebrates the glorious flavor of fresh green vegetables.

- **1 teaspoon salt**
- **8 ounces green beans, trimmed**
- **2 teaspoons vegetable oil**
- **4 ounces snow peas, trimmed and strings removed**
- **4 ounces sugar snap peas, trimmed and strings removed**
- **1 garlic clove, finely chopped**
- **1 tablespoon soy sauce**

1. In 12-inch skillet, combine 4 cups water and salt; heat to boiling over high heat. Add green beans and cook 3 minutes. Drain; wipe skillet dry with paper towels.

2. In same skillet, heat oil over high heat. Add green beans and cook, stirring frequently (stir-frying), until they begin to brown, 2 to 3 minutes. Add snow peas, sugar snap peas, and garlic; stir-fry until snow peas and sugar snap peas are tender-crisp, about 1 minute longer. Stir in soy sauce and remove from heat. Makes 4 accompaniment servings.

Each serving: About 63 calories (29 percent calories from fat), 3g protein, 8g carbohydrate, 2g total fat (0g saturated), 0mg cholesterol, 844mg sodium.

Peas and Fava Beans

Prep: 30 minutes plus cooling   Cook: 12 minutes

If you make this with fresh fava beans and peas, you'll have an extraordinary dish, but the frozen vegetables are almost as tasty.

4¹/₂ **pounds fresh fava beans or 2 packages (10 ounces each) frozen baby lima beans**

2 **ounces pancetta or 2 slices bacon, chopped**

1 **garlic clove, thinly sliced**

1 **package (10 ounces) frozen baby peas, thawed**

2 **tablespoons chopped fresh parsley**

¹/₄ **teaspoon salt**

¹/₈ **teaspoon ground black pepper**

1. Remove fava beans from shells and place in colander in sink. In 4-quart saucepan, heat 8 cups water to boiling over high heat. Pour boiling water over beans. When cool enough to handle, remove outer skins from fava beans. (If using lima beans, cook as label directs.)

2. In 10-inch skillet, cook pancetta and garlic over medium heat, stirring, until pancetta crisps, about 8 minutes.

3. Add peas, parsley, salt, and pepper and cook, stirring, 2 minutes. Add fava beans and cook, stirring, 2 minutes longer. Makes 6 accompaniment servings.

Each serving: About 149 calories (24 percent calories from fat), 10g protein, 19g carbohydrate, 4g total fat (1g saturated), 6mg cholesterol, 312mg sodium.

Zucchini and Sugar Snap Peas

Prep: 10 minutes   Cook: 20 minutes

1   **tablespoon vegetable oil**

3   **medium zucchini (8 ounces each), cut into 1¹/₂-inch chunks**

¹/₂   **pound sugar snap peas, stem and strings removed along both edges of each pea pod**

2   **green onions, cut into ¹/₂-inch pieces**

1   **tablespoon chopped fresh oregano or ¹/₂ teaspoon dried oregano leaves**

³/₄   **teaspoon salt**

¹/₄   **teaspoon coarsely ground black pepper**

Heat oil in nonstick 12-inch skillet over medium-high heat. Add zucchini, snap peas, green onions, oregano, salt, and pepper. Cook, stirring frequently, until vegetables are golden and tender-crisp, 8 to 10 minutes. Makes 6 accompaniment servings.

Each serving: About 275 calories (13 percent calories from fat), 17g protein, 47g carbohydrate, 4g total fat (1g saturated), 0mg cholesterol, 295mg sodium.

12 Low-fat Ways to Dress Your Veggies

Boost the flavor—not the fat—with these simple alternatives to classic butter, cheese, and cream sauces.

• Make a mock hollandaise by mixing light mayonnaise with Dijon mustard, fresh lemon juice, and a pinch of ground red pepper. Drizzle cool sauce over steamed cauliflower, broccoli or—the classic partner—asparagus.

• Cook minced garlic and a pinch of red pepper flakes in a teaspoon of olive oil until fragrant. Add fresh spinach or Swiss chard to pan and cook until wilted.

• Toss chopped mixed fresh herbs (such as basil, mint, and oregano) and grated lemon zest with boiled potato halves.

• Heat chopped fresh tomato with crushed fennel seeds in a skillet until hot. Spoon over baked or broiled eggplant slices.

• Toast bread crumbs with chopped garlic in a teaspoon of olive oil. Sprinkle over steamed yellow squash with chopped parsley.

• Slice Canadian bacon (it's surprisingly low-fat) into thin strips and cook in a nonstick skillet until golden. Toss with steamed collard greens or spinach.

• Chop some mango chutney (available in the supermarket international or gourmet-food section) and mix into carrots or cauliflower.

• Thin orange marmalade with water and heat with ground ginger. Stir into hot green beans or broccoli.

• When steaming bitter greens like Swiss chard, add a handful of raisins for sweetness.

• Blend prepared horseradish, Dijon mustard, and light mayonnaise; drizzle over steamed green beans.

• Whisk together seasoned rice vinegar, soy sauce, and grated fresh ginger to taste. Use as a dipping sauce for tender-crisp broccoli.

• Flavor cooked green beans with a dusting of freshly grated Parmesan cheese (a little goes a long way) and crackled black pepper.

Venetian-Style Zucchini

Prep: 20 minutes plus marinating   Roast: 20 minutes

In the traditional Italian method of preparing vegetables agrodolce (literally, "sweet and sour"), thin zucchini slices are fried in oil, then marinated in a mint, raisin, and balsamic vinegar mixture. Here we've roasted them instead.

3 **tablespoons golden raisins**

3 **tablespoons balsamic vinegar**

1 **tablespoon finely chopped fresh mint leaves**

1 **teaspoon dark brown sugar**

1/2 **teaspoon salt**

1/8 **teaspoon ground black pepper**

1 **garlic clove, peeled and cut in half**

8 **small zucchini (5 ounces each), cut crosswise into 1/4-inch slices**

1 **tablespoon vegetable oil**

1 **tablespoon pine nuts, toasted**

1. In large bowl, mix raisins, vinegar, mint, brown sugar, salt, pepper, and garlic; set aside.

2. Preheat oven to 450°F. Arrange zucchini in two 15 1/2" by 10 1/2" jelly-roll pans and drizzle with oil. Roast zucchini on 2 oven racks, rotating pans between upper and lower racks halfway through roasting time, until tender and golden at edges, about 20 minutes.

3. Stir hot zucchini into vinegar mixture in bowl. Let stand at room temperature at least 1 hour to marinate. Or, cover and refrigerate up to 3 days.

4. Serve at room temperature, topped with pine nuts. Makes about 3 cups or 6 accompaniment servings.

Each serving: About 95 calories (28 percent calories from fat), 3g protein, 12g carbohydrate, 3g total fat (1g saturated), 0mg cholesterol, 185mg sodium.

Roasted Beets and Red Onions

Prep: 20 minutes   Roast: 1 hour 30 minutes

Roasting brings out and concentrates the natural sweetness in vegetables. In this recipe, the beets and onions are roasted, then tossed with a simple balsamic sauce that enhances their rich flavors.

- 2 **pounds beets with tops (6 medium)**
- 3 **small red onions (1 pound), unpeeled**
  - **nonstick cooking spray**
- 1/3 **cup fat-free chicken broth**
- 1/4 **cup balsamic vinegar**
- 1 **teaspoon dark brown sugar**
- 1 **teaspoon fresh thyme leaves**
- 1/4 **teaspoon salt**
- 1/4 **teaspoon coarsely ground black pepper**
  - **finely chopped fresh parsley leaves**

1. Trim tops from beets, leaving about 1 inch of stems attached. Scrub beets well under cold running water.

2. Preheat oven to 400°F. Place beets and unpeeled red onions in 10-inch oven-safe skillet or 13" by 9" metal baking pan. Coat vegetables lightly with nonstick cooking spray. Roast vegetables, shaking skillet occasionally, until onions are soft to the touch and beets are fork-tender, at least 1 hour and 30 minutes, depending on size of vegetables. (Beets may take longer than onions to roast; remove onions as they are done and continue roasting beets.)

3. Transfer vegetables to plate to cool slightly. Meanwhile, add broth, vinegar, brown sugar, and thyme to same skillet. Heat to boiling over high heat. Boil, stirring and scraping bottom of skillet, until liquid is dark brown and syrupy and reduced to about 1/4 cup, 5 to 7 minutes. Stir in salt and pepper. Remove skillet from heat.

4. Peel beets and onions when cool enough to handle. Cut beets into 2" by 1/4" matchstick strips and onions into thin rings; place in bowl. Pour reduced liquid over vegetables. Serve at room temperature, sprinkled with parsley. Makes about 4 cups or 6 accompaniment servings.

Each serving: About 120 calories (0 percent calories from fat), 2g protein, 18g carbohydrate, 0g total fat, 0mg cholesterol, 195mg sodium.

Apricot-Ginger Carrots

Prep: 10 minutes   Cook: 20 minutes

Here's a great way to dress up pre-peeled baby carrots.

- **2 bags (16 ounces each) peeled baby carrots**
- **2 tablespoons margarine or butter**
- **2 green onions, finely chopped**
- **1 large garlic clove, finely chopped**
- **1 tablespoon minced, peeled fresh ginger**
- **1/3 cup apricot jam**
- **1 tablespoon balsamic vinegar**
- **1/4 teaspoon salt**
- **pinch ground red pepper (cayenne)**

1. Place steamer basket in deep 12-inch skillet with 1 inch water. Heat to boiling over high heat. Add carrots and reduce heat to medium. Cover and steam just until carrots are tender, 10 to 12 minutes. Remove carrots and rinse with cold running water to stop cooking; drain well.

2. In 12-inch skillet, melt margarine over medium heat. Add green onions, garlic, and ginger; cook, stirring often, until soft, about 3 minutes. Add apricot jam, vinegar, salt, and ground red pepper; cook, stirring often, 3 to 4 minutes longer.

3. Add carrots to glaze in skillet and cook over medium-high heat 5 minutes. Increase heat to high and cook, stirring occasionally, until carrots are well coated and heated through, 3 minutes. Makes about 6 1/2 cups or 8 accompaniment servings.

Each serving: About 115 calories (23 percent calories from fat), 1g protein, 22g carbohydrate, 3g total fat (1g saturated), 0mg cholesterol, 145mg sodium.

Baby Potatoes with Rosemary

Prep: 20 minutes   Roast: 30 to 40 minutes

For the best golden brown potatoes, roast them with olive oil and herbs in a hot oven. Instead of baby potatoes, you can also use larger potatoes cut into bite-size pieces.

- **5 pounds assorted small potatoes, such as red, white, purple, or golden, cut in half**
- **1/4 cup olive oil**
- **2 tablespoons chopped fresh rosemary or thyme or 1 teaspoon dried rosemary or thyme**
- **1 1/2 teaspoons salt**
- **1/2 teaspoon coarsely ground black pepper**

Preheat oven to 425°F. In large roasting pan (17" by 11 1/2"), toss potatoes, oil, rosemary, salt, and pepper to coat. Roast potatoes, turning occasionally, until golden and tender, 30 to 40 minutes. Makes 10 accompaniment servings.

Each serving: About 232 calories (23 percent calories from fat), 4g protein, 41g carbohydrate, 6g total fat (1g saturated), 0mg cholesterol, 366mg sodium.

Herbed Packet Potatoes

Prep: 15 minutes   Bake: 30 minutes

Potato chunks tossed with parsley and butter cook into tender morsels when foil-wrapped.

- **2** **tablespoons butter or margarine**
- **1** **tablespoon chopped fresh parsley**
- **1/2** **teaspoon freshly grated lemon peel**
- **1/2** **teaspoon salt**
- **1/8** **teaspoon coarsely ground black pepper**
- **1 1/2** **pounds small red potatoes, cut in half**

1. Preheat oven to 450°F. In 3-quart saucepan, melt butter with parsley, lemon peel, salt, and pepper over medium-low heat. Remove saucepan from heat; add potatoes and toss well to coat.

2. Place potato mixture in center of 24" by 18" sheet of heavy-duty foil. Fold edges over and pinch to seal tightly.

3. Place package in jelly-roll pan and bake until potatoes are tender when potatoes are pierced (through foil) with knife, about 30 minutes. Makes 6 accompaniment servings.

Each serving: About 126 calories (29 percent calories from fat), 2g protein, 20g carbohydrate, 4g total fat (2g saturated), 10mg cholesterol, 241mg sodium.

Mashed Potatoes with Horseradish Cream

Prep: 25 minutes   Bake: 20 minutes

We used buttery Yukon Golds for this addictive dish. You can make the potatoes a day ahead and refrigerate. When ready to serve, top with horseradish cream and bake until hot and golden.

- **4 pounds Yukon Gold potatoes (12 medium), peeled and cut into 1-inch chunks**
- **1 container (8 ounces) reduced-fat sour cream**
- **3 tablespoons snipped fresh chives**
- **1/2 cup reduced-fat (2%) milk, warmed**
- **1 teaspoon salt**
- **1/4 cup light mayonnaise**
- **2 tablespoons bottled white horseradish**
- **1/4 teaspoon coarsely ground black pepper**

1. Preheat oven to 450°F. In 6-quart saucepan, heat potatoes and enough water to cover to boiling over high heat. Reduce heat to low; cover and simmer until potatoes are fork-tender, about 15 minutes. Drain well and return potatoes to saucepan.

2. Meanwhile, reserve 1/4 cup sour cream and 1 tablespoon snipped chives to use later in topping.

3. With potato masher, mash potatoes with milk, salt, remaining sour cream, and chives until smooth. Spoon potato mixture into shallow 2 1/2-quart casserole.

4. In small bowl, stir mayonnaise with horseradish, pepper, reserved sour cream, and reserved snipped chives. Spread horseradish mixture over mashed potatoes.

5. Bake potatoes until hot and bubbly and top is lightly browned, about 20 minutes. Makes 10 cups or 12 accompaniment servings.

Each serving: About 130 calories (14 percent calories from fat), 4g protein, 25g carbohydrate, 2g total fat (0g saturated), 2g fiber, 7mg cholesterol, 275mg sodium.

Oven Fries

Prep: 10 minutes　Bake: 45 minutes

A quick way to make crispy "fries" without frying—just don't crowd them in the pan, or they won't crisp.

- **3　medium baking potatoes or sweet potatoes (8 ounces each), not peeled**
- **1　tablespoon vegetable oil**
- **1/2　teaspoon salt**
- **1/8　teaspoon ground black pepper**

1. Preheat oven to 425°F. Cut each potato lengthwise into quarters, then cut each quarter lengthwise into 3 wedges.

2. In jelly-roll pan, toss potatoes, oil, salt, and pepper to coat. Bake, turning occasionally, until tender, about 45 minutes. Makes 4 accompaniment servings.

Each serving: About 156 calories (23 percent calories from fat), 4g protein, 28g carbohydrate, 4g total fat (0g saturated), 0mg cholesterol, 301mg sodium.

Mashed Potatoes with Caramelized Onions

Prep: 25 minutes　Cook: 35 minutes

Sweet caramelized onions folded into creamy mashed potatoes are especially inviting when served with roasted meats.

- **3　tablespoons olive oil**
- **3　large red onions (2 1/4 pounds), thinly sliced**
- **2　teaspoons salt**
- **2 1/2　pounds baking potatoes (5 medium), peeled and cut into 1-inch pieces**
- **1/3　cup milk**
- **1/8　teaspoon coarsely ground black pepper**

1. In 12-inch skillet, heat oil over medium heat. Add onions and 1/4 teaspoon salt; cook, stirring occasionally, until very tender and deep golden brown, about 30 minutes.

2. Meanwhile, in 4-quart saucepan, combine potatoes, enough water to cover, and 1 teaspoon salt; heat to boiling over high heat. Reduce heat; cover and simmer until tender, about 15 minutes. Drain.

3. Return potatoes to saucepan. Coarsely mash potatoes with milk, remaining 3/4 teaspoon salt, and pepper. Stir in all but 2 tablespoons caramelized onions; heat through. Spoon potato mixture into serving bowl and top with remaining caramelized onions. Makes 6 accompaniment servings.

Each serving: About 242 calories (30 percent calories from fat), 6g protein, 40g carbohydrate, 8g total fat (1g saturated), 2mg cholesterol, 808mg sodium.

Potato Pointers

Select potatoes that are firm and smooth. Avoid any with wrinkled skins, bruises, discolorations, or sprouts. Store the potatoes in a cool, dark place—but not in the refrigerator, where the starch converts to sugar and the nutrient value is reduced. Also important: Do not store potatoes with onions. Each vegetable releases a gas that hastens the spoilage of the other.

Gently scrub potatoes with a vegetable brush just before using; washing them in advance shortens their storage life. For even cooking, pick ones of uniform size. To prevent peeled potatoes from turning dark, toss with lemon juice.

Twice-Baked Potatoes

Prep: 35 minutes   Bake: 1 hour 10 minutes

For this family favorite, you roast the garlic along with the potatoes. You can make the potatoes ahead: After stuffing the potatoes, cover the jelly-roll pan and refrigerate. Reheat in a preheated 350°F. oven for 30 minutes.

- **1** whole large head garlic
- **1** teaspoon olive oil
- **10** small baking potatoes (5 ounces each)*
- **1** tablespoon chopped fresh parsley leaves
- **1/2** teaspoon salt
- **1/4** teaspoon coarsely ground black pepper
- **1/4** cup plus 2 tablespoons grated Parmesan cheese
- **1/2** cup heavy or whipping cream

1. Preheat oven to 450°F. Remove any loose papery skin from garlic, leaving head intact. Cut top from head, just to tip of cloves (do not cut into cloves). Place head on sheet of heavy-duty foil; drizzle with olive oil. Loosely wrap foil around garlic, being careful that seam is folded to seal in oil.

2. Place potatoes and wrapped garlic on oven rack. Bake 45 minutes or until potatoes and garlic are fork-tender. Transfer to wire rack; cool slightly. Turn oven control to 350°F.

3. Open garlic package carefully and discard foil. Separate cloves from head and scrape or squeeze out

pulp from each clove into a large mixing bowl. Slice each potato lengthwise in half. With spoon, carefully scoop out potato flesh into bowl with garlic, leaving potato-skin shells intact. Place the 12 prettiest potato shells in 15½" by 10½" jelly-roll pan. If you like, refrigerate remaining 8 shells for another use.

4. With mixer at low speed, beat garlic and potatoes with parsley, salt, pepper, and ¼ cup Parmesan until garlic and potatoes are broken up. Add cream and beat until almost smooth, about 30 seconds (do not overbeat; potato mixture will become gummy).

5. Spoon mixture into potato shells on jelly-roll pan; sprinkle with remaining 2 tablespoons Parmesan.

6. Bake potatoes in jelly-roll pan until hot on the inside and golden on top, 20 to 30 minutes. Makes 12 accompaniment servings.

*Find small baking potatoes in 5-pound bags.

Each serving: About 150 calories (30 percent calories from fat), 4g protein, 23g carbohydrate, 5g total fat (3g saturated), 16mg cholesterol, 155mg sodium.

Sauté of Potatoes, Tomatoes and Fresh Corn
Prep: 30 minutes   Cook: 40 minutes

Accented with fresh tarragon and a lemony dressing, this simple side dish is perfect with steak.

- **4 tablespoons olive oil**
- **2 pounds small red potatoes, cut into 1-inch chunks**
- **2 pints cherry tomatoes**
- **4 cups corn kernels cut from cobs (about 8 ears)**
- **2 teaspoons chopped fresh tarragon leaves**
- **2 tablespoons fresh lemon juice**
- **3/4 teaspoon salt**
- **1/4 teaspoon coarsely ground black pepper**

1. In nonstick 12-inch skillet, heat 1 tablespoon olive oil over medium heat. Add potato chunks and cook, stirring occasionally, until potatoes are browned on the outside and tender on the inside, about 35 minutes. Transfer potatoes to large bowl.

2. In same skillet, heat 1 more tablespoon oil; add whole cherry tomatoes and cook, stirring, 2 minutes. Add corn and tarragon, and cook 2 minutes longer. Transfer tomato mixture to bowl with potatoes.

Nutrition Spotlight: Sweet Corn

Sweet corn is one of the tastiest sources of folic acid. It's often mistakenly dismissed as a dieter's foe, but rest assured: One ear of fresh yellow or white corn has only 80 calories (if it's not slathered in butter, of course). Because its natural sugars start converting to starch as soon as it's picked, corn should be bought fresh and cooked the same day to preserve its sweetness.

3. In cup, mix lemon juice, salt, pepper, and remaining 2 tablespoons olive oil; pour over potato mixture and toss to combine. Makes about 12 cups or 12 accompaniment servings.

Each serving: About 165 calories (27 percent calories from fat), 4g protein, 28g carbohydrate, 5g total fat (1g saturated), 0mg cholesterol, 150mg sodium.

Brown Butter Sweet Potatoes

Prep: 15 minutes   Cook: 20 minutes

Just four ingredients! This can be made well ahead and then, just before serving, reheated either in a microwave or a double boiler.

> **4** **pounds sweet potatoes (8 medium), peeled and cut into 2-inch chunks**
>
> **6** **tablespoons butter (do not use margarine)**
>
> **1/4** **cup light molasses**
>
> **1/2** **teaspoon salt**

1. In 5-quart saucepot, heat sweet potatoes and enough water to cover to boiling over high heat. Reduce heat to low; cover and simmer until sweet potatoes are fork-tender, about 20 minutes. Drain well and return sweet potatoes to saucepot.

2. Meanwhile, in 1-quart saucepan, cook butter over medium heat until browned but not burned, 5 to 7 minutes (butter should be the color of maple syrup).

3. With potato masher, mash sweet potatoes with brown butter, molasses, and salt until smooth. Makes 12 accompaniment servings.

Each serving: About 180 calories (30 percent calories from fat), 2g protein, 30g carbohydrate, 6g total fat (4g saturated), 15mg cholesterol, 160mg sodium.

Candied Sweet Potatoes

Prep: 30 minutes   Bake: 40 minutes

If there are marshmallow lovers in the family, top the already baked casserole with mini marshmallows and place in the oven for an extra 10 minutes. Do-ahead: This dish can be made through Step 1, covered, and refrigerated overnight. When ready to serve, continue with Steps 2 and 3.

> **4** **pounds sweet potatoes (8 medium), peeled and sliced into 1-inch-thick rounds**
>
> **1/2** **cup packed dark brown sugar**
>
> **1/4** **cup water**
>
> **4** **tablespoons margarine or butter**
>
> **3/4** **teaspoon salt**
>
> **1/4** **teaspoon coarsely ground black pepper**
>
> **pinch nutmeg**

1. In 6-quart saucepot, heat potatoes and enough water to cover to boiling over high heat. Reduce heat to low; cover and simmer until potatoes are barely fork-tender (slightly underdone), about 5 minutes. Drain well and place potatoes in shallow 2-quart casserole.

2. Preheat oven to 400°F. In 10-inch skillet, heat water, brown sugar, margarine, salt, pepper, and nutmeg over medium heat, stirring frequently, until margarine melts, about 3 minutes. Drizzle mixture evenly over potatoes.

3. Bake casserole, uncovered, basting potatoes occasionally with sugar mixture and turning slices over halfway through cooking, until potatoes are tender and lightly browned and sugar mixture thickens slightly, about 40 minutes. Makes 12 accompaniment servings.

Each serving: About 205 calories (18 percent calories from fat), 2g protein, 41g carbohydrate, 4g total fat (1g saturated), 0mg cholesterol, 205mg sodium.

Pan-Roasted Sweet Potato Chunks

Prep: 10 minutes   Cook: 22 minutes

Here's how to prepare sweet potatoes quickly: Cut them up and cook in a skillet on top of the stove.

1¹/₂   pounds sweet potatoes (2 large), peeled and cut into 1-inch pieces

2   tablespoons butter or margarine

1/4   teaspoon salt

1/8   teaspoon ground black pepper

In 12-inch skillet, melt butter over medium-low heat. Add sweet potatoes; cover and cook, turning occasionally, until tender and browned, about 20 minutes. Sprinkle with salt and pepper. Makes 4 accompaniment servings.

Each serving: About 180 calories (30 percent calories from fat), 2g protein, 30g carbohydrate, 6g total fat (4g saturated), 16mg cholesterol, 218mg sodium.

Aromatic Rice

Prep: 5 minutes   Cook: 25 minutes

Follow these basic directions to cook up fluffy rice, then add the desired flavoring for one of the six options below.

- **1   cup chicken broth**
- **3/4   cup water**
- **1   cup regular long-grain rice**
- **1/4   teaspoon salt**
- **seasonings (below)**

In 3-quart saucepan, heat broth and water to boiling over high heat. Stir in rice and salt; heat to boiling. Reduce heat to low; cover and simmer, without stirring or lifting lid, until rice is tender and all liquid has been absorbed, 18 to 20 minutes. Remove from heat and let stand 5 minutes. Fluff rice with fork and stir in seasonings. Makes about 3 cups or 4 accompaniment servings.

Each serving (without seasoning): About 176 calories (5 percent calories from fat), 4g protein, 37g carbohydrate, 1g total fat (0g saturated), 0mg cholesterol, 395mg sodium.

Lemon-Parsley Rice

Cook as directed. Stir in 2 tablespoons chopped fresh parsley and 1 teaspoon freshly grated lemon peel.

Asian Rice

Cook as directed but omit salt. Stir in 2 green onions, chopped, 2 teaspoons soy sauce, and 1/4 teaspoon Asian sesame oil.

Lemon-Parmesan Rice

Cook as directed. Stir in 1/4 cup freshly grated Parmesan cheese, 1 teaspoon freshly grated lemon peel, and 1/4 teaspoon ground black pepper.

Pepper Jack Rice

Cook as directed. Stir in 2 ounces (1/2 cup) Monterey Jack cheese with jalapeño chiles, shredded, and 3 green onions, thinly sliced.

Coconut Rice

Cook as directed. Stir in 1/2 cup unsweetened coconut milk, 1/2 teaspoon freshly grated lime peel, and pinch ground red pepper (cayenne).

Green Rice

Cook as directed but after the rice has cooked 15 minutes, stir in 1 package (10 ounces) frozen chopped spinach, thawed; cover and cook 5 minutes longer. Stir in 2 ounces (1/2 cup) feta cheese, finely crumbled.

Confetti Rice Pilaf

Prep: 35 minutes   Bake: 30 minutes

Tender rice with peas, carrots, and green onions—this colorful side dish goes well with a simple roast chicken or pork.

- **3   tablespoons margarine or butter**
- **2   medium carrots, finely chopped**
- **2   cups regular long-grain rice**
- **2   cups water**
- **1   can (14 1/2 ounces) chicken broth or 1 3/4 cups homemade**
- **1   small bay leaf**
- **1/2   teaspoon salt**
- **1/4   teaspoon coarsely ground black pepper**
- **1   package (10 ounces) frozen peas**
- **2   medium green onions, sliced**

1. In 3-quart saucepan, melt margarine over medium heat. Add carrots and cook, stirring occasionally, until slightly softened, 2 to 3 minutes. Add rice and cook, stirring, until grains are coated, 1 minute. Stir in water, broth, bay leaf, salt, and pepper; heat to boiling over high heat. Reduce heat to low; cover and simmer, without stirring or lifting lid, until all liquid is absorbed and rice is tender, 15 to 20 minutes.

2. Preheat oven to 350°F. Discard bay leaf from rice; stir in peas and green onions. Transfer mixture to shallow 2 1/2-quart baking dish.

3. Cover pilaf and bake until heated through, about 30 minutes. Makes about 8 cups or 12 accompaniment servings.

Each serving: About 165 calories (16 percent calories from fat), 4g protein, 29g carbohydrate, 3g total fat (1g saturated), 0mg cholesterol, 260mg sodium.

Wheat Berry Pilaf
Prep: 30 minutes   Cook: 1 hour

You'll love this veggie-flecked combination of nutty wheat berries and brown rice.

- **1 cup wheat berries (whole-grain wheat)***
- **1/2 cup long-grain brown rice**
- **3 teaspoons olive oil**
- **4 medium carrots, finely chopped**
- **2 medium stalks celery, finely chopped**
- **1 large onion, finely chopped**
- **1 can (14 1/2 ounces) chicken broth or 1 3/4 cup homemade**
- **1/2 pound green beans, trimmed and cut into 1 1/2-inch pieces**
- **3/4 teaspoon salt**
- **1/2 teaspoon freshly grated orange peel**
- **1/4 teaspoon coarsely ground black pepper**
- **1/4 teaspoon dried thyme**
- **3/4 cup dried cranberries**

1. In 3-quart saucepan, heat wheat berries and 4 cups water to boiling over high heat. Reduce heat to low; cover and simmer until wheat berries are firm to the bite but tender enough to eat, about 50 minutes. Drain and set aside.

2. Meanwhile, in 2-quart saucepan, prepare brown rice as label directs, but do not add butter or salt.

3. While wheat berries and brown rice are cooking, in deep 12-inch skillet, heat 2 teaspoons olive oil over medium heat. Add carrots and celery; cook, stirring occasionally, until almost tender, about 10 minutes. Add onion and 1 more teaspoon olive oil; cook, stirring occasionally, until vegetables are lightly browned, 12 to 15 minutes longer.

4. Increase heat to high; add broth, green beans, salt, orange peel, pepper, and thyme. Heat to boiling. Reduce heat to medium-high; cook, stirring often, until green beans are just tender, about 5 minutes.

5. Add cranberries, wheat berries, and brown rice to skillet, stirring to mix well; heat through. Makes about 8 cups or 8 accompaniment servings.

*Wheat berries are unmilled whole wheat kernels that have a delicious nutty, toasted flavor. Look for them in health-food stores and some supermarkets.

Each serving: About 210 calories (13 percent calories from fat), 7g protein, 42g carbohydrate, 3g total fat (1g saturated), 0mg cholesterol, 395mg sodium.

Wild Rice and Orzo Pilaf

Prep: 25 minutes Cook: 45 minutes

You can prepare this and refrigerate it for up to 2 days, then bake just before serving.

1¼ **cups orzo pasta (8 ounces)**

1 **cup wild rice (6 ounces)**

3 **tablespoons margarine or butter**

1 **small onion, finely chopped**

1 **medium stalk celery, finely chopped**

1 **pound medium mushrooms, trimmed and sliced**

2 **teaspoons chopped fresh thyme leaves**

1 **teaspoon salt**

¼ **teaspoon coarsely ground black pepper**

1. Prepare orzo and wild rice, separately, as labels direct.

2. Meanwhile, in 12-inch skillet, melt margarine over medium heat. Add onion and celery, and cook, stirring occasionally, until tender, about 10 minutes. Add mushrooms, thyme, salt, and pepper; cook, stirring occasionally, until mushrooms are tender and liquid evaporates, about 10 minutes longer.

3. Preheat oven to 350°F. In shallow 2½-quart baking dish, stir orzo, rice, and mushroom mixture until blended. Cover and bake until heated through, about 35 minutes. Makes about 9 cups or 12 accompaniment servings.

Each serving: About 155 calories (17 percent calories from fat), 5g protein, 26g carbohydrate, 3g total fat (1g saturated), 0mg cholesterol, 220mg sodium.

Mushroom Risotto

Prep: 20 minutes plus standing Cook: 45 minutes

Just a few dried porcini mushrooms add deep earthy flavor to ordinary white mushrooms. The flavorful soaking liquid is used, too, so don't throw it out.

½ **cup boiling water**

½ **ounce dried porcini mushrooms**

3¼ **cups water**

1 **can (14½ ounces) chicken or vegetable broth or 1¾ cups homemade**

2 **tablespoons butter or margarine**

1 **pound white mushrooms, trimmed and sliced**

1¼ **teaspoons salt**

¼ **teaspoon ground black pepper**

pinch dried thyme

1 **tablespoon olive oil**

1 **small onion, finely chopped**

2 **cups Arborio rice (Italian short-grain rice) or medium-grain rice**

½ **cup dry white wine**

½ **cup freshly grated Parmesan cheese**

2 **tablespoons chopped fresh parsley**

1. In small bowl, pour boiling water over porcini mushrooms; let stand 30 minutes. With slotted spoon, remove porcini. Rinse mushrooms to remove any grit, then chop. Strain mushroom liquid through sieve lined with paper towels into separate small bowl.

2. In 2-quart saucepan, heat water, broth, and mushroom liquid to boiling over high heat. Reduce heat to maintain simmer; cover.

3. Meanwhile, in 4-quart saucepan, melt butter over medium heat. Add white mushrooms, ½ teaspoon salt, pepper, and thyme. Cook, stirring occasionally, until mushrooms are tender and liquid has evaporated, about 10 minutes. Stir in chopped porcini. Transfer to bowl.

4. In same saucepan, heat oil over medium heat. Add onion and cook until tender, about 5 minutes. Add

rice and remaining 3/4 teaspoon salt and cook, stirring frequently, until rice grains are opaque. Add wine; cook until wine has been absorbed. Add about 1/2 cup simmering broth to rice, stirring until liquid has been absorbed. Continue cooking, adding remaining broth 1/2 cup at a time and stirring after each addition, until all liquid has been absorbed and rice is tender but still firm, about 25 minutes (risotto should have a creamy consistency). Stir in mushroom mixture, Parmesan, and parsley; heat through. Makes 4 main-dish servings.

Each serving: About 504 calories (27 percent calories from fat), 16g protein, 77g carbohydrate, 15g total fat (7g saturated), 25mg cholesterol, 1,447mg sodium.

Fast "Baked" Beans

Prep: 10 minutes   Cook: 15 minutes

Choose a variety of canned beans and add special seasonings and molasses for homemade flavor.

    2 **teaspoons olive oil**
    1 **small onion, finely chopped**
    1 **cup ketchup**
  1/2 **cup water**
    3 **tablespoons light molasses**
    1 **tablespoon Dijon mustard**
  1/2 **teaspoon Worcestershire sauce**
  1/4 **teaspoon salt**
       pinch ground cloves
    4 **cans (15 to 19 ounces each) beans, such as black, kidney, white, pink, and pinto, rinsed and drained**

1. In 4-quart saucepan, heat olive oil over medium-low heat. Add onion and cook, stirring occasionally, until tender and golden, 5 to 8 minutes.

2. Stir in ketchup, water, molasses, mustard, Worcestershire, salt, and cloves until blended. Increase heat to high; add beans and heat to boiling. Reduce heat to medium-low; cover and simmer 5 minutes. Makes about 6 cups or 8 accompaniment servings.

Each serving: About 320 calories (6 percent calories from fat), 19g protein, 62g carbohydrate, 2g total fat (0g saturated), 0mg cholesterol, 1,085mg sodium.

White Beans, French-Style

Prep: 10 minutes plus soaking beans   Cook: 1 hour 20 minutes

In French homes and bistros, white beans are the traditional accompaniment to roasted leg of lamb. Add leftovers to soups, or top them with buttered fresh bread crumbs and reheat in a shallow casserole.

- **1 package (16 ounces) dry Great Northern beans**
- **2 medium onions, 1 peeled and studded with 2 whole cloves**
- **1 bay leaf**
- **2 tablespoons butter or olive oil**
- **1 garlic clove, finely chopped**
- **1 can (14 to 16 ounces) tomatoes**
- **2 teaspoons salt**
- **1/4 teaspoon ground black pepper**
- **1/4 cup chopped fresh parsley**

1. Rinse beans with cold running water and discard any stones or shriveled beans. In large bowl, place beans and enough water to cover by 2 inches. Cover and let stand at room temperature overnight. (Or, in 6-quart saucepot, place beans and enough water to cover by 2 inches. Heat to boiling over high heat; cook 2 minutes. Remove from heat; cover and let stand 1 hour.) Drain and rinse beans.

2. In 5-quart Dutch oven, combine beans, clove-studded onion, bay leaf, and enough water to cover by 2 inches; heat to boiling over high heat. Reduce heat; cover and simmer until beans are tender, about 1 hour. Drain beans, discarding onion and bay leaf; return beans to Dutch oven.

3. Meanwhile, peel and finely chop remaining onion. In nonstick 10-inch skillet, melt butter over medium heat. Add onion and cook until tender, about 5 minutes. Stir in garlic and cook 30 seconds. Add tomatoes with their juice, salt, and pepper; heat to boiling over high heat, breaking up tomatoes with side of spoon. Reduce heat and simmer, stirring occasionally, until almost all liquid has evaporated, 10 to 15 minutes.

4. Gently stir tomato mixture and parsley into beans. Makes about 6 1/2 cups or 8 accompaniment servings.

Each serving: About 246 calories (15 percent calories from fat), 13g protein, 42g carbohydrate, 4g total fat (2g saturated), 8mg cholesterol, 709mg sodium.

Turkey and Mango Roll-Ups,
page 218

Turkey and Mango Roll-Ups

Prep: 25 minutes plus chilling

A lime-spiked curried chutney adds zip to this rolled sandwich. If you can't find lavash (an Armenian flatbread), divide the filling ingredients among four 8- to 10-inch flour tortillas.

 1 **large lime**
 1/4 **cup light mayonnaise**
 3 **tablespoons mango chutney, chopped**
 1/2 **teaspoon curry powder**
 1/8 **teaspoon paprika**
 1 **lavash flatbread (7 ounces)**
 1 **medium cucumber (8 ounces), peeled and thinly sliced**
 8 **ounces thinly sliced smoked turkey breast**
 1 **medium mango, peeled and finely chopped**
 6 **large green-leaf lettuce leaves**

1. From lime, grate 1/4 teaspoon peel and squeeze 1 tablespoon juice. In bowl, combine lime peel, lime juice, mayonnaise, chutney, curry powder, and paprika until blended.

2. Unfold lavash; spread evenly with mayonnaise mixture. Arrange cucumber slices over mayonnaise, then top with turkey, mango, and lettuce. From a short side, roll lavash up, jelly-roll fashion.

3. Wrap lavash roll in foil and refrigerate at least 2 hours or up to 4 hours to blend flavors and let bread soften. To serve, trim ends, then cut lavash roll into 4 pieces. Makes 4 main-dish servings.

Each serving: About 375 calories (17 percent calories from fat), 18g protein, 55g carbohydrate, 7g total fat (2g saturated), 29mg cholesterol, 939mg sodium.

Roast Beef–Waldorf Club Sandwiches

Prep: 20 minutes plus standing

Horseradish dressing and a crunchy celery-and-apple mixture make rare roast beef taste even better. Soaking in ice water crisps the onion and tames its bite.

 4 **very thin slices red onion**
 1/2 **Golden Delicious apple, peeled and finely chopped (1/2 cup)**
 2 **stalks celery, finely chopped**
 4 **tablespoons reduced-fat mayonnaise**
 2 **tablespoons sour cream**
 1/2 **teaspoon fresh lemon juice**
 1 **tablespoon bottled white horseradish**
 12 **slices pumpernickel bread, lightly toasted, if desired**
 8 **ounces thinly sliced rare roast beef**
 1 **bunch watercress (4 ounces), tough stems trimmed**

1. In small bowl, combine onion with enough ice water to cover; let stand 15 minutes. Drain.

2. In separate small bowl, combine apple, celery, 2 tablespoons mayonnaise, 1 tablespoon sour cream, and lemon juice until well blended. In cup, combine remaining 2 tablespoons mayonnaise, remaining 1 tablespoon sour cream, and horseradish until blended.

3. Spread horseradish mixture evenly on 4 bread slices. Layer roast beef, onion, and watercress on top. Spread celery mixture evenly on 4 bread slices and place, celery mixture side up, over roast beef. Top with remaining bread slices. To serve, cut sandwiches in half. Makes 4 main-dish servings.

Each serving: About 451 calories (30 percent calories from fat), 25g protein, 54g carbohydrate, 15g total fat (5g saturated), 50mg cholesterol, 842mg sodium.

Bistro Chicken and Roasted Vegetable Sandwiches

Prep: 20 minutes   Cook: 20 minutes

- **1 small eggplant (12 ounces), cut lengthwise into 1/2-inch-thick slices**
- **1 medium red onion, cut crosswise into 1/2-inch-thick slices**
- **1 teaspoon dried basil leaves**
- **2 tablespoons plus 1 1/2 teaspoons balsamic vinegar**
- **2 tablespoons extra virgin olive oil or olive oil**
- **1/2 teaspoon salt**
- **3/4 teaspoon coarsely ground black pepper**
- **2 teaspoons all-purpose flour**
- **4 medium skinless, boneless chicken breast halves (1 1/4 pounds)**
- **1 large round loaf crusty bread**
- **3 tablespoons Dijon mustard**

1. Preheat oven to 500°F. Spray 15 1/2" by 10 1/2" jelly-roll pan with nonstick cooking spray. Arrange eggplant and onion slices in 1 layer on jelly-roll pan.

2. In cup, mix basil with 2 tablespoons balsamic vinegar, 1 tablespoon oil, salt, and 1/2 teaspoon pepper. Brush half of balsamic vinegar mixture over vegetables.

3. Roast vegetables, turning them once and brushing with remaining balsamic vinegar mixture, until tender and beginning to brown, 10 to 12 minutes.

4. Meanwhile, on waxed paper, combine flour and remaining 1/4 teaspoon pepper; use to coat chicken. In 12-inch skillet, heat remaining 1 tablespoon oil over medium-high heat until very hot. Add chicken and cook 6 minutes. Reduce heat to medium; turn chicken over and cook until chicken is golden brown and loses its pink color throughout, 6 to 8 minutes longer. Holding knife almost parallel to the work surface, cut each breast into 3 slices.

5. To serve, from center of loaf of bread, cut four 3/4-inch-thick slices (reserve remaining bread for another use). Top bread with eggplant slices, slightly overlapping, onion slices, separated into rings, and chicken.

6. In cup, mix mustard with remaining 1 1/2 teaspoons balsamic vinegar; drizzle over chicken. Makes 4 main-dish servings.

Each serving: About 505 calories (21 percent calories from fat), 42g protein, 53g carbohydrate, 12g total fat (2g saturated), 82mg cholesterol, 1,160mg sodium.

BBQ Pork Sandwiches

Prep: 10 minutes   Broil: 15 to 20 minutes

- **3 tablespoons light molasses**
- **3 tablespoons ketchup**
- **1 tablespoon Worcestershire sauce**
- **1 teaspoon minced, peeled fresh ginger**
- **1/2 teaspoon grated lemon peel**
- **1 garlic clove, crushed with garlic press**
- **2 whole pork tenderloins (3/4 pound each)**
- **12 small, soft dinner rolls**

1. Preheat broiler. In medium bowl, combine molasses, ketchup, Worcestershire, ginger, lemon peel, and garlic; add pork, turning to coat.

2. Place pork tenderloins on rack in broiling pan. Spoon any remaining molasses mixture over pork. Place pan in broiler 5 to 7 inches from heat source; broil pork, turning once, until meat is browned on the outside and still slightly pink in the center (internal temperature of tenderloins should be 160°F. on meat thermometer), 15 to 20 minutes.

3. To serve, thinly slice pork. Serve on rolls with any juices from broiling pan. Makes 6 main-dish servings.

Each serving: About 390 calories (30 percent calories from fat), 32g protein, 35g carbohydrate, 13g total fat (4g saturated), 70mg cholesterol, 360mg sodium.

Tuscan Tuna Salad on Focaccia

Prep: 15 minutes

Tuna and cannellini beans are a popular combination in Italy. Tossed with a piquant dressing, it makes a great sandwich filling.

- 1 can (15 to 19 ounces) white kidney beans (cannellini), rinsed and drained
- 1/2 cup chopped fresh basil
- 3 tablespoons capers, drained and chopped
- 2 tablespoons fresh lemon juice
- 2 tablespoons olive oil
- 1/2 teaspoon salt
- 1/4 teaspoon coarsely ground black pepper
- 1 can (6 ounces) tuna packed in water, drained and flaked
- 1 bunch watercress (4 ounces), tough stems trimmed and sprigs cut in half
- 1 (8-inch) round or square focaccia or 4 pita breads, cut horizontally in half
- 2 ripe medium tomatoes (6 ounces each), thinly sliced

1. In large bowl, mash 1 cup beans. Stir in basil, capers, lemon juice, oil, salt, and pepper until well blended. Add tuna, watercress, and remaining beans; toss to mix.

2. Spoon tuna mixture onto bottom half of focaccia; top with tomato slices. Replace top half of focaccia. To serve, cut into 4 wedges. Makes 4 main-dish servings.

Each serving: About 522 calories (24 percent calories from fat), 33g protein, 69g carbohydrate, 14g total fat (3g saturated), 22mg cholesterol, 1,464mg sodium.

Chicken-Topped Pita Pizzas

Prep: 20 minutes   Broil: 2 minutes

- 2 teaspoons vegetable oil
- 1 medium red pepper, thinly sliced
- 1 medium green pepper, thinly sliced
- 1 medium onion, thinly sliced
- 3/4 cup bottled marinara sauce
- 1/4 teaspoon crushed red pepper
- 3 (6-inch) pitas
- 6 ounces smoked chicken, torn into fine shreds
- 1 cup shredded part-skim mozzarella cheese (4 ounces)
- 2 tablespoons sliced fresh basil leaves

1. In nonstick 12-inch skillet, heat oil over medium-high heat. Add red peppers, green peppers, and onion and cook until vegetables are tender-crisp. Stir in marinara sauce and crushed red pepper; heat through.

2. Preheat broiler. Split each pita horizontally into 2 halves. Place pita halves, split-side up, on cookie sheet. Place cookie sheet in broiler at closest position to heat source; broil pitas until lightly browned.

3. Spoon sauce on pita halves; top with chicken and mozzarella. Broil until cheese melts. Sprinkle with basil. Makes 6 main-dish servings.

Each serving: About 215 calories (29 percent calories from fat), 14g protein, 25g carbohydrate, 7g total fat (3g saturated), 26mg cholesterol, 735mg sodium.

Falafel Sandwiches

Prep: 10 minutes   Cook: 8 minutes per batch

We serve these small, flat bean patties in pita pockets with lettuce, tomatoes, cucumbers, and tangy plain low-fat yogurt.

- **4   green onions, cut into 1-inch pieces**
- **2   garlic cloves, peeled and cut in half**
- **1/2 cup packed fresh Italian parsley leaves**
- **2   teaspoons dried mint**
- **1   can (15 to 19 ounces) garbanzo beans, rinsed and drained**
- **1/2 cup plain dried bread crumbs**
- **1   teaspoon ground coriander**
- **1   teaspoon ground cumin**
- **1   teaspoon baking powder**
- **1/2 teaspoon salt**
- **1/4 teaspoon ground red pepper (cayenne)**
- **1/4 teaspoon ground allspice**
- **   olive oil nonstick cooking spray**
- **4   (6- to 7-inch) pitas**

ACCOMPANIMENTS:

sliced romaine lettuce, sliced tomatoes, sliced cucumber, sliced red onion, plain low-fat yogurt

1. In food processor with knife blade attached, finely chop green onions, garlic, parsley, and mint. Add garbanzo beans, bread crumbs, coriander, cumin, baking powder, salt, ground red pepper, and allspice; blend until a coarse puree forms.

2. Shape bean mixture, by scant 1/2 cups, into eight 3-inch round patties and place on sheet of waxed paper. Spray both sides of patties with olive oil spray.

3. Heat nonstick 10-inch skillet over medium-high heat until hot. Add half of patties and cook, turning once, until dark golden brown, 8 minutes. Transfer patties to paper towels to drain. Repeat with remaining patties.

4. Cut off top third of each pita to form a pocket. Place warm patties in pitas. Serve with choice of accompaniments. Makes 4 main-dish servings.

Each sandwich without accompaniments: About 365 calories (12 percent calories from fat), 14g protein, 68g carbohydrate, 5g total fat (1g saturated), 0mg cholesterol, 1,015mg sodium.

Flatbread Salad Pizza

Prep: 20 minutes plus time to prepare flatbread

Try this salad pizza as an alternative to the usual tomato-and-cheese kind. It's especially good because it starts with our crusty Grilled Flatbread.

Grilled Flatbread (page 255)

- 2 **tablespoons extra virgin olive oil**
- 2 **tablespoons red wine vinegar**
- 1 **teaspoon sugar**
- 1 **teaspoon Dijon mustard**
- 1/4 **teaspoon salt**
- 1/8 **teaspoon coarsely ground black pepper**
- 6 **cups salad greens, such as radicchio, endive, and arugula, cut into 1/2-inch pieces**
- 2 **ripe medium tomatoes, cut into 1/2-inch pieces**
- 1 **small cucumber, peeled and cut into 1/2-inch pieces**

1. Prepare Grilled Flatbread through step 5.

2. About 10 minutes before grilling flatbread, prepare salad: In large bowl, with wire whisk, mix oil, vinegar, sugar, mustard, salt, and pepper until dressing is blended.

3. Add salad greens, tomatoes, and cucumber to dressing in bowl; toss to coat well. Set salad aside.

4. Grill flatbreads as in step 6 of flatbread recipe.

5. To serve, top each flatbread with about 2 cups salad. Cut each round into quarters. Makes 8 first-course or 4 main-dish servings.

Each first-course serving: About 310 calories (20 percent calories from fat), 8g protein, 53g carbohydrate, 7g total fat (1g saturated), 0mg cholesterol, 625mg sodium.

Quick Homemade Pizza Dough

Prep: 20 minutes

Use this basic dough and method for all the pizza variations on the following pages—and for those you and your family create using favorite ingredients. To bake the pizza, layer dough with toppings and bake in a 450°F. degree oven until crust is browned, 20 to 25 minutes.

2½ **cups all-purpose flour**

1 **package quick-rise yeast**

1 **teaspoon salt**

1 **cup very warm water (120 to 130°F.)**

2 **teaspoons cornmeal**

1. In large bowl, combine 2 cups flour, yeast, and salt. Stir in very warm water until blended and dough comes away from side of bowl.

2. Turn dough onto floured surface and knead until smooth and elastic, about 8 minutes, working in more flour (about ½ cup) while kneading. Shape dough into a ball; cover with plastic wrap and let rest 10 minutes.

3. Grease 15-inch pizza pan; sprinkle with cornmeal. Pat dough onto bottom of pizza pan, shaping dough into ½-inch-high rim at edge of pan.

Take-Out Dough

To really save time when making pizza at home, many neighborhood pizza shops—and some supermarkets—will sell you raw, raised dough ready for you to roll and top. And some even have whole-wheat dough for more fiber, flavor, and vitamins.

Spinach and Feta Pizza

Prep: 20 minutes plus time to make the dough   Bake: 20 to 25 minutes

Quick Homemade Pizza Dough (recipe above)

1 **teaspoon olive oil**

1 **small onion, chopped**

1 **teaspoon finely chopped garlic**

1 **package (10 ounces) frozen chopped spinach, thawed and squeezed dry**

¼ **teaspoon dried dill or mint**

1 **cup tomato sauce**

2 **ounces feta cheese, crumbled**

12 **Kalamata olives**

1. Prepare Quick Homemade Pizza Dough.

2. Preheat oven to 450°F.

3. In small skillet, heat oil over medium-high heat; add onion and cook 5 minutes. Stir in garlic, spinach, and dill; heat through.

4. Spread pizza dough with tomato sauce. Top with spinach mixture. Sprinkle with crumbled feta and olives. Bake pizza until crust is browned, 20 to 25 minutes. Makes 8 main-dish servings.

Each serving: About 210 calories (17 percent calories from fat), 7g protein, 37g carbohydrate, 4g total fat (1g saturated), 6mg cholesterol, 660mg sodium.

Bistro Pizza

Prep: 20 minutes plus time to make the dough   Bake: 20 to 25 minutes

Quick Homemade Pizza Dough (page 224)

1 pound thin asparagus, trimmed and cut into 2-inch pieces

1 teaspoon olive oil

1/4 teaspoon salt

1 medium yellow pepper, cut into thin strips

1 cup part-skim ricotta cheese

2 tablespoons grated Parmesan cheese

1/4 teaspoon coarsely ground black pepper

1. Prepare Quick Homemade Pizza Dough.

2. Preheat oven to 450°F.

3. In small bowl, toss asparagus with oil and salt. Top pizza dough with pepper strips and asparagus. Dollop with teaspoons of ricotta; sprinkle with Parmesan and black pepper. Bake on bottom rack in oven until crust is browned, 20 to 25 minutes. Makes 8 main-dish servings.

Each serving: About 215 calories (17 percent calories from fat), 10g protein, 35g carbohydrate, 4g total fat (2g saturated), 11mg cholesterol, 405mg sodium.

Garden Pizza

Prep: 20 minutes plus time to make the dough   Bake: 20 to 25 minutes

Quick Homemade Pizza Dough (page 224)

1 tablespoon vegetable oil

1 small zucchini (6 ounces) cut into 1/4-inch pieces

1 small yellow straightneck squash (6 ounces), cut into 1/4-inch pieces

1 large tomato, seeded and cut into 1/4-inch pieces

1/2 teaspoon dried oregano

1/4 teaspoon ground black pepper

1/4 teaspoon salt

1 cup shredded part-skim mozzarella cheese

1. Prepare Quick Homemade Pizza Dough.

2. Preheat oven to 450°F.

3. In 12-inch skillet, heat oil over medium-high heat. Add zucchini and yellow squash and cook until tender. Stir in tomato, oregano, pepper, and salt.

4. Top pizza dough with squash mixture; sprinkle evenly with shredded mozzarella cheese. Bake pizza on bottom rack of oven until crust is golden and crisp, 20 to 25 minutes. Makes 8 main-dish servings.

Each serving: About 215 calories (21 percent calories from fat), 9g protein, 34g carbohydrate, 5g total fat (2g saturated), 10mg cholesterol, 455mg sodium.

Broccoli Pizza

Prep: 20 minutes plus time to make the dough   Bake: 20 to 25 minutes

Quick Homemade Pizza Dough (page 224)

1 **tablespoon light corn-oil spread (56% to 60% fat)**

1 **package (16 ounces) mushrooms, sliced**

1 **large garlic clove, crushed with garlic press**

1 **package (16 ounces) broccoli flowerets**

1/4 **teaspoon salt**

1/2 **cup packed basil leaves, chopped**

1/2 **cup tomato sauce**

1 **cup shredded part-skim mozzarella or Monterey Jack cheese**

1. Prepare Homemade Pizza Dough.

2. Preheat oven to 450°F.

3. In nonstick 12-inch skillet, melt corn-oil spread over medium-high heat. Add mushrooms and garlic; cook until mushrooms are golden. Meanwhile, in 10-inch skillet, heat 1 inch water to boiling over high heat. Place steamer basket in skillet; add broccoli. Reduce heat to medium; cover and steam until tender.

4. Remove broccoli; add to mushrooms with 1/4 teaspoon salt and toss well to mix.

5. Spread dough with tomato sauce. Spoon broccoli mixture on top. Sprinkle with basil and cheese. Bake 20 to 25 minutes. Makes 8 main-dish servings.

Each serving: About 230 calories (16 percent calories from fat), 12g protein, 38g carbohydrate, 4g total fat (2g saturated), 10mg cholesterol, 570mg sodium.

(From top to bottom)
Peach Salsa, Tomato Salsa and
Tomatillo Salsa, pages 228 and 229

Tomato Salsa

Prep: 20 minutes plus chilling

As a topping for burgers, this flavor-packed salsa is stiff competition for plain old ketchup.

- 1 **large lime**
- 1 1/2 **pounds ripe tomatoes (3 large), chopped**
- 1/2 **small red onion, finely chopped**
- 1 **small jalapeño chile, seeded and minced**
- 2 **tablespoons chopped fresh cilantro**
- 3/4 **teaspoon salt**
- 1/4 **teaspoon coarsely ground black pepper**

From lime, grate 1/2 teaspoon peel and squeeze 2 tablespoons juice. In medium bowl, gently stir lime peel, lime juice, tomatoes, onion, jalapeño, cilantro, salt, and pepper until well mixed. Cover and refrigerate at least 1 hour to blend flavors or up to 2 days. Makes about 3 cups.

Each 1/4 cup: About 15 calories (0 percent calories from fat), 1g protein, 3g carbohydrate, 0g total fat, 0mg cholesterol, 151mg sodium.

Peach Salsa

Prep: 30 minutes plus chilling

Be patient. Wait until it is the height of peach season to make this. Spoon over grilled chicken breasts or pork chops.

- 1 3/4 **pounds ripe peaches (5 medium), peeled, pitted, and chopped**
- 2 **tablespoons finely chopped red onion**
- 1 **tablespoon chopped fresh mint**
- 1 **teaspoon seeded, minced jalapeño chile**
- 1 **tablespoon fresh lime juice**
- 1/8 **teaspoon salt**

In medium bowl, gently stir peaches, onion, mint, jalapeño, lime juice, and salt until well mixed. Cover and refrigerate 1 hour to blend flavors or up to 2 days. Makes about 3 cups.

Each 1/4 cup: About 23 calories (0 percent calories from fat), 0g protein, 6g carbohydrate, 0g total fat, 0mg cholesterol, 25mg sodium.

Olive and Lemon Salsa

Prep: 10 minutes

- 2 **lemons**
- 2 **small navel oranges**
- 1/4 **cup coarsely chopped pimiento-stuffed olives**
- 2 **tablespoons chopped shallot**
- 2 **tablespoons chopped fresh parsley leaves**
- 1/2 **teaspoon sugar**
- 1/4 **teaspoon coarsely ground black pepper**

With knife, cut peel and white pith from lemons and oranges. Cut fruit into 1/4-inch slices, discarding seeds. Cut slices into 1/4-inch pieces. In small bowl, combine lemon pieces, orange pieces, olives, shallot, parsley, sugar, and black pepper, stirring gently. Cover and refrigerate if not serving right away. Makes about 2 cups.

Each 1/4 cup: About 130 calories (21 percent calories from fat), 3g protein, 28g carbohydrate, 3g total fat (1g saturated), 0mg cholesterol, 705mg sodium.

Tomatillo Salsa

Prep: 25 minutes plus chilling

The tomatillo, sometimes called a Mexican green tomato, is actually related to the gooseberry. It has an acidic fruity flavor that is excellent with grilled meats and fish.

1 **pound fresh tomatillos (10 medium), husked, washed well, and cut into quarters**

3/4 **cup loosely packed fresh cilantro leaves, chopped**

1/4 **cup finely chopped onion**

1 **or 2 serrano or jalapeño chiles, seeded and minced**

1 **garlic clove, minced**

1 **teaspoon sugar**

1/2 **teaspoon salt**

1. In food processor with knife blade attached, coarsely chop tomatillos.

2. In medium bowl, gently stir tomatillos, cilantro, onion, serranos, garlic, sugar, and salt until well mixed. Cover and refrigerate at least 1 hour to blend flavors or up to 3 days. Makes about 2 cups.

Each 1/4 cup: About 20 calories (0 percent calories from fat), 1g protein, 3g carbohydrate, 0g total fat (0g saturated), 0mg cholesterol, 146mg sodium.

Watermelon Salsa

Prep: 30 minutes plus chilling

A great way to use up that last piece of watermelon. Both red and yellow watermelon work well here.

1 **piece (2 1/2 pounds) watermelon, seeded and chopped**

2 **tablespoons fresh lime juice**

1 **tablespoon finely chopped red onion**

1 **tablespoon chopped fresh cilantro**

2 **teaspoons seeded, minced jalapeño chile**

1/8 **teaspoon salt**

In medium bowl, gently stir watermelon, lime juice, onion, cilantro, jalapeño, and salt until well mixed. Cover and refrigerate at least 1 hour to blend flavors or up to 2 days. Makes about 3 cups.

Each 1/4 cup: About 17 calories (0 percent calories from fat), 0g protein, 4g carbohydrate, 0g total fat, 0mg cholesterol, 26mg sodium.

Tomato Chutney

Prep: 25 minutes plus chilling   Cook: 55 minutes

Deep red and richly flavored, this is a delicious accent for grilled meats and vegetables, or a nice spread for cold meat sandwiches.

- 3 pounds ripe tomatoes (9 medium), peeled and chopped
- 1 medium Granny Smith apple, peeled, cored, and coarsely grated
- 1 small onion, chopped
- 1/2 cup cider vinegar
- 1/3 cup golden raisins
- 1/3 cup packed brown sugar
- 2 tablespoons minced, peeled fresh ginger
- 2 garlic cloves, finely chopped
- 1/2 teaspoon salt
- 1/2 teaspoon coarsely ground black pepper

1. In heavy nonreactive 12-inch skillet, combine tomatoes, apple, onion, vinegar, raisins, brown sugar, ginger, garlic, salt, and pepper; heat to boiling over high heat. Reduce heat to medium; cook, stirring occasionally, until mixture has thickened, 45 to 50 minutes.

2. Cover and refrigerate until well chilled, about 4 hours or up to 2 weeks. Makes about 3 1/2 cups.

Each 1/4 cup: About 59 calories (0 percent calories from fat), 1g protein, 15g carbohydrate, 0g total fat, 0mg cholesterol, 94mg sodium.

Sweet Red Pepper Chutney

Prep: 25 minutes plus chilling   Cook: 50 minutes

You can prepare and refrigerate this zesty-sweet relish up to two weeks before serving.

- 1 1/2 cups cider vinegar
- 1 cup sugar
- 6 large red peppers, chopped
- 3 firm medium pears, peeled, cored, and cut into 1/2-inch pieces
- 1 small red onion, chopped
- 1/3 cup dark seedless raisins
- 1 1/2 teaspoons mustard seeds
- 1 teaspoon salt
- 1/8 teaspoon ground allspice

1. In nonreactive 5-quart Dutch oven, combine vinegar and sugar; heat to boiling over high heat. Boil 10 minutes.

2. Add red peppers, pears, onion, raisins, mustard seeds, salt, and allspice; heat to boiling. Reduce heat to medium-high and cook, stirring occasionally, until syrupy, about 30 minutes. Cover and refrigerate until well chilled, about 4 hours or up to 2 weeks. Makes about 6 cups.

Each 1/4 cup: About 62 calories (0 percent calories from fat), 0g protein, 16g carbohydrate, 0g total fat, 0mg cholesterol, 99mg sodium.

Skinny Salad Dressings

These quick, flavor-packed versions of old favorites are so good, you'll forget you're eating low-fat.

Orange-Ginger Dressing

Prep: 5 minutes

- 1/2 **cup seasoned rice vinegar**
- 1/2 **cup orange juice**
- 1/2 **teaspoon grated, peeled fresh ginger**
- 1/2 **teaspoon soy sauce**
- 1/8 **teaspoon Asian sesame oil**

In small bowl, with wire whisk, mix vinegar, orange juice, ginger, soy sauce, and sesame oil until blended. Cover and refrigerate up to 5 days. Makes about 1 cup.

Each tablespoon: About 10 calories (0 percent calories from fat), 0g protein, 3g carbohydrate, 0g total fat, 0mg cholesterol, 110mg sodium.

Buttermilk-Chive Dressing

Prep: 5 minutes

- 1/2 **cup reduced-fat buttermilk**
- 2 **tablespoons distilled white vinegar**
- 2 **tablespoons chopped fresh chives**
- 1 **tablespoon low-fat mayonnaise dressing**
- 1/4 **teaspoon salt**
- 1/4 **teaspoon ground black pepper**

In small bowl, with wire whisk, mix buttermilk, vinegar, chives, dressing, salt, and pepper until blended. Cover and refrigerate up to 3 days. Makes about 3/4 cup.

Each tablespoon: About 6 calories (0 percent calories from fat), 0 grams protein, 1g carbohydrate, 0g total fat, 0mg cholesterol, 65mg sodium.

Tomato-Orange Vinaigrette

Prep: 5 minutes

- 1/2 **cup tomato juice**
- 1 **tablespoon balsamic vinegar**
- 1/4 **tablespoon grated orange peel**
- 1/4 **teaspoon sugar**
- 1/4 **teaspoon ground black pepper**

In small bowl, with wire whisk, mix tomato juice, vinegar, orange peel, sugar, and pepper until blended. Cover and refrigerate up to 3 days. Makes about 1/2 cup.

Each tablespoon: About 5 calories (0 percent calories from fat), 0g protein, 1g carbohydrate, 0g total fat, 0mg cholesterol, 55mg sodium.

Creamy Ranch Dressing

Prep: 5 minutes

- 3/4 **cup plain nonfat yogurt**
- 1/4 **cup low-fat mayonnaise**
- 1 **green onion, minced**
- 1 **tablespoon cider vinegar**
- 2 **teaspoons Dijon mustard**
- 1/4 **teaspoon dried thyme**
- 1/4 **teaspoon coarsely ground black pepper**

In small bowl, with wire whisk, mix yogurt, mayonnaise, green onion, vinegar, mustard, thyme, and pepper until blended. Cover and refrigerate up to 5 days. Makes about 1 cup

Each tablespoon: About 15 calories (0 percent calories from fat), 1g protein, 2g carbohydrate, 0g total fat, 0mg cholesterol, 60mg sodium.

Honey-Lime Vinaigrette

Prep: 5 minutes

- 1/3 **cup fresh lime juice (2 to 3 limes)**
- 4 **teaspoons honey**
- 1 **tablespoon rice vinegar**
- 1/8 **teaspoon salt**

In small bowl, with wire whisk, mix lime juice, honey, vinegar, and salt until blended. Cover and refrigerate up to 3 days. Makes about 1/2 cup.

Each tablespoon: About 13 calories (0 percent calories from fat), 0g protein, 4g carbohydrate, 0g total fat, 0mg cholesterol, 37mg sodium.

Secret-Recipe BBQ Sauce

Prep: 25 minutes   Cook: 40 minutes

Brush this over anything—from hamburgers to chicken. The recipe makes almost 5 cups, so you'll have enough for several dishes.

- **1 tablespoon olive oil**
- **1 large onion (12 ounces), chopped**
- **2 tablespoons chopped, peeled fresh ginger**
- **3 tablespoons chili powder**
- **3 garlic cloves, crushed with garlic press**
- **1 can (8 ounces) crushed pineapple in juice**
- **1 can (28 ounces) crushed tomatoes in puree**
- **1/3 cup ketchup**
- **1/4 cup cider vinegar**
- **3 tablespoons dark brown sugar**
- **3 tablespoons light (mild) molasses**
- **2 teaspoons dry mustard**
- **1 teaspoon salt**

1. In 5- to 6-quart saucepot, heat oil over medium heat until hot. (Do not use a smaller pan as the sauce bubbles up and splatters during cooking.) Add onion and ginger and cook until onion is tender and golden, about 10 minutes. Add chili powder and cook, stirring, 1 minute. Add garlic and pineapple with its juice; cook 1 minute longer.

2. Remove saucepot from heat. Stir in tomatoes with their puree, ketchup, vinegar, brown sugar, molasses, mustard, and salt.

3. Spoon one-fourth of sauce into blender; cover with center part of cover removed to let steam escape and puree until smooth. Pour sauce into bowl; repeat with remaining sauce. Return sauce to saucepot; heat to boiling over high heat. Reduce heat to medium-low and cook, partially covered and stirring occasionally, until reduced to about 4 3/4 cups, 25 minutes.

4. Serve warm, or cover and refrigerate up to 1 week or freeze up to 2 months. Makes about 4 3/4 cups.

Each 1/4 cup: About 60 calories (16 percent calories from fat), 1g protein, 12g carbohydrate, 1g total fat (0g saturated), 0mg cholesterol, 310mg sodium.

Flavored Vinegars: Make a Splash!

Flavored vinegars have gone from the exclusive domain of specialty-food shops to supermarket shelves everywhere—and with good reason. They perk up everything from salad dressings and marinades to fruit salad splashes, adding next to nothing in calories and zero fat. Plus, flavored vinegars are easy to prepare at home.

To start, you need a sterilized 3- to 4-cup-capacity decorative bottle, fitted with a sterilized cork stopper. For Raspberry-Mint Vinegar, place 3 or 4 sprigs of fresh mint in the bottle (you may need a skewer to push them in), and add 1 1/2 cups fresh raspberries. In a nonreactive saucepan, heat 3 to 4 cups (depending on the size of your bottle) white-wine vinegar to boiling. Pour through funnel into bottle. Insert cork; let stand in a cool, dark place about 2 weeks. (Note: If the storage place is too warm, the vinegar will ferment and develop an off flavor and odor.) Strain through a fine sieve into a glass measuring cup or pitcher. Discard herbs and fruits, pour vinegar back into bottle, and add fresh sprigs of mint. Store at room temperature up to 3 months.

It's fun to experiment with other flavors to create your own favorites. Here are two more ideas to get you started:

Lemon-Thyme Vinegar: Substitute fresh thyme for the mint, and the peel of one lemon for the raspberries.

Chili Pepper–Cilantro Vinegar: Substitute fresh cilantro for the mint and 1 to 4 chili peppers (depending on how hot you want the vinegar) for the raspberries.

Shortcut BBQ Sauce

Prep: 10 minutes   Cook: 20 minutes

Sweet and sassy—this sauce is great whether you're grilling in your backyard or broiling in your oven. Just brush it onto ribs, chicken, or pork during the last few minutes of cooking (makes enough for 4 pounds spareribs or 2 chickens).

- **1 tablespoon olive oil**
- **1 medium onion, chopped**
- **2 tablespoons grated, peeled fresh ginger**
- **3/4 cup chili sauce**
- **1/2 cup ketchup**
- **1/3 cup water**
- **1 tablespoon sugar**
- **2 tablespoons cider vinegar**
- **2 tablespoons soy sauce**
- **1 teaspoon Worcestershire sauce**

1. In nonstick 10-inch skillet, heat oil over medium heat. Add onion and ginger and cook until onion is tender and lightly browned, 12 minutes.

2. Stir in chili sauce, ketchup, water, sugar, vinegar, soy sauce, and Worcestershire. Cook 5 minutes, partially covered, to blend flavors.

3. Use to brush on meat immediately, or cover and refrigerate up to 1 week or freeze up to 2 months. Makes about 2 cups.

Each 1/4 cup: About 70 calories (26 percent calories from fat), 1g protein, 13g carbohydrate, 2g total fat (0g saturated), 0mg cholesterol, 750mg sodium.

Cranberry-Port Sauce

Prep: 5 minutes   Cook: 20 minutes

Serve this richly flavored cranberry sauce warm with baked ham, roast duck, pork, or venison.

- **1/2 (12-ounce bag) cranberries (11/2 cups)**
- **2/3 cup sugar**
- **1/2 cup orange juice**
- **1/3 cup port wine**
- **1/8 teaspoon salt**

In nonreactive 3-quart saucepan, combine cranberries, sugar, orange juice, port, and salt; heat to boiling over high heat, stirring occasionally. Reduce heat; cover and simmer, stirring occasionally, until thickened, about 15 minutes. Makes 13/4 cups.

Each 1/4 cup: About 111 calories (0 percent calories from fat), 0g protein, 25g carbohydrate, 0g total fat, 0mg cholesterol, 43mg sodium.

McIntosh Applesauce

Prep: 15 minutes   Cook: 15 minutes

Cooking the apples with the cores and peels adds flavor and body to applesauce; pressing the mixture through a sieve makes it silky smooth. If the apples you use are red-skinned, the sauce will turn a lovely shade of pink.

1¹/₂ pounds cooking apples (6 small), preferably McIntosh

¹/₄ cup water

¹/₃ cup sugar or more to taste

1 teaspoon fresh lemon juice

1. Cut apples into quarters but do not peel or remove cores. In 4-quart saucepan, combine apples and water; heat to boiling over high heat. Reduce heat; cover and simmer, stirring occasionally, until very tender, 10 to 15 minutes. Stir in sugar and lemon juice.

2. Press apple mixture through sieve or food mill set over large bowl; discard skin and seeds. Taste and add more sugar, if desired. Serve warm, or cover and refrigerate to serve chilled. Makes about 3¹/₂ cups.

Each 1/2 cup: About 84 calories (0 percent calories from fat), 0g protein, 22g carbohydrate, 0g total fat, 0mg cholesterol, 0mg sodium.

Ginger Applesauce

Prepare as directed but add 1¹/₂ teaspoons grated, peeled fresh ginger to apples.

Lemon Applesauce

Prepare as directed but add 2 strips (2" by 1" each) lemon peel to apples.

Spiced Applesauce

Prepare as directed but add 1 cinnamon stick (3 inches) and 3 whole cloves to apples.

Horseradish Applesauce

Prepare as directed but after straining, stir 2 tablespoons bottled white horseradish into applesauce. (Serve with pork.)

Cranberry Applesauce

Prepare as directed but add 1¹/₂ cups fresh or frozen cranberries to apples.

Best Blueberry Sauce

Prep: 5 minutes   Cook: 5 to 8 minutes

Perfect with vanilla ice cream for a cooling, easy summer dessert.

- **3 cups blueberries**
- **1/2 to 3/4 cup confectioners' sugar**
- **3 tablespoons water**
- **1 to 2 teaspoons fresh lemon or lime juice**

1. In nonreactive 2-quart saucepan, combine blueberries, 1/2 cup confectioners' sugar, and water; cook over medium heat, stirring occasionally, until berries have softened and sauce has thickened slightly, 5 to 8 minutes.

2. Remove saucepan from heat; stir in 1 teaspoon lemon juice. Taste and stir in additional sugar and lemon juice, if desired. Serve warm, or cover and refrigerate up to 1 day. Reheat to serve, if you like. Makes about 2 cups.

Each tablespoon: About 17 calories (0 percent calories from fat), 0g protein, 4g carbohydrate, 0g total fat, 0mg cholesterol, 1mg sodium.

Freezer Strawberry Jam

Prep: 25 minutes plus overnight to stand   Cook: 8 to 10 minutes

A quick way to prepare jam and keep it handy, freezer jam is super fresh-tasting, jewel-bright in color, and very sweet. Peak-season farm stand strawberries work best.

- **5 half-pint freezer-safe containers with tight-fitting lids**
- **1 quart fully ripe strawberries, hulled**
- **4 cups sugar**
- **2 tablespoons fresh lemon juice**
- **3/4 cup water**
- **1 package (13/4 ounces) powdered fruit pectin**

1. Prepare containers and lids: Slowly pour boiling water into and over the outside of clean containers and lids. Invert onto a clean kitchen towel and drain dry. Or place the clean containers and lids in the dishwasher. Run the rinse cycle using very hot water (at least 150°F or higher). Leave them in the dishwasher until ready to use.

2. In large bowl, thoroughly crush enough strawberries to equal 2 cups. Stir in sugar and lemon juice until well blended; let stand 10 minutes.

3. In 1-quart saucepan, combine water and pectin and heat to boiling over high heat. Boil, stirring constantly, 1 minute. Stir pectin mixture into fruit until sugar has dissolved and mixture is no longer grainy, 3 to 4 minutes. A few sugar crystals will remain.

4. Quickly ladle jam into containers to within 1/2 inch of top. Wipe container rims clean; cover tightly with lids.

5. Let stand at room temperature until set, about 24 hours. Refrigerate up to 3 weeks or freeze up to 1 year. To use, place frozen jam in refrigerator until thawed, about 4 hours. Refrigerate after opening; use within 3 weeks. Makes five 8-ounce containers.

Each tablespoon: About 43 calories (0 percent calories from fat), 0g protein, 11g carbohydrate, 0g total fat, 0mg cholesterol, 1mg sodium.

Freezer Raspberry Jam

Prep: 20 minutes plus overnight to stand   Cook: 10 minutes

4 half-pint freezer-safe containers with tight-fitting lids

2 pints fully ripe raspberries

4 cups sugar

1 pouch (3 ounces) liquid fruit pectin

2 tablespoons fresh lemon juice

1. Prepare containers and lids: Slowly pour boiling water into and over the outside of clean containers and lids. Invert onto a clean kitchen towel and drain dry. Or place the clean containers and lids in the dishwasher. Run the rinse cycle using very hot water (at least 150°F or higher). Leave them in the dishwasher until ready to use.

2. In large bowl, thoroughly crush raspberries. If you like, with spoon, press half of crushed berries through sieve into medium bowl to remove seeds; discard seeds. In large bowl, combine fruit. Stir in sugar until thoroughly mixed; let stand 10 minutes.

3. In small bowl, combine pectin and lemon juice. Stir pectin mixture into fruit until sugar has dissolved and mixture is no longer grainy, 3 to 4 minutes. A few sugar crystals will remain.

4. Quickly ladle jam into containers to within 1/2 inch of top. Wipe container rims clean; cover with lids.

5. Let stand at room temperature until set, about 24 hours. Refrigerate up to 3 weeks or freeze up to 1 year. To use, place freezer jam in refrigerator until thawed, about 4 hours. Refrigerate after opening; use within 3 weeks. Makes four 8-ounce containers.

Each tablespoon: About 52 calories (0 percent calories from fat), 0g protein, 13g carbohydrate, 0g total fat, 0mg cholesterol, 0mg sodium.

Farmhouse White Bread, page 239

White Bread

Prep: 25 minutes plus rising   Bake: 30 minutess

The all-American bread—beautiful tall loaves for sandwiches and toast or for serving with meals.

- 1/2 **cup warm water (105° to 115°F)**
- 2 **packages active dry yeast**
- 1 **teaspoon plus 1/4 cup sugar**
- 2 1/4 **cups warm milk (105° to 115°F)**
- 4 **tablespoons butter or margarine, softened**
- 1 **tablespoon salt**
- 7 1/2 **cups (approx.) all-purpose or bread flour**

1. In large bowl, combine warm water, yeast, and 1 teaspoon sugar; stir to dissolve. Let stand until foamy, about 5 minutes. Add milk, butter, remaining 1/4 cup sugar, salt, and 4 cups flour. Beat well with wooden spoon. Gradually stir in 3 cups flour to make soft dough.

2. Turn dough onto floured surface and knead until smooth and elastic, about 8 minutes, working in enough of remaining 1/2 cup flour just to keep dough from sticking.

3. Shape dough into ball; place in greased large bowl, turning dough to grease top. Cover bowl with greased plastic wrap and let dough rise in warm place (80° to 85°F) until doubled in volume, about 1 hour.

4. Grease two 9" by 5" metal loaf pans. Punch down dough. Turn dough onto lightly floured surface and cut in half. Shape each half into rectangle about 12" by 7". Roll up from a short side. Pinch seam and ends to seal. Place dough, seam side down, in prepared pans. Cover pans loosely with greased plastic wrap and let rise in warm place until almost doubled, about 1 hour.

5. Meanwhile, preheat oven to 400°F. Bake until browned and loaves sound hollow when lightly tapped on bottom, 30 to 35 minutes. Remove loaves from pans; cool on wire racks. Makes 2 loaves, 12 slices each.

Each slice: About 187 calories (14 percent calories from fat), 5g protein, 34g carbohydrate, 3g total fat (2g saturated), 8mg cholesterol, 323mg sodium.

Cinnamon-Raisin Bread

Prepare as directed but stir 2 cups dark seedless raisins into yeast mixture with milk. Spread each rectangle with 2 tablespoons butter or margarine, softened, leaving 1/2-inch border. In small cup, combine 1/3 cup firmly packed brown sugar and 1 tablespoon ground cinnamon; sprinkle over butter. Roll up each loaf from a short side. Pinch seam and ends to seal. Makes 2 loaves, 12 slices each.

Each slice: About 244 calories (15 percent calories from fat), 5g protein, 47g carbohydrate, 4g total fat (2g saturated), 11mg cholesterol, 335mg sodium.

Farmhouse White Bread

Prep: 24 hours for starter plus 1 hour 30 minutes plus rising   Bake: 25 minutes

This two-loaf recipe is a "plan-ahead" bread that requires two overnight risings. First, a sponge starter is made of flour, water, and yeast; after 24 hours in the refrigerator, it's light and bubbly. Once the starter is combined with the remaining ingredients, the dough requires two 1-hour rises at warm room temperature, then another 3 to 24 hours in the refrigerator. Don't imagine that you need to spend the whole time in the kitchen, though! While the dough is rising, it doesn't need any attention at all.

SPONGE STARTER:

- 3 cups all-purpose flour or 2¹/₂ cups bread flour
- ¹/₂ teaspoon active dry yeast
- 1¹/₃ cups warm water (105° to 115°F)

DOUGH:

- 1 cup warm water (105° to 115°F)
- ³/₄ teaspoon active dry yeast
- ¹/₄ teaspoon sugar
- 1 tablespoon plus 1 teaspoon salt
- 3¹/₃ cups (approx.) all-purpose flour or 3¹/₄ cups bread flour
- 12 ice cubes

1. Prepare starter: In large bowl, combine flour, yeast, and warm water. With mixer at low speed, beat 3 minutes to develop a smooth, elastic batter. Cover bowl and refrigerate at least 15 hours, or up to 24 hours. Starter is ready to use when it has thinned out slightly, the volume has tripled, and small bubbles appear on the surface.

2. Next day, let starter stand, covered, at room temperature 30 minutes before using. Meanwhile, prepare dough: In very large bowl, combine warm water, yeast, and sugar; stir to dissolve. Let stand until foamy, about 5 minutes.

3. Add starter to yeast mixture in bowl, breaking up starter with hand (it will not be completely blended). Stir in salt and 3 cups flour. With floured hands, knead to combine in bowl.

4. Turn dough onto lightly floured surface and knead until smooth and elastic, 10 to 12 minutes, working in enough of remaining flour just to keep dough from sticking. Shape dough into ball and place in greased large bowl, turning dough to grease top. Cover bowl and let dough rise in warm place (80° to 85°F) until doubled in volume, about 1 hour.

5. Punch down dough. In same bowl, shape dough into ball. Cover bowl and let dough rise again until doubled, about 1 hour.

6. Turn dough onto floured surface and cut in half; cover and let rest 15 minutes for easier shaping. Sprinkle large cookie sheet with flour.

7. Shape each dough half into 7-inch round loaf. Place loaves at opposite corners on prepared cookie sheet. Cover and let dough rise in refrigerator at least 3 hours, or up to 24 hours.

8. Preheat oven to 500°F. Remove loaves from refrigerator and sprinkle with flour. With serrated knife or single-edge razor blade, cut 2 parallel slashes, 1¹/₂ inches apart, on top of each loaf, then cut 2 more slashes, perpendicular to first lines (final effect will be a grid, like tic-tac-toe box). Place ice cubes in 13" by 9" metal baking pan. Place pan in bottom of oven. Bake loaves on middle rack 10 minutes. Turn oven control to 400°F. Bake until loaves golden and sound hollow when lightly tapped on bottom, 15 minutes longer. Transfer to wire racks to cool. Makes 2 loaves, 12 slices each.

Each slice: About 125 calories (0 percent calories from fat), 4g protein, 26g carbohydrate, 0g total fat, 0mg cholesterol, 385mg sodium.

Baguettes

Prep: 20 minutes plus rising   Bake: 30 minutes

Long, crisp French baguettes taste best the day they are made. Eat one and freeze the other to have in reserve.

2 cups warm water (105° to 115°F)

1 package active dry yeast

1 tablespoon sugar

1 tablespoon plus ¹/₄ teaspoon salt

5 cups (approx.) all-purpose flour or bread flour

1 large egg white

1. In large bowl, combine warm water, yeast, and sugar; stir to dissolve. Let stand until foamy, about 5 minutes. Add 1 tablespoon salt and 3 cups flour. Beat well with wooden spoon until smooth. Gradually stir in 1¹/₂ cups flour to make soft dough.

2. Turn dough onto lightly floured surface; knead until smooth and elastic, 6 to 8 minutes, working in enough of remaining ¹/₂ cup flour just to keep dough from sticking.

3. Shape dough into ball; place in greased large bowl, turning dough to grease top. Cover bowl with greased plastic wrap and let dough rise in warm place (80° to 85°F) until doubled in volume, about 1¹/₂ hours.

4. Grease two large cookie sheets. Punch down dough. Turn dough onto lightly floured surface and cut in half. With rolling pin, roll each dough half into 18" by 7" rectangle. From a long side, with hands, roll up tightly, rolling dough back and forth to taper ends. Place each loaf on diagonal on one prepared cookie sheet. Cover loosely with greased plastic wrap and let rise in warm place until almost doubled, about 1 hour.

5. Meanwhile, preheat oven to 400°F. With serrated knife or single-edge razor blade, cut five ¹/₄-inch-deep diagonal slashes in top of each loaf. In small cup, beat egg white and remaining ¹/₄ teaspoon salt; brush over loaves. Bake until well browned, 30 to 35 minutes, rotating cookie sheets between upper and lower oven racks halfway through baking. Transfer loaves to wire racks to cool. Makes 2 loaves, 8 slices each.

Each slice: About 156 calories (6 percent calories from fat), 5g protein, 32g carbohydrate, 1g total fat (0g saturated), 0mg cholesterol, 477mg sodium.

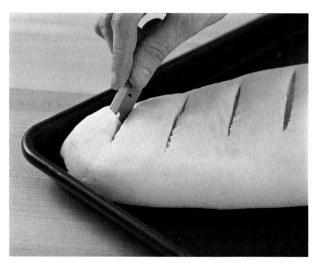

Cloverleaf Rolls

Prep: 30 minutes plus rising   Bake: 10 to 12 minutes

1/2 **cup warm water (105° to 115°F)**

2 **packages active dry yeast**

1 **teaspoon plus 1/3 cup sugar**

3/4 **cup warm milk (105° to 115°F)**

4 **tablespoons butter or margarine, softened**

3 3/4 **cups (approx.) all-purpose flour**

1 1/2 **teaspoons salt**

2 **large eggs**

1 **egg yolk mixed with 1 tablespoon water**

1. In large bowl, combine warm water, yeast, and 1 teaspoon sugar; stir to dissolve. Let stand until foamy, about 5 minutes.

2. With wooden spoon or mixer at low speed, beat in remaining 1/3 cup sugar, warm milk, butter, 1/2 cup flour, salt, and eggs to make a thick batter; continue beating, scraping bowl frequently, 2 minutes longer. Gradually stir in 3 cups flour to make a soft dough.

3. Turn dough onto lightly floured surface and knead until smooth and elastic, about 10 minutes, working in enough remaining 1/4 cup flour just to keep dough from sticking. Shape dough into ball; place in greased large bowl, turning dough to grease top. Cover bowl and let rise in warm place (80° to 85°F) until doubled in volume, about 1 hour.

4. Punch down dough. Turn onto lightly floured surface; cover and let rest 15 minutes for easier shaping.

5. Grease twenty-four 2 1/2-inch muffin-pan cups. Cut dough in half. Cut 1 dough half into 36 equal pieces; shape each piece into ball. Place 3 balls in each prepared muffin-pan cup. Repeat with remaining dough. Cover and let rise in warm place until doubled, about 30 minutes.

6. Preheat oven to 400°F. Brush rolls with egg-yolk mixture. Bake rolls until golden, 10 to 12 minutes, rotating sheets between upper and lower racks halfway through baking. Transfer to wire racks. Serve warm or let cool to serve later. Makes 24 rolls.

Each roll: About 130 calories (28 percent calories from fat), 3g protein, 19g carbohydrate, 4g total fat (2g saturated), 33mg cholesterol, 175mg sodium.

Dinner Rolls

Prep: 30 minutes plus rising   Bake: 15 minutes

For an extra special touch, these easy rolls are sprinkled with sesame or poppy seeds before baking.

- **1 package quick-rise yeast**
- **2 tablespoons sugar**
- **1¹/₂ teaspoons salt**
- **3¹/₄ cups all-purpose flour or bread flour**
- **1 cup very warm water (120° to 130°F)**
- **3 tablespoons butter or margarine, softened**
- **1 large egg**
- **¹/₄ cup sesame seeds or poppy seeds**

1. In large bowl, combine yeast, sugar, salt, and 3 cups flour. With wooden spoon, gradually stir very warm water and butter into flour mixture to make soft dough.

2. Turn dough onto lightly floured surface; knead until smooth and elastic, about 5 minutes, working in enough of remaining ¹/₄ cup flour just to keep dough from sticking. Shape into ball. Cover with plastic wrap and let rest 15 minutes. Grease large cookie sheet.

3. Cut dough into 12 equal pieces. On lightly floured surface, roll each piece of dough into ball. Place 2 inches apart on prepared cookie sheet. Cover and let rise in warm place (80° to 85°F) until doubled, about 30 minutes.

4. Meanwhile, preheat oven to 375°F. In small cup, beat egg and 1 teaspoon water; brush over tops of rolls. Sprinkle with sesame seeds. Bake rolls until golden, 15 to 20 minutes. Serve rolls warm, or cool on wire racks to serve later. Makes 12 rolls.

Each roll: About 184 calories (24 percent calories from fat), 5g protein, 29g carbohydrate, 5g total fat (2g saturated), 25mg cholesterol, 327mg sodium.

Challah

Prep: 30 minutes plus rising   Bake: 30 minutes

This Jewish egg bread, made in the traditional double-braid shape, can be served anytime but is a must for holiday meals. If you wish, divide the dough in half and make two single-braided loaves instead.

- **³/₄ cup warm water (105° to 115°F)**
- **1 package active dry yeast**
- **1 teaspoon plus ¹/₄ cup sugar**
- **3 large eggs, lightly beaten**
- **¹/₄ cup vegetable oil**
- **1 teaspoon salt**
- **4¹/₄ cups (approx.) all-purpose flour or 3¹/₂ cups bread flour**

1. In large bowl, combine warm water, yeast, and 1 teaspoon sugar; stir to dissolve. Let stand until foamy, about 5 minutes. Measure 1 tablespoon beaten egg into small cup; cover and refrigerate. Add remaining ¹/₄ cup sugar, remaining eggs, oil, salt, and 2 cups flour to yeast mixture; with wooden spoon, beat well. Stir in enough flour (about 1³/₄ cups all-purpose flour or 1¹/₄ cups bread flour) to a make soft dough.

2. Turn dough onto lightly floured surface and knead until smooth and elastic, about 8 minutes, working in enough of remaining ¹/₂ cup all-purpose flour or ¹/₄ cup bread flour just to keep dough from sticking.

3. Shape dough into ball; place in greased large bowl, turning dough to grease top. Cover bowl with plastic wrap and let dough rise in warm place (80° to 85°F) until doubled in volume, about 1 hour.

4. Punch down dough. Grease large cookie sheet. Turn dough onto lightly floured surface and cut two-thirds of

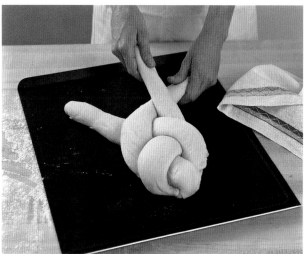

dough into 3 equal pieces; with hands, roll each piece into 13-inch-long rope. Place ropes side by side on prepared cookie sheet; braid ropes, pinching ends to seal. Cut remaining third of dough into 3 pieces. With hands, roll each piece into 14-inch-long rope. Place ropes side by side and braid; pinch ends to seal. Place small braid on top of large braid. Tuck ends of top braid under bottom braid, stretching top braid if necessary; pinch ends to seal. Cover loosely with greased plastic wrap and let rise in warm place until doubled, about 45 minutes.

5. Meanwhile, preheat oven to 375°F. Brush reserved beaten egg over loaf. Bake until browned and loaf sounds hollow when lightly tapped on bottom, 30 to 35 minutes. Transfer loaf to wire rack to cool completely. Makes 1 loaf, 12 slices.

Each slice: About 250 calories (25 percent calories from fat), 7g protein, 40g carbohydrate, 7g total fat (1g saturated), 53mg cholesterol, 211mg sodium.

Portuguese Peasant Bread

Prep: 20 minutes plus rising and cooling   Bake: 35 minutes

This dense bread is called broa in Portugal. The "secret" ingredient for its unusual flavor and texture? Barley cereal for babies! The loaves are also sprayed with water during baking to help give them the characteristic crisp and chewy crust.

- **3 cups warm water (105° to 115°F)**
- **2 packages active dry yeast**
- **2 tablespoons sugar**
- **1 package (8 ounces) barley cereal (4¹/₂ cups),* uncooked**
- **2¹/₂ cups stone-ground cornmeal, preferably white**
- **4 teaspoons salt**
- **4³/₄ cups (approx.) all-purpose flour**

1. In small bowl, combine 1/2 cup warm water, yeast, and sugar; let stand until foamy, about 5 minutes.

2. In large bowl, combine barley cereal, cornmeal, salt, and 4 cups flour. With wooden spoon, stir in yeast mixture and remaining 2¹/₂ cups warm water until combined. With floured hands, shape dough into a ball in bowl. Cover bowl with plastic wrap and let dough rise in warm place (80° to 85°F) until doubled in volume, about 1 hour.

3. Punch down dough. Turn dough onto well-floured surface and knead until smooth, about 5 minutes, working in enough remaining 3/4 cup flour just to keep dough from sticking.

4. Grease large cookie sheet. Cut dough in half and shape each half into a 6-inch round. Dust each round with flour; place on prepared cookie sheet. Cover loaves with towel and let rise in warm place until doubled, about 1 hour.

5. Preheat oven to 400°F. Bake loaves until golden brown, about 35 minutes, using spray bottle to spritz loaves with water after first 5 minutes of baking, and again 10 minutes later. Cool on wire racks. Makes 2 loaves, 12 slices each.

*Barley cereal can be found in the baby-food section of supermarkets.

Each slice: About 170 calories (5 percent calories from fat), 5g protein, 36g carbohydrate, 1g total fat (0g saturated), 0mg cholesterol, 360mg sodium.

Honey-Wheat Bread

Prep: 25 minutes plus rising   Bake: 40 minutes

Honey accentuates the sweetness of whole-wheat flour. These loaves emerge crusty from the oven but soften a bit when cool.

- **1¹/₂ cups warm water (105° to 115°F)**
- **2 packages active dry yeast**
- **1 teaspoon sugar**
- **¹/₂ cup honey**
- **¹/₃ cup butter or margarine, softened**
- **1 large egg**
- **1¹/₂ teaspoons salt**
- **3 cups whole-wheat flour**
- **3 cups (approx.) all-purpose flour**

1. In large bowl, combine 1/2 cup warm water, yeast, and sugar; stir to dissolve. Let stand until foamy, about 5 minutes. Stir in remaining 1 cup warm water, honey, butter, egg, salt, and whole-wheat flour until smooth. Gradually stir in 2¹/₂ cups all-purpose flour.

2. Turn dough onto lightly floured surface and knead until smooth and elastic, 7 to 10 minutes, working in enough of remaining 1/2 cup flour to make slightly sticky dough.

3. Shape dough into ball; place in greased large bowl,

turning dough to grease top. Cover bowl with plastic wrap and let dough rise in warm place (80° to 85°F) until doubled in volume, about 1½ hours.

4. Punch down dough. Turn dough onto lightly floured surface and cut in half; cover and let rest 10 minutes. On two ungreased cookie sheets, shape each dough half into 6" by 4½" oval. Cover loosely with plastic wrap; let rise in warm place until doubled, about 30 minutes. With serrated knife or single-edge razor blade, cut three 3-inch-long and ¼-inch-deep diagonal slashes across tops of loaves.

5. Preheat oven to 375°F. Lightly dust loaves with all-purpose flour. Bake until loaves sound hollow when lightly tapped on bottom, about 40 minutes. Transfer loaves to wire racks to cool. Makes 2 loaves, 12 slices each.

Each slice: About 161 calories (17 percent calories from fat), 4g protein, 30g carbohydrate, 3g total fat (2g saturated), 16mg cholesterol, 175mg sodium.

Whole Wheat–Oatmeal Bread

Prep: 45 minutes plus rising   Bake: 35 minutes

This recipe makes two slightly flat breads with a sweet flavor and dense texture.

2	cups warm water (105° to 115°F)
2	packages active dry yeast
½	teaspoon sugar
½	cup honey
4	tablespoons butter or margarine
1	cup quick-cooking or old-fashioned oats, uncooked
1	tablespoon salt
4	cups whole-wheat flour
1	large egg
2½	cups (approx.) all-purpose flour or 2 cups bread flour

1. In large bowl, combine ½ cup warm water, yeast, and sugar; stir to dissolve. Let stand until foamy, about 5 minutes. Stir in remaining 1½ cups warm water, honey, butter, oats, salt, and 2 cups whole-wheat flour until smooth. Stir in egg. Gradually stir in remaining 2 cups whole-wheat flour, then 2 cups all-purpose flour or 1½ cups bread flour.

2. Turn dough onto lightly floured surface and knead until smooth but slightly sticky, about 7 minutes, working in enough of remaining ½ cup flour just to keep dough from sticking.

3. Shape dough into ball; place in greased large bowl, turning dough to grease top. Cover bowl with plastic wrap and let dough rise in warm place (80° to 85°F) until doubled in volume, about 1 hour.

4. Punch down dough. Turn dough onto lightly floured surface and cut in half; cover and let rest 15 minutes. Grease large cookie sheet.

5. Shape each dough half into 7" by 4" oval; place on prepared cookie sheet. Cover and let rise in warm place until doubled, about 1 hour.

6. Preheat oven to 350°F. With serrated knife or single-edge razor blade, cut three to five ¼-inch-deep criss-cross slashes across top of each loaf. Lightly dust tops of loaves with all-purpose flour. Bake until loaves sound hollow when lightly tapped on bottom, 35 to 40 minutes. Transfer to wire racks to cool. Makes 2 oval loaves, 12 slices each.

Each slice: About 177 calories (15 percent calories from fat), 5g protein, 33g carbohydrate, 3g total fat (1g saturated), 14mg cholesterol, 315mg sodium.

Multigrain Bread

Prep: 40 minutes plus rising   Bake: 35 minutes

The trick to maintaining the light texture of these loaves is to keep the dough slightly sticky while kneading. Adding more flour than what's called for will make your bread too dense.

- **1 cup old-fashioned oats, uncooked**
- **2 cups warm water (105° to 115°F)**
- **2 packages active dry yeast**
- **1 tablespoon sugar**
- **1 cup whole-wheat flour**
- **1 cup stone-ground rye flour**
- **1/3 cup flax seeds, ground**
- **1/4 cup light (mild) molasses**
- **3 tablespoons olive oil**
- **2 1/2 teaspoons salt**
- **2 3/4 cups (approx.) all-purpose flour**
- **1 cup pitted prunes, coarsely chopped**

1. Preheat oven to 350°F. Place oats in small baking pan and bake, stirring occasionally, until lightly toasted, 10 minutes.

2. Meanwhile, in cup, combine 1/2 cup warm water, yeast, and sugar; stir to dissolve. Let mixture stand until foamy, about 5 minutes.

3. In large bowl, with wooden spoon, stir oats, yeast mixture, whole-wheat flour, rye flour, ground flax seeds, molasses, oil, salt, and remaining 1 1/2 cups warm water until smooth. Gradually stir in 2 1/2 cups all-purpose flour. With hand, knead in bowl until dough comes together.

4. Turn dough onto lightly floured surface and knead until elastic and almost smooth, about 8 minutes, working in remaining 1/4 cup all-purpose flour while kneading (dough will be sticky). Knead in prunes.

5. Shape dough into a ball; place in greased large bowl, turning dough to grease top. Cover bowl with plastic wrap and let dough rise in warm place (80° to 85°F) until doubled in volume, about 1 hour.

6. Punch down dough. Turn dough onto floured surface; cut in half. Lightly sprinkle large cookie sheet (17" by 14") with flour. With hands, shape half of dough on 1 end of cookie sheet to a 10" by 8" rectangle. Fold dough over lengthwise to make a 10" by 4" rectangle. Turn dough seam side down and pinch edges to seal; shape into 11" by 4" loaf. Repeat with remaining dough on other end of same cookie sheet.

7. Cover loaves loosely with greased plastic wrap and let rise in warm place until doubled, about 45 minutes.

8. Preheat oven to 350°F. With serrated knife or single-edge razor, cut six 1/4-inch-deep diagonal slashes across top of each loaf. Lightly dust tops of loaves with all-purpose flour. Bake until loaves are lightly browned and sound hollow when lightly tapped on bottom, about 35 minutes. Transfer loaves to wire rack to cool. Makes 2 loaves, 12 slices each.

Each serving: About 160 calories (17 percent calories from fat), 4g protein, 30g carbohydrate, 3g total fat (0g saturated), 0mg cholesterol, 225mg sodium.

Healthy Flax

The tiny brown, nut-flavored seeds of the age-old grain called flax are the best source of plant substances called lignans—which are attracting attention as potential cancer fighters. Experts believe lignans (a type of plant estrogen) block some effects of the body's estrogen, thereby inhibiting the formation of certain types of breast and ovarian tumors. Flax is also the primary plant source of alpha-linolenic acid, the garden's version of the healthful omega-3 fatty acids found in fish oil. Flax seeds serve up cholesterol-reducing soluble fiber too.

You can buy flax seeds already ground for recipes like our Multigrain Bread. Problem is, they may have been sitting in the health-food store for months, and be past their prime. The beneficial omega-3 fatty acids in flax can rapidly become rancid after the seeds are milled; you'll notice a strong paintlike smell if this happens. (In its other life, flax seeds are used to make linseed oil, a key ingredient in paint, varnish, and linoleum.)

Buy seeds whole, store in an airtight container in a cool area, and pulverize as needed in a coffee grinder. The seeds should keep well up to 1 year. If you have leftover ground flax seeds, refrigerate for up to 1 month or freeze for up to 6 months.

Bread-Machine Multigrain Loaf

Prep: 10 minutes   Bake: per bread machine's instructions

Bread machines have become the favorite appliance of many home bakers. To make this loaf, be sure to add the ingredients according to your machine's instructions. This recipe uses the setting for a 1 1/2-pound whole-wheat loaf. Do not use the "delay" start mode; this dough contains buttermilk, which should not be left at room temperature for an extended period of time.

2 **cups whole-wheat flour**

1 **cup all-purpose flour**

1/4 **cup bulgur wheat**

1/4 **cup old-fashioned oats, uncooked**

2 **tablespoons toasted wheat germ**

1 1/2 **teaspoons salt**

1 1/4 **cups buttermilk**

1/4 **cup honey**

3 **tablespoons vegetable oil**

1 **package active dry yeast**

Prepare recipe according to your bread machine's instructions. Makes 1 loaf, 16 slices.

Each slice: About 143 calories (19 percent calories from fat), 4g protein, 25g carbohydrate, 3g total fat (0g saturated), 1mg cholesterol, 240mg sodium.

Chocolate-Cherry Bread

Prep: 25 minutes plus rising   Bake: 20 minutes

This contemporary classic is unique: Not overly rich, sweet, or "dessert," it nonetheless satisfies a chocolate-craver's deepest needs! Dutch-process cocoa gives the bread a darker brown color than natural cocoa.

1/4 **cup warm water (105° to 115°F)**

1 **package active dry yeast**

3 **teaspoons granulated sugar**

1/3 **cup unsweetened Dutch-process cocoa**

1/3 **cup packed dark brown sugar**

13/4 **teaspoons salt**

31/2 **cups (approx.) all-purpose flour**

1 **large egg, separated**

1 **cup freshly brewed coffee, cooled to warm (105° to 115°F)**

4 **tablespoons butter or margarine, softened**

3/4 **cup dried tart cherries**

3 **ounces bittersweet chocolate, coarsely chopped**

1. In small cup, combine warm water, yeast, and 1 teaspoon granulated sugar; stir to dissolve. Let stand until foamy, about 5 minutes. In large bowl, combine cocoa, brown sugar, salt, and 3 cups flour; stir to blend.

2. Cover egg white and reserve in refrigerator. With wooden spoon, stir egg yolk, warm coffee, butter, and yeast mixture into flour mixture. With floured hands, knead to combine in bowl.

3. Turn dough onto lightly floured surface and knead until smooth and elastic, about 10 minutes, working in enough of remaining 1/2 cup flour just to keep dough from sticking. Knead in cherries and chocolate.

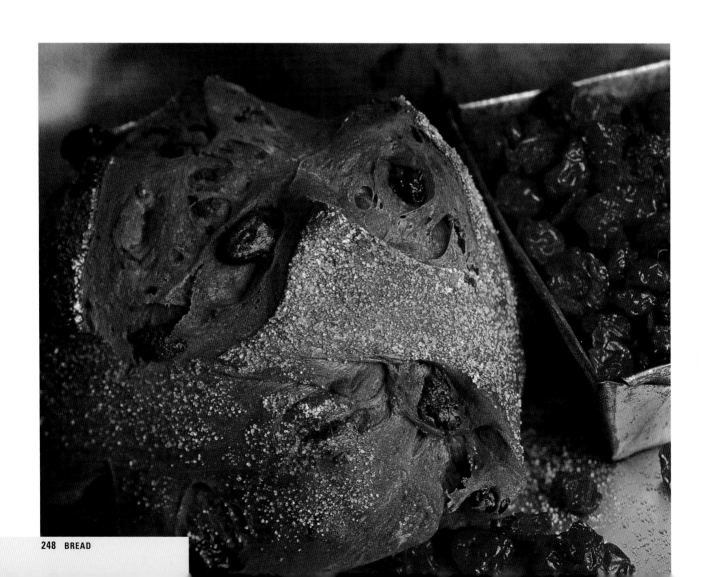

4. Place dough in greased large bowl, turning dough to grease top. Cover bowl and let dough rise in warm place (80° to 85°F) until doubled in volume, about 1 1/2 hours.

5. Punch down dough. Turn dough onto lightly floured surface and cut in half; cover and let rest 15 minutes for easier shaping. Shape each dough half into 5-inch round loaf. Place loaves, about 3 inches apart, in opposite corners of ungreased large cookie sheet. Cover and let rise in warm place until doubled, about 1 hour.

6. Preheat oven to 400°F. In cup, mix reserved egg white with 1 teaspoon water. Brush egg-white mixture on tops of loaves. Sprinkle loaves with remaining 2 teaspoons granulated sugar. With serrated knife or single-edge razor blade, cut shallow "x" on top of each loaf. Bake until crusty and loaves sound hollow when lightly tapped on bottoms, about 20 minutes. Transfer loaves to wire racks to cool. Makes 2 loaves, 12 slices each.

Each slice: About 135 calories (27 percent calories from fat), 3g protein, 24g carbohydrate, 4g total fat (2g saturated), 14mg cholesterol, 200mg sodium.

Pumpernickel Bread

Prep: 30 minutes plus rising   Bake: 40 minutes

A medley of ingredients—molasses, chocolate, espresso powder, and prune juice—gives this loaf its distinctive dark color and complex flavor; dark rye flour makes it a hearty loaf.

- 3/4 **cup warm water (105° to 115°F)**
- 2 **packages active dry yeast**
- 1 **tablespoon brown sugar**
- 2 **teaspoons instant espresso-coffee powder**
- 1 **cup prune juice**
- 1/3 **cup light (mild) molasses**
- 4 **tablespoons butter or margarine, softened**
- 1 **square (1 ounce) unsweetened chocolate, melted**
- 1 **tablespoon caraway seeds**
- 1 **tablespoon salt**
- 3 **cups rye flour, preferably dark**
- 1/2 **cup whole-wheat flour**
- 2 1/2 **cups (approx.) all-purpose flour**
- 1 **large egg white**

1. In large bowl, combine 1/2 cup warm water, yeast, and brown sugar; stir to dissolve. Let mixture stand until foamy, about 5 minutes.

2. Meanwhile, in cup, dissolve espresso-coffee powder in remaining 1/4 cup warm water. Stir into yeast mixture along with prune juice. Stir in molasses, butter, chocolate, caraway seeds, salt, and rye and whole-wheat flours until smooth. Gradually stir in 2 cups all-purpose flour. Knead mixture in bowl until dough holds together.

3. Turn dough onto lightly floured surface and knead until smooth and elastic, about 10 minutes, working in enough of remaining 1/2 cup all-purpose flour to make a slightly sticky dough.

4. Shape dough into ball; place in greased large bowl, turning dough to grease top. Cover bowl with plastic wrap and let dough rise in warm place (80° to 85°F) until doubled in volume, about 1 hour.

5. Punch down dough. Turn dough onto floured surface; cut in half. Shape each dough half into ball: Using the sides of your hands, tuck sides of dough under to meet in center. Rotate dough and repeat to form taut balls. Grease two large cookie sheets. Place balls on prepared cookie sheets. Cover and let rise in warm place until doubled, about 1 hour.

6. Meanwhile, preheat oven to 350°F. With serrated knife or single-edge razor blade, cut three 1/4-inch-deep slashes across top of each loaf. In small cup, beat egg white and 1 teaspoon water; brush over loaves. Bake until loaves sound hollow when lightly tapped on bottom, about 40 minutes. Transfer to wire racks to cool. Makes 2 loaves, 12 slices each.

Each slice: About 163 calories (22 percent calories from fat), 5g protein, 29g carbohydrate, 4g total fat (2g saturated), 5mg cholesterol, 316mg sodium.

Fig-Walnut Bread

Prep: 25 minutes plus rising   Bake: 30 to 35 minutes

Breads like this are loved in Europe. A popular Portuguese version is studded with almonds and raisins.

1¹/2   **cups warm water (105° to 115°F)**
  1   **package active yeast**
  1   **teaspoon sugar**
4¹/4   **cups (approx.) all-purpose flour**
  2   **tablespoons olive oil**
  1   **tablespoon honey**
  2   **teaspoons salt**
  2   **cups dried figs, finely chopped**
  1   **cup walnuts, toasted and coarsely chopped**

1. In large bowl, combine 1 cup warm water, yeast, and sugar; stir to dissolve. Let stand until foamy, about 5 minutes. Stir in 1 cup flour. Cover bowl and let stand at room temperature until mixture is thick and bubbly, about 45 minutes.

2. Stir in 3 cups flour, 1 tablespoon oil, honey, salt, and remaining ¹/2 cup warm water until well combined. Turn dough onto lightly floured surface and knead until smooth and elastic, 5 to 8 minutes, adding enough of remaining ¹/4 cup flour as needed. Flatten dough; press figs and walnuts into dough. Fold dough over onto fruit and nuts and knead until well combined. Place in greased large bowl, turning dough to grease top. Cover bowl and let dough rise in warm place (80° to 85°F) until doubled in volume, about 2 hours.

3. Punch down dough; cover and let rest 10 minutes for easier shaping. Grease large cookie sheet. Cut dough in half. Shape each half into 6-inch round loaf. Place loaves at opposite corners of prepared cookie sheet. Cover and let rise until doubled, about 45 minutes.

4. Preheat oven to 425°F. With serrated knife or single-edge razor blade, make several slashes in top of each loaf. Brush loaves with remaining 1 tablespoon oil. Bake until loaves sound hollow when lightly tapped on bottoms, 30 to 35 minutes. Cool 10 minutes on cookie sheet. Transfer to wire racks to cool completely. Makes 2 loaves, 12 slices each.

Each slice: About 170 calories (26 percent calories from fat), 4g protein, 30g carbohydrate, 5g total fat (1g saturated), 0mg cholesterol, 195mg sodium.

Olive-Rosemary Loaves

Prep: 30 minutes plus rising   Bake: 30 minutes

Kalamata olives and fresh rosemary give this peasant loaf robust flavor. Using high-gluten bread flour guarantees your baking success.

1¹/2   **cups warm water (105° to 115°F)**
  4   **tablespoons extra virgin olive oil**
  2   **packages active dry yeast**
  1   **tablespoon sugar**
  1   **cup Kalamata or green olives, pitted and chopped**
  2   **tablespoons finely chopped fresh rosemary**
  2   **teaspoons salt**
5¹/4   **cups (approx.) all-purpose flour**

1. In large bowl, combine ¹/2 cup warm water, 3 tablespoons oil, yeast, and sugar; stir to dissolve. Let stand until foamy, about 5 minutes. Stir in remaining 1 cup warm water, olives, rosemary, salt, and 4 cups flour until combined.

2. Turn dough onto lightly floured surface and knead until smooth and elastic, about 8 minutes, working in enough of remaining 1¹/4 cups flour just to keep dough from sticking.

3. Shape dough into ball; place in greased large bowl, turning dough to grease top. Cover bowl and let dough

rise in warm place (80° to 85°F) until doubled in volume, about 1 hour.

4. Punch down dough. Turn dough onto lightly floured surface and cut in half; cover and let rest 15 minutes for easier shaping. Grease large cookie sheet.

5. Shape each dough half into 7 1/2" by 4" oval; place 3 inches apart on prepared cookie sheet. Cover and let rise in warm place until doubled, about 1 hour.

6. Preheat oven to 400°F. Brush tops of loaves with remaining 1 tablespoon oil. With serrated knife or single-edge razor blade, cut three diagonal slashes across top of each loaf. Bake until golden and loaves sound hollow when tapped on bottom, about 30 minutes. Cool on wire rack. Makes 2 loaves, 12 slices each.

Each slice: About 148 calories (24 percent calories from fat), 4g protein, 23g carbohydrate, 4g total fat (1g saturated), 0mg cholesterol, 296mg sodium.

Marble Rye Bread

Prep: 30 minutes plus rising   Bake: 35 minutes

A handsome two-tone rye looks great on a buffet table. Slices of this old-country bread would fit right in with a hearty offering of cold meats, cheeses, mustards, chutneys, pickles— and beer.

1¼ **cups medium rye flour**

2¼ **cups (approx.) all-purpose flour or 2 cups bread flour**

¼ **cup warm water (105° to 115°F)**

1 **package active dry yeast**

1 **teaspoon sugar**

¾ **cup warm milk (105° to 115°F)**

3 **tablespoons butter or margarine, softened**

3 **teaspoons caraway seeds**

1½ **teaspoons salt**

½ **cup whole-wheat flour**

2 **tablespoons dark molasses**

2 **teaspoons unsweetened cocoa**

1 **teaspoon instant coffee powder**

cornmeal

1 **large egg, lightly beaten**

1. In medium bowl, combine rye flour and 1¼ cups all-purpose or bread flour.

2. In large bowl, combine warm water, yeast, and sugar; stir to dissolve. Let stand until foamy, about 5 minutes. With wooden spoon, stir in 1½ cups of the rye-flour mixture, warm milk, butter, 2½ teaspoons caraway seeds, and salt; beat well. Transfer ¾ cup batter to medium bowl.

3. To mixture in large bowl, add whole-wheat flour, molasses, cocoa, and coffee powder and beat well with wooden spoon. Gradually stir in ¾ cup of the rye-flour mixture until dough forms and leaves side of bowl.

4. Turn dough onto lightly floured surface and knead until smooth and elastic, 5 minutes, working in additional ¼ cup all-purpose flour or 2 tablespoons bread flour as needed just to keep dough from sticking.

Shape dough into ball and place in greased medium bowl, turning dough to grease top. Cover.

5. To batter in medium bowl, stir in remaining ¼ cup rye-flour mixture and ½ cup all-purpose flour or ¼ cup bread flour until dough leaves side of bowl. Turn dough onto floured surface and knead until smooth and elastic, 5 minutes, working in enough of remaining ¼ cup all-purpose flour or 2 tablespoons bread flour just to keep dough from sticking. Place dough in greased bowl, turning dough to grease top. Cover. Let both doughs rise in warm place (80° to 85°F) until doubled in volume, about 1½ hours.

6. Grease large cookie sheet and sprinkle with cornmeal. Punch down doughs. Divide each into 6 pieces. Lightly knead pieces together, alternating light and dark pieces. Shape into 10-inch-long loaf. Place loaf on prepared cookie sheet, cover with greased plastic wrap, and let rise in warm place until almost doubled, about 45 minutes.

7. Preheat oven to 375°F. With serrated knife or single-edge razor blade, make 4 diagonal slashes across top of loaf. Brush with beaten egg, avoiding slashes. Sprinkle with remaining 1/2 teaspoon caraway seeds. Bake loaf until browned and sounds hollow when lightly tapped on bottom, about 35 minutes. Transfer to wire rack to cool. Makes 1 loaf, 16 slices.

Each slice: About 160 calories (23 percent calories from fat), 4g protein, 26g carbohydrate, 4g total fat (2g saturated), 21mg cholesterol, 250mg sodium.

Potato Bread

Prep: 1 hour 30 minutes plus rising   Bake: 25 minutes

Mashed potatoes and eggs make these loaves moist and delectable. They make perfect toast or French toast the next day.

    1   **pound all-purpose potatoes (3 medium), peeled and cut into 1-inch chunks**
    1   **cup warm water (105° to 115°F)**
    2   **packages active dry yeast**
    2   **tablespoons sugar**
 4 1/4 **teaspoons salt**
    4   **tablespoons butter or margarine, softened**
 9 3/4 **cups (approx.) all-purpose flour or 8 3/4 cups bread flour**
    2   **large eggs**

1. In 2-quart saucepan, combine potatoes and 4 cups water; heat to boiling over high heat. Reduce heat; cover and simmer until potatoes are tender, about 15 minutes. Drain, reserving 1 cup potato water. Return potatoes to saucepan; mash until smooth.

2. In large bowl, combine warm water, yeast, and 1 tablespoon sugar; stir to dissolve. Let stand until foamy, about 5 minutes. Stir in reserved potato water, remaining 1 tablespoon sugar, 4 teaspoons salt, butter, and 3 cups flour.

3. With mixer at low speed, beat just until blended. Increase speed to medium; beat 2 minutes, occasionally scraping bowl with rubber spatula. Separate 1 egg. Cover egg white and reserve in refrigerator. Beat in egg yolk, remaining egg, and 1 cup flour to make a thick batter; continue beating 2 minutes, frequently scraping bowl. With wooden spoon, stir in mashed potatoes, then 5 cups all-purpose flour or 4 cups bread flour, 1 cup at a time, to make a soft dough. (You may want to transfer mixture to larger bowl for easier mixing.)

4. Turn dough onto well-floured surface and knead until smooth and elastic, about 10 minutes, working in enough of remaining 3/4 cup flour just to keep dough from sticking.

5. Shape dough into ball; place in greased large bowl, turning dough to grease top. Cover bowl with plastic wrap and let dough rise in warm place (80° to 85°F) until doubled in volume, about 1 hour.

6. Grease two 9" by 5" metal loaf pans. Punch down dough. Turn dough onto lightly floured surface and cut in half. Shape each dough half into rectangle about 12" by 7". Roll up from a short side. Pinch seam and ends to seal. Place, seam side down, in prepared pans. Cover pans and let dough rise in warm place until doubled, about 40 minutes, or refrigerate up to overnight.

7. Preheat oven to 400°F. (If dough has been refrigerated, remove plastic wrap and let stand 10 minutes before baking.) Beat reserved egg white with remaining 1/4 teaspoon salt; brush over loaves. Bake until golden and loaves sound hollow when lightly tapped on bottom, 25 to 30 minutes. Remove loaves from pans; cool on wire racks. Makes 2 loaves, 12 slices each.

Each slice: About 231 calories (12 percent calories from fat), 6g protein, 43g carbohydrate, 3g total fat (1g saturated), 23mg cholesterol, 439mg sodium.

Tomato Focaccia

Prep: 20 minutes plus rising   Bake: 35 to 40 minutes

The dough for this popular Italian bread is "dimpled" (indented) just before baking. The dimples catch some of the olive oil drizzled on at the end for added flavor.

- **6 tablespoons olive oil**
- **1¹/3 cups water**
- **1 package quick-rise yeast**
- **4 cups (approx.) all-purpose flour**
- **2 teaspoons salt**
- **cornmeal**
- **1 pound ripe plum tomatoes (5 medium), sliced ¹/4 inch thick**
- **1 tablespoon chopped fresh rosemary or 1 teaspoon dried rosemary leaves, crushed**
- **¹/2 teaspoon coarsely ground black pepper**

1. In 1-quart saucepan, heat 4 tablespoons oil and water over medium heat, until very warm (120° to 130°F). In large bowl, combine yeast, 1¹/2 cups flour, and 1¹/2 teaspoons salt.

2. With mixer at low speed, beat oil mixture into flour mixture just until blended. Increase speed to medium; beat 2 minutes, scraping bowl often with rubber spatula. Add ¹/2 cup flour; beat 2 minutes. With spoon, stir in 1¹/2 cups flour to make a soft dough.

3. On lightly floured surface, with floured hands, knead dough 8 minutes, working in more flour (about ¹/2 cup) while kneading. Cover dough and let rest 15 minutes.

4. Grease 15¹/2" by 10¹/2" jelly-roll pan; sprinkle with cornmeal. Press dough evenly into pan; cover and let rise in warm place (80° to 85°F) until doubled in volume, about 30 minutes.

5. Preheat oven to 400°F. Press fingers into dough almost to bottom of pan, making indentations 1 inch apart. Drizzle with 1 tablespoon olive oil. Arrange sliced tomatoes over top; sprinkle with remaining ¹/2 teaspoon salt, chopped rosemary, and pepper.

6. Bake focaccia in top third of oven until top is lightly browned, 35 to 40 minutes. Transfer to wire rack; drizzle with remaining 1 tablespoon oil. Cool slightly and serve warm. Makes 12 servings.

Each serving: About 225 calories (28 percent calories from fat), 5g protein, 35g carbohydrate, 7g total fat (1g saturated), 0mg cholesterol, 360mg sodium.

Soft Pretzels

Prep: 30 minutes plus rising   Bake: 16 minutes

These soft pretzels, a specialty of Pennsylvania Dutch country, are best served warm with mustard. Freeze them after shaping, if you like. Let them thaw, then dip in the baking-soda mixture and bake as directed. The pretzels can be sprinkled with sesame or poppy seeds in addition to the salt.

- **2 cups warm water (105° to 115°F)**
- **1 package active dry yeast**
- **1 teaspoon sugar**
- **1 teaspoon salt**
- **4 cups (approx.) all-purpose flour**
- **2 tablespoons baking soda**
- **1 tablespoon kosher or coarse sea salt**

1. In large bowl, combine 1¹/2 cups warm water, yeast, and sugar; stir to dissolve. Let stand until foamy, about 5 minutes. Add salt and 2 cups flour; beat well with wooden spoon. Gradually stir in 1¹/2 cups flour to make soft dough.

2. Turn dough onto floured surface and knead until smooth and elastic, about 6 minutes, kneading in enough of remaining ¹/2 cup flour just to keep dough from sticking.

3. Shape dough into ball; place in greased large bowl, turning dough to grease top. Cover bowl with plastic

wrap and let dough rise in warm place (80° to 85°F) until doubled in volume, about 30 minutes.

4. Preheat oven to 400°F. Grease two cookie sheets. Punch down dough and cut into 12 equal pieces. Roll each piece into 24-inch-long rope. Shape ropes into loop-shaped pretzels.

5. In small bowl, whisk remaining 1/2 cup warm water and baking soda until soda has dissolved.

6. Dip pretzels in baking-soda mixture and place 1 1/2 inches apart on prepared cookie sheets; sprinkle with kosher salt. Bake until browned, 16 to 18 minutes, rotating cookie sheets between upper and lower oven racks halfway through baking. Serve pretzels warm, or transfer to wire racks to cool. Makes 12 pretzels.

Each pretzel: About 167 calories (5 percent calories from fat), 5g protein, 33g carbohydrate, 1g total fat (0g saturated), 0mg cholesterol, 1192mg sodium.

Grilled Flatbread

Prep: 15 minutes plus rising   Grill: about 5 minutes per flatbread

Cooking this bread on the grill gives it a unique look and imparts a rustic flavor. Serve simply with herb-infused olive oil and fresh herbs, or top with our chopped salad

1 1/4 **cups warm water (105° to 115°F)**
    1 **package active dry yeast**
    1 **teaspoon sugar**
    4 **cups (approx.) all-purpose flour**
    3 **tablespoons (approx.) olive oil**
    2 **teaspoons salt**

1. In large bowl, combine 1/4 cup warm water, yeast, and sugar; stir to dissolve. Let stand until foamy, about 5 minutes. With wooden spoon, stir in 1 1/2 cups flour, 2 tablespoons oil, salt, and remaining 1 cup warm water until combined. With spoon, gradually stir in 2 cups flour. With floured hands, knead mixture to combine in bowl.

2. Turn dough onto lightly floured surface and knead until smooth and elastic, about 10 minutes, working in remaining 1/2 cup flour while kneading.

3. Shape dough into a ball and place in greased large bowl, turning dough to grease top. Cover and let rise in warm place (80° to 85°F) until doubled in volume, about 1 hour. (After dough has risen, if not using dough right away, punch down and leave in bowl, covered loosely

with greased plastic wrap. Refrigerate until ready to use, up to 24 hours. When ready to use, follow directions below.)

4. Prepare grill. Punch down dough. Turn dough onto lightly floured surface. Cover and let rest 15 minutes for easier shaping.

5. Shape dough into 4 balls. On lightly floured surface, with floured rolling pin, roll 1 dough ball at a time into a 12-inch round about 1/8 inch thick. (The diameter or shape of the round is not as important as an even thickness.) Place rounds on greased large cookie sheets; lightly brush tops with some remaining oil.

6. With hands, place 1 round at a time, greased side down, on grill over medium heat. Grill until grill marks appear on underside and dough stiffens (dough may puff slightly), 2 to 3 minutes. Brush top with some oil. With tongs, turn bread over and grill until grill marks appear on underside and bread is cooked through, 2 to 3 minutes longer. Transfer flatbread to tray; keep warm. Repeat with remaining dough rounds. Makes 4 flatbreads, 12 servings.

Each serving: About 185 calories (19 percent calories from fat), 5g protein, 32g carbohydrate, 4g total fat (1g saturated), 0mg cholesterol, 355mg sodium.

Traditional Irish Soda Bread

Prep: 15 minutes   Bake: 1 hour

This bread is rich and tender, and even better when served warm with butter.

4 cups all-purpose flour
1/4 cup sugar
1 tablespoon baking powder
1 1/2 teaspoons salt
1 teaspoon baking soda
6 tablespoons cold butter or margarine, cut into pieces
1 1/2 cups buttermilk

1. Preheat oven to 350°F. Grease cookie sheet. In large bowl, combine flour, sugar, baking powder, salt, and baking soda. With pastry blender or two knives used scissor-fashion, cut in butter until mixture resembles coarse crumbs. Stir in buttermilk just until flour is moistened (dough will be sticky).

2. Turn dough onto well-floured surface; with lightly floured hands, knead 8 to 10 times to mix. (Do not overknead, or bread will be tough.) Shape into ball; place on prepared cookie sheet.

3. Dust dough lightly with all-purpose flour. With serrated knife or single-edge razor blade, in center, cut an "x" 4 inches long and about 1/4 inch deep. Bake until toothpick inserted in center comes out clean, about 1 hour. Transfer loaf to wire rack to cool. Makes 1 loaf, 12 slices.

Each slice: About 235 calories (27 percent calories from fat), 5g protein, 38g carbohydrate, 7g total fat (4g saturated), 17mg cholesterol, 609mg sodium.

Golden Raisin and Dried Cranberry Soda Bread

Prep: 15 minutes   Bake: 50 to 55 minutes

This wonderfully moist quick bread will satisfy any craving for soda bread. We like to use cranberries during the holiday season, but other dried fruits, such as chopped apricots or cherries, can be used. Enjoy slices fresh out of the oven or toasted and buttered the next day.

2 1/2 cups all-purpose flour
1/2 cup whole wheat flour
1/2 cup plus 2 teaspoons sugar
2 teaspoons baking soda
1/4 teaspoon salt
4 tablespoons cold margarine or butter, cut into pieces
1/2 cup golden raisins
1/2 cup dried cranberries
1 1/2 cups buttermilk

1. Preheat oven to 350°F. Grease 9" by 5" metal loaf pan.

2. In large bowl, combine all-purpose flour, whole-wheat flour, 1/2 cup sugar, baking soda, and salt. With pastry blender or two knives used scissor-fashion, cut in margarine until mixture resembles fine crumbs. With spoon, stir in raisins and cranberries, then buttermilk just until batter is combined.

3. Spoon batter into prepared loaf pan. Sprinkle top with remaining 2 teaspoons sugar. Bake until toothpick inserted in center of loaf comes out clean, 50 to 55 minutes. Cool loaf in pan on wire rack 10 minutes; remove from pan and cool completely on wire rack. Makes 1 loaf, 12 slices.

Each slice: About 230 calories (20 percent calories from fat), 5g protein, 44g carbohydrate, 5g total fat (1g saturated), 1mg cholesterol, 340mg sodium.

Southern Corn Bread

Prep: 10 minutes   Bake: 25 minutes

For a golden brown crust, bake this unsweetened corn bread in a cast-iron skillet. Eat it warm!

4	tablespoons butter or margarine
1 1/2	cups cornmeal
1	cup all-purpose flour
2	teaspoons baking powder
1	teaspoon salt
1/4	teaspoon baking soda
1 3/4	cups buttermilk
2	large eggs

1. Preheat oven to 450°F. Place butter in 10-inch cast-iron skillet or 9-inch square baking pan; place in oven just until butter melts, 3 to 5 minutes. Tilt skillet to coat evenly.

2. Meanwhile, in large bowl, combine cornmeal, flour, baking powder, salt, and baking soda. In medium bowl, with fork, beat buttermilk and eggs until blended. Add melted butter to buttermilk mixture, then add to flour mixture. Stir just until flour is moistened (batter will be lumpy).

3. Pour batter into prepared skillet. Bake until golden at edges and toothpick inserted in center comes out clean, about 25 minutes. Serve warm. Makes 8 servings.

Each serving: About 243 calories (30 percent calories from fat), 7g protein, 35g carbohydrate, 8g total fat (4g saturated), 71mg cholesterol, 584mg sodium.

Corn and Black-Pepper Scones

Prep: 10 minutes   Bake: 20 to 25 minutes

These are at their peak when warm, so serve straight from the oven or reheat.

2 1/4	cups all-purpose flour
2	tablespoons sugar
2	teaspoons baking powder
1/2	teaspoon coarsely ground black pepper
1/4	teaspoon salt
4	tablespoons cold margarine or butter, cut into pieces
1	can (8 1/2 ounces) cream-style corn
1	large egg, beaten

1. Preheat oven to 400°F. In large bowl, mix flour, sugar, baking powder, pepper, and salt. With pastry blender or 2 knives used scissor-fashion, cut in margarine until mixture resembles coarse crumbs. With fork, stir corn and egg into flour mixture just until blended.

2. Spoon dough onto ungreased large cookie sheet. With floured hands, pat dough into 9-inch round (dough will be sticky).

3. Bake until golden, 20 to 25 minutes. Transfer cookie sheet to wire rack to cool scones slightly, about 10 minutes. Cut into 12 wedges and serve warm. Makes 12 scones.

Each scone: About 150 calories (30 percent calories from fat), 3g protein, 24g carbohydrate, 5g total fat (1g saturated), 18mg cholesterol, 220mg sodium.

Cranberry-Orange Bread

Prep: 20 minutes   Bake: 55 minutes

Bake this tasty bread a day ahead to allow the flavors to develop.

- **1 large orange**
- **2¹/₂ cups all-purpose flour**
- **1 cup sugar**
- **2 teaspoons baking powder**
- **¹/₂ teaspoon baking soda**
- **¹/₂ teaspoon salt**
- **4 tablespoons butter or margarine, melted**
- **2 large eggs**
- **2 cups cranberries, coarsely chopped**
- **³/₄ cup walnuts, chopped (optional)**

1. Preheat oven to 375°F. Grease 9" by 5" metal loaf pan. From orange, grate 1 teaspoon peel and squeeze ¹/₂ cup juice.

2. In large bowl, combine flour, sugar, baking powder, baking soda, and salt. In small bowl, beat orange peel, orange juice, melted butter, and eggs until blended. With wooden spoon, stir egg mixture into flour mixture just until blended (batter will be stiff). Stir in cranberries and walnuts, if using.

3. Pour batter into prepared pan. Bake until toothpick inserted in center comes out clean, 55 to 60 minutes. Cool loaf in pan on wire rack 10 minutes; remove from pan and cool completely on wire rack. Makes 1 loaf, 12 slices.

Each slice without walnuts: About 223 calories (20 percent calories from fat), 4g protein, 40g carbohydrate, 5g total fat (3g saturated), 46mg cholesterol, 281mg sodium.

Lowfat Banana Bread

Prep: 20 minutes   Bake: 40 minutes

For a whole-grain variation, substitute ¹/₂ cup whole-wheat flour for the same amount of all-purpose flour.

1³/4   cups all-purpose flour
¹/2   cup sugar
1   teaspoon baking powder
¹/2   teaspoon baking soda
¹/2   teaspoon salt
1   cup mashed very ripe bananas (2 medium)
¹/3   cup fruit-based substitute for fat or unsweetened applesauce
2   large egg whites
1   large egg
¹/4   cup pecans, chopped

1. Preheat oven to 350°F. Grease 9" by 5" metal loaf pan. In large bowl, combine flour, sugar, baking powder, baking soda, and salt. In medium bowl, with fork, mix bananas, fat substitute, egg whites, and egg until well blended. Stir banana mixture into flour mixture just until flour mixture is moistened.

2. Pour batter into prepared pan; sprinkle with chopped pecans. Bake until toothpick inserted in center comes out almost clean, 40 to 45 minutes. Cool in pan on wire rack 10 minutes; remove from pan and cool completely on wire rack. Makes 1 loaf, 16 slices.

Each slice: About 119 calories (15 percent calories from fat), 3g protein, 23g carbohydrate, 2g total fat (0g saturated), 13mg cholesterol, 155mg sodium.

Skinny Carrot Muffins

Prep: 15 minutes   Bake: 30 minutes

Moist muffins studded with raisins and carrots—perfect for a light breakfast or dessert.

2¹/4 **cups all-purpose flour**
¹/2 **cup granulated sugar**
1 **teaspoon ground cinnamon**
1 **teaspoon salt**
1 **teaspoon baking soda**
¹/2 **teaspoon baking powder**
¹/4 **teaspoon ground ginger**
3 **medium carrots, peeled and finely shredded (1¹/2 cups)**
1 **container (8 ounces) vanilla nonfat yogurt**
¹/2 **cup thawed, frozen egg substitute**
¹/2 **cup unsweetened applesauce**
¹/2 **cup dark seedless raisins**
¹/3 **cup packed light-brown sugar**
1 **teaspoon vanilla extract**
1 **teaspoon confectioners' sugar**

1. Preheat oven to 350°F. Spray eight 6-ounce brioche pans or jumbo (3" by 1¹/2") muffin-pan cups with non-stick cooking spray. Place the prepared brioche pans in a 15¹/2" by 10¹/2" jelly-roll pan for easier handling.

2. In medium bowl, combine flour, granulated sugar, cinnamon, salt, baking soda, baking powder, and ginger. In large bowl, with wire whisk or fork, mix shredded carrots, yogurt, egg substitute, applesauce, raisins, brown sugar, and vanilla until well blended. Stir flour mixture into carrot mixture just until flour mixture is moistened.

3. Spoon batter into brioche pans or muffin cups. Bake until toothpick inserted in center of muffins comes out clean, about 30 minutes. Cool muffins in pans on wire racks 10 minutes; remove muffins from pans and cool slightly on wire racks. Sprinkle with confectioners' sugar. Makes 8 muffins.

Each muffin: About 290 calories (3 percent calories from fat), 7g protein, 65g carbohydrate, 1g total fat (0g saturated), 1mg cholesterol, 505mg sodium.

Oranges with Caramel, page 262

Oranges with Caramel

Prep: 30 minutes plus chilling   Cook: 10 minutes

Serve as a light and elegant finale to a rich meal. When the caramel-drizzled orange rounds are refrigerated, the caramel melts into a luscious golden syrup.

- **6 large navel oranges**
- **2 tablespoons brandy (optional)**
- **1 cup sugar**

1. From oranges, with vegetable peeler, remove 6 strips (3" by 3/4" each) peel. Cut strips lengthwise into slivers. Cut remaining peel and white pith from oranges. Slice oranges into 1/4-inch-thick rounds and place on deep platter, overlapping slices slightly. Sprinkle with brandy, if desired, and orange peel.

2. In 11/2-quart saucepan, cook sugar over medium heat, stirring to dissolve any lumps, until sugar has melted and turned deep amber. Drizzle caramel over orange slices. Cover and refrigerate until caramel melts, about 2 hours. Makes 6 servings.

Each serving: About 208 calories (0 percent calories from fat), 2g protein, 53g carbohydrate, 0g total fat, 0mg cholesterol, 2mg sodium.

Orange Slices Marinated in Marmalade

Prep: 15 minutes plus chilling

A super-simple dessert with triple orange flavor.

- **5 medium navel oranges, peeled and sliced into rounds**
- **1/2 cup sweet or bitter orange marmalade**
- **1 tablespoon orange-flavored liqueur (optional)**

Arrange orange slices on platter, overlapping them slightly; brush with marmalade. Sprinkle with liqueur, if you like. Cover and refrigerate at least 30 minutes or up to several hours. Makes 4 servings.

Each serving: About 179 calories (0 percent calories from fat), 2g protein, 47g carbohydrate, 0g total fat , 0mg cholesterol, 24mg sodium.

Flambéed Bananas

Prep: 5 minutes   Cook: 8 minutes

Be sure to use dark Jamaican rum in this classic dessert: It gives the bananas an irresistible flavor.

- **3 tablespoons butter or margarine**
- **3/4 cup packed brown sugar**
- **1 tablespoon fresh lemon juice**
- **4 ripe medium bananas, each peeled, cut crosswise in half, and then lengthwise in half**
- **1/3 cup dark Jamaican rum or brandy**
  vanilla ice cream (optional)

1. In 12-inch skillet, melt butter over medium heat. Stir in brown sugar and lemon juice. Place bananas in single layer in skillet; cook until just slightly softened, about 2 minutes per side. Reduce heat to low.

2. In 1-quart saucepan, heat rum over low heat. With long match, carefully ignite rum; pour over bananas. Spoon rum over bananas until flames die out. Serve with ice cream, if you like. Makes 8 servings.

Each serving: About 179 calories (25 percent calories from fat), 1g protein, 34g carbohydrate, 5g total fat (3g saturated), 12mg cholesterol, 53mg sodium.

Strawberries in White Wine

Prep: 10 minutes

Make this simple Italian treat with perfectly ripe, fragrant fruit.

1/3 cup dry white wine, such as riesling or sauvignon blanc

2 tablespoons sugar

1 pint strawberries, hulled and cut in half

In small bowl, stir wine and sugar together until sugar has dissolved. Divide strawberries among four goblets. Pour wine mixture over fruit. Makes 4 servings.

Each serving: About 61 (0 percent calories from fat), 0g protein, 12g carbohydrate, 0g total fat, 0mg cholesterol, 2mg sodium.

Peaches in Red Wine

Prepare as directed but substitute 1/3 cup red wine for white wine and 2 cups sliced, peeled peaches (3 to 4 peaches) for strawberries. Makes 4 servings.

Each serving: About 75 calories (0 percent calories from fat), 1g protein, 16g carbohydrate, 0g total fat, 0mg cholesterol, 1mg sodium.

Nutrition Spotlight: Strawberries

Easy to find all year long, strawberries are at their sweet-juice peak in spring. Delicious and nutritious, 12 medium berries weigh in at 45 calories, 3 grams of fiber, and about 135 percent of the Daily Value for vitamin C.

Broiled Pineapple Wedges

Prep: 20 minutes   Broil: 10 to 15 minutes

1 medium pineapple

3 tablespoons brown sugar

2 tablespoons margarine or butter

1. Preheat broiler. Line broiling pan with foil (do not use rack). Cut pineapple lengthwise into 4 wedges, through crown to stem end, leaving on leafy crown. Loosen fruit from each pineapple wedge by cutting close to rind. Leaving fruit in shell, cut flesh crosswise into 1/2-inch-thick slices for easier serving. Place pineapple wedges, cut-side up, in prepared broiling pan.

2. In small saucepan, heat brown sugar and margarine over low heat until melted and smooth. Brush pineapple wedges with brown sugar mixture. Place pan in broiler at closest position to heat source. Broil until golden brown, 10 to 15 minutes. Makes 4 servings.

Each serving: About 220 calories (29 percent calories from fat), 1g protein, 43g carbohydrate, 7g total fat (1g saturated), 0mg cholesterol, 75mg sodium.

Broiled Amaretti Plums

Prep: 5 minutes   Broil: 2 to 3 minutes

Turn ripe, juicy plums into a great warm dessert that you can make at the last minute—with only two ingredients!

- **6 ripe medium red or purple plums (1¹/₂ pounds), each cut in half**
- **16 amaretti cookies, crushed**
  vanilla nonfat frozen yogurt (optional)

Preheat broiler. On rack in broiling pan, arrange plums, cut side up, in one layer. Sprinkle crushed amaretti cookies over plums. Place pan in broiler about 5 inches from heat source. Broil until crumbs are lightly browned and plums are heated through, 2 to 3 minutes. Serve warm, with frozen yogurt if you like. Makes 6 servings.

Each serving: About 130 calories (14 percent calories from fat), 2g protein, 26g carbohydrate, 2g total fat (0g saturated), 0mg cholesterol, 10mg sodium.

Fresh Apple Soufflés

Prep: 45 minutes plus cooling   Bake: 12 minutes

A fresh fruit puree is the base for these little soufflés. So much sophistication and flavor for so few calories.

- **4 cups peeled, cored and coarsely chopped apples (4 to 5 medium), such as McIntosh or Cortland**
- **1 tablespoon fresh lemon juice**
- **1 tablespoon butter or margarine, melted**
- **2 tablespoons plus ¹/₄ cup sugar**
- **6 large egg whites**
- **¹/₂ teaspoon cream of tartar**
- **1 teaspoon vanilla extract**

1. In nonreactive 2-quart saucepan, combine apples and lemon juice. Cover and cook over medium-high heat until apples are soft, about 10 minutes. Remove cover and cook, stirring occasionally, until almost all liquid has evaporated and apples are reduced to 1 cup, about 10 minutes longer.

2. In blender with center of cover removed to allow steam to escape, or in food processor with knife blade attached, puree apple mixture until smooth. Transfer to large bowl; cool to room temperature.

3. Meanwhile, preheat oven to 425°F. Brush six 6-ounce custard cups or ramekins with melted butter and sprinkle with 2 tablespoons sugar.

4. In large bowl, with mixer at high speed, beat egg whites and cream of tartar until soft peaks form when beaters are lifted. Sprinkle in remaining ¹/₄ cup sugar, 1 tablespoon at a time, beating until sugar has dissolved. Add vanilla; continue beating until egg whites stand in stiff, glossy peaks when beaters are lifted. With rubber spatula, fold beaten egg whites, one-third at a time, into apple mixture just until blended.

5. Spoon into prepared custard cups. Place cups in jelly-roll pan for easier handling. Bake until soufflés have puffed and begin to brown, 12 to 15 minutes. Serve immediately. Makes 6 servings.

Each serving: About 127 calories, (14 percent calories from fat) 4g protein, 24g carbohydrate, 2g total fat (1g saturated), 5mg cholesterol, 75mg sodium.

Fresh Pear Soufflés

Prepare soufflés as directed but prepare pear puree instead of apple puree: In nonreactive 2-quart saucepan, combine 4 cups peeled, cored, and coarsely chopped fully ripe pears (5 to 6 medium), 1 tablespoon fresh lemon juice, and 2 teaspoons minced, peeled fresh ginger. Cover and cook over medium-high heat until pears have softened, about 15 minutes. Remove cover and cook, stirring occasionally, until almost all liquid has evaporated and pears are reduced to 1 cup, 10 to 15 minutes longer. In blender with center of cover removed to allow steam to escape or in food processor with knife blade attached, puree pear mixture until smooth. Cool to room temperature. Fold beaten egg whites into pear puree and bake as directed.

Banana Soufflés

Prepare soufflés as directed but prepare banana puree instead of apple puree: In blender or in food processor with knife blade attached, puree 3 very ripe large bananas, cut into large pieces, with 1 tablespoon fresh lemon juice and 1/4 teaspoon ground cinnamon until smooth. Fold beaten egg whites into banana puree and bake as directed.

Peach or Apricot Soufflés

Prepare soufflés as directed but prepare peach or apricot puree instead of apple puree: Drain 1 can (1 pound, 13 ounces) peaches in heavy syrup or 2 cans (16 ounces each) apricots in heavy syrup. In blender or food processor with knife blade attached, puree peaches or apricots until smooth. Transfer to 4-quart saucepan and heat to boiling over medium-high heat. Reduce heat to medium-low and cook, stirring occasionally, until puree has reduced to 1 cup, 15 to 20 minutes. Cool to room temperature. Stir in 1 tablespoon fresh lemon juice and 1/8 teaspoon almond extract. Fold beaten egg whites into fruit puree and bake as directed.

Apple Charlotte

Prep: 1 hour   Bake: 20 minutes

This traditional French farmhouse dessert is simply intensely flavored applesauce baked in a buttery sliced-bread shell.

- 1 **lemon**
- 5 **pounds Golden Delicious apples, peeled, cored, and cut into 3/4-inch pieces (15 cups)**
- 6 **tablespoons butter or margarine, softened**
- 2/3 **cup sugar**
  - **pinch salt**
- 15 **slices firm white bread, crusts removed**

1. From lemon, with vegetable peeler, remove 2 strips (3" by 1" each) peel; squeeze 1 tablespoon juice.

2. In 5-quart Dutch oven, combine lemon peel, apples, and 2 tablespoons butter. Cover and cook over medium-high heat, stirring occasionally, until apples are almost tender, about 15 minutes.

3. Discard lemon peel and stir in sugar. Increase heat to high. Cook, mashing apples with spoon and stirring frequently to prevent burning, until apples are tender and lightly caramelized and almost all liquid has evaporated, 15 to 25 minutes. Stir in lemon juice and salt.

4. Meanwhile, preheat oven to 425°F. Spread remaining 4 tablespoons butter over one side of bread slices. Line bottom and sides of 9" by 5" metal loaf pan with some of bread, placing buttered side against pan and trimming bread to fit.

5. Spoon apple mixture into bread-lined pan; top with remaining bread, placing buttered side up. Bake 20 minutes. Invert onto serving plate. To serve, cut into slices with serrated knife while warm. Makes 10 servings.

Each serving: About 326 calories (25 percent calories from fat), 3g protein, 61g carbohydrate, 9g total fat (5g saturated), 19mg cholesterol, 290mg sodium.

Fast Baked Apples with Oatmeal Streusel

Prep: 8 minutes   Microwave: 12 to 14 minutes

Cooking apples in the microwave, rather than the regular oven, yields plumper, juicier, less shriveled fruit—and saves a big chunk of time!

- **4   large Rome or Cortland apples (10 ounces each)**
- **1/4   cup packed brown sugar**
- **1/4   cup quick-cooking oats, uncooked**
- **2   tablespoons chopped dates**
- **1/2   teaspoon ground cinnamon**
- **2   teaspoons margarine or butter**

1. Core apples, cutting out a 1 1/4-inch-diameter cylinder from center of each, almost but not all the way through to bottom. Remove peel about one-third of the way down from top. Place apples in shallow 1 1/2-quart ceramic casserole or 8" by 8" glass baking dish.

2. In small bowl, combine brown sugar, oats, dates, and cinnamon. Fill each cored apple with equal amounts of oat mixture. (Mixture will spill over top of apples.) Place 1/2 teaspoon margarine on top of filling in each apple.

3. Microwave apples, covered, on medium-high until tender, 12 to 14 minutes, turning each apple halfway through cooking time. Spoon cooking liquid from baking dish over apples to serve. Makes 4 servings.

Each serving: About 240 calories (11 percent calories from fat), 2g protein, 54g carbohydrate, 3g total fat (1g saturated), 0mg cholesterol, 30mg sodium.

Lemon-Anise Poached Pears

Prep: 20 minutes plus chilling　Cook: 1 hour

Serve these tender pears and their bracing aromatic syrup in a large glass bowl, and garnish with glistening orange slices.

- **1　lemon**
- **8　firm-ripe pears, such as Bosc or Anjou (8 to 9 ounces each), peeled and cored**
- **6　cups water**
- **1　cup sugar**
- **3　whole star anise or 1 teaspoon anise seeds**
- **1　small orange, thinly sliced**

1. From lemon, with vegetable peeler, remove 3 strips (3" by 3/4" each) peel; squeeze 2 tablespoons juice. In nonreactive 8-quart saucepot, combine lemon peel, pears, water, sugar, and star anise; heat to boiling over high heat. Reduce heat; cover and simmer until pears are tender, about 30 minutes. With slotted spoon, transfer pears to large bowl. Stir lemon juice into bowl with pears. Strain syrup through sieve into separate large bowl. Return syrup to saucepot.

2. Heat syrup to boiling over high heat; cook, uncovered, until reduced to 3 cups, about 15 minutes. Pour hot syrup over pears. Cover and refrigerate, turning occasionally, until pears are well chilled, at least 6 hours.

3. Serve pears with syrup, garnished with orange slices. Makes 8 servings.

Each serving: About 236 calories (4 percent calories from fat), 1g protein, 61g carbohydrate, 1g total fat (0g saturated), 0mg cholesterol, 1mg sodium.

Roasted Pears with Marsala

Prep: 25 minutes   Bake: 40 to 50 minutes

Roasting pears at high heat intensifies their flavor, and the Marsala adds a sweet nuttiness. Ruby port is a delicious alternative.

- **1 lemon**
- **8 medium Bosc pears**
- **2 teaspoons plus 1/3 cup sugar**
- **1/2 cup sweet Marsala wine**
- **1/3 cup water**
- **2 tablespoons butter or margarine, melted**

1. Preheat oven to 450°F. From lemon, with vegetable peeler, remove peel in strips (2½" by ½" each); squeeze juice.

2. With melon baller or small knife, remove cores from pears by cutting through blossom end (bottom) of unpeeled pears (do not remove stems). With pastry brush, brush cavity of each pear with lemon juice, then sprinkle each cavity with 1/4 teaspoon sugar.

3. In shallow 1½- to 2-quart baking dish, combine lemon peel, wine, and water. Place remaining 1/3 cup sugar on waxed paper. With pastry brush, brush pears with melted butter, then roll in sugar to coat. Stand pears in baking dish. Sprinkle any remaining sugar into baking dish.

4. Bake pears, basting occasionally with syrup in dish, until tender, 40 to 45 minutes.

5. Cool slightly to serve warm, or cool completely and cover and refrigerate up to 1 day. Reheat to serve warm, if you like. Makes 8 servings.

Each serving: About 201 calories (18 percent calories from fat), 1g protein, 45g carbohydrate, 4g total fat (2g saturated), 8mg cholesterol, 31mg sodium.

Quick Poached Pears with Ruby-Red Raspberry Sauce

Prep: 10 minutes   Microwave: 5 to 6 minutes

- **2 medium, ripe Bosc pears**
- **1/2 lemon**
- **2 teaspoons granulated sugar**
- **2 tablespoons water**
- **1 1/2 cups fresh or frozen (thawed) raspberries (reserve 10 raspberries for garnish)**
- **1/3 cup confectioners' sugar**
- **1 tablespoon black currant-flavor or orange-flavor liqueur**

1. With melon baller or small knife, remove cores from pears by cutting through blossom end (bottom) of pears. Peel pears almost to top but do not remove stems. Rub pears with lemon half; sprinkle with granulated sugar.

2. In glass pie plate, arrange pears on their sides with stems toward center; add water. Microwave, uncovered, on high until tender, 5 to 6 minutes, turning pears over halfway through cooking. Transfer pears, stem ends up, to 2 dessert plates; set aside until ready to serve.

3. In blender at high speed, puree raspberries. Sift confectioners' sugar through coarse sieve into small bowl. Press raspberry puree through same sieve into same bowl to remove seeds. Discard seeds. Stir liqueur into raspberry mixture.

4. To serve, spoon raspberry sauce over poached pears. Garnish with reserved raspberries. Makes 2 servings.

Each serving: About 245 calories (4 percent calories from fat), 1g protein, 59g carbohydrate, 1g total fat (0g saturated), 0mg cholesterol, 2mg sodium.

Skillet Blueberry Crisps

Prep: 10 minutes   Cook: 5 minutes

Homespun and delicious, but easy to stir up in a saucepan!

- **1 medium lemon**
- **1/2 cup cold water**
- **2 tablespoons brown sugar**
- **2 teaspoons cornstarch**
- **2 teaspoons almond-flavor liqueur**
- **1 tablespoon margarine or butter, softened**
- **1 pint blueberries**
- **10 amaretti cookies, coarsely crushed**
  confectioners' sugar

1. From lemon, grate 1/4 teaspoon peel and squeeze 1 teaspoon juice. In 2-quart saucepan, combine lemon peel, lemon juice, water, brown sugar, cornstarch, and liqueur. Add margarine and half of blueberries; lightly crush blueberries with potato masher or side of spoon. Bring to a boil over medium heat, stirring constantly. Stir in remaining blueberries and cook, stirring, 2 minutes longer.

2. Spoon hot blueberry mixture into 4 dessert or custard cups; top with cookie crumbs and sprinkle with confectioners' sugar. Serve warm. Makes 4 servings.

Each serving: About 160 calories (23 percent calories from fat), 1g protein, 30g carbohydrate, 4g total fat (1g saturated), 0mg cholesterol, 50mg sodium.

Plum Dessert Pizza

Prep: 30 minutes plus chilling   Bake: 1 hour

As easy as it is impressive, this rustic fruit tart is too fabulous to save for special occasions. Make sure plums are ripe to guarantee their juicy sweetness.

SWEET PIZZA CRUST:

- **1 1/3 cups all-purpose flour**
- **1/2 cup sugar**
- **1 tablespoon baking powder**
  pinch salt
- **2 tablespoons cold margarine or butter, cut up**
- **1/3 cup part-skim ricotta cheese**
- **2 teaspoons water**
- **1 1/4 teaspoons vanilla extract**
- **2 large egg whites, lightly beaten**

FRUIT TOPPING:

- **8 ripe medium red or purple plums (2 pounds), each cut into eighths**
- **3 tablespoons sugar**
- **1/2 cup blueberries**

1. Prepare crust: In food processor with knife blade attached, pulse flour, sugar, baking powder, salt, and margarine until mixed. Add ricotta, water, vanilla, and half of beaten egg whites; pulse just until dough forms a ball. Wrap dough in plastic wrap and refrigerate at least 1 hour or overnight.

2. Preheat oven to 350°F. Spray large cookie sheet with nonstick cooking spray.

3. With rolling pin, roll dough between 2 sheets of lightly floured waxed paper into 11-inch round. Remove top sheet of waxed paper and invert dough round onto prepared cookie sheet; remove remaining sheet of paper. Fold in edge of round to make 1/2-inch rim. Bake 10 minutes. Remove from oven and brush top of crust with remaining egg white.

4. Top warm crust with fruit topping: Arrange plum slices, peel side down, in concentric circles on crust; sprinkle evenly with sugar. Bake pizza 40 minutes; top with blueberries and bake until crust is golden brown

and plums are cooked through, 10 minutes longer. Cool pizza on cookie sheet 10 minutes. Slide pizza onto platter or cutting board and cut into wedges. Serve warm. Makes 12 servings.

Each serving: About 155 calories (17 percent calories from fat), 3g protein, 30g carbohydrate, 3g total fat (1g saturated), 2mg cholesterol, 145mg sodium.

Country Plum Cobbler

Prep: 20 minutes plus cooling   Bake: 50 to 60 minutes

Comfort food at its best: fresh, sugared summer plums baked until bubbly, under a golden biscuit crust.

2¹/2	**pounds ripe red or purple plums (about 10 medium), each cut into quarters**
¹/2	**cup sugar**
2	**tablespoons all-purpose flour**
1³/4	**cups reduced-fat all-purpose baking mix**
¹/4	**cup yellow cornmeal**
³/4	**cup water**

1. Preheat oven to 400°F. In large bowl, toss plums with sugar and flour. Spoon plum mixture into shallow 2-quart ceramic or glass baking dish. Cover loosely with foil. Bake until plums are very tender, 30 to 35 minutes.

2. Meanwhile, prepare topping: In medium bowl, stir baking mix, cornmeal, and water just until combined.

3. Remove baking dish from oven. Drop 10 heaping spoonfuls of batter randomly on top of plum mixture. Return cobbler to oven and bake, uncovered, until biscuits are browned and plum mixture is bubbling, 20 to 25 minutes longer. Cool slightly to serve warm, or cool completely to serve later. Reheat if desired. Makes 10 servings.

Each serving: About 190 calories (9 percent calories from fat), 3g protein, 41g carbohydrate, 2g total fat (0g saturated), 0mg cholesterol, 230mg sodium.

Peach Cobbler

Prep: 45 minutes   Bake: 45 minutes

A true summer treat, bursting with the flavor of ripe peaches and topped with lemon-scented biscuits. Serve with vanilla frozen yogurt.

PEACH FILLING:

- 6 pounds ripe medium peaches (16 to 18), peeled, pitted, and sliced (13 cups)
- 1/4 cup fresh lemon juice
- 2/3 cup granulated sugar
- 1/2 cup packed brown sugar
- 1/4 cup cornstarch

LEMON BISCUITS:

- 2 cups all-purpose flour
- 1/2 cup plus 1 teaspoon granulated sugar
- 2 1/2 teaspoons baking powder
- 1 teaspoon freshly grated lemon peel
- 1/4 teaspoon salt
- 4 tablespoons cold butter or margarine, cut into pieces
- 2/3 cup plus 1 tablespoon half-and-half or light cream

1. Prepare filling: Preheat oven to 425°F. In non-reactive 8-quart saucepot, toss peaches with lemon juice; add granulated sugar, brown sugar, and cornstarch, tossing to coat. Heat over medium heat, stirring occasionally, until bubbling; boil 1 minute. Spoon hot peach mixture into 13" by 9" baking dish. Place baking dish on foil-lined cookie sheet to catch any overflow during baking. Bake 10 minutes.

2. Meanwhile, prepare biscuits: In medium bowl, combine flour, 1/2 cup granulated sugar, baking powder, lemon peel, and salt. With pastry blender or two knives used scissor-fashion, cut in butter until mixture resembles coarse crumbs. Stir in 2/3 cup half-and-half just until mixture forms soft dough that leaves side of bowl.

3. Turn dough onto lightly floured surface. With lightly floured hands, pat into 10" by 6" rectangle. With floured knife, cut rectangle lengthwise in half, then cut each half crosswise into 6 pieces.

4. Remove baking dish from oven. Arrange biscuits on top of fruit. Brush biscuits with remaining 1 tablespoon half-and-half and sprinkle with remaining 1 teaspoon granulated sugar. Return cobbler to oven and bake until filling is hot and bubbling and biscuits are golden, about 35 minutes longer. To serve warm, cool cobbler on wire rack about 1 hour. Makes 12 servings.

Each serving: About 331 calories (16 percent calories from fat), 4g protein, 69g carbohydrate, 6g total fat (3g saturated), 16mg cholesterol, 199mg sodium.

Three-Fruit Salad with Vanilla Bean Syrup

Prep: 30 minutes plus chilling   Cook: 10 minutes

Perfect alone but also a delicious accompaniment to pound cake. If you don't have a vanilla bean, stir one-half teaspoon vanilla extract into the chilled syrup.

- 2 **large lemons**
- 1 **vanilla bean**
- 3/4 **cup water**
- 3/4 **cup sugar**
- 3 **ripe mangoes, peeled and cut into 1-inch pieces**
- 2 **pints strawberries, hulled and cut in half, or into quarters if large**
- 1 **medium honeydew melon, peeled and cut into 1-inch pieces**

1. From 1 lemon, with vegetable peeler, remove 1-inch-wide continuous strip of peel; from lemons, squeeze 1/4 cup juice. Cut vanilla bean lengthwise in half. With small knife, scrape seeds from vanilla bean; reserve seeds and pod.

2. In 1-quart saucepan, combine lemon peel, vanilla-bean seeds and pod, water, and sugar; heat to boiling over high heat. Reduce heat to medium and cook until syrup has thickened slightly, about 5 minutes. Pour syrup mixture through sieve into small bowl; stir in lemon juice. Cover and refrigerate syrup until chilled, about 2 hours.

3. Place mangoes, strawberries, and melon in large bowl; add syrup and toss. Makes 12 servings.

Each serving: About 138 calories (0 percent calories from fat), 1g protein, 35g carbohydrate, 0g total fat, 0mg cholesterol, 13mg sodium.

Watermelon Bowl

Prep: 1 hour plus chilling   Cook: 10 minutes

For a great presentation, serve this colorful mixture of sweet summer fruits and minty syrup in the hollowed-out water-melon. It makes a very large amount, so it's just right for casual summer get-togethers.

- 1 1/2 **cups water**
- 1 **cup sugar**
- 1 1/2 **cups loosely packed fresh mint leaves and stems, chopped**
- 3 **tablespoons fresh lime juice**
- 1 **large watermelon (20 pounds), cut lengthwise in half**
- 1 **small cantaloupe**
- 6 **large plums, each cut in half and pitted**
- 4 **large nectarines, each cut in half and pitted**
- 1 **pound seedless green grapes**

1. In 2-quart saucepan, combine water and sugar; heat to boiling over medium heat, stirring occasionally until sugar has dissolved. Cook 5 minutes. Stir in mint and lime juice and refrigerate until well chilled.

2. Meanwhile, cut watermelon flesh into bite-size pieces; discard seeds. Cut cantaloupe flesh into bite-size pieces. Cut plums and nectarines into wedges. Combine cut-up fruit with grapes in very large bowl or in shell of watermelon. Hold sieve over fruit and pour chilled syrup through. Gently toss to mix well. Cover and refrigerate about 2 hours to blend flavors, stirring occasionally. Makes about 32 cups.

Each cup: About 111 calories (8 percent calories from fat), 2g protein, 26g carbohydrate, 1g total fat (0g saturated), 0mg cholesterol, 7mg sodium.

Summer Fruit Compote

Prep: 15 minutes.

Refreshing and fat-free—great for Sunday brunch. Leftovers will keep in the refrigerator for up to 3 days.

- 1 tablespoon sugar
- 1 tablespoon dark Jamaican rum
- 1 tablespoon fresh lime juice
- 2 large mangoes, peeled and cut into 3/4-inch pieces
- 1 pint blueberries

In medium bowl, combine sugar, rum, and lime juice. Add mangoes and blueberries; toss to coat. Cover and refrigerate until serving. Makes 6 servings.

Each serving: About 85 (0 percent calories from fat), 1g protein, 21g carbohydrate, 0g total fat, 0mg cholesterol, 5mg sodium.

Autumn Fruit Compote

Prep: 20 minutes plus chilling   Cook: 25 minutes

Dried fruits and fresh apples are poached together for a sweet compote with just a touch of citrus and cinnamon. Serve after a rich entrée such as pork or roast goose.

- 1 orange
- 1 lemon
- 4 medium Golden Delicious or Jonagold apples, each peeled, cored, and cut into 16 wedges
- 1 package (8 ounces) mixed dried fruit (with pitted prunes)
- 1 cup dried Calimyrna figs (6 ounces)
- 1/2 cup sugar
- 1 cinnamon stick (3 inches)
- 3 cups water

1. From orange and lemon, with vegetable peeler, remove peel in 1-inch-wide strips. From lemon, squeeze 2 tablespoons juice (reserve orange for another use).

2. In nonreactive 4-quart saucepan, combine orange and lemon peels, lemon juice, apples, mixed dried fruit, figs, sugar, cinnamon stick, and water; heat to boiling over high heat. Reduce heat; cover and simmer until apples are tender, 15 to 20 minutes.

3. Pour fruit mixture into bowl; cover and refrigerate at least 4 hours to blend flavors. Serve chilled. Store in refrigerator up to 4 days. Makes 8 servings.

Each serving: About 211 calories (4 percent calories from fat), 1g protein, 55g carbohydrate, 1g total fat (0g saturated), 0mg cholesterol, 8mg sodium.

Spicy Plum Compote

Prep: 10 minutes plus chilling   Cook: 6 minutes

Plum slices are simmered just long enough in a lemony-allspice syrup to give them a hint of exotic flavor.

1/2 **cup sugar**

3 **strips lemon peel (3" by 1/2" each)**

4 **whole allspice berries**

2 **cups water**

4 **ripe medium red, purple, and/or green plums (1 pound), cut into 1/2-inch slices**

1/2 **teaspoon vanilla extract**

low-fat yogurt (optional)

1. In 2-quart saucepan, combine sugar, lemon peel, allspice, and water; heat to boiling over high heat. Boil 5 minutes.

2. Stir plums into syrup; heat to boiling over high heat. Reduce heat to low; simmer 1 minute or just until plums are tender.

3. Pour mixture into bowl; stir in vanilla. Cover and refrigerate until cold, about 2 hours. Serve with yogurt if you like. Makes 4 servings.

Each serving: About 135 (0 percent calories from fat), 1g protein, 34g carbohydrate, 0g total fat, 0mg cholesterol, 0mg sodium.

Double Blueberry Pie

Prep: 30 minutes plus chilling   Bake: 8 minutes

In this old New England recipe, the blueberry flavor is intensi-fied by stirring raw berries into the cooked filling. We like it with a simple gingersnap crust to make it especially easy for casual summer entertaining.

1²/₃ **cups gingersnap cookie crumbs (about 25 cookies)**

   5 **tablespoons butter or margarine, melted**

   2 **tablespoons plus ¹/₂ cup sugar**

   2 **tablespoons cornstarch**

   2 **tablespoons cold water**

   3 **pints blueberries**
      whipped cream (optional)

1. Preheat oven to 375°F. In 9-inch pie plate, with fork, mix cookie crumbs, melted butter, and 2 tablespoons sugar until moistened. With hand, press mixture firmly onto bottom and up side of pie plate. Bake 8 minutes. Cool on wire rack.

2. Meanwhile, in 2-quart saucepan, blend cornstarch and water until smooth. Add half of blueberries and remaining ¹/₂ cup sugar to cornstarch mixture; heat to boiling over medium-high heat, pressing blueberries against side of saucepan with back of spoon. Boil, stir-ring constantly, 1 minute. Remove from heat; stir in remaining blueberries.

3. Pour blueberry filling into cooled crust. Press plastic wrap onto surface and refrigerate until thoroughly chilled, about 5 hours. Serve with whipped cream, if desired. Makes 10 servings.

Each serving: About 241 calories (30 percent calories from fat), 2g protein, 42g carbohydrate, 8g total fat (4g saturated), 16mg cholesterol, 201mg sodium.

Raspberry-Peach Pie

Prep: 30 minutes plus cooling   Bake: 1 hour 15 minutes

Make this top-crust-only dessert in a shallow baking dish or deep-dish pie plate.

1¹/₄ **cups all-purpose flour**

 ¹/₂ **plus ¹/₈ teaspoon salt**

   2 **tablespoons shortening**

   6 **tablespoons cold margarine or butter**
      about 4 tablespoons cold water

1¹/₄ **cups sugar**

 ¹/₃ **cup cornstarch**

   3 **pounds ripe peaches (9 medium)**

2¹/₂ **cups raspberries**

   1 **tablespoon lemon juice**

1. In medium bowl, combine flour and ¹/₂ teaspoon salt. With pastry blender or two knives used scissor-fashion, cut in shortening and 4 tablespoons margarine until mixture resembles coarse crumbs. Sprinkle cold water, 1 tablespoon at a time, into flour mixture, mixing lightly with a fork after each addition until dough is just moist enough to hold together. Shape dough into a disk; wrap with plastic wrap and refrigerate until ready to use.

2. Preheat oven to 425°F. In large bowl, combine sugar, cornstarch, and remaining ¹/₈ teaspoon salt. Peel and slice peaches; toss with sugar mixture in bowl. With rubber spatula, gently stir in raspberries and lemon

juice. Spoon peach mixture into 6-cup baking dish or 9 1/2-inch deep-dish pie plate; dot with remaining 2 tablespoons margarine.

3. On lightly floured surface, with floured rolling pin, roll dough 1 1/2 inches larger all around than top of baking dish. Center dough over filling. Trim pastry edge, leaving 1-inch overhang. Fold overhang under; pinch dough onto rim of baking dish to seal. With tip of knife, cut slits in piecrust to allow steam to escape during baking.

4. Place sheet of foil underneath baking dish; crimp foil edges to form a rim to catch any drips during baking. Bake pie until filling is bubbling and crust is golden, about 1 hour and 15 minutes. If necessary to prevent overbrowning, cover pie loosely with a tent of foil after 1 hour of baking. Cool pie on wire rack 1 hour to serve warm or cool completely to serve later. Makes 10 servings.

Each serving: About 315 calories (29 percent calories from fat), 3g protein, 56g carbohydrate, 10g total fat (2g saturated), 0mg cholesterol, 225mg sodium.

Deep-Dish Apple Pie
Prep: 40 minutes plus cooling   Bake: 1 hour 15 minutes

This is the easiest apple pie you'll ever make!

APPLE FILLING:

- 6 pounds Granny Smith apples (12 large), peeled, cored, and each cut into 16 wedges
- 3/4 cup sugar
- 1/3 cup all-purpose flour
- 2 tablespoons fresh lemon juice
- 1/2 teaspoon ground cinnamon

CRUST:

- 2 cups all-purpose flour
- 1/4 cup plus 1 tablespoon sugar
- 2 teaspoons baking powder
- 1/2 teaspoon salt
- 4 tablespoons margarine or butter
- 1 large egg, beaten
- 2/3 cup plus 2 tablespoons heavy cream

1. Prepare apple filling: In large bowl, combine apples, sugar, flour, lemon juice, and cinnamon; toss to coat well. Spoon apple mixture into 13" by 9" glass baking dish; set aside.

2. Preheat oven to 400°F. Prepare crust: In medium bowl, mix flour, 1/4 cup sugar, baking powder, and salt. With pastry blender or 2 knives used scissor-fashion, cut in margarine until mixture resembles coarse crumbs. Stir in egg and 2/3 cup cream until blended.

3. With floured hands, shape dough into a ball. Divide dough into 6 pieces; flatten each to about 1/2-inch thickness and arrange on top of apple mixture. (It is not necessary to completely cover top; as dough bakes, it will spread.) Brush dough with remaining 2 tablespoons cream, and sprinkle with remaining 1 tablespoon sugar.

4. Place sheet of foil underneath baking dish; crimp foil edges to form a rim to catch any drips during baking. Bake pie until apples are tender when pierced with knife, filling is bubbling, and crust is golden, about 1 hour 15 minutes. If necessary to prevent overbrowning, cover pie loosely with a tent of foil halfway through baking time. Cool pie on wire rack 1 hour to serve warm, or cool completely to serve later. Makes 12 servings.

Each serving: About 355 calories (30 percent calories from fat), 4g protein, 64g carbohydrate, 11g total fat (5g saturated), 39mg cholesterol, 210mg sodium.

Plum Yogurt Pops

Prep: 15 minutes plus freezing

Forget store-bought popsicles: This super-fruity refresher will be a cool hit with kids of all ages. Make a day in advance to allow enough time for freezing.

1 pound ripe red or purple plums (4 medium), coarsely chopped

1/2 cup sugar

1 tablespoon fresh lemon juice

2 cups vanilla low-fat yogurt

1. In blender, at medium speed, puree plums, sugar, and lemon juice. Pour plum puree into medium-mesh sieve set over medium bowl. With spoon, press purée against sieve to push through pulp and juice. Discard solids in sieve.

2. With wire whisk, mix yogurt and plum mixture until well combined.

3. Spoon yogurt mixture into sixteen 3-ounce paper cups; freeze 4 hours or until partially frozen. Insert wooden ice-cream-bar sticks and freeze until completely frozen. (Or, spoon yogurt mixture into sixteen 2-ounce popsicle molds; seal and insert wooden sticks as manufacturer directs. Freeze overnight.) Makes 16 pops.

Each pop: About 60 calories (15 percent calories from fat), 1g protein, 13g carbohydrate, 1g total fat (0g saturated), 2mg cholesterol, 20mg sodium.

Lemon Ice in Lemon Cups

Prep: 30 minutes plus freezing   Cook: 5 minutes

Serve these at your next dinner party with a sprightly sprig of mint on each.

- **6 large lemons**
- **1 cup sugar**
- **1 envelope unflavored gelatin**
- **2¼ cups water**

1. Cut off top one-third of each lemon. Grate peel from lemon tops. Wrap 1 teaspoon grated peel in plastic wrap for garnish and refrigerate; reserve remaining grated peel. Squeeze ¾ cup juice from lemons. With melon baller, remove all pulp and membrane; discard. Cut thin slice off bottom of each lemon cup so it sits flat. Place lemon cups in plastic bag and freeze until ready to fill.

2. In 2-quart saucepan, combine sugar and gelatin; stir in water. Let stand 2 minutes to soften gelatin slightly. Cook over medium-low heat, stirring constantly, until gelatin has completely dissolved. Remove saucepan from heat. Stir in lemon juice and reserved grated peel.

3. Pour lemon mixture into 9-inch square metal baking pan. Cover and freeze, stirring occasionally, until partially frozen, about 2 hours. Meanwhile, place large bowl in refrigerator to chill.

4. Spoon lemon mixture into chilled bowl. With mixer at medium speed, beat until smooth but still frozen. Return mixture to pan. Return bowl to refrigerator. Cover mixture in pan and freeze until partially frozen, about 2 hours. Spoon lemon mixture into chilled bowl and beat until smooth but still frozen. Cover and freeze until firm, about 3 hours.

5. Spoon lemon ice into frozen lemon cups. Sprinkle with remaining 1 teaspoon grated lemon peel. Serve immediately, or freeze up to 2 hours. Makes 6 servings.

Each serving: About 141 (0 percent calories from fat), 1g protein, 36g carbohydrate, 0g total fat, 0mg cholesterol, 3mg sodium.

Chocolate Sorbet

Prep: 10 minutes plus chilling and freezing   Cook: 12 minutes

An alternative to rich ice cream, with lots of chocolate flavor.

- **¾ cup sugar**
- **2½ cups water**
- **2 squares (2 ounces) unsweetened chocolate, chopped**
- **¼ cup light corn syrup**
- **1½ teaspoons vanilla extract**

1. In 2-quart saucepan, combine sugar and water; heat to boiling over high heat, stirring until sugar has dissolved. Reduce heat to medium and cook 3 minutes. Remove from heat.

2. In heavy 1-quart saucepan, combine chocolate and corn syrup; heat over low heat, stirring frequently, until chocolate is melted and smooth.

3. With wire whisk, stir 1 cup sugar syrup into chocolate mixture until well blended. Stir chocolate mixture into remaining sugar syrup in saucepan; stir in vanilla. Pour into medium bowl; cover and refrigerate until well chilled, about 1½ hours.

4. Freeze in ice-cream maker as manufacturer directs. Makes about 4 cups or 8 servings.

Each serving: About 141 calories (26 percent calories from fat), 1g protein, 29g carbohydrate, 4g total fat (2g saturated), 0mg cholesterol, 14mg sodium.

Frozen Chocolate Kahlua Mousse

Prep: 10 minutes plus freezing

When company's coming unexpectedly, or you need a special dessert at the last minute, this delicate, rich-tasting confection rises to the occasion—and it's fat-free, to boot.

- **1 envelope unflavored gelatin**
- **1 cup cold water**
- **1/2 cup nonfat ricotta cheese**
- **1/2 cup cold fat-free (skim) milk**
- **6 tablespoons sugar**
- **1/2 cup Kahlua liqueur**
- **3 tablespoons unsweetened cocoa**
   pinch salt

1. In 1-quart saucepan, evenly sprinkle gelatin over cold water; let stand 2 minutes to soften gelatin slightly. Cook over medium heat, stirring frequently, until gelatin has completely dissolved (do not boil).

2. In blender, combine gelatin mixture, ricotta, milk, sugar, liquor, and cocoa. Blend until smooth, about 1 minute. Pour into dessert glasses and freeze at least 2 hours. Makes 6 servings.

Each serving: About 100 calories (0 percent calories from fat), 5g protein, 16g carbohydrate, 0g total fat, 3mg cholesterol, 80mg sodium.

Peach Granita

Prep: 20 minutes plus freezing

Be sure the peaches or nectarines are as ripe as possible.

- **1 cup sugar**
- **1 1/4 cups water**
- **1 3/4 pounds peaches or nectarines (5 medium), unpeeled and cut into wedges**
- **2 tablespoons fresh lemon juice**

1. In 1-quart saucepan, heat sugar and water to boiling over high heat, stirring occasionally. Reduce heat to medium; cook mixture about 1 minute or until sugar dissolves completely. Transfer to small bowl to cool.

2. In blender, at medium speed, blend unpeeled peach wedges until smooth. Pour puree into medium-mesh sieve set over medium bowl. With spoon, press puree against sieve to push through pulp and juice. You should have 3 cups puree; discard solids in sieve.

3. Stir sugar syrup and lemon juice into puree. Pour peach mixture into 9" by 9" metal baking pan.

4. Cover with foil or plastic wrap. Freeze until partially frozen, about 2 hours; stir with fork. Freeze until completely frozen, at least 3 hours or overnight.

5. To serve, let granita stand at room temperature until softened slightly, about 15 minutes. With spoon or fork, scrape across surface of granita to create pebbly texture. Makes about 8 cups or 16 servings.

Each serving: About 65 calories (0 percent calories from fat), 0g protein, 17g carbohydrate, 0g total fat, 0mg cholesterol, 0mg sodium.

Blueberry Granita

Prepare as directed but substitute 3 pints blueberries for the peaches.

Each serving: About 80 calories (0 percent calories from fat), 0g protein, 20g carbohydrate, 0g total fat, 0mg cholesterol, 5mg sodium.

Raspberry Granita

Prepare as directed but substitute 6 half-pints raspberries for the peaches and 2 tablespoons lime juice for the lemon juice.

Each serving: About 70 calories (0 percent calories from fat), 0g protein, 18g carbohydrate, 0g total fat, 0mg cholesterol, 0mg sodium.

Watermelon Granita

Prepare as directed but substitute 1 piece (5 1/2 pounds) watermelon, seeded and cut into chunks, for the peaches, 2 tablespoons lime juice for the lemon juice, and decrease the water to 3/4 cup.

Each serving: About 70 calories (0 percent calories from fat), 1g protein, 17g carbohydrate, 0g total fat, 0mg cholesterol, 2mg sodium.

Banana-Maple Sorbet

Prep: 5 minutes plus freezing

Here's what to do with very ripe bananas—just freeze them, then buzz in the food processor.

  4 **very ripe medium bananas**
1/3 **cup maple syrup**
  1 **teaspoon vanilla extract**
     pinch salt

1. Peel bananas and place in large self-sealing plastic bag; freeze overnight or until very firm.

2. Slice frozen bananas. In food processor with knife blade attached, process bananas, syrup, vanilla, and salt until creamy, about 2 minutes. Serve immediately. Makes about 3 cups or 6 servings.

Each serving: About 115 calories (0 percent calories from fat), 1g protein, 29g carbohydrate, 0g total fat, 0mg cholesterol, 25mg sodium.

Orange Sherbet

Prep: 10 minutes plus chilling and freezing   Cook: 10 minutes

No need to pull out your ice-cream machine for this rich and creamy sorbet.

1½   **cups milk**

½   **cup sugar**

5   **large oranges**

⅛   **teaspoon salt**

1. In heavy 2-quart saucepan, combine milk and sugar; cook over medium-high heat, stirring occasionally, until bubbles form around edge and sugar has completely dissolved, about 2 minutes. Pour into medium bowl; press plastic wrap onto surface. Refrigerate until well chilled, about 1 hour or up to 4 hours.

2. From oranges, grate 1 teaspoon peel and squeeze 2 cups juice. Stir orange peel, orange juice, and salt into chilled milk mixture. Pour into 9-inch square metal baking pan; cover and freeze until firm, at least 4 hours.

3. With spoon, scoop sherbet into food processor with knife blade attached. Process sherbet until smooth but still frozen. Return mixture to pan; cover and freeze until firm, 1 to 2 hours longer.

4. To serve, let sherbet stand at room temperature until just soft enough to scoop, about 10 minutes. Makes about 4 cups or 8 servings.

Each serving: About 104 calories (17 percent calories from fat), 2g protein, 21g carbohydrate, 2g total fat (1g saturated), 6mg cholesterol, 60mg sodium.

Lime Pavlova

Prep: 30 minutes plus cooling and chilling   Bake: 1 hour 15 minutes

This dessert is very low in fat but rich in flavor; a creamy fresh lime filling is spooned into a crisp meringue nest. The meringue can be made several days ahead and stored in an airtight container. Fill the shell up to four hours before serving.

3   **large egg whites**

¼   **teaspoon cream of tartar**

¼   **teaspoon salt**

½   **cup sugar**

1   **teaspoon vanilla extract**

4   **to 6 limes**

1   **can (14 ounces) lowfat sweetened condensed milk**

1   **container (8 ounces) plain low-fat yogurt**

1   **envelope unflavored gelatin**

¼   **cup cold water**

5   **strawberries, hulled and each cut in half**

1. Preheat oven to 275°F. Line cookie sheet with foil. Using 9-inch round cake pan or plate as guide, with toothpick, outline circle on foil.

2. In medium bowl, with mixer at high speed, beat egg whites, cream of tartar, and salt until soft peaks form when beaters are lifted. Sprinkle in sugar, 2 tablespoons at a time, beating until sugar has dissolved. Add vanilla; continue beating until egg whites stand in stiff, glossy peaks when beaters are lifted.

3. Spoon meringue inside circle on cookie sheet. With back of tablespoon, make well in center to form "nest" about 1½ inches high at edge. Bake meringue 1 hour 15 minutes. Turn off oven; leave meringue in oven 1 hour to dry. Cool completely on cookie sheet on wire rack.

4. Meanwhile, prepare filling: From limes, grate 2 teaspoons peel and squeeze ½ cup juice. In medium bowl, with wire whisk, beat lime peel, lime juice, condensed milk, and yogurt until well blended.

5. In 1-quart saucepan, evenly sprinkle gelatin over cold water; let stand 2 minutes to soften gelatin. Cook over medium-low heat, stirring until gelatin has completely dissolved. Add gelatin to lime mixture and whisk until blended.

6. Set bowl with lime mixture in larger bowl filled with ice water. With rubber spatula, stir mixture occasionally until it begins to thicken, about 20 minutes. Remove bowl from water bath.

7. With metal spatula, carefully loosen and separate meringue shell from foil; place on serving plate. Spoon lime filling into meringue shell; refrigerate until set, about 1 hour. Garnish with strawberries and serve. Makes 10 servings.

Each serving: About 234 calories (8 percent calories from fat), 7g protein, 45g carbohydrate, 2g total fat (2g saturated), 8mg cholesterol, 147mg sodium.

Valentine Sundaes

Prep: 10 minutes plus freezing

Special finale: frozen yogurt hearts drizzled with ruby red raspberry sauce. To soften the frozen yogurt for spooning into the molds, place in a microwave and heat, uncovered, on medium-low for 45 seconds to 1 minute.

1 pint vanilla frozen yogurt, softened
1 package (12 ounces) frozen raspberries, thawed
1/4 cup sugar
fresh raspberries for garnish

1. Line four 4-ounce heart-shaped molds (or small bowls) with plastic wrap. Spoon the softened frozen yogurt into molds. Fold wrap over to cover. Freeze until firm, about 2 hours.

2. In food processor, with knife blade attached, puree thawed raspberries and sugar. Pour puree into fine-mesh sieve set over medium bowl. With spoon, press puree against sieve to push through pulp and juice. Discard seeds.

3. Unmold hearts and serve drizzled with raspberry sauce and garnished with fresh berries. Makes 4 servings.

Each serving: About 225 calories (8 percent calories from fat), 4g protein, 52g carbohydrate, 2g total fat (1g saturated), 5mg cholesterol, 60mg sodium.

5-Minute Frozen Peach Yogurt

Prep: 15 minutes plus standing

A food processor makes quick work of this dessert. Try it with strawberries, blueberries, or your favorite combination of flavorful frozen fruits.

1 bag (20 ounces) frozen unsweetened peach slices
1 container (8 ounces) plain low-fat yogurt
1 cup confectioners' sugar
1 tablespoon fresh lemon juice
1/8 teaspoon almond extract

1. Let frozen peaches stand at room temperature 10 minutes. In food processor with knife blade attached, process peaches until fruit resembles finely shaved ice, occasionally scraping down side with rubber spatula.

2. With processor running, add yogurt, confectioners' sugar, lemon juice, and almond extract; process until mixture is smooth and creamy, occasionally scraping down side. Serve immediately. Makes about 4 cups or 8 servings.

Each serving: About 107 calories (8 percent calories from fat), 2g protein, 25g carbohydrate, 1g total fat (0g saturated), 2mg cholesterol, 20mg sodium.

Rice Pudding

Prep: 10 minutes   Cook: 1 hour 15 minutes

Cooking the rice very slowly in lots of milk makes this pudding especially creamy.

4 cups milk

1/2 cup regular long-grain rice

1/2 cup sugar

1/4 teaspoon salt

1 large egg

1 teaspoon vanilla extract

1. In heavy 4-quart saucepan, combine milk, rice, sugar, and salt; heat to boiling over medium-high heat. Reduce heat; cover and simmer, stirring occasionally, until rice is very tender, about 1 hour.

2. In small bowl, lightly beat egg; stir in 1/2 cup hot rice mixture. Slowly pour egg mixture back into rice mixture, stirring rapidly to prevent curdling. Cook, stirring constantly, until rice mixture has thickened, about 5 minutes (do not boil, or mixture will curdle). Remove from heat; stir in vanilla. Serve warm, or spoon into medium bowl and refrigerate until well chilled, about 3 hours. Makes 4 cups or 6 servings.

Each serving: About 234 calories (23 percent calories from fat), 7g protein, 37g carbohydrate, 6g total fat (4g saturated), 58mg cholesterol, 187mg sodium.

Sticky Toffee Pudding

Prep: 20 minutes plus standing and cooling   Bake/Broil: 31 minutes

This traditional British pudding, with its sticky caramel topping, is a favorite of kids and adults alike.

1 cup chopped pitted dates

1 teaspoon baking soda

1 1/2 cups boiling water

10 tablespoons (1 1/4 sticks) butter or margarine, softened

1 cup granulated sugar

1 large egg

1 teaspoon vanilla extract

2 cups all-purpose flour

1 teaspoon baking powder

1 cup packed brown sugar

1/4 cup heavy or whipping cream

1. Preheat oven to 350°F. Grease 13" by 9" baking pan. In medium bowl, combine dates, baking soda, and boiling water; let stand 15 minutes.

2. In large bowl, with mixer at medium speed, beat 6 tablespoons butter until creamy. Beat in granulated sugar until light and fluffy. Add egg and vanilla; beat until blended. Reduce speed to low; add flour and baking powder, beating to combine. Add date mixture and beat until well combined (batter will be very thin). Pour batter into prepared pan. Bake until golden and toothpick inserted in center of pudding comes out clean, about 30 minutes.

3. Meanwhile, in 2-quart saucepan, combine remaining 4 tablespoons butter, brown sugar, and cream; heat to boiling over medium-high heat. Boil 1 minute; remove saucepan from heat.

4. Turn oven control to broil. Spread brown-sugar mixture evenly over top of hot pudding. Broil at position closest to heat source until bubbling, about 30 seconds. Cool in pan on wire rack 15 minutes. Serve warm. Makes 12 servings.

Each serving: About 362 calories (30 percent calories from fat), 3g protein, 62g carbohydrate, 12g total fat (7g saturated), 50mg cholesterol, 259mg sodium.

Holiday Baked Alaska with Raspberry Sauce

Prep: 1 hour 30 minutes plus freezing   Bake: 2 to 3 minutes

For this new take on an old favorite, line a dish with ladyfingers and fill with vanilla ice cream and ruby-red sorbet. Then spoon on a dome of meringue, and brown lightly in the oven right before serving. Do-ahead: Make and freeze cake without meringue up to 2 weeks before serving. The sauce can be made up to 3 days ahead. Baked meringue-topped cake can be frozen up to 4 hours before serving. Just remember to remove from freezer 20 minutes before serving for easier slicing.

ICE-CREAM CAKE:

- 2 pints vanilla ice cream
- 3 packages (3 to 4 1/2 ounces each) sponge-type ladyfingers
- 2 pints raspberry sorbet

RASPBERRY SAUCE:

- 1 package (10 ounces) frozen raspberries in quick-thaw pouch, thawed
- 2 tablespoons seedless raspberry jam
- 1 tablespoon orange-flavor liqueur

MERINGUE:

- 4 large egg whites
- 3/4 cup sugar
- 4 teaspoons water
- 1/4 teaspoon salt
- 1/4 teaspoon cream of tartar

1. Prepare ice-cream cake: Place vanilla ice cream in large bowl; let stand at room temperature to soften slightly, stirring occasionally, until spreadable.

2. Meanwhile, split each ladyfinger in half lengthwise. Line bottom and side of 10" by 11/2" round baking dish, shallow 11/2-quart round casserole, or 91/2-inch deep-dish pie plate with about two-thirds of ladyfingers, placing ladyfingers with rounded side out around side and allowing ladyfingers to extend above rim of baking dish.

3. Spoon vanilla ice cream into lined dish. Smooth with small metal spatula; place in freezer 30 minutes or until ice cream is firm.

4. Place raspberry sorbet in large bowl; let stand at room temperature to soften slightly, stirring occasionally, until spreadable. Spoon raspberry sorbet on top of ice cream, smoothing with spatula. Top sorbet with remaining ladyfingers. Cover cake with waxed paper and foil; freeze until firm, at least 6 hours.

5. Prepare raspberry sauce: In food processor, puree raspberries, jam, and liquor until smooth. Pour sauce into small pitcher to serve. Refrigerate until ready to use. Makes about 11/3 cups sauce.

6. About 30 minutes before serving, prepare meringue: Preheat oven to 500°F. In large bowl set over simmering water or in top of double boiler, with handheld mixer at medium speed, beat egg whites, sugar, water, salt, and cream of tartar until soft peaks form when beaters are lifted and temperature on thermometer reaches 160°F, 12 to 14 minutes. Transfer bowl with meringue to work surface. Beat meringue until stiff peaks form, 8 to 10 minutes longer.

7. Remove cake from freezer. Spoon meringue over top of cake, swirling with spoon to make attractive top. Bake until meringue top is lightly browned, 2 to 3 minutes. Place on heat-safe platter and serve immediately, passing Raspberry Sauce at table. Makes 16 servings.

Each serving: About 250 calories (18 percent calories from fat), 4g protein, 40g carbohydrate, 5g total fat (3g saturated), 73mg cholesterol, 95mg sodium.

Lowfat Crème Caramel

Prep: 15 minutes plus cooling and chilling   Bake: 40 minutes

Lowfat milk and a moderate number of eggs make this a guilt-free caramel custard.

3/4	**cup sugar**
1	**large egg**
2	**large egg whites**
2	**cups lowfat milk (1%)**
1/2	**teaspoon vanilla extract**

1. Preheat oven to 350°F. In heavy 1-quart saucepan, heat 1/2 cup sugar over medium heat, swirling pan occasionally, until sugar has melted and is amber in color. Immediately pour into eight 4- to 5-ounce ramekins.

2. In large bowl, with wire whisk, beat remaining 1/4 cup sugar, egg, and egg whites until well blended. Beat in milk and vanilla; pour into ramekins. Skim off foam.

3. Place ramekins in medium roasting pan; cover loosely with foil. Place pan on rack in oven. Carefully pour enough very hot water into pan to come halfway up sides of ramekins. Bake until knife inserted 1 inch from center comes out clean, 40 to 45 minutes. Transfer ramekins to wire rack to cool. Refrigerate until well chilled, 3 hours or up to overnight.

4. To serve, run tip of small knife around edge of custards. Invert ramekins onto dessert plates, shaking cups gently until custards slip out, allowing caramel syrup to drip onto custards. Makes 8 servings.

Each serving: About 112 calories (8 percent calories from fat), 4g protein, 22g carbohydrate, 1g total fat (1g saturated), 29mg cholesterol, 52mg sodium.

Brownie Pudding Cake

Prep: 20 minutes   Bake: 30 minutes

*Two desserts for the price of one! It separates during baking
into a fudgy brownie atop a silky chocolate pudding.*

- **2 teaspoons instant-coffee powder (optional)**
- **2 tablespoons plus 1³/4 cups boiling water**
- **1 cup all-purpose flour**
- **³/4 cup unsweetened cocoa**
- **¹/2 cup granulated sugar**
- **2 teaspoons baking powder**
- **¹/4 teaspoon salt**
- **¹/2 cup milk**
- **4 tablespoons butter or margarine, melted**
- **1 teaspoon vanilla extract**
- **¹/2 cup packed brown sugar**
-   **whipped cream or vanilla ice cream (optional)**

1. Preheat oven to 350°F. In cup, dissolve coffee powder in 2 tablespoons boiling water, if using.

2. In bowl, combine flour, ¹/2 cup cocoa, granulated sugar, baking powder, and salt. In 2-cup measuring cup, combine coffee, if using, milk, melted butter, and vanilla. With wooden spoon, stir milk mixture into flour mixture until just blended. Pour into ungreased 8-inch square baking dish.

3. In small bowl, thoroughly combine brown sugar and remaining ¹/4 cup cocoa; sprinkle evenly over batter. Carefully pour remaining 1³/4 cups boiling water evenly over mixture in baking dish; do not stir.

4. Bake 30 minutes (batter will separate into cake and pudding layers). Cool in pan on wire rack 10 minutes. Serve hot, with whipped cream, if you like. Makes 8 servings.

Each serving: About 238 calories (26 percent calories from fat), 4g protein, 43g carbohydrate, 7g total fat (5g saturated), 18mg cholesterol, 267mg sodium.

Light Chocolate-Buttermilk Bundt Cake

Prep: 30 minutes plus cooling   Bake: 45 minutes

*This is sure to satisfy any chocolate craving, with or without
the glaze.*

- **2¹/4 cups all-purpose flour**
- **1¹/2 teaspoons baking soda**
- **¹/2 teaspoon baking powder**
- **¹/2 teaspoon salt**
- **³/4 cup unsweetened cocoa**
- **1 teaspoon instant espresso-coffee powder**
- **³/4 cup hot water**
- **2 cups sugar**
- **¹/3 cup vegetable oil**
- **2 large egg whites**
- **1 large egg**
- **1 square (1 ounce) unsweetened chocolate, melted**
- **2 teaspoons vanilla extract**
- **¹/2 cup buttermilk**
-   **Mocha Glaze (page 289)**

1. Preheat oven to 350°F. Grease 10-inch Bundt pan.

2. In medium bowl, combine flour, baking soda, baking powder, and salt.

3. In 2-cup measuring cup, stir cocoa, espresso powder, and hot water until blended.

4. In large bowl, with mixer at low speed, beat sugar, oil, egg whites, and egg until blended. Increase speed to high; beat until creamy, about 2 minutes. Reduce speed to low; beat in cocoa mixture, melted chocolate, and vanilla. Add flour mixture alternately with buttermilk,

beginning and ending with flour mixture. Beat just until blended, occasionally scraping bowl with rubber spatula.

5. Scrape batter into prepared pan; spread evenly with rubber spatula. Bake until toothpick inserted in center comes out clean, about 45 minutes. Cool in pan on wire rack 10 minutes. Run tip of thin knife around edge of cake to loosen. Invert onto rack to cool completely.

6. Meanwhile, prepare Mocha Glaze. Place cake on cake plate; pour glaze over cooled cake. Makes 16 servings.

Each serving without Mocha Glaze: About 235 calories (27 percent calories from fat), 4g protein, 42g carbohydrate, 7g total fat (2g saturated), 14mg cholesterol, 226mg sodium.

Mocha Glaze

In medium bowl, combine 1/4 teaspoon instant espresso-coffee powder and 2 tablespoons hot water; stir until dissolved. Stir in 3 tablespoons unsweetened cocoa, 3 tablespoons dark corn syrup, and 1 tablespoon coffee-flavored liqueur until blended. Add 1 cup confectioners' sugar; stir until smooth.

Each serving with Mocha Glaze: About 280 calories (23 percent calories from fat), 4g protein, 53g carbohydrate, 7g total fat (2g saturated), 14mg cholesterol, 232mg sodium.

Golden Sponge Cake

Prep: 20 minutes   Bake: 15 minutes

This cake is just made for soaking up fruit juices. Serve with fresh fruit or use as the base for a shortcake or trifle.

- 3/4 **cup all-purpose flour**
- 2 **tablespoons cornstarch**
- 3 **large eggs**
- 1/2 **cup sugar**
- 1 **tablespoon butter or margarine, melted**

1. Preheat oven to 375°F. Grease and flour 9-inch square baking pan.

2. In small bowl, combine flour and cornstarch.

3. In large bowl, with mixer at high speed, beat eggs and sugar until thick and lemon colored and mixture forms ribbon when beaters are lifted, about 10 minutes, occasionally scraping bowl with rubber spatula. Fold in flour mixture until well blended, then fold in melted butter.

4. Scrape batter into prepared pan; spread evenly. Bake until cake is golden and springs back when lightly pressed, 15 to 20 minutes. Cool in pan on wire rack 10 minutes. Run thin knife around cake to loosen from sides of pan; invert onto rack to cool completely. Makes 8 servings.

Each serving: About 148 calories (24 percent calories from fat), 4g protein, 24g carbohydrate, 4g total fat (2g saturated), 84mg cholesterol, 39mg sodium.

Pumpkin Snack Cake

Prep: 15 minutes plus cooling   Bake: 25 to 30 minutes

Moist little squares full of aromatic spices—and only three grams of fat per serving.

- 1 **cup packed light brown sugar**
- 4 **tablespoons light corn-oil spread (56% to 60% fat)**
- 1 **cup canned solid-pack pumpkin (not pumpkin-pie mix)**
- 1/2 **cup thawed, frozen egg substitute**
- 1/2 **cup low-fat milk (1%)**
- 1 **tablespoon vanilla extract**
- 2 **cups cake flour (not self-rising)**
- 2 **teaspoons baking soda**
- 11/2 **teaspoons ground cinnamon**
- 11/2 **teaspoons ground ginger**
- 1 **teaspoon baking powder**
- 1/2 **teaspoon ground allspice**
- 1/2 **teaspoon salt**
  confectioners' sugar for garnish

1. Preheat oven to 350°F. Generously spray 13" by 9" ceramic or glass baking dish with nonstick cooking spray.

2. In large bowl, with mixer at high speed, beat brown sugar and corn-oil spread until well mixed, about 2 minutes, scraping bowl with rubber spatula.

3. Reduce speed to medium; beat in pumpkin, egg substitute, milk, and vanilla. With mixer at low speed, add flour, baking soda, cinnamon, ginger, baking powder, allspice, and salt; beat just until well blended.

4. Pour batter into prepared baking dish; spread evenly with spatula. Bake until toothpick inserted in center of cake comes out clean, 25 to 30 minutes. Cool cake completely in baking dish on wire rack. When cool, dust lightly with confectioners' sugar. Makes 12 servings.

Each serving: About 170 calories (16 percent calories from fat), 3g protein, 35g carbohydrate, 3g total fat (1g saturated), 0mg cholesterol, 385mg sodium.

Angel Food Cake

Prep: 30 minutes   Bake: 35 minutes

Angel food cake, beloved for its clean flavor and light texture, has an added attraction—it's virtually fat-free.

- **1 cup cake flour (not self-rising)**
- **1/2 cup confectioners' sugar**
- **1²/₃ cups egg whites (12 to 14 large egg whites)**
- **1¹/₂ teaspoons cream of tartar**
- **1/2 teaspoon salt**
- **1¹/₄ cups granulated sugar**
- **2 teaspoons vanilla extract**
- **1/2 teaspoon almond extract**

1. Preheat oven to 375°F. Sift flour and confectioners' sugar through sieve set over small bowl.

2. In large bowl, with mixer at medium speed, beat egg whites, cream of tartar, and salt until foamy. Increase speed to medium-high; beat until soft peaks form when beaters are lifted. Sprinkle in granulated sugar, 2 tablespoons at a time, beating until sugar has dissolved and egg whites stand in stiff, glossy peaks when beaters are lifted. Beat in vanilla and almond extracts.

3. Transfer egg-white mixture to larger bowl. Sift flour mixture, one-third at a time, over beaten egg whites; fold in with rubber spatula just until flour mixture is no longer visible. Do not overmix.

4. Scrape batter into ungreased 9- to 10-inch tube pan; spread evenly. Bake until cake springs back when lightly pressed, 35 to 40 minutes. Invert cake in pan onto large metal funnel or bottle; cool completely in pan. Run thin knife around cake to loosen from side and center tube of pan. Remove from pan and place on cake plate. Makes 16 servings.

Each serving: About 115 calories (0 percent calories from fat), 3g protein, 25g carbohydrate, 0g total fat, 0mg cholesterol, 114mg sodium.

Cappuccino Angel Food Cake

Prepare as directed but add 4 teaspoons instant espresso-coffee powder and 1/2 teaspoon ground cinnamon to egg whites before beating; use 1¹/₂ teaspoons vanilla extract and omit almond extract. In cup, mix 1 tablespoon confectioners' sugar with 1/8 teaspoon ground cinnamon; sprinkle evenly over cooled cake.

Banana Snack Cake with Brown-Butter Frosting

Prep: 30 minutes plus cooling   Bake: 25 to 30 minutes

BANANA CAKE:

1¹/₃ cups mashed fully ripe bananas (about 4
     medium)

  1 tablespoon fresh lemon juice

  2 teaspoons vanilla extract

  2 cups all-purpose flour

  1 teaspoon baking powder

¹/₂ teaspoon baking soda

¹/₂ teaspoon salt

¹/₈ teaspoon ground cinnamon

³/₄ cup packed brown sugar

¹/₂ cup granulated sugar

¹/₂ cup margarine or butter (1 stick), softened

  2 large eggs

BROWN-BUTTER FROSTING:

  6 tablespoons butter (do not use margarine or any
     other substitution)

  3 cups confectioners' sugar

  5 tablespoons milk

  2 teaspoons vanilla extract

1. Preheat oven to 350°F. Grease 13" by 9" metal baking pan and dust with flour.

2. In small bowl, mix bananas, lemon juice, and vanilla. On waxed paper, mix flour, baking powder, baking soda, salt, and cinnamon.

3. In large bowl, with mixer at medium speed, beat brown sugar, granulated sugar, and margarine until light and creamy, about 5 minutes, scraping bowl often with rubber spatula. Add eggs, 1 at a time, beating well after each addition. At low speed, add flour mixture alternately with banana mixture, beginning and ending with flour mixture; beat just until smooth.

4. Spoon batter into pan and spread evenly with rubber spatula. Bake cake until toothpick inserted in center comes out clean, 25 to 30 minutes. Cool cake in pan on wire rack.

5. Prepare frosting: In 1-quart saucepan, heat butter over medium heat, stirring occasionally, until melted and dark nutty-brown in color but not burned, 6 to 8 minutes. Immediately transfer butter to pie plate; refrigerate until firm, about 30 minutes.

6. In large bowl, with mixer at medium speed, beat chilled butter, confectioners' sugar, milk, and vanilla until creamy and smooth. Spread frosting evenly over cooled cake. Makes 24 servings.

Each serving: About 225 calories (28 percent calories from fat), 2g protein, 39g carbohydrate, 7g total fat (3g saturated), 26mg cholesterol, 175mg sodium.

Applesauce Spice Cake

Prep: 20 minutes   Bake: 40 minutes

For a quick snack, make this easy cake. You probably have all the ingredients on hand.

- **2 cups all-purpose flour**
- **1¹/2 teaspoons ground cinnamon**
- **1 teaspoon baking powder**
- **¹/2 teaspoon baking soda**
- **¹/2 teaspoon ground ginger**
- **¹/4 teaspoon ground nutmeg**
- **¹/2 teaspoon salt**
- **¹/2 cup butter or margarine (1 stick), softened**
- **¹/4 cup granulated sugar**
- **1 cup packed dark brown sugar**
- **2 large eggs**
- **1¹/4 cups unsweetened applesauce**
- **¹/2 cup dark seedless raisins**
- **confectioners' sugar**

1. Preheat oven to 350°F. Grease and flour 9-inch square baking pan.

2. In medium bowl, combine flour, cinnamon, baking powder, baking soda, ginger, nutmeg, and salt.

3. In large bowl, with mixer at low speed, beat butter, granulated sugar, and brown sugar until blended. Increase speed to medium-high; beat until light and fluffy, about 3 minutes. Add eggs, one at a time, beating well after each addition. Reduce speed to low; beat in applesauce. Mixture may appear curdled. Beat in flour mixture until smooth, occasionally scraping bowl with rubber spatula. Stir in raisins.

4. Scrape batter into prepared pan; spread evenly. Bake cake until toothpick inserted in center comes out clean, about 40 minutes. Cool completely in pan on wire rack. To serve, dust with confectioners' sugar. Makes 9 servings.

Each serving: About 369 calories (29 percent calories from fat), 5g protein, 62g carbohydrate, 12g total fat (7g saturated), 75mg cholesterol, 383mg sodium.

Jelly Roll

Prep: 20 minutes plus cooling   Bake: 10 minutes

Jelly rolls are easy to make and look sensational on a decorative platter.

5 **large eggs, separated**
1/2 **cup granulated sugar**
1 **teaspoon vanilla extract**
1/2 **cup all-purpose flour**
 confectioners' sugar
2/3 **cup strawberry jam**

1. Preheat oven to 350°F. Grease 151/2" by 101/2" jelly-roll pan. Line with waxed paper; grease paper.

2. In large bowl, with mixer at high speed, beat egg whites until soft peaks form when beaters are lifted. Sprinkle in 1/4 cup granulated sugar, 1 tablespoon at a time, beating until egg whites stand in stiff, glossy peaks when beaters are lifted. Do not overbeat.

3. In small bowl, with mixer at high speed, beat egg yolks, remaining 1/4 cup granulated sugar, and vanilla until very thick and lemon colored, 8 to 10 minutes. Reduce speed to low; stir in flour until blended. With rubber spatula, gently fold egg-yolk mixture into beaten egg whites just until blended.

4. Evenly spread batter in prepared pan. Bake until cake springs back when lightly pressed, 10 to 15 minutes.

5. Sift confectioners' sugar onto clean kitchen towel. Run thin knife around edges of cake to loosen from sides of pan; invert onto towel. Carefully remove

waxed paper. Trim 1/4 inch from edges of cake. From a short side, roll cake up with towel jelly-roll fashion. Place rolled cake, seam side down, on wire rack; cool completely.

6. Unroll cooled cake. With narrow metal spatula, spread evenly with jam. Starting from same short side, roll cake up (without towel). Place rolled cake, seam side down, on platter and dust with confectioners' sugar. Makes 10 servings.

Each serving: About 163 calories (17 percent calories from fat), 4g protein, 30g carbohydrate, 3g total fat (1g saturated), 106mg cholesterol, 40mg sodium.

Tomato-Soup Cake

Prep: 10 minutes plus cooling   Bake: 30 minutes

  2 **cups all-purpose flour**
  1 **tablespoon baking powder**
1 1/2   **teaspoons ground cinnamon**
  1 **teaspoon ground ginger**
  1 **teaspoon baking soda**
1/2 **teaspoon salt**
1/4 **teaspoon ground nutmeg**
1/8 **teaspoon ground cloves**
1 1/3 **cups sugar**
  4 **tablespoons light corn-oil spread (60 to 70% fat)**
  1 **can (10 3/4 ounces) condensed tomato soup**
1/4 **cup water**
  2 **large egg whites**
  1 **teaspoon vanilla extract**
     confectioners' sugar for garnish

1. Preheat oven to 350°F. Spray 13" by 9" metal baking pan with nonstick cooking spray.

2. In medium bowl, combine flour, baking powder, cinnamon, ginger, baking soda, salt, nutmeg, and cloves. In large bowl, with mixer at high speed, beat sugar and corn-oil spread until blended, about 2 minutes, scraping bowl with rubber spatula. Reduce speed to low; beat in undiluted tomato soup, water, egg whites, and vanilla. With mixer at low speed, gradually add flour mixture and beat until just blended.

3. Pour batter into prepared pan; spread evenly with rubber spatula. Bake cake until toothpick inserted in center comes out clean, about 30 minutes. Cool completely in pan on wire rack. To serve, dust lightly with confectioners' sugar. Makes 16 servings.

Each serving: About 160 calories (17 percent calories from fat), 2g protein, 32g carbohydrate, 3g total fat (1g saturated), 0mg cholesterol, 390mg sodium.

Butterscotch Blondies

Prep: 15 minutes   Bake: 35 minutes

These chewy treats are one of our test kitchen's favorites—it's hard to believe there's only three grams of fat in each one!

- **1   cup all-purpose flour**
- **1/2 teaspoon baking powder**
- **1/4 teaspoon salt**
- **3   tablespoons butter or margarine**
- **3/4 cup packed dark brown sugar**
- **2   large egg whites**
- **1/3 cup dark corn syrup**
- **2   teaspoons vanilla extract**
- **2   tablespoons finely chopped pecans**

1. Preheat oven to 350°F. Grease 8-inch square baking pan. In bowl, combine flour, baking powder, and salt.

2. In large bowl, with mixer at medium speed, beat butter and brown sugar until well blended, about 2 minutes. Reduce speed to low; beat in egg whites, corn syrup, and vanilla until smooth. Beat in flour mixture just until combined. Spread batter evenly in prepared pan. Sprinkle with pecans.

3. Bake until toothpick inserted in center comes out clean and edges are lightly browned, 35 to 40 minutes. Cool completely in pan on wire rack.

4. When cool, cut into 4 strips, then cut each strip crosswise into 4 pieces. Makes 16 blondies.

Each blondie: About 117 calories (23 percent calories from fat), 1g protein, 21g carbohydrate, 3g total fat (1g saturated), 6mg cholesterol, 94mg sodium.

Fudgy Brownies

Prep: 15 minutes   Bake: 18 minutes

Moist, chocolaty, and lowfat. Need we say more? Serve with cold skim milk for a healthful and delicious treat.

- **1   teaspoon instant espresso-coffee powder**
- **1   teaspoon hot water**
- **3/4 cup all-purpose flour**
- **1/2 cup unsweetened cocoa**
- **1/2 teaspoon baking powder**
- **1/4 teaspoon salt**
- **3   tablespoons butter or margarine**
- **3/4 cup sugar**
- **2   large egg whites**
- **1/4 cup dark corn syrup**
- **1   teaspoon vanilla extract**

1. Preheat oven to 350°F. Grease 8-inch square baking pan. In cup, dissolve espresso powder in hot water; set aside. In large bowl, combine flour, cocoa, baking powder, and salt.

2. In 2-quart saucepan, melt butter over low heat. Remove from heat. With wooden spoon, stir in espresso, sugar, egg whites, corn syrup, and vanilla until blended. Stir sugar mixture into flour mixture just until blended (do not overmix). Pour batter into prepared pan.

3. Bake until toothpick inserted in center comes out almost clean, 18 to 22 minutes. Cool brownies completely in pan on wire rack.

4. When cool, cut brownies into 4 strips, then cut each strip crosswise into 4 pieces. If brownies are difficult to cut, use knife dipped in hot water and dried; repeat as necessary. Makes 16 brownies.

Each brownie: About 103 calories (26 percent calories from fat), 2g protein, 19g carbohydrate, 3g total fat (2g saturated), 6mg cholesterol, 88mg sodium.

Date Bars

Prep: 40 minutes plus cooling   Bake: 45 to 50 minutes

These beloved triple-layer sweets have a simple streusel topping.

OAT CRUST AND TOPPING:

1¹/4 **cups all-purpose flour**

1 **cup old-fashioned or quick-cooking oats, uncooked**

1/2 **cup packed light brown sugar**

1/2 **cup butter (1 stick), softened**

1/4 **teaspoon baking soda**

1/4 **teaspoon ground cinnamon**

1/4 **teaspoon salt**

DATE FILLING:

1 **container (10 ounces) pitted dates, chopped**

3/4 **cup water**

2 **tablespoons light brown sugar**

1. Preheat oven to 375°F. Grease 9" by 9" metal baking pan. Line pan with foil; grease foil.

2. Prepare crust and topping: In large bowl, with hand, mix flour, oats, brown sugar, butter, baking soda, cinnamon, and salt until mixture comes together. Transfer 2 cups mixture to prepared baking pan; reserve remaining mixture for crumb topping. With hand, press mixture evenly onto bottom of pan to form a crust. Bake crust 10 minutes. Cool completely in pan on wire rack. Turn off oven.

3. While crust is cooling, prepare filling: In 2-quart saucepan, combine dates, water, and brown sugar. Cook over medium heat, stirring frequently, until mixture thickens and all liquid is absorbed, 6 to 8 minutes. Spoon filling into bowl and refrigerate until cool, about 30 minutes.

4. When filling is cool, preheat oven to 375°F. Spread filling over crust; top with reserved crumb mixture. Bake until topping is golden, 35 to 40 minutes. Cool completely in pan on wire rack.

5. When cool, transfer with foil to cutting board and remove foil. Cut into 4 strips, then cut each strip crosswise into 3 pieces. Makes 12 bars.

Each bar: About 275 calories (29 percent calories from fat), 4g protein, 47g carbohydrate, 9g total fat (5g saturated), 21mg cholesterol, 155mg sodium.

Gingerbread Cutouts

Prep: 45 minutes plus cooling and decorating   Bake: 12 minutes per batch

Most gingerbread cookie doughs need to be chilled; ours can be rolled out right away. For wreath or tree decorations, tie a loop of nylon fishing line through a hole in each cookie for hanging.

- 1/2 **cup sugar**
- 1/2 **cup light (mild) molasses**
- 1 1/2 **teaspoons ground ginger**
- 1 **teaspoon ground allspice**
- 1 **teaspoon ground cinnamon**
- 1 **teaspoon ground cloves**
- 2 **teaspoons baking soda**
- 1/2 **cup butter or margarine (1 stick), cut into pieces**
- 1 **large egg, beaten**
- 3 1/2 **cups all-purpose flour**
  Ornamental Frosting (see recipe below)

1. In 3-quart saucepan, combine sugar, molasses, ginger, allspice, cinnamon, and cloves; heat to boiling over medium heat, stirring occasionally with wooden spoon. Remove from heat; stir in baking soda (mixture will foam up). Stir in butter until melted. Stir in egg, then flour.

2. On floured surface, knead dough until thoroughly blended. Divide dough in half; wrap one piece in plastic wrap and set aside.

3. Preheat oven to 325°F. With floured rolling pin, roll remaining piece of dough slightly less than 1/4 inch thick. With floured 3- to 4-inch assorted cookie cutters, cut dough into as many cookies as possible; reserve trimmings for rerolling. Place cookies, 1 inch apart, on two ungreased large cookie sheets. If desired, with drinking straw or skewer, make 1/4-inch hole in top of each cookie for hanging.

4. Bake until brown around edges, about 12 minutes, rotating cookie sheets between upper and lower oven racks halfway through baking. With wide spatula, transfer cookies to wire racks to cool completely. Repeat with remaining dough and trimmings.

5. When cookies are cool, prepare Ornamental Frosting; use to decorate cookies as desired. Allow frosting to dry completely, about 1 hour. Makes about 36 cookies.

Each cookie without frosting: About 93 calories (29 percent calories from fat), 1g protein, 15g carbohydrate, 3g total fat (2g saturated), 13mg cholesterol, 100mg sodium.

Ornamental Frosting

Prep: 5 minutes

This glossy, hard-drying frosting is often made with raw egg whites, but we prefer meringue powder, which is available at many supermarkets and cake supply stores.

- 1 **package (16 ounces) confectioners' sugar**
- 3 **tablespoons meringue powder**
- 1/3 **cup warm water**

1. In large bowl, with mixer at medium speed, beat confectioners' sugar, meringue powder, and water until stiff and knife drawn through leaves path, about 5 minutes.

2. Keep tightly covered to prevent drying out. With small metal spatula, artists' paintbrushes, or decorating bags with small plain tips, decorate cookies with frosting. (You may need to thin frosting with a little warm water to obtain right spreading or piping consistency.) Makes about 3 cups.

Each tablespoon: About 39 calories (0 percent calories from fat), 0g protein, 10g carbohydrate, 0g total fat, 0mg cholesterol, 2mg sodium.

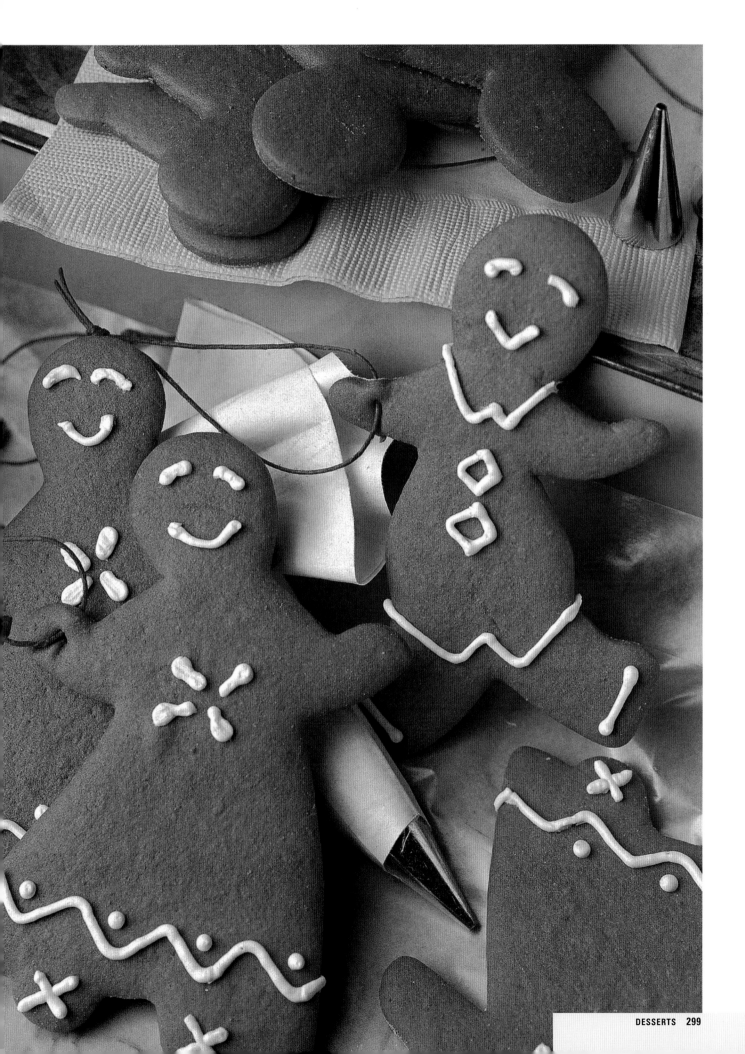

Ricotta-Cheese Cookies

Prep: 30 minutes plus cooling   Bake: 15 minutes per batch

These soft, Italian-style cookies will be a hit with everyone. The baked cookies freeze well.

   2 **cups sugar**
   1 **cup margarine or butter (2 sticks), softened**
   1 **container (15 ounces) ricotta cheese**
   2 **teaspoons vanilla extract**
   2 **large eggs**
   4 **cups all-purpose flour**
   2 **tablespoons baking powder**
   1 **teaspoon salt**
1 1/2 **cups confectioners' sugar**
   3 **tablespoons milk**
     red and green sugar crystals

1. Preheat oven to 350°F. In large bowl, with mixer at low speed, beat sugar and margarine until blended. Increase speed to high; beat until light and fluffy, about 5 minutes. At medium speed, beat in ricotta, vanilla, and eggs until well combined.

2. Reduce speed to low. Add flour, baking powder, and salt; beat until a dough forms.

3. Drop dough by level tablespoons, 2 inches apart, onto ungreased large cookie sheet. Bake until cookies are very lightly golden (they will be soft), about 15 minutes. With pancake turner, transfer cookies to wire rack to cool. Repeat with remaining dough.

4. When cookies are cool, prepare icing: In small bowl, stir confectioners' sugar and milk until smooth. With small metal spatula or knife, spread icing on cookies; sprinkle with red or green sugar crystals. Set cookies aside to allow icing to dry completely, about 1 hour. Makes about 6 dozen cookies.

Each cookie: About 90 calories (30 percent calories from fat), 1g protein, 14g carbohydrate, 3g total fat (1g saturated), 3mg cholesterol, 100mg sodium.

Oatmeal-Raisin Cookies

Prep: 15 minutes   Bake: 10 minutes per batch

If you thought the words "delicious" and "low-fat" could never be used to describe the same cookie, think again. This one's chewy and sweet, yet it has only two grams of fat per cookie.

   2 **cups all-purpose flour**
   1 **teaspoon baking soda**
 1/2 **teaspoon salt**
 1/2 **cup light corn-oil spread (1 stick), 56 to 60% fat**
 3/4 **cup packed dark brown sugar**
 1/2 **cup granulated sugar**
   2 **large egg whites**

   1 **large egg**
   2 **teaspoons vanilla extract**
   1 **cup quick-cooking oats, uncooked**
 1/2 **cup dark seedless raisins**

1. Preheat oven to 375°F. Grease two large cookie sheets. In medium bowl, combine flour, baking soda, and salt.

2. In large bowl, with mixer at low speed, beat corn-oil spread, brown, and granulated sugar until well combined. Increase speed to high; beat until mixture is light and fluffy. Add egg whites, whole egg, and vanilla; beat until blended. With wooden spoon, stir in flour mixture, oats, and raisins until combined.

3. Drop dough by level tablespoons, 2 inches apart, on prepared cookie sheets. Bake until golden, 10 to 12 minutes, rotating cookie sheets between upper and lower oven racks halfway through baking. With wide spatula, transfer cookies to wire racks to cool completely.

4. Repeat with remaining dough. Makes about 48 cookies.

Each cookie: About 67 calories (27 percent calories from fat), 1g protein, 12g carbohydrate, 2g total fat (0g saturated), 4mg cholesterol, 72mg sodium.

Almond-Anise Biscotti

Prep: 25 minutes plus cooling   Bake: 55 minutes

Soaking the anise seeds in liqueur softens them and releases their delicious flavor.

- **1 tablespoon anise seeds, crushed**
- **1 tablespoon anise-flavored aperitif or liqueur**
- **2 cups all-purpose flour**
- **1 cup sugar**
- **1 cup whole almonds (4 ounces), toasted and coarsely chopped**
- **1 teaspoon baking powder**
- **1/8 teaspoon salt**
- **3 large eggs**

1. Preheat oven to 325°F. In medium bowl, combine anise seeds and anise-flavored aperitif; let stand 10 minutes.

2. Grease large cookie sheet. In large bowl, combine flour, sugar, chopped almonds, baking powder, and salt. With wire whisk, beat eggs into anise mixture. With wooden spoon, stir egg mixture into flour mixture until blended. Divide dough in half. On prepared cookie sheet, with floured hands, shape each half into 15-inch log, placing them 3 inches apart (dough will be sticky).

3. Bake until golden and toothpick inserted in center comes out clean, about 40 minutes. Cool 10 minutes on cookie sheet on wire rack; then transfer logs to cutting board. With serrated knife, cut each log crosswise on diagonal into 1/4-inch-thick slices. Place slices, cut side down, on two ungreased cookie sheets. Bake 15 minutes, turning slices over once and rotating cookie sheets between upper and lower oven racks halfway through baking. With spatula, transfer biscotti to wire racks to cool completely. Makes about 84 biscotti.

Each biscotti: About 33 calories (27 percent calories from fat), 1g protein, 5g carbohydrate, 1g total fat (0g saturated), 8mg cholesterol, 12mg sodium.

Meringue Fingers

Prep: 25 minutes plus cooling   Bake: 1 hour

These ethereal meringue cookies are dipped into chocolate, which gives them fabulous flavor.

    3 **large egg whites**
  1/4 **teaspoon cream of tartar**
  1/8 **teaspoon salt**
  1/2 **cup sugar**
    1 **teaspoon vanilla extract**
    2 **squares (2 ounces) semisweet chocolate, chopped**
    1 **teaspoon vegetable shortening**

1. Preheat oven to 200°F. Line two large cookie sheets with foil or parchment paper.

2. In small bowl, with mixer at high speed, beat egg whites, cream of tartar, and salt until soft peaks form when beaters are lifted. Beating at high speed, gradually sprinkle in sugar, 2 tablespoons at a time, beating until sugar has dissolved. Add vanilla; continue beating until meringue stands in stiff, glossy peaks when beaters are lifted.

3. Spoon meringue into pastry bag fitted with 1/2-inch star tip. Pipe meringue into 3 inch lengths, 1 inch apart, on prepared cookie sheets.

4. Bake cookies until set, about 1 hour, rotating cookie sheets between upper and lower oven racks halfway through baking. Cool 10 minutes on cookie sheets on wire racks; then, with spatula, transfer cookies to wire racks to cool completely.

5. When cookies have cooled, in heavy 1-quart saucepan, melt chocolate and shortening over low heat, stirring frequently, until smooth; remove from heat. Dip one end of each cookie into melted chocolate; let dry on wire racks set over waxed paper. Makes about 48 cookies.

Each cookie: About 16 calories (0 percent calories from fat), 0g protein, 3g carbohydrate, 0g total fat, 0mg cholesterol, 10mg sodium.

Limeade, page 304

Limeade

Prep: 25 minutes plus standing and chilling   Cook: 10 minutes

Some people find limeade even more refreshing than lemonade. This one is especially good with fresh berries added—try raspberries, blueberries, or sliced strawberries.

  2 cups sugar
3¹/₂ cups cold water
1¹/₄ cups fresh lime juice (about 10 limes)
    ice cubes

1. In 2-quart saucepan, combine sugar and water; heat to boiling over high heat, stirring until sugar has dissolved.

Reduce heat to medium and cook 2 minutes. Remove from heat; cover and let stand 10 minutes.

2. Add lime juice to sugar syrup in saucepan; pour limeade into 1¹/₂-quart heatproof pitcher. Cover and refrigerate until well chilled, about 3 hours. To serve, fill tall glasses with ice cubes and pour limeade over. Makes about 6 cups or 6 servings.

Each serving: About 272 calories (0 percent calories from fat), 0g protein, 71g carbohydrate, 0g total fat, 0mg cholesterol, 1mg sodium.

Strawberry-Lemon Spritzer

Prep: 10 minutes

You may need to add a bit of sugar if the strawberries are less than fully ripe or if you substitute frozen.

  2 cups fresh ripe strawberries, hulled and
    quartered (1 quart)
  1 tablespoon lemon juice
  1 quart club soda
    lemon wedges and fresh mint leaves (optional)

In food processor or blender, process strawberries and lemon juice until smooth. Stir in club soda. Garnish with lemon wedges and fresh mint leaves, if you like, and serve. Makes 6 servings.

Each serving: About 15 calories (0 percent calories from fat), 0g protein, 4g carbohydrate, 0g total fat, 0mg cholesterol, 35mg sodium.

Fizzy Cranberry-Lemonade Punch

Prep: 5 minutes

One of the easiest and most refreshing punches. If you wish, offer guests vodka or dark rum on the side to spike their drinks.

  4 cups cranberry-juice cocktail, chilled
  1 container (6 ounces) frozen lemonade
    concentrate, thawed
  1 bottle (1 liter) plain seltzer or club soda, chilled
    ice cubes (optional)
  1 small orange, cut into ¹/₄-inch-thick slices and
    each slice cut in half

In large pitcher, stir cranberry-juice cocktail and lemonade concentrate until blended. Stir in seltzer and ice cubes, if you like. Add orange slices and serve. Makes about 9 cups or 12 servings.

Each serving: About 81 calories (0 percent calories from fat), 0g protein, 21g carbohydrate, 0g total fat, 0mg cholesterol, 23mg sodium.

Mango-Strawberry Smoothie

Prep: 5 minutes

All you need to whip up a fruit-filled smoothie for breakfast or a snack is a blender. Blend different fruits and juices with the yogurt and ice cubes to vary the drinks. If you use frozen fruit, skip the ice cubes.

- **1 cup fresh or frozen unsweetened strawberries**
- **1 cup mango or apricot nectar**
- **1/2 cup plain or vanilla yogurt**
- **4 ice cubes**

In blender, process strawberries, mango nectar, yogurt, and ice cubes until smooth and frothy. Pour into two tall glasses. Serve with straws, if you like. Makes 2 servings.

Each serving: About 129 calories (7 percent calories from fat), 4g protein, 27g carbohydrate, 1g total fat (1g saturated), 3mg cholesterol, 44mg sodium.

Peach Smoothie

Prepare as directed but substitute 1 cup peeled, sliced fresh or frozen unsweetened peaches for strawberries and 1 cup peach juice or nectar or apple juice for mango nectar.

Banana Smoothie

Prepare as directed but substitute 1 ripe medium banana for strawberries and 1 cup pineapple or orange juice for mango nectar. Add 1/2 teaspoon vanilla extract, if desired.

Strawberry-Pear Frothy

Prep: 10 minutes

You can make this up to 1 day ahead and refrigerate until ready to serve.

  4 cups fresh ripe strawberries, hulled and quartered (2 quarts)

  2 ripe pears, peeled, cored, and sliced

  1 cup plain low- or nonfat yogurt

  1/2 cup fresh orange juice

  fresh mint leaves, additional strawberries, or orange slices (optional)

In blender, process berries, pears, yogurt, and orange juice until smooth. Garnish with fresh mint leaves, strawberries, or orange slices if desired. Makes 4 servings.

Each serving with low-fat yogurt: About 145 calories (12 percent calories from fat), 4g protein, 30g carbohydrate, 2g total fat (1g saturated), 4mg cholesterol, 40mg sodium.

Frosty Cappuccino

Prep: 5 minutes

Better than store-bought! A deceptively rich blender drink.

  1 cup low-fat milk (1%)

  1 tablespoon chocolate-flavored syrup

  1 teaspoon instant espresso-coffee powder

  2 ice cubes

  sugar (optional)

  1/8 teaspoon ground cinnamon

In blender at high speed, process milk, chocolate syrup, espresso powder, and ice cubes 1 minute. Pour into 2 chilled glasses. Add sugar to taste, if you like. Sprinkle with cinnamon to serve. Makes 2 servings.

Each serving: About 75 calories (12 percent calories from fat), 4g protein, 12g carbohydrate, 1g total fat (1g saturated), 5mg cholesterol, 65mg sodium.

Italian Lemon Cordial

Prep: 10 minutes plus 1 week standing, cooling, and chilling   Cook: 5 minutes

Known as limoncello, this potent after-dinner drink is best served in tiny glasses right from the freezer so it's very cold and syrupy.

> 6 **lemons**
> 1 **bottle (750 milliliters) 100-proof vodka**
> 1³/4 **cups sugar**
> 3¹/4 **cups water**

1. From lemons, with vegetable peeler, remove peel in strips. (Refrigerate lemons for another use.) Pour vodka into 8-cup glass measuring cup or large pitcher and add lemon peel. Cover measuring cup with plastic wrap and let stand 1 week at room temperature.

2. After 1 week, strain vodka through paper towel–lined sieve set over large bowl. Discard lemon peel.

3. In 2-quart saucepan, combine sugar and water; heat to boiling over high heat, stirring until sugar has dissolved. Reduce heat to medium and cook 2 minutes. Remove from heat and cool completely.

4. Add cooled syrup to vodka in bowl. Pour cordial into small decorative bottles with tight-fitting stoppers or lids. Store in refrigerator up to 3 months or in freezer up to 6 months. Serve very cold. Makes about 6¹/2 cups or 34 servings.

Each serving: About 89 calories (0 percent calories from fat), 0g protein, 10g carbohydrate, 0g total fat, 0mg cholesterol, 0mg sodium.

Sangria

Prep: 15 minutes

This sparkling summer refresher looks lovely in a glass pitcher.

> 2 **oranges**
> 2 **lemons**
> 1 **bottle (750 milliliters) dry red wine, chilled**
> ¹/4 **cup brandy**
> ¹/4 **cup orange-flavored liqueur**
> ¹/3 **cup sugar**
> 3 **cups plain seltzer or club soda, chilled**
>   **ice cubes (optional)**

1. With vegetable peeler, remove peel from 1 orange and 2 lemons. Squeeze juice from both oranges. (Refrigerate lemons for another use.)

2. In 2¹/2-quart pitcher, combine orange juice, wine, brandy, orange liqueur, and sugar; stir until sugar has completely dissolved.

3. Stir in orange peel, lemon peel, and seltzer. To serve, half-fill wine glasses with ice, if desired, and pour sangria over. Makes about 7 cups or 14 servings.

Each serving: About 82 calories (0 percent calories from fat), 0g protein, 7g carbohydrate, 0g total fat, 0mg cholesterol, 14mg sodium.

White Sangria

Prepare as directed but substitute 1 bottle (750 milliliters) dry white wine for red wine and add 1 ripe peach, peeled, pitted, and cut into thin wedges, or 1 cup sliced unsweetened frozen peaches with citrus peel in Step 3.

Hot Mulled Wine

Prep: 10 minutes   Cook: 20 minutes

If you wish, add other whole spices, such as cardamom pods, allspice berries, or even black peppercorns. The toasted sliced almonds are a traditional Scandinavian garnish.

- **2 cups sugar**
- **1 cup water**
- **1 small orange, thinly sliced**
- **1 small lemon, thinly sliced**
- **3 cinnamon sticks (3 inches each)**
- **8 whole cloves**
- **1 bottle (750 milliliters) dry red wine**

1. In nonreactive 4-quart saucepan, combine sugar, water, orange slices, lemon slices, cinnamon sticks, and cloves; heat to boiling over high heat, stirring until sugar has dissolved. Reduce heat to medium and cook 3 minutes.

2. Add wine to saucepan and heat, stirring, until hot (do not boil). Serve hot. Makes 8 generous cups or 16 servings.

Each serving: About 170 calories (0 percent calories from fat), 0g protein, 28g carbohydrate, 0g total fat, 0mg cholesterol, 5mg sodium.

Wassail

Prep: 10 minutes   Cook: 25 minutes

This classic Christmas beverage is traditionally made with wine, ale, or hard cider, but we like this less potent combination of sweet cider and apple brandy.

- **1/2 gallon apple cider or juice**
- **1 lemon, thinly sliced**
- **2 tablespoons brown sugar**
- **2 cinnamon sticks (3 inches each)**
- **12 whole allspice berries**
- **12 whole cloves**
- **6 lady apples or 1 Golden Delicious apple**
- **1 cup applejack or apple brandy**

1. In nonreactive 5-quart Dutch oven, combine cider, lemon slices, brown sugar, cinnamon sticks, and all-spice berries; heat to boiling over medium-high heat. Reduce heat and simmer 10 minutes.

2. Insert 2 cloves into each lady apple or all cloves into Golden Delicious apple. Add apples and applejack to cider and cook until heated through, about 2 minutes. Makes about 8 cups or 16 servings.

Each serving: About 108 calories (0 percent calories from fat), 0g protein, 18g carbohydrate, 0g total fat, 0mg cholesterol, 5mg sodium.

Holiday Champagne Punch

Prep: 20 minutes   Freeze: 3 hours

This pretty punch is refreshing and only slightly sweet.

- **1 pint strawberries**
- **1 pound seedless green grapes, stemmed**
- **2 cups orange juice**
- **1/4 cup orange-flavored liqueur**
- **1 bottle (1 liter) ginger ale, chilled**
- **1 bottle (750 milliliters) champagne or sparkling white wine, chilled**
- **1 bunch fresh mint**

1. Prepare ice ring: Fill 5-cup ring mold with 1/4 inch cold water; freeze until hard, about 45 minutes. Reserve 8 strawberries; hull and slice remaining strawberries. On top of ice in ring mold, decoratively arrange half of sliced strawberries and 1/2 cup grapes. Add just enough water to cover to prevent fruit from floating. Freeze until hard, about 45 minutes. Repeat with remaining strawberry slices, another 1/2 cup grapes, and enough water to cover fruit; freeze until hard, about 45 minutes.

2. With kitchen shears, cut remaining grapes into small bunches; arrange grape bunches and reserved whole strawberries alternately in ring mold. Add enough water to come up to rim of mold, allowing some fruit to be exposed above water; freeze until hard, about 45 minutes or up to 6 hours.

3. About 15 minutes before serving, in 5-quart punch bowl or bowl large enough to hold ice ring, combine orange juice and orange liqueur. Stir in ginger ale and champagne.

4. Unmold ice ring and turn, fruit side up. Tuck small mint sprigs between grapes and strawberries. Add ice ring to punch bowl. Makes about 10 cups or 20 servings.

Each serving: About 85 calories (0 percent calories from fat), 0g protein, 14g carbohydrate, 0g total fat, 0mg cholesterol, 7mg sodium.